Mozart the Dramatist

MOZART THE DRAMATIST

*The value of his
operas to him, to his
age and to us*

———— ❈ ————

*Revised edition
with a Preface*

BRIGID BROPHY

Libris

1988

First published by Faber and Faber, 1964
Second, revised, edition first published 1988

Copyright © Brigid Brophy, 1964, 1988

Libris, 10 Burghley Road, London NW5 1UE

British Library Cataloguing in Publication Data available.
ISBN 1 870352 35 1

Typeset in Monotype Bell
New material set by
Merrion Letters, London
Produced by Cinamon and Kitzinger
Printed in Great Britain by
Redwood Burn Ltd, Trowbridge

Contents

Contents

To
ROSEMARY AND CHRISTOPHER WHITE
who initiated us into
Glyndebourne

Note

Two extracts from this book have appeared in *The London Magazine*.

The notes which are collected at the back of the book supply dates, sources, often the original wording of a quotation (when the text has given a translation) and occasionally additional information. Notes essential to the text are placed on the pages. I am grateful to the Executors of the late Emily Anderson, and her publishers, Messrs. Macmillan & Co., for permission to use throughout my book her translation of Mozart's and his family's Letters (London, 1938); references to the scores of the operas are to English editions: details of these and all the other books referred to are to be found at the end in the List of Articles and Books Cited. I take much pleasure in thanking Mrs David Wood for help about musical theory, and Mr R. Newland for help about German.

BRIGID BROPHY

"On the contrary they adore—we all adore here
—the rococo"

HENRY JAMES : THE AMBASSADORS

A new world of love and beauty broke upon her
when she was introduced to those divine compositions: this lady had the keenest and finest sensibility, and how could she be indifferent when
she heard Mozart? The tender parts of 'Don Juan'
awakened in her raptures so exquisite that she
would ask herself when she went to say her prayers
of a night whether it was not wicked to feel so much
delight as that with which 'Vedrai Carino' and
'Batti Batti' filled her gentle little bosom.

W. M. THACKERAY : VANITY FAIR

Brief Chronology

(Dates for the operas are of first performances)

1756   Johann* Wolfgang Amadeus Mozart born 27 January, youngest child of Leopold and Maria Anna† (Pertl) Mozart

1775   *Il Re Pastore*, K. 208

1778   death of Mozart's mother

1781   *Idomeneo*, K. 366

1782   *Die Entführung aus dem Serail (Il Seraglio)*, K. 384
       Mozart's marriage to Constanze Weber

1784   Mozart became a Mason

1785   Leopold Mozart became a Mason

1786   *Le Nozze di Figaro*, K. 492

1787   death of Mozart's father
       Don Giovanni, K. 527

1788   Symphonies K. 543, 550, 551

1790   *Così Fan Tutte*, K. 588

1791   *La Clemenza di Tito*, K. 621
       Die Zauberflöte, K. 620
       Requiem, K. 626 (finished by Süssmayr)
       Mozart died on 5 December

* See Alfred Einstein: *Mozart His Character His Work*, 3, footnote.
† Maria Anna according to Emily Anderson; Anna Maria according to Einstein.

Preface to the 1988 Edition

In this new edition of a book originally published in 1964 I have expanded and amended several passages. I have made reference to books published after 1964, some of which I reviewed in periodicals. A tolerably detailed note about one such book appears at the back of this volume. When I want to mention *Die Entführung aus dem Serail* by a shorter title, I call it *Il Seraglio*. That I have not altered, because it is correct. In English-speaking countries *Il Seraglio* is the title of countless performances and of the standard British vocal score. I do not know why an opera composed to sung and spoken words in German was given an English title consisting of two words of Italian, especially when to call it 'The Seraglio' would accord with eighteenth-century English idiom and with present-day comprehension.

Were I now writing a book about Mozart and his operas, my design would incorporate a section in praise of *Idomeneo* and *La Clemenza di Tito*. In 1964 I knew both operas to be musical masterpieces, but at that time it was rare for a performance, even in the theatre, to allow the music to point up the drama. The drama had probably been frightened into hiding by musicologists, who put it about that anything couched in the form of *opera seria* (in Italian, with sung recitative and with a plot taken from the mythology or the history of ancient Greece or Rome) was 'unfeeling'. From that notion, which is as senseless and as destructive of delight as it would be to write of Shakespeare's tragedies as unfeeling in comparison with his comedies or the other way about, audiences have now been rescued by performers, notably Charles Mackerras, who have moved them to joy and tears by placing before them the masterpieces in the *opera seria* form which Handel created towards the beginning and Mozart towards the end of the eighteenth century.

7

Mozart was commissioned in autumn 1780 to compose an opera for the carnival season at Munich. The Bavarian court, besides appointing as librettist Giambattista Varesco, Mozart's fellow-resident of Salzburg and fellow-employee of the ecclesiastical court, chose the subject of Idomeneus. His story is one of those about the return of the Greek heroes from the Trojan War. King of Crete, Idomeneus is on the voyage home when his ship is beset by a storm. He vows that, should he succeed in setting foot on land, he will sacrifice the first living entity he sees. The vow saves his life but impales him on a moral dilemma. The first live being he sees turns out to be his son, grown up while his father was away at the long, indeed the Homeric war. Cast safe on the coast of Crete, out of the sea, he sings in Mozart's opera; he has a sea in his breast.

Whether Idomeneus is more obliged to fulfil his oath, for his tardiness in discharging which he is magically and monstrously punished, though most of the actual affliction falls on the population of Crete, than he is obliged to love his son is a dilemma of the type by which ancient Greek tragedy regularly splits its heroes and heroines. Greek mythology is uncertain whether Idomeneus kills his son or only tries to, but his action or attempt revolts the people of Crete and they expel him from his kingdom. Fitting though the theme was for ancient Greek tragedy, no surviving Greek tragedy, so far as I know, took it up. It was left to eighteenth-century opera. It was treated in French in an opera I do not know, *Idomenée*, by André Campra, performed in 1712. Varesco may have borrowed from that his softened but dramatically cogent ending, where the dilemma is resolved not by the sacrifice of the son but by the voluntary quasi-sacrifice of the father, who abdicates his throne in his son's favour.

Late in the autumn of 1780 Mozart went to stay, alone, in Munich in order to compose the bulk of his opera in acquaintance with the orchestra and the singers who were to perform it. Leopold Mozart and the librettist were tethered, by their employment at the ecclesiastical court there, in Salzburg. Mozart wanted Varesco to alter the text, chiefly by cutting it, into accordance with Mozart's sense of drama and the abilities and disabilities he perceived in the singers. The negotiation was conducted by letter. Mozart wrote to his father and his father negotiated with Varesco. Mozart's letters bridging the turn of the year (1780 to 1781) are a casement opening uniquely on not only his dramatic method but the crucial relationship of his life. Mozart conducts a double negotiation : by argument and by tellingly applying the lessons taught him, he persuades his father, his earliest tutor in music, drama and worldly wisdom, to persuade Varesco.

Like Idomeneo's son, Mozart had matured unseen by his father. He reports that the dress rehearsal is scheduled for 27 January 1781 and adds 'my birthday, mark you'. It was the birthday on which he became twenty-five. Yet the Munich court had set him a theme through which he could also and did also express his compunction and his sympathy with the man who is worked on by magical and elemental forces into resigning his mastery to his son. The moral dilemma of Mozart the son was that the better he pleased his father, and obeyed his teaching, the more would posterity be bound to read the name Mozart as meaning not the father but the son.

Just conceivably, Leopold Mozart recognised that the son who shared his surname was adult and destined to eclipse him. Leopold Mozart's letters to his wife and his children are habitually signed 'Mozart' or 'MZT'. On 11 January 1781 he signed a letter to W. A. Mozart 'L. Mozart'. Mozart was meanwhile treating his father as business manager, negotiator and housekeeper, requesting the despatch by mail coach of everything from trumpet mutes to the black suit which Mozart needed in Munich because of an imperial death and which Leopold Mozart reported that he had to have mended before he sent it. After correspondence where Mozart played housekeeper on the subject of stoves and sleeping accommodation, his father and his sister managed to be in Munich for the first performance of *Idomeneo* on 29 January 1781.

During the composition of the opera, Mozart quoted, in a letter to his father, an aria by Metastasio as a model for an aria he wanted Varesco to write in to the text of *Idomeneo*; and to Metastasio my *opera seria* extension should include a shrine. His is one of the geat names which have dropped through the slats of fashion. So devalued is he that, about the time of this book's original publication, Michael Levey and I (who are married to one another) were able to buy in London for ten shillings (half a pound sterling) his complete works contained in ten small (roughly five by three inches) volumes published in Venice in 1800 and 1801, by virtue of which we became two of the rather, I suspect, rare twentieth-century people to have read him before commenting on him.

Metastasio's career and perhaps some of his literary personality were formed by the most derided of political fictions, the claim that there was a continuity between the empire of ancient Rome and the Holy (in the sense of Catholic) Roman Empire. Several basically German-speaking states were electorates and their rulers Electors with the right to choose the Holy Roman Emperor from among themselves, a right they exercised to choose with tolerable regularity the head of the royal house of Austria. Ludicrous the fiction indeed was but it did vital work to preserve the culture of ancient Rome and, through the prism of Rome and the prism of the renaissance, the culture of ancient Greece.

Thanks to the Austrian territorial possessions in Italy, Italian was one of the languages of the Empire. The establishment of an Italian opera company at Vienna came, wobbled and went according to fashion and resources, but the capital of any monarchy or principality within the Empire was likely to commission an Italian opera in the way that Munich commissioned *Idomeneo* from Mozart. The language was not foreign; it was hung about with prestige; slowed down by singing and amplified by the repetition of words and phrases in arias, it was apprehensible to the ear—or at least to the eye in the libretto, which was usually available to opera audiences. As Mozart's life demonstrates, the route was open for an Austrian citizen to study musical composition under an Italian master in Italy; and the route was open back to the cities of the constituent states of the Empire for Italian composers, performers and librettists.

In pursuit of its holy fiction the imperial court at Vienna called its laureate the Poeta Cesario. The job of the Cesarian poet was to provide Italian libretti. Metastasio was appointed to the office in 1729 and held it until his death in 1782.

He was born in Rome in 1698 and, to begin with, had the name Pietro Trapassi. Pietro continued to be his first name but Trapassi, which as an ordinary Italian word means 'crossings over', was translated into the ancient Greek word 'metastasis' and then given an italianate form again. The name he made famous throughout Europe was a pun. The component that begins it, 'meta', often has in Greek the significance of a change of state and is the same component that introduces 'metaphor' and 'metamorphosis'. The simplest meaning of 'metastasis' is 'removal from one place to another', which Metastasio fulfilled in his shift from Rome to Vienna.

Metastasio is a pun in the spirit in which Lorenzo da Ponte named the bossy and efficient maidservant in *Così Fan Tutte* by an italianised form of the ancient Greek word for the mistress of the house, Despina. In Greek the word is 'despoina', the feminine of the word that the English language abbreviates to 'despot'. Perhaps da Ponte was respectfully satirising the dead Metastasio.

Many of Metastasio's texts were repeatedly set, by different composers, and virtually from his childhood Mozart was one of the many composers who set extracts snipped from them to create an aria or a scena-and-aria for concert performance. In the edition published in Venice in 1800, each libretto is prefaced by a record or the name of the first composer and the occasion of the first performance. *La Clemenza di Tito* was first set by Caldara and first performed in Vienna on 4 November 1734 to celebrate the name-day of the Emperor Charles VI at the order of the Empress Elizabeth. Such records have misled posterity into dismissing Metastasio as a flagrant flatterer. Flatter he indeed did, often through the fictitious continuity with the ancient world and on themes that were surely approved and no doubt often chosen by the court; yet he did it with unparalleled dexterity. Perhaps the high point of the flattery, for which posterity too should be grateful, was that he expected his patrons to appreciate his skilled manipulation of literary technique. One of the figurative meanings of 'metastasis' is 'revolution'. His *Tito* libretto was composed again, to a commission for Prague, by Mozart in 1791, which turned out to be the last year of his life.

The story of Idomeneus served Mozart as an opportunity to reconcile his father to the son's independence and maturity of judgement. Almost immediately, Leopold Mozart was alarmed again: Mozart quit his employment with the Salzburg court and moved to Vienna. In terms that suggest he was still imaginatively identified with the son of Idomeneus he wrote to his father on 13 June 1781 that he would have gladly sacrificed his best years to his father by remaining in Salzburg, ill paid though he was there, had he not been scoffed at as well. On 15 December 1781 he wrote that he wanted to secure in Vienna what many freelance artists have yearned for, 'a small but *certain* income' on which to live and marry. He did marry, but none of the career slots that would produce a regular salary opened to him and he had to piece together a living. He had been famous since infancy. As composer and performer he had travelled much of Europe and filled the whole of it with his renown. As he demonstrated in his letter of 13 February 1782 to his sister, giving details of a day's work in Vienna, he worked with regularity and intense application. Yet he scratched a living by scratching for commissions and pupils.

Leopold Mozart himself made a conciliatory gesture when, in 1785, the year after that in which his son did the same thing, he disobeyed though he did not quarrel with the Catholic church by becoming a Freemason; and it was in terms of Masonic doctrine, which sought to vanquish the fear of death, that Mozart wrote to his father when he knew him to be dying. Masonic ceremony explains, through its ritual spokesman, that because not all Masons are 'operative', in the sense of being practical building workers, Masonry interprets the tools of practical building in symbolic senses. From Michael Levey's book *The Life and Death of Mozart* I learned that the paternal grandfather of Leopold Mozart had been a practical builder, and I think it likely that that fact, which was probably known to him, emotionally and psychologically eased the passage of Leopold Mozart into Masonry.

Thanks to its ceremonies and its secrecy, Masonry, I conceive, provided Mozart with both an ideology and a game, an enlarged and more varied version of the code which the Mozart family letters used, for fear of interception, in discussions of powerful employers. In both his operas of 1791 Mozart is, I believe, making posthumous amends to his father, who was by then four years dead. *Tito* was the vehicle of his reconciliation with authority in his own life. The text was by the dead Metastasio, whose death evidently made Mozart fear, with reason, that another master he admired would tumble. After composing *Tito* he noted that Metastasio's text had been made into a 'real opera' by Caterino Mazzolà, the court poet at Dresden, to whom he no doubt ascribed sympathetic editorial updating of the kind Mozart lovingly worked on the music of Handel. In Titus Mozart had for hero the most clement and forgiving of ancient emperors. Stabbed in the back emotionally and politically, Titus abnegates the revenge he has both the right and the power to deal. In an almost Masonic renunciation of vengeance he does what Selim does and Sarastro preaches.

Mozart's letters of 1790 to a 'brother' Mason are heartbreaking requests for small loans. The recipient has sometimes noted on the manuscript the despatch of sums smaller than Mozart requested. Mozart gives an account of his finances, hopes and hopes disappointed.

To write begging letters, it is clear from reading them, abraded Mozart's pride—which his father had held suspect. His very need to beg provoked, I think, the thought that Leopold Mozart had been correct in fearing that, in his quarrel with the Salzburg court, Mozart had sabotaged his chances of securing a similar post, with its regular salary, elsewhere. Even the obligation Mozart felt to set out to the man he sought to borrow from his precise financial situation was bound to resurrect his father in his thoughts, because he had not written letters of such detailed frankness since Leopold Mozart died.

Masonic society thus restored to Mozart the frankness of a child in relation to his father. Probably with greater success than the fantasies about excretion with which he filled his letters to members of his family who had been children when he was a child, Masonry gave him the childhood he had been too precocious to have. It mimicked the uninhibited and unpretentious society of childhood equals.

In *Die Zauberflöte* Mozart affirms Masonic principles in music of miraculous solemnity to his fellow-Mason Leopold Mozart. Yet the totality of the opera he created is a scherzo, a magical work of imagination that uses Masonic symbols, theatrical machinery and the devices of stagecraft in order to win reconciliation with his dead father, as he had sought to do during his father's lifetime by means of letters full of puns, drawings and doggerel.

13

The quasi-friendly-society effects of Freemasonry were intended to seem to an outsider like the effects of magic. By a transposition long enshrined in the history of music, the power of Masonry becomes in the opera the power of music and is incarnated in the magic bells which the Three Ladies give Papageno, the flute they give Tamino and the pipe that Papageno already possesses, a stunted version of the flute and one whose magic is effective on birds.

It is a curiosity that Mozart at least consented to and probably took an active part in the decision to make the prime instrument of magic a flute. There was scarcely reason enough in Schikaneder's success of two years earlier with an opera contrived from a story whose sub-title (alternative title) was 'The Magic Flute'. Piecing together his living, Mozart accepted commissions for (among other things) flute music. He gave lessons at the keyboard to a young pupil who later recorded his memory, collected by O. E. Deutsch under the year 1852, that Mozart had told him that he 'loathed' the flute. I think the paradox is resolved by the symbolism of Masonry. The practical building tools that Masonry interpreted moralistically included the square (in the sense of T-square) and the level. A candidate for initiation to a Lodge is asked by the spokesman 'How did you and I first meet?' and has been instructed in advance to give the ritual reply 'On the Square'. To 'How do we hope to part?' the answer is 'On the Level'. The ritual has deposited in English idiom 'on the square' and 'on the level' as slang synonyms for 'honestly'. The Masonic candidate is told that 'All Squares, Levels and Perpendiculars are true and proper signs to know a Mason by'. The instruction continues : 'You are therefore expected to stand perfectly erect, your feet formed in a square'.

The flute is a transverse instrument. In August 1791, as Deutsch's *Documentary Biography* of Mozart records, the *Wiener Zeitung* called it, in I am not sure which language, the 'Flaut travers'. Tamino has only to stand upright and play his flute and he becomes a living and amusing rebus, a visible pun, exerting the magic and power of the Masonic Square.

BRIGID BROPHY
1988

I

The Importance of Mozart's Operas

———————— ❋ ————————

Our century, which will surely be the most execrated in history (always provided it allows history to continue so that there is someone to execrate it) has this to its credit: it is recognising Mozart.

Mozart's orchestral music had never dropped out of the repertory. But it is his operas that lifted his genius to its highest and most sustained pitch, and operas which, as his letters make plain, he himself pre-eminently *wanted* to compose: and here, though some of the music from them was never wholly lost to the public's ears, it is the twentieth century which has resurrected the works as wholes and made it comparatively easy to hear good performances of the five major operas and not too difficult to hunt down most of the minor ones.

Even so, all that can be accurately said for the twentieth century is that it is in process of recognising Mozart. We have accomplished the resurrection but do not always perceive its value or even its content. Indeed, the very conjurers who have revived the operas and put them on the stage often go out of their way to prevent us from taking in their content, no doubt because they themselves do not fully believe that the operas *are* alive. Producers dare not take with Mozart today quite the liberties Victorian impresari took with Shakespeare when they mounted his plays as spectacular pantomimes: yet plenty of well sung and well played Mozart performances bury their virtues—sometimes under cheap and farcical business, but more often under picturesque and extremely expensive business. Whole 'crowds', corps de ballet or, worst of all, other singers coached ad hoc in the craft of acting are deployed to distract the eye while one singer gets on with the aria that has been reduced to a mere accompaniment. Most recent productions of Mozart have been designed on the theory that audiences would perish of boredom if the producer left them for a moment unattended with Mozart's music.

This is gross slander not only on Mozart the supreme artist and dramatist (he is more than capable of keeping audiences entertained by his own methods) but on Mozart the melodist. Mozart was probably borne back into the repertory simply on the wings of his own melodic fertility. He shares with Donizetti, Irving Berlin, Handel and Sir Arthur Sullivan the sheer gift of inventing tunes to be sung: a fertility so rare that we cannot afford to neglect for very long any composer who possesses it, but which does not in itself guarantee, though it is indispensable to, great opera. Yet if his tunes brought him back, it is fashion which makes much of him and lets producers expensively loose on him: and if we have no better reason for staging his operas, fashion may equally well carry him away again from our great grandchildren.

Nowadays almost everything eighteenth-century is allowed to be charming—as readily as, a hundred years ago, it was written off as frivolous, monotonous and worthless. The reversal of fashion began, in the last decade of the nineteenth and the first decade of this century, as a serious artistic revolution, nurtured half inside the mauve cloak of the 'decadent' movement and half in reaction against it. It was as a weapon against (among other things) 'art for art's sake' that Bernard Shaw revived eighteenth-century rationalism in the form of what he called[1] 'my own Irish eighteenth-centuryism', taking up the Mozart-da Ponte story of Don Giovanni and turning it into *Man And Superman*, restoring to modern prose the Canalettesque clarity of Voltaire, and transmuting Voltaire's Candide into Candida. In opera, a taste for the eighteenth century was revived by a pioneer whose artistic personality was almost the opposite of Shaw's (it was the ornamental, monumental eighteenth-centuryism of Dresden, as opposed to the four-square simplicity of Dublin classicism): far from seeking to contradict the received idea of the eighteenth century as frivolous and immoral, Richard Strauss was exploiting it for his own 'decadent', post-fin-de-siècle purposes when he set *Der Rosenkavalier* in 'Vienna, early in the reign of Maria Theresa' and created the dramatic personality of the Rosenkavalier himself out of material already supplied by Mozart in Cherubino. In the same year that *Der Rosenkavalier* was first performed—1911—Gustav Mahler died. As his widow wrote long afterwards,[2] 'It was he who gave the signal to the whole world for the Mozart renaissance'—by the directorship during which he restored to the Vienna repertory *Die Zauberflöte*, *Il Seraglio*, *Figaro* (with recitatives re-written by himself) and even, for a few, financially unsuccessful performances in 1902, *Zaide*. As Mahler lay dying, 'There was a smile on his lips and twice he said "Mozart!"'

While the nineteenth century was still in its long-drawn 'fin', the route back to the eighteenth was prospected, in another art, by another 'decadent'—Aubrey Beardsley, whose genius, like many that are going to die young, hurried on in advance of contemporary taste. 'In 1896' (so Oscar Wilde's friend Robert Ross wrote in 1909[*]) 'Beardsley, many people think to the detriment of his style, turned his attention to the eighteenth century, in the literature of which he was always deeply interested. Eisen, Moreau, Watteau, Cochin, Pietro Longhi, now became his masters.' The course of Beardsley's taste was, in fact, anticipating the course of Strauss's. From his illustrations to Wilde's *Salome* in 1894, Beardsley progressed to the eighteenth century in 1896, with his illustrations to *The Rape Of The Lock*: Strauss was presently to arrive at the neo-rococo of *Der Rosenkavalier* (whose original sets seem tinged with the influence of Beardsley[†]) from *his* version of Wilde's *Salome* in 1905.

The eighteenth-century revival as a whole was a three-part fugue, in three separate arts, woven by the highly independent geniuses of Strauss, Beardsley and Shaw. It seems the merest accident when Beardsley and Shaw coincide (as they did on 21 April, 1894, when an adaptation of a Beardsley poster[3] appeared as the programme for *Arms And The Man*—not to mention that Beardsley was Mrs Patrick Campbell's portraitist

* In a little book *Aubrey Beardsley* (John Lane), which is almost a handbook to the decadent movement: it is dedicated to Ronald Firbank's friend, Sir Coleridge Arthur Fitzroy Kennard.

† There is nothing unlikely in such an influence. As Robert Ross pointed out in 1909, 'Italy, Austria, and Germany recognised in him a master some time before his death. At Berlin his picture of *Mrs Patrick Campbell*, the actress, is now in a place of honour in the Museum.'

and Shaw her photographer*). Yet as a matter of fact, the three masters were united by the influence of music (at which Beardsley, as well as Shaw, was proficient†). In particular, all three were Wagnerites. If Strauss made himself Wagner's direct operatic heir, Beardsley made himself Wagner's and the Wagnerites' illustrator[4] and Shaw made himself (with *The Perfect Wagnerite* of 1898) Wagner's propagandist.

Under their feet, it was Wagner who became the stepping-stone back to the eighteenth century—an anomalous stepping-stone so far as style is concerned: and yet Wagner's conception of music-drama is essentially close to Mozart's. For both Strauss and Beardsley, some of Wagner's attractiveness must have lain in the perverse element in both his music and his dramas; from the brother-and-sister love of Siegmund and Sieglinde, both Wagnerites quested perversity through the necrophilism of *Salome* until they came to the eighteenth century, Beardsley drawn to Pope's epic about the perverse compulsion to assault women's hair and Strauss to the transvestite frisson of opening an opera with one prima donna newly arisen from the bed of another. Shaw, vestry-man and advocate of public and private healthiness, who would certainly have refuted the suggestion (though it may be true) that his own heroines are not a whit less transvestite than Octavian, was attracted to Wagner's dramatic scope. His own dramatic practice borrowed from both the Mozartian and the Wagnerian music-drama. *The Ring*, which Shaw (like, indeed, Wagner himself) was capable of reading as a socialist tract, became the model for Shaw's own 'metabiological pentateuch', where in the twilight of the old gods he switched on his neo-eighteenth-century enlightenment and revived the biological outlook of Goethe.

Pioneered from no matter what different directions, the eighteenth-century revival quickly became the twentieth-century mode (except according to the *Oxford Dictionary*, whose Pocket edition was still, in 1939, defining *rococo* as '. . . with much conventional decoration, tastelessly florid . . .

---

* He photographed her in bed. The photograph (reproduced in, e.g. Margaret Shenfield's pictorial biography of Shaw) shews the bed to have been purest fin-de-siècle rococo; it would serve very well for the first act of *Der Rosenkavalier*.

† Like another Mozart, Beardsley at the age of ten 'made his first public appearance as an infant musical phenomenon, playing at concerts in company with his sister' (Robert Ross: *Aubrey Beardsley*, p. 11).

antiquated, out of date'). From *Der Rosenkavalier* on, nothing could stop the twentieth century accelerating, with cries of 'charming', towards anything it could label *rococo*, *Georgian* or *Regency*, until nowadays the least pretending suburban drawing-room does not consider itself furnished unless it is satin-striped all over.

Unfortunately, all this is fashion, not passion. As anyone can see by reading the *Guardian** (the only newspaper in Britain with a conscience towards good buildings), or by walking about London and noting how many excellent Georgian and Regency houses have lately been or are soon to be demolished, our taste for the eighteenth-century manner is much too flimsy to stand up either to the impersonal† activity of governments and local governments or to the conscienceless spoliation which financialists—do they *mean* to be sardonic?—call 'development'. Fashion, which is merely a race to get into midstream before the stream changes direction, has no time for the pioneers of the eighteenth-century revival and precious little for the eighteenth-century originals themselves, which are liable to get knocked down in the rush. It hardly distinguishes between the eighteenth century's masterpieces, its mediocrities and its few but very deep abysms. They are all 'charming'.

This label is really only a kindlier translation of the Victorian judgment 'frivolous'. We still depend very largely on Victorian artistic judgments, especially in our official, academic taste, which has to stick to Victorian standards because it still has not replaced Victorian standard reference books. We are still disposed to accept that the general character of eighteenth-century art is frivolous: we differ from the Victorians only in that we like frivolity. Naturally, the eighteenth century's works of bad or indifferent art *are*, like any other century's, frivolous. But

* 'Georgian fronted house threatened with demolition' (by Colchester Town Council's road-widening scheme). 'Plan to demolish house', sc. 'a Georgian house used as the post office at Dereham, Norfolk'; plan by the Ministry of Works. '£10,000 appeal to save Georgian house', sc. 5 Beauford Square, Bath—'It is in good condition and structurally sound and the inside has been left largely untouched'; threatener: Bath Corporation. 'Regency houses threatened by traffic ramp', sc. Nos. 48 to 55 Clarence Square, Brighton. (*Guardian* of 29 August, 16 December, 1961, 5 January, 9 January, 17 March, 1962.)

† Under the first of the *Guardian* headlines cited in the previous note, the Chairman of Colchester Corporation Highways Committee is quoted as saying 'To me personally it is a very unpleasant prospect to have to demolish a house of that character, but personal feelings must not be taken into consideration'.

anyone who supposes Watteau's paintings, *Les Liaisons Dangereuses* or the death duet—the rococo Liebestod—between Constanze and Belmonte in *Il Seraglio* to be frivolous is a person who would titter during *King Lear*.

In the shadow of all those Victorian beards we still make the terrible mistake of assuming that because the rococo spirit did not take to high tragedy as practised by the old masters (a genre many eighteenth-century artists tried, but unsuccessfully) eighteenth-century art had no tragic sense. It had. Its tragedies are its ironical satires, like *The Rape Of The Lock* and *Così Fan Tutte*. Very often—this is the common matter between, for example, the poignant dots of light which glance off the clothes of Watteau's characters and the lucid child's-eye vision of Candide—eighteenth-century tragedy is the tragedy of intelligence in a block-headed world (one of the great discoveries of the eighteenth century was that intelligence is beautiful) and of the frail instinct of pleasure in a world block-headedly going on committing old atrocities and working up to worse ones: a poignancy to which our own world situation makes us more than ever vulnerable.

Official taste has always been perceptive enough to admit Mozart to the canon of perpetual remembrance: and popular taste is perfectly correct when it calls him charming, even though it giggles at the inane producer's business which so often coarsens the charm on our stages. Mozart *is* charming—indeed, ravishing—up to the very limit of our tolerance of pleasure. Our only just quarrel with either popular or official taste is that neither goes deep enough. Appreciation of Mozart is a matter of being moved.

Official taste, at least, has a number of excuses on its side—as well as the fact that it always is rather ponderous about coming round to doing justice to great artists. Mozart, because he was not, in the narrow sense, a technical innovator, does not attach himself to pure musicological scholarship. Again, there is no question of rehabilitating him by restoring a reputation colossal in his own period and unfairly left to lapse since. Neither is there any question of rescuing a genius no one noticed at the time. The result is that he does not exercise any of those holds on the romantic imagination of scholars which usually are the unacknowledged legislators of the major changes in academic taste. From the point of view of the academies, Mozart is there, and has always been there. It is merely that the academies do not know quite what to make of him. The only claim he exerts on posterity is his excellence.

This claim, which in the long run is the strongest an artist can put forward, is probably in any case the one which official taste takes longest to recognise. In Mozart's case the difficulty is doubled, because his excellence is couched in the idiom of the eighteenth century. Although we have tried to redress the grosser Victorian misjudgments, we are still not wholly at ease with any eighteenth-century work of art.

For this there is a very sufficient reason. The eighteenth century itself, and in particular its dominant intellectual temper, which was rationalistic, was not wholly at ease with *any* work of art. Eighteenth-century rationalism, being enlightened in every direction except psychologically, was at a loss when it was confronted with artistic fictions. It had made allowance in the most liberal way for everything except fantasy; it thought nothing human alien to itself except the unconscious. Art, as a fantasy worked on and recognised as untrue by the conscious but originating in the unconscious, it found the utmost difficulty in fitting in to the ideal, 'natural', sincere, truthtelling societies it was busy planning.

Mozart, who was technically no more an eccentric than an innovator, was not in the least a man born out of his time. The great difficulty he presents to academic taste is that his idiom and many of his ideas swim quite happily with the current of his time; and that current, at least if we judge its nature by its prolific theoretical manifestoes instead of its actual masterpieces in the arts, had an anti-artistic direction. Mozart's own practice, of course, (like Watteau's, Tiepolo's, Gainsborough's, Balthasar Neumann's, Laclos's, Pope's) is the opposite of anti-artistic. To illuminate in what sense Mozart was *of* his century and in what sense he countered and transcended it, it will be necessary to look deep into both his and his century's psychology and to search the relationship between eighteenth-century rationalism and psychology itself. This would constitute, if he had no other, his historical importance: if we take a sounding in his artistic practice, the top level will shew us at its most readable the grain of eighteenth-century thinking, and the depths, by shewing what Mozart alone achieved, will shew up the deficiencies in the temper of his time. But even before taking soundings, we can see that, while it is fair to recognise a *tendency* in the eighteenth century to blight the arts, it is sheer defiance of what our sensibilities tell us to imagine that the tendency was fulfilled—most particularly in music, where the unparalleled quartet of J. S. Bach, Handel, Haydn and Mozart makes the Age of Reason the Golden Age.

Fortunately, both official and popular taste have been outstripped by a group of people (which by now probably includes the majority of serious musicians and serious audiences) who have recognised Mozart as a transcendent case. Some of them will not listen to any operas except Mozart's. More, and commanding more respect, love both music and opera, and have recognised Mozart not only as *the* operatic composer but as *the* composer—perhaps as *the* artist.

For the moment, these people have also outstripped their own articulateness. But there is no doubt of their existence, which has been objectively observed. A writer in one of the Sunday papers can rely on his readers taking the force of the comparison when he throws off a remark that someone 'loved the Arabic language as other people love Mozart'.[5] Indeed, his readers have only to attend a Mozart opera and they will see some of these people coming away after the performance wrapped in a look which means that their Egos have been identified with the artistic Ego of Mozart (not by the conversion of the artist into flesh: but by taking of the manhood into the artist). It is a look which asserts '*my* Mozart'. Significantly, it is to be seen elsewhere only after the performance of a Shakespeare play. It is my intention in this book to speak for, and to, these Mozartians.

One of the most misleading of the Victorian judgments we have still with us is that it is Beethoven who is the Shakespeare among composers. 'More than any other composer he deserves to be called the Shakespeare of music' is the categorical assertion of the article on Beethoven in even the 1950 edition of *The Oxford Companion To Music*; and the whole volume is presided over, by way of frontispiece, by a (long posthumous) portrait of Beethoven. One way or another, we have all grown up under this presidency—indeed, under the presidency of a bogus, long-posthumous, idolatrous image of Beethoven. Anyone who acquainted himself with the musical repertory during an adolescence passed in London will have had dinned into him the liturgical tag of the Promenade Concerts, 'Friday night is Beethoven night'.

I steadfastly refuse to be bounced by all this into petulance against Beethoven. Indeed, anyone who claims to love Mozart and refuses a hearing to Beethoven is demonstrating that, whatever it is he loves in Mozart, it is not music, to which he is obviously deaf in just the way that Beethoven was never deaf. But it is time to point out that Beethovenolatry, a Victorian movement which did not reach its culmination until 1927 with the publication of J. W. N. Sullivan's famous book, leads to absurdities: such as Sullivan's 'People already saw in him a second Mozart, and Beethoven, we may be sure, felt that he was destined to something even greater';[6] and 'That' (it does not matter what) 'is, in fact, the weakness of Bach as compared with Beethoven'.[7]

It is absurd to talk about things greater than Mozart or about weaknesses in Bach as compared with anything. And it is not only absurd but in the most pointed way inept to call Beethoven a Shakespeare. An artist whose work, though often hearty, shews not the first stirrings of either wit or comedy cannot be a Shakespeare.

What Beethoven does have in common with Shakespeare is untidiness; and here both are in contrast with Mozart, who always achieves perfection of design in his immediate musical material and usually (the great exception is *Don Giovanni*) in the operatic scheme as a whole. Shakespeare, however, is untidy with the divine carelessness of a creator who, when the moment of shewing up comes, will simply invent something to patch up the gap he carelessly left to start with; whereas Beethoven's untidiness is inclusive, almost obsessional. He flings himself on the stone in a frenzy to liberate the statue inside; yet he wants the finished work to contain the chippings as well. He is one of the artists who present us not only with the final sum but with the sheaves of scrap paper on which they did their rough working.

Beethoven impresses us, in fact, by his tremendous labours to be a genius, like Herakles's to be a hero. He has every right to be a genius by this method. But we should not subscribe to the artist-as-Titan myth (a myth which probably began in Giorgio Vasari's attachment to the personality of Michelangelo) so exclusively that we let ourselves suppose that genius working by this method is ipso facto better genius than that which works otherwise. That is like supposing that the baby born of the more tremendous labour is a better and more valid baby or, as opponents of painless childbirth used to maintain, that it will be better loved by its mother.

In reality we know that what method an artist adopts, though infinitely interesting as gossip, is not directly correlated to the results. And in art it is only results that count. This last is a bitter truth, which we forget whenever a romantic myth offers us the opportunity. We should always prefer that the man who tries hardest should be the greatest artist—or at least (for in the deepest sense it really may be the one who tries hardest who is), the man who tries most visibly or in the way most appealing to us. We should like artistic merit to be a clutch of M.B.E.'s which we could distribute to the people who have slogged away. But the full bitterness of the truth is that art is a realm where the aristocratic principle rules, and must rule— if the whole business is not to be reduced to nonsense. Perhaps when we abolish the aristocratic principle in our social and political life, where it is the aristocratic principle which makes nonsense, we will stop trying to quiet our consciences by denying it in art: when wealth and birth can no longer purchase social merit, we may be brave enough to admit that artistic merit is not to be purchased by any of the things we consider virtues, whether being a decent chap or being a romantic and appealing indecent chap or slogging Titanically away. The Titan method produces a Benjamin Haydon quite as often as a Michelangelo or a Beethoven; and though Herakles *was* a hero, so was the wily Odysseus, who never laboured when he could think instead.

We are, as a matter of fact, inclined to deny that thought may be as forceful and effective as labour. Very few intellectual thinkers, especially if they are of left-wing persuasions (which often means believing in some special merit in labour beyond the work it gets done) would describe themselves—would think themselves worthy to be described—as workers. The note which J. W. N. Sullivan reiterates like a road-drill in his panegyric on Beethoven is *power*. Quite possibly power, if we mean power to move the emotions, really is the criterion of greatness in art. But it is only on the very naïvest interpretation of power that we can consider Beethoven *more* powerful than Mozart—as naïve as supposing that the weight-lifter is necessarily more virile than the fencer or that the navvy disposes of more force than the skilled workman who waits till he sees the chink where he may apply the lever. Beethoven assaults our emotions head on, heroically hurling his forces over the top, at no matter what cost to himself. Mozart is the strategist who takes our breath away by the audacity of his plans. He is upon us and has captured the citadel before we had time to conceive that he might come by that route.

In art, the only criterion is the effectiveness of the capture. If the citadel succumbs to him, Mozart is no less effective than Beethoven. Whether a person does succumb, only that person can know; and there is no arbitrating between two people's different experiences. One may object only when a person does succumb to Mozart and admits he does, and yet afterwards inclines to think there is, after all, more merit in Beethoven's head-on assault. There may be; but it is in some moralistic world, not the world of art. The head-on assault at least looks as if it cost its practitioner more pain (in reality, we cannot assess what it has cost the strategist to keep his mind and muscles controlled, to *be* intelligent); and so, in the world of moralistic magic where we unthinkingly pass so much of our time, we ascribe more merit to it—just as, in that world, we believe it is only medicine which tastes nasty that does the patient good. But if, in fact, both medicines work, then it is pure bias against intelligence which makes us think the painful one better.

In all probability it is a disesteem of intelligence which lies at the root of Beethovenolatry (as distinct from appreciating Beethoven). Even this disesteem is not wholly wrong-headed. It is a muddled apprehension of the aristocratic principle in art. It knows that art depends not on patiently and intellectually thinking up ideas but on the ideas coming up of their own accord. (The aristocratic principle goes on to insist that the distribution of such ideas is capricious, non-egalitarian and extremely unjust to the many who wait for them but are passed by.) But we ought not to confuse the irrational, unconscious origin and impulse of art with its conscious working out. The greatest (the most emotionally effective) art is that which achieves the most rigorously—indeed, ruthlessly—logical and intelligent working out of a germ which the conscious intellect and will can neither create nor justify. The *purpose* of art, like the purpose of life, is nonexistent (or at least it does not declare itself): artist and biologist must respectively accept art and life as activities which *are*—and have no further justification. Art, in this respect, is aping life. It is setting up to be another instinctual, self-justifying, self-existent activity, an extra life, an organic growth *on* life.

Mozart's beautifully lucid and forceful artistic intelligence is exercised on the perfect working out of his images. He is the classical artist par excellence. But the images themselves are such that the most masterly intellect could not in a thousand years have hit on them if it had gone in search of them by working through the possible permutations of notes. (If it could, Gluck's strong and classical intellect *would* have hit on them.) The melody of 'Voi che sapete' or 'Là ci darem la mano' takes us by surprise and captures us precisely because not only could *we* not have thought it up but nobody could have thought it up. To suppose Beethoven a more inspired artist than Mozart is a contradiction in terms (*inspiration* being a perfectly precise—psychological—term: for an image which visits the artist from a source of which he is unconscious). We can see Beethoven tearing his hair and calling down inspiration. But Mozart does not set a note on paper until the Muse has dictated the entire sequence.

What is more, the Muse dictates so remorselessly that Mozart has no time for tearing his hair. He has no time to be a genius: only to write works of genius. In one sense, Mozart has no more 'personality' than a stenographer working at high pressure: it is only we, with our unified conception of psychology, who insist that stenographer and dictator are in this case one and the same and that the source of the notes Mozart takes down is in fact the personality he seems not to possess.

The marvellous rationality and balance of Mozart's mind argue the very opposite of a cold, ratiocinative art. As with all great art, especially classical great art (Bach's is the most obviously similar case), the whole vigour of his splendid intelligence is devoted to holding his vessel steady to receive these overwhelming visitations from another source.

Once we let ourselves disesteem artistic intelligence, we are moving towards a disesteem of art. Beethoven has come to occupy his presidential niche because he appeals to us, in his squalor, his bad temper, his physical affliction, his celibacy, his inarticulateness like a vow of silence, as a monkish saint. We praise him as spiritual—the word Sullivan hit on when he entitled his book *Beethoven: His Spiritual Development*. The over-adulation of Beethoven is comparable to the over-adulation —though this has not been going on nearly so long—of another spiritual artist, El Greco.

This word *spiritual* represents another attempt to dodge the truth that nothing counts in art except the results. It is judging by a non-artistic criterion. The adulators of Beethoven are on the point of claiming that his art is the greatest because it goes beyond art. In art, however, nothing goes beyond art.

Religious people will always maintain that there is something in the universe which does go beyond art. But this must not be allowed to masquerade as an artistic judgment. It is not an *artistic* judgment if they tell us that St Luke was the greatest portrait painter. Similarly, religionists will always maintain that the spiritual goes beyond the psychological. Psychology, however, is meaningless unless it claims to be inclusive. Either it must take as its material every manifestation of the human psyche, including both art and spirituality, or it is nothing. Much lies outside it: much that comes within its sphere it cannot yet give an account of, and any or all the accounts it has so far given may be wrong: but nothing can lie beyond it.

If we recognise (as Alfred Einstein did*) that it is not Beethoven but Mozart who is to be properly and with exactitude compared to Shakespeare, the claim rests on his being, like Shakespeare, a supremely *intelligent* and a supremely *psychological* artist; and it is a claim which will make sense only to those who agree that, in art at least, nothing goes beyond psychology and nothing goes beyond art. It is *not* a claim which

* '. . . his achievement in opera can in fact be compared only with that of Shakespeare, who gave his characters the reality of living human beings: eternal types, and yet completely living embodiments of those types.' (*Mozart . . .* , 3)

asserts (this would be to be as obtuse in Mozart's behalf as J. W. N. Sullivan was in Beethoven's) that Mozart is a better or even a greater composer than Beethoven, Handel or Bach, any more than Shakespeare is a better poet than Donne or Keats. Not for a moment does Mozart make Beethoven superfluous— just as Shakespeare does not make Donne superfluous: there is material in Beethoven's final quartets which would have been as inaccessible to Mozart as Donne's passionate sensuality and passionate spirituality to Shakespeare. We can only super-adduce a quality of universality in Mozart and say of him what Keats said of Shakespeare, 'His genius was an innate universality'.

If we are talking about *universal*, presumably we do not mean some least common denominator of universal appeal, but the capacity to create universes seemingly as wide and as deep as the real universe. Beethoven creates no universes. His magnificent and moving opera is a failure, though an immortal failure, for the very reason that it does not realise a single character, let alone circumscribe a universe in which they all live and are inter-related. Each of Mozart's major operas is its own cosmos, as vivid and self-sufficient as the cosmoi created by Shakespeare's major plays. This is art setting up as an extra life, as the biological activity of the human imagination. A human is the only animal who is not limited to one self, one life history and the progeny he can beget of his body. It is not merely that a man may, as artistic creator, leave behind him the only sort of progeny in which the originator's stake is not watered down with each new generation. Whether as creator or appreciator, man may inhabit a thousand selves—and not only through the arts which create characters in the literary sense. The shape, proportions and progression of a symphony, and likewise the form of a picture, even though a picture does not proceed through time, constitute the shape of a certain experience, a shape which is in a sense a narrative, a life history which, in the objective world, has never taken place, which the creator animates and the appreciator re-animates.

In Mozart's cosmos, art has aped not the appearance reality has to the artist's eyes but the self-sufficiency of reality. If the spiritual really is transcendent, then it is transcendent in Mozart, too; if it is not, then it is not, there, too. Mozart's supreme excellence lies in the fact that, though he does not fall short of reality, in which case we could not ask the question about his cosmos, he does not tell us the answer, any more than reality does. With Beethoven, we have to agree that the spiritual *is* transcendent in the world of reality outside art before we can —on those grounds—agree to his claim to supremacy. Beethoven may be right; but his is not *artistic* rightness. It is Mozart's cosmos which has re-created the ambiguity, the purposelessness, the pointlessness, of life.

The most obvious overlapping, in the comparison between Mozart and Shakespeare, is that both are dramatists: respectively music-dramatist and poetry-dramatist. Only Shakespearean comedy makes the exact mixture of romantic with comedic, and artificial convention with piercingly real psychology, which are the constituents of the atmosphere of *Die Zauberflöte* and *Figaro*. Shakespearean tragedy at the pitch of *King Lear* Mozart never attempted: his tragic sense shewed itself in tragedy's eighteenth-century manifestation, irony: but in his one heavy drama, *Don Giovanni*, he produced a remarkable (and as I mean to shew not accidental) doublet of *Hamlet*. *Don Giovanni* is what Freud perceived *Hamlet* to be, an unconscious autobiography. Like *Hamlet*, it is one of the world's imperfect masterpieces; and again like *Hamlet*, it is, thanks to the nature of its unconsciously autobiographical material, an eternal enigma, an unstaunchable wound in the cultural consciousness of civilisation.

We need not hesitate to accept *Don Giovanni* as Mozart's own unconscious autobiography, although the story was an old one and the actual libretto by da Ponte. No more was the story of *Hamlet* original to Shakespeare: it became his by adoption. A process of psychological adoption is what one can see taking place between Mozart and all his major dramatic themes. The fact that Mozart was during most of his life short of money can be made the pretext for believing that he set to music whatever literary hackwork came his way: but that belief is possible only to people who have not read his letters. The letters shew him at the utmost pains to secure the best available librettists and then at the utmost pains to work the raw material they supplied into a shape acceptable—adoptable—to himself. Mozart was not one of the composers who set words to music: he was a composer who believed and explicitly said that in a successful opera the words are 'written solely for the music'[8]—a composer, in fact, of the Wagnerian pattern, for whom both drama and music are inextricably present from the moment of conception. 'The best thing of all', Mozart continued in the same letter, 'is when a good composer, who understands the stage and is talented enough to make sound suggestions, meets an able poet, that true phoenix.'

Mozart stopped short of the Wagnerian practice of writing the whole libretto himself—but only just short. From early in his career he had quite enough faith in his own talent for the stage to make very considerable 'suggestions' about shaping the raw material. As early as *Idomeneo* he was correcting the implausibilities his librettist had let slip by—indeed, redrafting the whole scheme of entrances and exits.* By the time (which was later in the same year) of *Seraglio*, he was reporting to his father 'I have explained to Stephanie the words I require for this aria—indeed I had finished composing most of the music for it before Stephanie knew anything whatever about it'.[9] This last must mean that Mozart had in fact more or less written the words of the aria before Stephanie knew anything whatever about them: he must at least have fixed their rhythm unalterably. And certainly Mozart was not (witness, if nothing else, the letters themselves) one of the musical people who feel afraid of or, through ignorance, superstitious about words. When he made a musical scena of Goethe's *Das Veilchen* he did not scruple to improve Goethe with a final line of his own.[10]

The truth is (and the firmest witnesses to it are the operas themselves) that Mozart's was a dramatic genius: his approach to opera was that of a dramatic composer (which he had always principally intended himself to be), for whom the drama and the music were inseparable. To the operatic face of Mozart's genius, the meeting with that true phoenix an able dramatic poet was as indispensable as meeting with a fertile woman is to fatherhood. Mozart was for ever mentally riffling through the

* 'For example, in Scene 6, after Arbace's aria, I see that Varesco has Idomeneo, Arbace, etc. How can the latter re-appear immediately? Fortunately he can stay away altogether . . . After the mourning chorus the king and all his people go away; and in the following scene the directions are, "*Idomeneo in ginocchione nel tempio*". That is quite impossible. He must come in with his whole suite. A march must be introduced here . . .' (Mozart to Leopold Mozart from Munich, 3 January, 1781.)

available librettists* to select the best; it is fair conjecture that he equally riffled through their ideas to select the ones he could adopt. Indeed, more than once we can detect him in the process of learning from experience which ones he could not adopt. Nothing is more telling about Mozart's care in picking texts than the ones he discarded because his dramatic genius could not make them its own. When Varesco, who had previously supplied him with *Idomeneo*, gave him *L'Oca del Cairo*, Mozart specifically complained to his father that it was through not trusting his own theatrical judgment that he had come to take up the theme at all; and in fact *L'Oca* remains fragmentary precisely because it was not a drama Mozart could adopt to himself.[11] He was capable, too, of leaving a commissioned song unfinished because the text offended him.[12] With his major operatic themes, the ones he could and did adopt, it was in one case at least Mozart himself who made the selection—direct from the theatrical repertory: it was he who proposed Beaumarchais's *Figaro* to da Ponte, the librettist whom he had selected. It was by a very scrutinising selection over a very wide field, followed up by his personal re-working of the material obtained by careful selection, that Mozart adopted into his own psychology characters and situations which had been in the first place Varesco's, Stephanie's, Beaumarchais's, da Ponte's. Don Giovanni and Count Almaviva are by the end of the process Mozart's characters, just as Oedipus is Sophocles's character by virtue of the selection Sophocles exercised through the field of Greek mythology and the re-working he then made of the substance of the myth he had selected.

Mozart's letters make it plain that we should be doing violence not merely to his intentions but to the actual psychology

* 'I believe and hope too that he himself may write an opera libretto for me.' ('He' is Gottlieb Stephanie the younger, librettist of *Seraglio*.) 'Whether he has written his plays alone or with the help of others, whether he has plagiarised or created, he still understands the stage . . . I have not the slightest doubt about the success of the opera, provided the text is a good one.' (Mozart to Leopold Mozart, from Vienna, 16 June, 1781.) 'Our poet here is now a certain Abbate Da Ponte. He has an enormous amount to do in revising pieces for the theatre and he has to write *per obbligo* an entirely new libretto for Salieri . . . He has promised after that to write a new libretto for me. But who knows whether he will be able to keep his word—or will want to? . . . If he is in league with Salieri, I shall never get anything out of him . . . So I have been thinking that unless Varesco is still very much annoyed with us about the Munich opera, he might write me a new libretto for seven characters.' (Mozart to Leopold Mozart, from Vienna, 7 May, 1783.)

of his genius if we did not accept his operas whole, as dramatic musical conceptions. Indeed, it is to the operas themselves as works of art that we should be doing most violence. They are not stories to which Mozart has added music—a point which many people have accidentally put to the test by making first acquaintance with some of the arias as concert or gramophone-record pieces and then discovering how much is lost by hearing them out of dramatic context or, rather, how much remains to discover by hearing them in it. Wilfully to separate music from drama in Mozart is to mutilate works of art by a world master of drama—a mutilation by elegant extract such as the eighteenth century itself performed on Shakespeare when it tried to have his verse, rhetoric and sententiousness without the play. And in fact Shakespeare is the clue to one of the problems which make academic taste uneasy, namely on what dramatic level we should take Mozart's operas. The rationalism of the eighteenth century and the puritanism of the nineteenth are here in a conspiracy, suggesting—even nowadays—that we should not take them at all but should try to have the music without the opera by writing off the dramatic part. Even nowadays, when the operas are performed and performed whole, reputable writers can be found dismissing the plots as nonsense. So they are, if one takes them as naturalistic stories. *Die Zauberflöte* is very nearly as nonsensical as *The Tempest*, *Così* as artificial as *The Two Gentlemen* and *Figaro* as improbable as *Twelfth Night*. However, they should be taken, not naturalistically but perfectly seriously, as metaphors and conceits—witty in themselves like the very shape on the printed page of metaphysical poetry —whose structural purpose is to frame within a convention the universe and the characters Mozart is creating. The convention in which Mozart sets his operatic world is the utmost development of the operatic—indeed, of the artistic—convention itself, and in developing it he accomplished the deepest exploitation of opera's potentialities; for opera of all arts offers the opportunity of the most direct expression of emotions by the least naturalistic method. Nature does not endow bereaved fathers with blank verse like King Lear's or permit bereaved daughters, like Donna Anna, to burst into soprano flames at a touch to the blue paper. The sounds which issue from the lips of King Lear and Donna Anna would, if they were sounds alone, without context, provoke us to an ecstasy of pleasure. Yet both Shakespeare and Mozart are psychologists of such expertise that we cannot doubt that King Lear and Donna Anna are 'real' characters feeling genuine grief. At the same time their authors are artists so versed and masterly that they can introduce into their pleasing texture recognisable hieroglyphs of the sounds people really do make in grief, so that at the end we are almost gulled into thinking we have truly listened to a naturalistic transcription of their sorrow and yet remain aware that the texture of delight has never in fact been flawed. This is, of course, the height and the very definition of dramatic art. Mozart practises it through the ravishment of his music, Shakespeare through the ravishment of his poetry, for which no one has ever found any synonym except music.

The arts of the mid twentieth century are in danger precisely of forgetting that art *is* art. Artistic intelligence is so little prized, and so much substance is wasted on frontal attacks—often of the noblest kind, sheer liberal good feeling—that there is nothing our audiences, critics and artists need so badly as an astringent course in Mozart's artistry. But this immediate remedial need is the lowliest reason for taking to Mozart. If we open our hearts to him, it must be for his own sake: which is only a different way of saying for our own sake. Our species is engaged in an evolutionary struggle to survive not the threats of the environment but the top-heaviness of our own destructive impulse. Nature as such does not attach any more purpose to our instinct to survive this struggle than it does to the ants' to survive their struggles; but since it has allowed us to evolve into psychic beings, we are capable of giving ourselves a purpose. A humanity which does not number its masterpieces of art among the reasons why human beings capable of appreciating them *must* remain on the earth has reduced itself to the condition of an ant society—and has probably lessened both its will and its capacity to survive.

Mozart was a classical artist, which was not unusual in the eighteenth century: but by carrying the common artistic idiom of his century to unique extremes (that is, by being intelligent enough to push the logic of classicism further than anyone else) he became the world's *most* classical artist. In his perfectly constructed vehicle he mounted what was, in the eighteenth century, the rarest and least wanted of gifts: psychological understanding. Eighteenth-century literature is short on nothing but characters: its lack can be supplied from Mozart's operas. With the nineteenth-century development of the novel, which influenced all the other arts (most obviously and deleteriously, Victorian painting), psychology in art became less rare, but classical form became rarer—until, by the mid twentieth century, literature at least has almost lost the ability or the desire to design, and concision, logic and sensuous beauty are neither required nor admired. Mozart's unique excellence lies in his double supremacy: as classical artist, and as psychological artist. Psychology can never transcend its immediate relevance to ourselves and become absolute, unless it is mounted in a classical vehicle; and unless classicism is psychological as well, it can never transcend its immediate irrelevance to ourselves and move us.

Mozart's supreme importance is as an artist, tout court. The Mozart of the operas is a music-dramatist in exactly the sense that Shakespeare is a poetry-dramatist. His characters (and he has made them by adoption utterly *his*) 'exist' and deserve serious scrutiny (which I propose to give them) to the same extent as Shakespeare's. They have the same importance to us as Shakespeare's—for their own sakes: that is, for our own sakes. The touchy problem of how to 'place' Mozart admits of only one solution. He stands on the very pinnacle of Parnassus.

II

Women and Opera

———————— ❋ ————————

In any of the arts, creative or executant, women *may* be the
equals of men. There is only one respect in which physiology
insists they must be not merely equal but dominant: they have
more interesting singing voices.

This is not to deny the beauty of men's voices or their
indispensability to opera—whose quintessential form is, indeed,
developed out of the relationship between men and women. But
it is the female voice, and par excellence the soprano, which
exerts the most vivid pressure on our imagination. Our attention
goes as naturally and immediately to the part sung by the
soprano as it does to the first violins when we listen to an
orchestra or look at an orchestral score; if the composer wants
us to pay more heed to some other part, he must pick it out and
force it on our notice. And then the soprano, having captured
our ear in the first place, has the best qualifications for holding
it, either because the soprano really is the most flexible voice
or because our ear is more sensitive to subtlety and variety
couched in its register.

Opera is a creation not exclusively for but round the soprano.
Prima donna is a term without a masculine. However, it did
have throughout the eighteenth century—that is, throughout
the formative and well into the formed period of opera—a
neuter. The castrati (who included, of course, alto as well as
treble voices) enjoyed all the public fuss and put on all the airs
of the prima donna. What they did not take were the prima
donna's arias. Whereas in church music boys and castrati had
excluded women from the choir altogether, in opera, where the
voices belong to characters, women quickly began to take possession of the women's parts. It was the male voices, and particularly the tenor, which the castrati drove out. In a sense, the

reign of the castrati was actually the period of utmost triumph for the female *voice*, though that voice had been partly usurped by men. (So had the female rôles: a young castrato might sing a female part;[1] but that was only fair exchange, since women quite often sang male rôles, too.) The truly male voices were pushed into a department which supplied harsh* and unsensuous noise, the tenor being conceived heroically rather than lyrically. Though the bass might be given, especially in Handel's scheme of things, a bravura aria or two in which to match his warrior-like temper against the trumpet, the male singers on the whole supplied weight and impressiveness, and characterised, in the persons of parents and rulers, the circumstances and authorities of the plot rather than its emotional moving principles. The male voices were a dark background for the more glamorously attractive characters—par excellence, of course, the young man and young woman in love, both of whom were likely to be vocally soprano. Dramatic attention was focused where the ear naturally leads it, namely on the register which among adults, if nature is left untampered-with, belongs exclusively to women. Mozart, who wrote the soprano jeune premier part in *Idomeneo* for Vincenzo del Prato ('my *molto amato castrato*', to whom 'I shall have to teach the whole opera . . . as if he were a child'[2]), was brought up in this tradition,† and it left its traces in his operas even when he dispensed with castrato rôles, in the form of his rather unloving treatment of the tenor voice. His Tamino and Belmonte, being heroic tenors, come off not so badly; it is in lyrical tenor arias such as 'Dalla sua pace' and 'Un'aura amorosa', and only there, that Mozart approaches—or at least gives his singers the opportunity to approach—vulgarity and banality.

It was really only in nineteenth-century opera, after the eclipse of the castrato, that the lyrical tenor could come forward with a bid to rival the soprano. Nineteenth-century music

---

* Angus Heriot (*The Castrati In Opera*, II) remarks on the seventeenth- and eighteenth-century prejudice against tenor and bass voices and the common accusation that they were rough, an accusation he thinks may have been justified and attributable to the training methods of the time.

† Mozart himself at the age of eight, in London, took singing lessons from the famous castrato Giovanni Manzuoli, who later sang in Mozart's *Ascanio in Alba* in Milan in 1771. (See Mozart's letter to his sister, from Milan, 24 November, 1771; and Angus Heriot: *The Castrati In Opera*, V.)

enabled him to make a splash, but it could not equip him to drown out the prima donna. He is obliged to make his appeal in a more limited mood and by less musical means. Emotionally, he is more or less confined to the two extremes of the jolly and the love-lorn; technically, he must rest his case on the weight-lifting ability whereby he hurls his sustained high notes into the auditorium. Moreover, he astounds us only when he is on his heights; and if he tries to bounce between high and low he achieves not coloratura but yodelling. Even the great tenors have none of the soprano's power, which Mozart so tenderly exploits, to move us by the gravity and density of what are, for her, low notes. In *Così Fan Tutte*, Mozart musically distinguishes Fiordiligi's character from her sister's largely by virtue of the astonishing low notes which play so heroic a part in her big arias—particularly, of course, in 'Come scoglio'; and this despite the fact that it is Dorabella who is technically the mezzo-soprano. Fiordiligi, in fact, has the greater compass: in music as in personality. Her depths suggest that her character has more—in the eighteenth-century word which Dr Johnson was so affronted to find made his auditors laugh—bottom. The profound notes with which she affirms her rock-solidity against temptation adumbrate the greater tragedy of her fall.

Opera being an exploitation of the female voice, it was bound to be the eighteenth century in which the operatic form emerged (after being conceived in the century before*), since it is in the eighteenth century that women first emerge into the full light of social history. Both emergences are parts of a greater whole, namely the psychological emancipation of European humanity which was the eighteenth century's major achievement. Once reason was set free to plead for justice in place of the inherited social order, liberal sympathy was drawn to women as a long oppressed class; and the cause of their emancipation was bound to be implicitly helped by the arrival of opera, which not merely drew attention to women but pointed up the injustice of assuming that nature had made them in every respect inferior to men.

However, opera did not have an easy growing-up in the age of reason. Reason was continually protesting against its

---

* Or, strictly speaking, a year or two before that—if Jacopo Peri's *Daphne* of 1597 really was the first opera as opposed to musical play.

absurdity and—at a period when every branch of aesthetics was insisting on 'nature' as the ideal—its blatant anti-naturalism. Even so, what Voltaire called 'ce beau monstre de l'opéra' inexorably became the voguish form of art, from which position it was able to render women a service quite reasonably and justly. But it reached that position not by direct help from the eighteenth-century passion for reason but because reason licensed mankind to go in search of pleasure, which reason recognised as the most natural of occupations. Opera was created in the first place out of the natural desire to be entertained by the artificial. Its patrons were in quest of pleasure; and opera directed their attention to women as a neglected class in a different sense—as a class long undervalued as a source of pleasure.

Not, of course, that the eighteenth century was the first to appreciate the pleasures of sex. But it probably was the first in the modern world to appreciate the pleasures of a public, socialised sexuality—of the kind which is now quite familiar though still exciting to us under the name, which we have borrowed from the technology of witchcraft, of glamour. The enlightened city-culture of ancient Greece seems to have taken this kind of stimulus from its athletes; the enlightened city-culture of eighteenth-century Europe took it from its vocal athletes. And it is not difficult to read both the prodigies of muscular exertion and the prodigies of breath control as metaphors of virtuoso performance in bed. For public exhibition, the virtuosity *must* be transposed into metaphor if it is not to provoke a riot in the opera house. That eighteenth-century opera houses sometimes were the scene of riots is perhaps a sign that sexual rivalry among the patrons was imperfectly under control: but it is also a sign that internal control of some sort existed. The patrons, instead of being divided as rivals one against the other, acted in groups: the audience as a whole against the management, or the partisans of one singer against those of another. The remarkable phenomenon is that the partisan of a singer considers other partisans of the same singer not as his rivals and enemies, but as his allies. Freud pointed out[3] just this remarkable phenomenon among girl 'fans' of a public figure: the seemingly obvious and natural course would be for each girl to detest all the other rivals who share her infatuation;

instead of which the rivals all seek solidarity with one another in a group.

This almost magical effect is wrought by glamour. Glamour in the performer makes a socialising effect among the audience; it turns the audience into a miniature tribe or nation (subject, of course, to civil wars), whose internal control is a microcosm of social control. The result can be achieved only by the numinous remoteness of the performer from the audience, which is to all intents and purposes an *equal* remoteness from each member. The stalls may be nearer the stage than the gallery is, but it is equally unthinkable for the stalls and the gallery to storm the stage and put the audience's infatuation with the performer into physical effect. Only because the members of the audience are all equally debarred from acting on the erotic stimulation that emanates from the stage can that stimulation make them members of one another instead of rivals.

An audience shares the 'democratic character' which Freud remarked running through social groups such as the Catholic church—'for the very reason that before Christ everyone is equal'.[4] Freud goes on to observe that it 'is not without a deep reason that the similarity between the Christian community and a family is invoked, and that believers call themselves brothers in Christ'. The core of Freud's analysis of the relation of groups to their leaders is that he saw it to be a cultural extension of the relation of the family to its parents. In the nursery there are rivalries and a hierarchy of age: but let the nursery door open and a parent enter, and these vanish; vis-à-vis the parent, older and younger children are solidified into a social group, 'the children', through which runs a 'democratic character'.

Since psycho-analysis obliged us to notice the obvious, everyone has observed that small children are intensely concerned with the sexuality of their parents and the sexual differences between the mother and the father. This interest stimulates, and is stimulated by, the child's own sexual ambitions towards the parents; but the child is debarred from acting on his ambitions by the fact that he has not reached the age of potency, both in the sexual sense and in the sense that he is not big and strong enough to assault the parents. This infantile situation is recreated in the theatre or opera house. The audience's attention and curiosity is concentrated on the stage. (Often this is done by the same physical means, the manipulation of light and darkness, and with an almost equally intense result, as in hypnosis, another phenomenon which Freud traced to the child-to-parent relationship.) And yet the audience is debarred—by its being unthinkable, 'impossible'—from assaulting the stage. The architecture of theatres usually arranges that a member of the audience really is too small to jump up or down on to the stage; and it goes further still when it fosters an illusion that the players are bigger than the audience (the glamour of being larger than life) by making sure that they are, like genuinely tall objects, visible from a distance. The invention of the cinema, civilisation's widest disseminator of glamour, really did make the players as large in comparison with the audience as parents are in comparison with children; and it completed the remoteness and unattainableness of the performer by letting the audience know that anyone who did storm the screen would find nothing but a shadow to embrace. The cinema might have been invented to illustrate what psycho-analysis meant by the image of a parent.

Because it re-establishes the infantile situation, the theatre, which has already democratised the audience by abolishing its social hierarchy, can also abolish its division into men and women—and even its hidden division into heterosexuals and homosexuals. It has long been remarked that women are just as precise and interested judges of sex appeal in women film idols as men are. Indeed, the genuine glamorous idol, of whichever sex, like the genuine religious idol of whichever sex, seems as a rule to inspire a cult among worshippers of both sexes. Our usual explanation, that the boy who worships a film actor is modelling himself on the actor, whereas the girl who worships him is imagining him as her lover, is probably superficial and may even be a touch disingenuous. It seems more likely that when the glamour-situation places the audience in the position of the infant (quite literally so: the audience renounces the power of speech in favour of the persons on the stage and signifies its own feelings only by the infantile methods of inarticulate cries and hand-clapping), it reconstitutes the infantile bisexuality. To be more accurate, bisexual impulses still exist in the adult, but in most individual (as distinct from group) relationships they are sieved and sorted out according to the adult's sexual disposition; an unconscious censorship and suppression is exercised on the inadmissible impulses, whichever ones those may be (the homosexual person being a repressed heterosexual just as truly as vice versa). But the group infatuation with an idol, precisely because it is impossible to act on, does not need to call out the whole apparatus of suppression, and what are usually inadmissible impulses may become conscious. (It is by no means uncommon for a homosexual man, utterly incapable of falling in love with a woman he has met face to flesh-and-blood face, to be devotedly and lastingly in love with the Madonna or Marlene Dietrich.) The adulation which patrons of both sexes poured out on the castrato singers of the eighteenth century may well have been homosexual: directly so when the patron was a man (the very idea of the castrati still provokes a sexualised excitement among homosexual men who are patrons of opera); and, when the patron was a woman, as a token of that unconscious predisposition towards homosexuality which consists in the wish to emasculate men.

All these characteristics of opera make it apt to the point of inevitability that opera should have been the favourite and special nursling of the eighteenth century. Opera had the peculiarity of nullifying the social distinctions of the old era, against which the enlightenment was in rebellion, and at the same time creating a coherent social order to replace them. The eighteenth-century enlightenment was above all social in its thinking and planning; and its social ideal was just that orderly egalitarianism which the opera house achieved between ranks and between the sexes.

Straight theatre, which had in any case never been so darling to the beau monde, did not accord predominance to women performers and had sometimes not admitted them at all. Women were always completely excluded, and the very image of the mother was kept to a pointedly less than divine place, by the church—whose Mass was the direct predecessor of the opera, creating the same near-hypnotised egalitarianism among the audience, and putting a still more numinous distance between the audience and the drama. The eighteenth century, however, was playing down the magic in religion or had actually made a deliberate and conscious rejection of the church's ceremonies.

It was the opera which it propounded as—implicitly—a secular alternative. If reason was persuaded to swallow the anti-natural absurdities of opera at all, it was on the grounds that at least they were not the *super*natural ones which a believer had once claimed to believe *because* they were absurd.

The culture of the eighteenth century was also engaged in cutting across the groups formed by the other great communal loyalty, nationalism. Opera was precisely suited to serve as the vessel of cultural internationalism—which it did by launching itself everywhere under an Italianate flag of convenience. English audiences made a departure from the chauvinism which was to characterise them ever after, and insisted on hearing Italian singers almost exclusively—which has brought on them posthumously the displeasure of chauvinistic critics; at Vienna not only was Italian the language, as it was everywhere, in which the composer indicated with what expression his music was to be played, but it might also be the language in which the music printer composed the title-page, his own name and description included.*

The mysteries of religion, which must be celebrated only by priestly fathers and which reside ultimately in the universal progenitor, are a fairly well disguised symbol of the mysteries of sex which are known to and practised by parents, and which children spend so much time and curiosity contemplating. When the eighteenth century abandoned religious mysteries and took up those of opera, the children—the audience—remained in the dark, but the sexual nature of what provoked their interest and excitement was quite explicitly displayed. Indeed, curiosity and the pursuit of sexual pleasure were precisely what the eighteenth century was emancipating from the embargoes laid on them by religion. Yet if the socialising purpose of the century was to be served, the sexual content must be disguised in metaphor, the sexual stimulus softened, and the stage kept inviolable. The aptness of opera was complete. Distance is kept between performer and audience not only by the physical structure of the opera house but also by the barrier of technique, the very

* E.g. the title-page, 1785 (reproduced in H. Gal: *The Golden Age Of Vienna*) of the six quartets Mozart dedicated to Haydn: 'Sei Quartetti . . . Composti e Dedicati al Signor Giuseppe Haydn . . . Dal Suo Amico W. A. Mozart . . . In Vienna presso Artaria Comp. Mercanti ed Editori di Stampe, Musica, e Carte Geografiche'.

barrier which separates parent from child. The technical superiority of the performers is much more specialised and conspicuous in the opera house than it is in the straight theatre: the barrier is correspondingly electrified with a higher degree of numinous awe. The auditors, who can perhaps sing but cannot sing like *that*, are even deeper sunk in the impotence of the child; and the performers' virtuosity is of a kind precisely calculated to figure to the unconscious as a metaphor of sexual virtuosity, since the fluctuation of lovers' breathing is the indication of sexual intercourse which children most commonly contrive to eavesdrop. Moreover, the question which is so consumingly important to the child, the puzzle of the physiological differences between men and women, is not merely displayed but made the whole point of the operatic performance —yet in such a softened form as not to excite rivalry among the audience: it is the essence of opera to insist on a physiological sexual distinction, but a secondary one.

Eighteenth-century opera wears that unmistakable but delicate mist of eroticism which suffuses so much eighteenth-century painting. Painting quickly lost or hid this quality when or even before the eighteenth century came to an end; but in opera it was less easily disguised, there being virtually no neutral pretexts for performing an opera at all—no operatic equivalents of landscape or still life; and opera continues to incur the sort of reproach which is sometimes addressed to eighteenth-century painting. The eighteenth century's own puritanism, of course, did not spare its own painting or opera; and then the reproaches came in the idiom of the age and were made in behalf of reason. Latterday protests against opera were more openly puritanical—until people became ashamed of puritanism, which has had to assume various specious disguises.

Occasionally the protest is the social one that opera is extravagant and snobbish (just as people who are ashamed of their human decency and fear to hear it called sentimental sometimes attack fox-hunting as a sport of the rich: as though its atrocities would instantly become loving kindnesses if they were committed by paupers). More often the reproach claims to be aesthetic: opera is stigmatised as an impure art because it is both drama and music. On the reasonable face of it, however, one might suppose that two arts would create an art not half but twice as good; and one can guess that this formal impurity is only a synonym for another kind of 'impurity'—which in fact is probably the original source of opera's vitality.

III

Opera, Cities and Enlightenment

————— ❈ —————

The emancipation which women achieved in the eighteenth century was sporadic and altogether informal. Women's rights were not written-in to the constitutions either of nations or of professions. It was this which made it easy for the Victorians to go back on the emancipation, re-impose restrictions and argue as though they belonged to a tradition that had never been broken. (And in general one of the nineteenth century's strongest wishes was that some moralistic magic would ordain that the eighteenth had never in fact taken place.) When emancipation was achieved once and for all, the reformers took care to make it conclusive by having it written down formally; but to reach that point they had to fight through much heavier opposition than if they had been able to take up their cause where Mary Wollstonecraft had left it in 1792.

All the same, her *Vindication Of The Rights Of Woman* needed to be written. The eighteenth century had left fair-minded people plenty of scope to protest women's rights, both in the realm of manners and on the official level, where women were excluded from the corporate and more formally constituted professions and likewise from political office. Those states which had given the vote to some men had not given it to any women.

Nevertheless, the *Vindication*—or the first volume of it—*was* written (but heavily criticised): and written by a woman. Women could be kept out of corporate, ritualistic professions: but once they had acquired the necessary education and, which is just as necessary, enough psychological independence to conceive the desire to enter, there was no keeping them out of the creative professions, which are practised in informal solitude. Mrs Aphra Behn became Great Britain's first female professional

45

writer in the second half of the seventeenth century; and women had practised as painters, usually in tolerated eccentricity, since the renaissance: but during the eighteenth century English and French literature bristled with authoresses, and all civilised Europe (including, in one case, Russia) accorded the tribute of fashion to the pastels of Rosalba Carriera and (with smaller justification) the paintings of Angelica Kauffmann and Élisabeth Vigée-Lebrun.

It was in and on the fringes of art and learning that women became emancipated. Mary Wollstonecraft's own unhappy, vagabond but emancipated life was spent in literary-journalistic circles; her daughter married Shelley and invented science fiction. It is in this setting that women's emancipation shews as part of mankind's. It is not only the women who have come out of hiding or oppression. Social emancipation is accompanied by the tremendous intellectual and emotional emancipation which is what we mean by the enlightenment; and the enlightenment is manifested in hundreds of men as well as women who, by the class system of previous centuries, would have been condemned to servile and probably unlettered obscurity.

If we ask to what *class* Mary Wollstonecraft and William Godwin belonged—or Mozart and the Webers (the family of professional musicians which he worked, lodged and flirted with and eventually married into)—we cannot return an answer in terms that held good before the eighteenth century. To the middle ages, and again to the incurious and inarticulate bourgeoisie of Victorian times, the figures of the enlightenment would have seemed socially anomalous. Were the Mozarts *respectable*? Were the Godwins *gentlefolk*? Half. Yet a half-world is just what we cannot call it, because it is anything but half-lit. The enlightenment is characterised by a new attainment of self-consciousness; and the enlightened society is brilliantly illuminated by its members' own awareness of it and themselves. Precisely because of their self-consciousness, articulately expressed in their letters, diaries, memoirs, journalism, portraits and genre paintings, we have to think of this seeming half-world as *the* eighteenth-century world.

The enlightened society (which outlasted the eighteenth century, in the strict numerical sense of *century*, by a couple of decades, during which it withstood the shock of the French

Revolution, though it was that shock which shattered it in the end) came into being by mentally knocking down the barriers which had for so long defined the structure of Christendom. Externally, the barriers had held Christendom snug and withdrawn from contact, except the hostile one of the Crusades, with its non-Christian surroundings. The internal barriers had consigned everyone to his social and ecclesiastical place, and had very largely delimited the thoughts each person might express, and probably those which might even enter his head.

The old dispensation rested on feudalism and theology. The social and intellectual constitution was held rigid by a superstitious belief in the magic properties of pedigree and ordination. For this the eighteenth century substituted an all but superstitious belief in the potency of reason. Applying reason, the enlightenment thought away the divine right of princes and either thought away the divinity himself or diminished him to a nonsectarian and un-interfering Supreme Being, who was credited with such universal benevolence that he quite lost the old divine attributes of punishment and menace. Anyone who could acquire enough education to reason at all was emotionally free (though there were still plenty of earthly punishments and menaces to censor his expression of his thoughts) to think anything he could reasonably sustain.

The old prestige of high birth did not vanish: it could not while it was supported by inherited wealth. The world may even have become more snobbish, but at the same time less feudally awe-struck. Madame de Staël's cardinal and international position in the European enlightenment owed something to her father's fortune and her husband's (not quite his by right[1]) barony; Lord Byron's international glamour owed more than a little to the 'Lord'. But snobbery and flattery, having been denuminised, were becoming a matter of open expediency ('The known style of a dedication', according to Dr Johnson,[2] 'is flattery: it professes to flatter') or of deliberate self-indulgence in romantic imagination ('Were it not for imagination, Sir, a man would be as happy in the arms of a chambermaid as of a Duchess'[3]). Birth still had something to add, but it was no longer self-sufficient. (Thus Dr Johnson on 'a nobleman raised at a very early period to high office':— 'His parts, Sir, are pretty well for a Lord; but would not be distinguished in a man who had nothing else but his parts'.[4]) Pedigree must be supplemented by the qualities which make people agreeable in social intercourse; and of these qualities the appointed judge was reason, greatest of social levellers because its laws are true for everyone and the faculty of applying them is not distributed according to class or the laying on of hands. Pamela, in Goldoni's dramatisation of Samuel Richardson's novel,* begins her tirade against her employer and would-be seducer by pointing out the levelling effect of reason (which she couples with honour): 'Sir, I am a poor maidservant, you are my master. You were born a gentleman, I a wretched woman; but we have two things equally, and those are reason and honour' ('ma due cose eguali abbiam noi, e sono queste, la ragione e l'onore').[5] 'What is done' was no longer what is in practice done by the well-born, including the seduction of maidservants like Pamela and the Beaumarchais-Mozart character of Susanna, but what must be done if polite society was to work; and the honorary LL.D. from Lichfield could rule that the precepts of a fourth earl on this subject taught only 'the morals of a whore, and the manners of a dancing master'.[6]

Though there were still lumps that had not been mixed. in, the enlightened society was approaching a fluid condition where any interesting person might meet any other interesting person. In breaking up the accepted social order of Christendom, the enlightenment had incurred the responsibility of designing a new one, and its intellectual attention was chiefly given to social questions. It judged individuals not by fore-ordained social standing but by their contributions to a social setting actively created by their contributions; it was on the whole tolerant of those who contributed eccentricity, which might be entertaining, and less tolerant of genius, which might be socially disruptive. Societies it judged by the independence they accorded the individual to pursue reason without pressure from social and religious taboos. (It was persistence in propounding ancient communal taboos when they were no longer supported by the propounder's individual commonsense that Dr Johnson attacked as *cant*.) Society was to be not only of but for people. The arts were in process of being emancipated from patronage and handed over to the judgment of a public. Learning was no longer

* See further chapters VII and X.

shut up in cabalistic and hierarchical institutions, the monastery, the cathedral close, the university (all of which suffered a decline during the eighteenth century), but was set loose in coffee houses and—where, incidentally, women could get at it— drawing-rooms and circulating libraries. Women became not merely literate but fluently so: eighteenth-century novels could plausibly place the burden of their narrative on letters written by the women characters.

To facilitate the freer meetings which were the fluid in which its freedom consisted, the enlightened society created round itself a new—and, in eighteenth-century hands, ravishing—art form: the city. (Two examples survive intact: Dublin, which is perishing of neglect; and Bath, which is preserved but—by the wide world—hardly less neglected.) Urbanity was the tone of the eighteenth century. People fell in love with cities as they had done with princesses in romaunts, and with the idea of foreign cities as with the princesse lointaine—a romantic longing which even wars did not embitter: 'There is nothing . . . I long for so much as to see Paris', wrote Sydney Smith three years after the Battle of Waterloo, 'and I pray my life may be spared for this great purpose'.[7] The English even attempted to transplant urbanity to the country, replacing castles and palaces by country houses or sham castles, like Ralph Allen's at Bath,[8] designed to improve the view from urban residences. Even in France and Austria, where powerful aristocratic courts held out in their ancient rôle of citadel, the court had been supplemented by a capital city. In London ('when a man is tired of London, he is tired of life'[9]), the court was virtually lost to notice in the town, a physical expression of the fact that the real power lay with the House of Commons—which was another victory of house over palace. The small German courts became almost merged with their towns, to the point where we can hardly tell an Electorate from a watering-place. Their rulers were subjected to bour- geoisation, a process the Hanoverian kings imported to England, where it culminated in the monarchy succumbing for ever to the current middle-class ideal of the gentleman. George IV accepted it as a prouder title to be the first gentleman of Europe than to be prince of the realm.

The glory of eighteenth-century Dublin was the number and distinction of its public buildings.[10] The same is true of Bath:[11]

the idea of 'assembly rooms' is the very key of eighteenth-century society. The function these public buildings served in society (this time in London) is displayed in Fanny Burney's *Evelina*,[12] where the story employs them as meeting-places between the sexes and the classes. Assemblies, ridotti, pleasure gardens, exhibitions, theatres, the opera house (the last two places to talk in as much as to listen in*): the eighteenth-century city spontaneously provided itself with those 'community centres' which we have self-consciously to plant in our new towns. These are places where acquaintance can be scraped: in them Evelina, who, through mésalliances in her ancestry, has connections in both high and low life, becomes the pretext for the story to display a complete social promiscuity; earls encounter silver-smiths; baronets make up pleasure parties with characters of Hogarthian coarseness capable of spitting in one another's faces.[13] Fanny Burney's intellectualising eighteenth-century morality (which, together with the whole Fanny Burney manner, was presently borrowed—but completely refashioned—by Jane Austen) is careful to condemn the coarseness not the class, and to imply, in the true enlightenment tone, that breeding alone is not enough to make good-breeding. She sets up her hero, Lord Orville, as a model of true good-breeding; but his sister, the languid Lady Louisa Larpent, though from the identical stock, represents very nearly its opposite.

City life, being more succinct, minimised the difference between the wealthy man and the bourgeois, who could now live at the centre of influence without the hereditary qualifications or the expense of setting up as a courtier; and once at the centre he could exert influence through social means, without basing his claim on country estates and retainers exclusively his. To use restaurants and clubs, in the city fashion begun by the eighteenth century, is precisely to have a 'seat' and to employ a whole staff of servants while cutting the expense by sharing it with the other customers. The city was also the home of another great leveller, the stock exchange. The great capital speculations of the early part of the century in England and France had the effect of

---

* When Mozart talked through an opera, it was his comment on the performance: 'In regard to the performance of this opera I can give no definite opinion because I talked a lot; but that quite contrary to my usual custom I chattered so much may have been due to . . . Well, never mind!' (letter to Baron Gottfried von Jacquin, from Prague, 14 January, 1787).

shaking up aristocracy and bourgeoisie in a bag together and giving them equal chances of a fortune or ruin. And the eighteenth-century clubs, as though to emphasise the equality of chance between all the members, became centres of gambling second only to the stock exchange.

If the city promoted the bourgeoisie nearer equality with the landowners, it also promoted the other oppressed class, women, a little nearer social equality with men. In the country, where there are large distances between social meeting-places, and where mud and puddles, which were common enough in eighteenth-century cities, may be met with miles from home and a change of clothes, women were always at a disadvantage in social freedom—at least while they kept their long skirts and their belief in their own fragility. The English attempt to urbanise the country was only an attempt and belonged in any case only to the great houses. In middle-class country life, at the end of the century and the beginning of the next, women were much less mobile than men—as Jane Austen's novels make clear: brothers and suitors jump on their horses and ride off for a day or two in London; but for her heroines riding is a pleasure and a rare one at that; journeys are great bustles; and often it is only by undertaking the journey and passing a city holiday in London or Bath (the season temporarily transformed a provincial watering-place into a city) that the heroine can attain that basic social freedom which consists in meeting and considering a sufficiency of men to choose one's husband wisely.

This new creation, the city, formed itself into the setting for the opera house—which, especially in Germany, commands the eighteenth-century city as the cathedral commanded the medieval town. Even more than straight theatre, opera must have a city (Glyndebourne itself hangs by the train service back to London): not only because the personnel of an opera house is so cumbersome to take on tour, but also because the actual cost of opera and, still more, its air of costliness demand an urban and urbane public—in fact, a city bourgeoisie. Peasants and city proletarians may spend money, but they do not like expenditure to be seen. (Evelina's proletarian kinsmen, though Londoners to a man and proud of it, take the peasant attitude towards the opera: they are amazed to find the price of admission higher than at the theatre—'And, finally, they all agreed, that it was *monstrous dear*'[14]). An opera public came into being for the first time in the eighteenth-century cities.

If the city was originally a supplement to the court, now bidding to swallow up the court, the opera in its turn was a development of the spectacles whereby courtiers and kings had tried to alleviate the boredom of their state; and physically the opera house might remain the property of the court, its personnel in the court's employ, and its musical policy under a monarch's direction. But the point which is so often made,[15] with polite regrets towards democracy, that opera was created as the sport not of democrats but of kings, is not wholly fair. It was not—certainly on the continent of Europe—democracy in practice which produced opera, but neither had the heyday of absolutism produced it; and opera is pronouncedly different from the forms of art which absolutism at its most secure did produce or permit. The triumph of opera in the eighteenth century belongs to an atmosphere in which absolutism was everywhere threatened (which often made it more absolute on the surface and in the short run, by making it bad-tempered); and democratic or enlightened aspirations abounded at even the most servile courts. The old-fashioned Catholic absolutism of the Austrian court did not prevent Mozart from writing Masonic cryptograms into his music and making an opera from a banned subversive play. In Prussia, the most dictatorial of opera's regal patrons, Frederick the Great, himself a composer and a librettist, set the new fashion of enlightened despotism and expressly intended opera to be an instrument of the enlightenment.*

Before the citizens perfected the habit of clubbing together to support extravagancies (a habit which also promoted commercial capitalism and rapidly made them corporately richer than the kings), kings had been the only people with both the taste and the resources for spectacular expenditure. Kings, however, until the enlightenment obliged them to turn gentlemen, who are by definition unostentatious, glossed over their boredom by displaying their magnificence; the display was not to provoke an intelligent question about the king's moral right to his magnificence or to suggest (which attacks kings from a contradictory point of view) that magnificence was not the route to happiness.

* See further chapter XVII, p. 216.

Opera has a long tradition, begun, a touch timidly, in the eighteenth century and more than kept up in the nineteenth, of proclaiming the bliss of true love: even, or perhaps especially, impoverished true love. Admittedly, opera, like socialism, was caught in a dilemma: should it argue that the poor will never be happy until they share the wealth of the rich; or should it imply that the poor, simply by being poor, have virtues and happinesses the rich cannot share—a cogent argument for keeping the poor poor? (It was probably this argument which eighteenth-century genre painting and its patrons were implicitly putting forward when they developed a taste for sentimentalised peasants and picturesque cripples and beggars.) However, dilemma or no dilemma, contradiction or no contradiction, opera raised or at least hinted the question; and that in itself marks it as a non-monarchical entertainment. At court even so simple a competitor as true love is not permitted to challenge the theory that all the warmth and light enjoyed by the nation emanates from the Sun King. The entertainment form promoted by courts is the masque and its subsidiary the ballet, a form which is the successor to, and only in technique an improvement on, the courtly pageants of the Middle Ages. To a more than medieval extent, it was, though given to elaborate allegories and personifications, incapable of characters. All the technique, together with the spectacle and the very music, was designed to saturate the senses and drown out the sense. The difference between this and opera is precisely the difference between the absolutism of Louis XIV and the enlightened despotism of Frederick. The latter is at least based on an idea.

Opera, too, may occasionally drown out the sense, but never the emotion. It is anything but mute. At an absolute court, as Saint-Simon shews us, only the king may have emotions freely; other people must have them in relation to his. Protocol—that is, primitive taboo—governs other people's behaviour; the king alone may twitch according to his whims, and acquires thereby a puppet's semblance of the personal and independent psychology which in reality he is not free to develop in his artificial vacuum. Puppet-psychology, together with a measure of allegory (usually through classical prototypes), which fore-ordained the characteristics of the dramatis personae as predictably as protocol fore-ordained the behaviour of courtiers, survived from the masque into the early, rhetorical days of opera. But since an emancipated public existed, opera quickly threw off the masque and fairly soon the classical masks as well, and developed into the world's most unconstrained vehicle for personal emotions.

As a form, opera is ill-adapted to depicting the massy and seemingly impersonal forces of taboo. Even its dignity, that quality most necessary to absolute monarch, totters. (For dignity the enlightened despot substituted something opera *could* depict: panache.) Its crowd scenes are its most dangerous moments. On the stage, the chorus moves as well as sings in consort; and its drilledness, which impresses us in a church or a concert hall, easily gives us the giggles in the opera house. For re-inforcing its choruses or characters with the weight of centuries of numinous awe, opera possesses no acceptable metaphor: hence the unhistorical, fancy-dress-ball air of nineteenth-century opera's costume dramas; and hence, at another remove, the cheapness of effect when Puccini pierces his own admirably blown bubble of operatic convention by introducing touches of Christian liturgy. Opera can no more portray the mass psychology of taboo than it can tracts of landscape or lapses of historical time. (Or, at least, it could not portray those until Wagner made splendid effects of mass and time by the literal method of deploying masses of singers and instrumentalists and keeping the audience in the theatre for great lengths of time.) What opera excels in creating, by its nature (Wagner, though magnificently, was working against its nature), is, as Mozart was to shew, precisely what the enlightenment had created: not a society but a nexus of characters on whom external social forces impose nothing more constraining than good manners and who reflect society at large only in the freedom it has given them to form and express their personal inter-relationships.

IV

Singing and Theology

———————— ❀ ————————

The superiority which belongs to women's singing voices is certainly not to be found in their speaking voices, which lack even the elementary pre-requisite of carrying the words clearly to a wide audience. If it is true that *The Odyssey* was originally committed not to writing but to an audience, then Samuel Butler must have been wrong in thinking that its author was really an authoress. In the ancient world, where juries might be five hundred strong, and where political assemblies consisted not of representatives but of the entire citizenry and their votes might be registered by acclamation, women would have remained at a vocal disadvantage even if they had been allowed to practise law and politics. And indeed they did remain at a disadvantage, though it was perhaps carried on as much through tradition as for practical reasons, so long as culture remained to any extent oral: that is to say, both in the ancient world, dominated as it was by rhetoric, and in Christendom, dominated as that was by a theological rhetoric incarnated in the disputation and (whether preached by mendicant friars or by protestant divines) the sermon—both of which forms survived in a scholastic version at the universities, in, respectively, the oral examination and the lecture system. If women achieved an unprecedented measure of emancipation in the eighteenth century, it was made possible by the fact that written culture was at that time overtaking oral, through the wider and cheaper dissemination of print.

Even the male speaking voice, however, could not stand up to the acoustics of gothic architecture, and had to be supplemented by the singing voice. For liturgical purposes, two kinds of vocal music were developed: singing proper, performed by the choir, whose members need not be clerical (but must be male); and intoning, which was really only a resonant extension of speech

—and in fact could not be more, since it had to be performable by anyone who became a monk or a priest, regardless of whether he possessed a voice or even an ear.

Both kinds of singing passed from the liturgy into opera, where the old distinction is preserved in the distinction between aria and recitative. But in opera the performer who quasi-speaks the recitative must also be able to sing. Again, the ecclesiastical class-distinction between clergy and laity survives in opera; but it is muted to the distinction (though that is still pretty numinous) between soloists and chorus. And, most important change of all, opera has admitted women on both sides of all these distinctions.

The church did not need women's speaking or intoning voices, and, after its primitive period, it did not want their persons in the sanctuary. (It expressly denied itself the use of their singing voices at all, on the strength of the Pauline injunction that 'woman be silent in the church'.*) No sooner had Christianity completed its victory over ancient civilisation than it began to develop a feeling that women were closer to unredeemed nature than men, and thus less sanctifiable. Women were eligible for canonisation, a personal distinction and payable only post-humously, and they shared the common sacraments and the hope of salvation with the male laity; but the whole class of women was excluded from the sacrament of ordination, whose touch was sufficient to transform a man into an officer of the church who, when considered *in* his office, represented God to the people. Setting aside nunship as a reserved and sealed compart-ment for women, from which there was no access to the ecclesiastical hierarchy,† the church was busy from the fourth century onwards turning women out of the clergy, forbidding them to administer the sacraments and even to approach the altar.

This did not mean that the church choir had to forgo the alto and soprano singing voices, with all the soprano's superior power of catching and delighting the attention. The church simply drew on the fact that these registers are really the

---

* 'Mulier taceat in ecclesia' (see Angus Heriot: *The Castrati In Opera*, I).

† The nun, who had originally ranked as an officer of the church, though a minor one, was in practice downgraded to equality with the monk. (See Tuker and Malleson: *Handbook To Christian And Ecclesiastical Rome*, III and IV.)

common property of women, girls and boys. This, incidentally, is probably *why* these voices (and in particular the soprano, because it is the more extremely differentiated from the other voices) have their natural claim on our ear. We are all, men and women, born with a high voice, and we all pass our infancy in the orbit of a mother or nurse. The result may well be that all our life long, whenever we are given the choice of two voices, we feel that it is the higher which speaks more directly to our emotions. It is equipped both to command attention and sympathy by speaking *as* a mother and also to speak more intimately—from further back in our personal history—on behalf of ourselves.

The church called on boys' voices and supplemented them by the device of turning a boy chorister into a castrato*—a device which allowed it to use the child's voice at the same time as the adult's training and musical understanding. For opera, however, these sources of soprano and alto sound were not sufficient, and the reason lies deep in both the nature and the circumstances of opera.

The mere fact that female characters were to be represented would not in itself have been enough to get women on to the operatic stage. Elizabethan drama had female characters, but not actresses to play them. Perhaps because it had not long severed itself from its religious origins, it followed the ecclesiastical precedent and made up the deficiency with boys. It may even be this convention we have to thank for liberating Shakespeare's genius into the theatre. To judge from the sexual disgust he attributes to many of his later characters, and also from the Sonnets, which are more trustworthy as being utterances in his own person, he was, though by no means exclusively homosexual, more inclined to conceive romantic love in homosexual terms; it may be that his deeply appreciative and psychological portraiture of women became possible only because he could imagine his women characters through the provocative trans-

---

* The practice began no one is sure when, became common about 1600 and was not abandoned as a means of staffing the Sistine Choir until 1884. Recordings were made by a Sistine Chapel castrato in 1902–3. In eighteenth-century Italy, as Angus Heriot points out, the practice was, although at the height of its popularity, against both secular and ecclesiastical law; the operation had to be carried out secretly and accounted for by fictions. (See Angus Heriot: *The Castrati In Opera*, and the Appendix to it by Desmond Shaw-Taylor.)

vestite cloak of their really being boys. The social attitude which permitted such a position had been revolutionised full-circle by the time that Beaumarchais decreed that the part of the page in *Le Mariage de Figaro* 'can only be played, as it has been, by a young and very pretty woman', on the grounds that young actors were not up to it ('nous n'avons point à nos théâtres de très-jeune homme assez formé pour en sentir bien les finesses'[1]). Beaumarchais's ruling held when his play became Mozart and da Ponte's opera, and the precedent was followed by Richard Strauss in the creation of his latterday Cherubino, Octavian.

When the English theatre re-emerged after the puritan fast, it had not only female characters but female players. It was not, to begin with, that opera emancipated women but rather that women were allowed into opera because they were just sufficiently emancipated already. They naturally went into opera because they were already making their way into the theatre in most parts of Europe,* though often at the cost of disrepute; and as opera developed, it was not the women but some of the men who were driven out when the castrati, who already existed to serve ecclesiastical music, moved into opera.

Yet, once they were *in* opera and opera was in fashion, the women singers could not fail to procure a further degree of emancipation for women in general. Psycho-analysis has shewn us that we can understand both the social history and the psychology of women through the all-important discovery made by the little girl that she lacks—or, as the childish imagination reconstructs it, has actually been deprived of—an esteemed and adulated instrument which boys still possess.[2] In psychological terms, emancipation depends on women's success in adopting a substitute for their loss. To this nothing could have made a more apt contribution than opera. Here, at the centre of fashionable society, a tremendous fuss was being made of another esteemed and adulated instrument, the high singing voice— and this was actually an instrument which originally belongs to boys and girls but which the boy, unless he forgoes his manhood, is deprived of.

Even after triumphing in opera, women were not invited into church music. What counted against them was not merely their

* In Rome, throughout the eighteenth century, women could not legally appear in public either in plays or in operas. (See Angus Heriot: *The Castrati In Opera*, I.)

descent from Eve but the fact that in church music the voices are not characterised but must actually play an impersonal part. It was otherwise with oratorio, which might be either sacred or profane but remained, even at its most sacred, non-canonical; and which was, at its utmost point of development, a characteristically protestant form. Oratorio became most prolific when it addressed itself to filling in the dreary spaces of the English Lent; and here, although it often took Lenten themes of religious meditation, it was substituting not for the churches but for the theatres, which were closed for dramatic performances. Suitably for this substitution, the voices in oratorio were at least partly characterised, and the singers might include women.

In contrast to this, the church service is a transaction between the people en bloc and their God. The voices cannot be characterised because they must be representative. Whenever voices are thought of schematically rather than for the creation of character, there is a tendency for a true fact, namely that it is adolescence which lowers the boy's voice, to be elaborated into an artificial system whereby the lower the voice the greater the age represented. If the treble is a boy, then, by a false extension of the same token, we expect the vigorous and virile grown man to be a tenor and interpret the bass as a greybeard. So automatically do we think by this scheme that one of our difficulties with the everlasting problem opera, *Don Giovanni*, is that Don Giovanni himself, in keeping with Mozart's lack of love for the tenor voice, is a baritone. *Don Giovanni* alone of Mozart's stories is easy to imagine as it would have been treated (which, indeed, it was) by a nineteenth-century composer;* and one of our uneasinesses with a baritone Don Giovanni is our near-certainty that a Verdi would have made such a celebrated lover a tenor. It is even rather disconcerting that the legendary Don Juan's surname is Tenorio.

In the church choir, the notion that the deeper the voice the greater the age represented probably lent itself to an interpretation whereby the various pitches were taken in a schematic sense as representing the various Ages of Man, a concept which, though it survived to serve Shakespeare and the renaissance

---

* —though it would not have done for Beethoven, who (Einstein: *Mozart . . .*, 22) eschewed the plot of *Così* for what he took to be its frivolity and thought even *Don Giovanni* scandalous.

painters, was essentially and deeply medieval. (It is[3] the subject
of a chapter in *De Proprietatibus Rerum*, the encyclopaedia compiled in the thirteenth century by Bartholomew Anglicus.[4]) The
ensemble of voices could be held to represent man in the generic,
under whom woman is subsumed, singing his praises to God.
For that purpose there was a special aptness not merely in the
unemotional and inexpressive purity of boys' voices but actually
in the connotation of sexlessness inherent in the very thought
of the castrato voice.

Indeed, church music was continuing to exemplify the impersonal concepts of psychology against which the eighteenth
century, taking opera as one of its chief vehicles, was in rebellion. There is no such thing, of course, as a psychology which is
impersonal in fact. The rules and forces of taboo, like the very
image of God, emanate from the human mind; but the people
who are governed by them do not know that they do. (Eighteenth-century rationalism had realised that they must in fact
do so, but was at a loss to explain *how*; and this was its great
disability in dealing with religion.) The savage sees the world
swayed by taboos acting as automatically and impersonally as
an infection. The Christian has decided to entertain his taboos
via God; like a radio signal transmitted up to the moon and
bounced down again, the taboo laws are now sent up to heaven
and returned to man from heaven; the idea of free will has been
introduced, and is attributed to both man and God. Yet God's
personality remains partly impersonal. Ultimately, perhaps, he
responds only by his personal whim (his grace) to an act of will
made by man; but there is still (rationalised by the idea that
God has bound himself by unbreakable promises) some automatic virtue in certain sacred objects and spells—most notably
in the regularly repeated offices of the church—and they are
far too potent to be dispensed with.

Already the protestant revolution had begun to destroy the
taboo picture of the world by taking the emphasis of Christianity
away from the church's automatic infallibility and the Mass's
automatic effectiveness, and placing it on the individual's
personal and emotional relationship to God—an emphasis
presently reflected, in oratorio, in Bach's emotive meditations
for the solo voice. Martin Luther's protest against indulgences,
however camouflaged in theological rationalisations, had been

understood as a protest against the belief that objects impregnated with magic power retained an automatic efficacy. In the long run, Europe elected to read straight through the manifest message of protestantism, which was every bit as authoritarian, disciplinarian, taboo-ridden and puritanical as Catholicism itself, and respond only to the emotional import beneath. By the eighteenth century, protestantism had led into (the last thing it consciously wanted to lead into, but the result the Catholic church had foreseen all along) scepticism, and individuals were questioning not only the terms of their relationship to God but the very existence of a God bearing the smallest resemblance to any of the sects' portraits of him.

The enlightenment was above all a self-recognition and a self-assertion on the part of the Ego. It brought tumbling down all the external representatives of the jealous father who had hitherto constrained the Ego's intellectual freedom and its pleasures: gods, priests, kings, the taboo barriers of class; and it also demolished, tamed or transformed the internal perpetuation of the father, the conscience, which had, especially in the preceding century, made the Ego's life a torment of religious (and in England loyalist) scruples. In the eighteenth century it was the Ego which proclaimed its positive duty towards itself.

V

The Quest for Pleasure

———— ❈ ————

Everyone knows (thanks to Tom Paine, who christened the
enlightenment the Age of Reason) that the immediate duty of
the emancipated Ego was to reason out its own moral judgments. However, as soon as reason was set free to act on
behalf of the individual Ego, it began to accomplish another
liberation even more fundamental to the character of the age:
the emancipation of pleasure. The eighteenth century's great
perception was that the desire for pleasure motivated all living
conduct. For centuries Christian puritanism had looked at
pleasure askance. Theology recognised the 'natural law', a
moral obligation to prefer good to evil, which it held to be
implanted by nature in all human beings; but it maintained that
the natural instinct towards good had been so weakened by the
Fall (which man had incurred while in quest of pleasure) as to
need constant re-inforcement by the church. The eighteenth
century swept away the Fall and restored natural innocence.
The 'natural man', whether exemplified in contemporary
savages or in antique shepherds, was no longer pitied for having
missed the Christian redemption, but was admired as not in
need of redemption of any kind; and pleasure was recognised as
moral in its own right.

Socrates had discovered by inquiry that the only possible
answer to 'What do men mean by "the good"?' was 'What
pleases them'. Men could not avoid the choice between pleasure
and displeasure, and they could not help choosing pleasure; a
man who chose to deny himself pleasure could do so only
because that gave him greater pleasure or the hope of it in the
future. The quest for pleasure was the instinctual motivation of
behaviour; and since 'the good' was synonymous with 'the
pleasing', man could not choose evil unless he made an intel-

lectual mistake about the pleasure values involved. Self-destructive and anti-social conduct could come into existence only through miscalculations. Wickedness thus became intellectual error; and the cure was education.

This was precisely the conclusion reached by the eighteenth-century enlightenment. Edward Young pointed out that the saint and the assassin were moved by exactly the same consideration, pleasure—whose 'despotic pow'r' was, indeed, universal. The 'black' desires of the assassin could be formed only through a mistake or through ignorance: they were what resulted when natural and normally blameless passions 'Mistake their objects or transgress their bounds'.[1] The cure prescribed by the eighteenth century was, once again, education*—or, in another word, enlightenment. What was good, in both the moral and the aesthetic sense, was what was pleasing; instruction and exercise would make the natural capacity for pleasure a more precise instrument; the advancement of both morals and taste depended on refining the capacity for pleasure.

In the process of refinement, reason was the Ego's natural—indeed, its only possible—guide. John Locke had pointed out that if man was to make moral judgments at all he could not help using reason to make them, since even the decision to prefer authority to reason had to be reached by reasoning, albeit bad reasoning. The enlightenment was in no doubt that man in fact *must* make moral judgments, because he could not help discriminating between the pleasing and the unpleasing; and he could not help at least trying to choose the pleasing and, therefore, the good. If he failed, it was through intellectual short-sight. Reason was necessary to illuminate him, but it was never the enlightenment's main objective, because it could not supply the motive-power of life or even any reason for living at all. Those had to be provided by the natural instinct towards pleasure. The business of reason was to distinguish between long- and short-term, genuine and specious, pleasures. When reason had accomplished this, it would have set instinct back on the path which nature had originally designed for it but which,

---

* Whether the Memoirs of Madame du Barri published in 1829 are really by her or are an informed forgery, they perfectly capture the eighteenth-century tone when they have her say of her royal lover 'The vices of Louis were the result of bad education' (vi).

in the course of history, had become overgrown and obscured by the short-term, and therefore wrong, self-interest of tyrannical rulers and scheming priests. Reason could not compel man to take the right course; but once reason had made the right course plain, man *would* be compelled to take it, by his own instinctual nature.

The habitual clarity of eighteenth-century prose and even the legibility of eighteenth-century lettering are analogues of the fundamental purpose of eighteenth-century literature, which is always to cut a clear path back to the true nature of human beings by clearing away cant and affectation. What cant is to thought, affectation is to behaviour; with both the contrast is nature. This purpose, pro-knowledge, pro-education and anti-affectation, enunciated early in the century by Pope* and obvious in the contes of Voltaire, is also the purpose in the novel of manners and morals as it was developed by Fanny Burney and carried to perfection by Jane Austen. Fanny Burney's blatant contrasts between grossness and politeness and the subtle and sardonic contrast Jane Austen is always drawing between affected emotions and sincere (that is, natural) ones are alike contributions to the great eighteenth-century educative programme of discovering how to choose between, and how to refine on the choice between, short-term and long-term pleasures.

The remarkably uniform philosophy of eighteenth-century thinkers was based on the scientific discoveries and formulations of the preceding century—or, rather, on the whole scientific view of the universe which natural science had by then achieved. The age of reason was not so much logical as biological. It viewed man as a species (one which it often disparaged in contrasts with the animal species), and held him, of course, to be a species capable of reason. But where Christendom had taken man's reasonable capacity as a sign that he was unique, divinely favoured and detached from the rest of nature, the age of reason, being in a sense less impressed by reason, was concerned to fit man back into his natural setting. Its deepest interest was in the nature of man in relation to the nature of the universe.

* Spence's *Anecdotes* quotes Pope as holding that 'the great matter to write well is, "to know thoroughly what one writes about", and "not to be affected".' (1820 edition, p. 59.)

Nature as a whole it took to be inherently benevolent and harmonious, the unquestionable guide to morals and taste: indeed, it came near to promoting nature to the place left empty by the Christian god.

This near-deification of nature, which is sometimes attributed to the second half of the eighteenth century and interpreted as a break with the strict rationalism of the enlightenment, really runs all through the century and is the necessary basis of a rationalism which was not broken until the triumph of romanticism and industrialism. Pope had early admitted

> *Yes, nature's road must ever be preferr'd;*
> *Reason is here no guide, but still a guard.*[2]

The age of reason was in fact the age of reason and nature; and when, in the middle of the next century, Dickens created in Betsey Trotwood a survivor from that age, he accurately ascribed to her the precept that her great-nephew should 'always be natural and rational'.[3]

This biological rationalism, lacking a coherent hypothesis of evolution, could not dispense with God the creator of nature; it is with his benevolence that the natural system, as his hand created it, is stamped. The mistakes which distorted the natural design could, however, be corrected by the natural faculty of reason, without God's resorting to a further creative dispensation in the form of a miraculous redemptive act breaking the fabric he had created in the first place. The enlightenment, although it believed that God had fathered the natural world, did not really believe that he had begotten a son. It saw no need for him to have done so. Once the mistakes of man had been corrected by the reason of man, the universe would return to its primitive condition, which contained nothing which should set man against man or even, according to Pope, man against society: since the individual and society were mutually dependent on one another's natural quest for pleasure, it must be that, when God created them, he 'bade self-love and social be the same'.[4]

The instinct of a self towards pleasure was at once, and by the same token, natural, benevolent and virtuous. As Edward Young insisted,

Pleasure is nought but virtue's gayer name . . .
*Virtue the root, and pleasure is the flower.**

Although misjudgment might have led natural instincts to 'transgress their bounds', man had only to search his own nature to discover what the correct bounds were, since (in Pope's words)

> *God, in the nature of each being, founds*
> *Its proper bliss, and sets its proper bounds.*[5]

Only in those proper, natural bounds, as opposed to the artificial and wrongly calculated interferences with them practised by the old social system, would reason concur. When the Ego asserted itself against the old system, it was asserting the naturalness, and therefore the reasonableness and benevolence, of its quest for pleasure. The duty of the Ego towards itself was hedonism. It was in the direct and acknowledged exercise of hedonism that the enlightened society, with its new and more convenient unit, the city, was formed. Its motto was struck by Pope: 'Oh Happiness! our being's end and aim!'[6]

A society with such an end and aim was a reversal of Christendom, which had located Happiness in heaven and considered the search for it on earth to be natural but not by any means necessarily benevolent and virtuous; and which, so far from seeking positive pleasures on its own account, was fully occupied in paying off the incalculable debt to God which every mortal incurred at the moment of being conceived in sin. John Donne had asked God the Father in 1623

> *Wilt thou forgive that sinne where I begunne,*
> *Which is my sin, though it were done before?*[7]

But by the end of the next century Tom Paine, as passionate a Deist as Donne was a Christian, was protesting that God had been brought into contempt, and the relation between man and God sullied, by man's being taught 'to contemplate himself as an

* (*Night Thoughts*, VIII) Young's next line is 'And honest EPICURUS' foes were fools'. The enlightenment's classical patron for this argument was not so much Socrates as Empedocles (who greatly impressed Pope) or Epicurus; and it is poetically just that at Herculaneum, whose re-discovery in 1720 became so widely influential on the theory and practice of the arts in the eighteenth century, the enlightenment should have at last found fragments of Epicurus's writings (which Johann Kaspar Orelli published in 1818).

outlaw . . . as a mumper, as one thrown, as it were, on a dung-hill, at an immense distance from his Creator, and who must make his approaches by creeping and cringing to intermediate beings'.[8] The enlightenment adhered to the creator and to the God of love, but threw out original sin, for which it substituted original benevolence subject to intellectual error: the sin of Adam and Eve had been no more than a miscalculation of the value of apples.

The existence of the enlightened society was a protest against the notion that society could draw its sanction and stability only from bouncing an account of its structure up to heaven and getting it sent back as God-ordained. The enlightenment often denied that love between a man and a woman must be referred to heaven via the church, though it usually believed that love still needed social approval; still more strenuously it denied that man was capable of loving his fellow men only through Christ's love for mankind. Against that Christian theory it put forward its own cardinal idea of natural benevolence: mankind would recover a peaceful and co-operative Garden of Eden as soon as the unreasonable and unnatural interference of parental tyrants was removed. The enlightenment put no trust in the systems evolved ad hoc by its immediate forefathers: it was revolutionary in that it was radically conservative—nothing would satisfy it as reasonable but to go right back to the beginning, to the original datum of human nature.

Opera reflected the enlightened mood when it took as its principal subject love—which is the dominating force in all Mozart's major operas, and which in *Così Fan Tutte* he beautifully placed in the middle of an informal social setting, a nexus of family and friends such as Jane Austen might have assembled. It is true that Christianity had also placed love at the heart of the scheme of things, and that the servants of the Christian god of love were capable of infatuated, ecstatic emotions towards him; but again the point is that they were unaware of the natural and instinctual quality of their love, and regarded it as a special visitation coming on them from outside. Moreover, to love God, although mankind is invited to arrive at it by an act of will, is in a sense obligatory on all mankind, mankind as a social bloc, the class next below the angels. There are

67

stringent, eternal penalties for failing to love God. The enlightenment was trying to achieve a society that should cohere without threat of penalties. It placed its reliance solely on the power of natural love, which included self-love; self-love, working through the instinctual choice of pleasure rather than pain, was enough to draw human beings into matrimony and into social relationships, and thus to serve the socially benevolent purposes of perpetuating life and amenity.

Opera concerned itself with the very type of love which is most obviously natural and which can least be compelled. It is not by chance that one of its standard plots was a case of young lovers who choose one another against the decree of parents and social convention and who may even have to refuse to enter into arranged marriages with the wrong people. Not that the plot always had the courage of its rebellious convictions; it was more likely to call on coincidence to reconcile the two sides. The frowned-on suitor would win over the frowning parent, possibly by a display of nobility of character but more probably by turning out to be a lost or disguised scion of the hereditary nobility. The romantic novel, which marched with the opera* as a reflection of the enlightenment's fundamental theme of rebellion against parental authority, was often bolder, or at least wilder, than opera in supporting young hearts against parental heads. In the same year[9] that Mozart composed *Così*, the adolescent Jane Austen was privately satirising the romantic novel for placing a quite unreasonable, and therefore not really enlightened, reliance on the heart. The romantic heroines of *Love And Freindship* are a much wilder pair than Fiordiligi and Dorabella: their criterion for young men is whether or not they have read *The Sorrows of Werter*.[10] One of them is made by her satirical creator to write: 'Convinced as you must be from what I have already told you concerning Augustus and Sophia, that there never were a happier Couple, I need not I imagine, inform you that their union had been contrary to the inclinations of their Cruel and Mercenary Parents; who had vainly endeavoured with obstinate Perseverance to force them into a Marriage with those whom they had ever abhorred; but with an Heroic Fortitude worthy to be related and admired, they

---

* 'It's like a printed book' ('Pare un libro stampato') is Leporello's comment on Donna Elvira's story in *Don Giovanni* (Act I, No. 3).

had both, constantly refused to submit to such despotic Power.'[11]

However, if opera was less bold to start with, it built itself a more impregnable folly than the novel; and deep into the nineteenth century, when novelists and playwrights had to be circumspect about even mentioning love outside marriage, opera not only felt free to do so but virtually offended the operatic conventions if it let its lovers be respectablised by a wedding ceremony.

Once opera had devoted itself to love stories, the castrati were doomed to be rejected from opera and returned to church music—not because they broke any naturalistic illusion (opera did not offer that in any case) but because the sight of them was a particularly discomfiting affront to the Egos in the audience, who had come to the opera, as they did not go to church, in conscious pursuit of hedonism. Freud has demonstrated that the most momentous threat apprehended by the infantile Ego (and so for ever after by the unconscious Ego) is the possibility of being castrated. For the girl this is a fait accompli in which she must eventually, with greater or smaller reluctance, and with or without compensation, acquiesce; but for the boy the price of keeping what he has is the perpetuation of his dread of losing it; and this dread is deepened by his acquaintance with people—par excellence women—who apparently have lost the valuable possession, thus proving that the loss really can take place. Mr G. Rattray Taylor has shewn[12] that the fear of impotence, common to all men at all times, became an absolutely crucial unconscious factor in the social life of the eighteenth century—'perhaps the most significant . . . strain in the sexuality of the period'. The result, as he shews, was obsessive and over-protesting attempts to counter the fear by denying it, such as Don Juanism and 'the hair-trigger sensitivity of the gallant' in springing into duels. Here, surely, is another occasion where we can trace the influence of the operatic vogue in social history. In most modern societies the awful truth that castration can take place is presented only by women; if the dread became particularly acute in the eighteenth century, it was (though not caused) re-inforced by the fashionably conspicuous existence of the castrati.

The castrati lasted so long, despite the threat they re-inforced, thanks to the persistence of opera seria in classical themes. Towards pagan religion, which no longer threatened it, the enlightenment could afford to be more indulgent than towards Christianity. It would even swallow political autocracy providing that was wearing a toga. Admittedly, the republicanism of Pope and Addison had adduced in its favour the republicanism of ancient Rome; but monarchs and imperial highnesses could in their turn adduce imperial Rome. They commonly believed that their own autocracy could be attractively presented through the veil of a classical prototype of mercy and noblemindedness in power. Metastasio's *La Clemenza di Tito* had been serving this propaganda purpose of wiping autocracy's modern face clean for fifty years and was already a soiled towel when[13] Mozart set it again for the celebration of Leopold II's coronation as king of Bohemia. The orderly stability of the ancient world (or what was taken for such) served the eighteenth century as an imaginary resting place after its own practical and anarchical scepticism. In artistic style the century actually did accept a near dictatorship from the rules of classical practice. But in religious and social matters there could be no serious question of reviving the classical system. The classicising habit created a restful fantasy of an organised world which presented no threat of actually coming true.

This was, indeed, the deepest re-assurance offered by the classics. Here was a world whose tyrants and whose religion had been completely conquered. Loyalty to the tyrants and belief in the gods had simply evaporated. Reason was believed without dissent or even misgiving when it said that the pantheon, or the deification of Nero, was nonsense. The eighteenth century returned to the ancient world in artistic fantasies in much the same manner as people who have in real life been good at passing examinations return to examinations—apparently anxiously—in their dreams. The dream fantasy is a re-assurance in some present difficulty that the dreamer will overcome it as he in fact overcame the difficulty of examinations.[14] Whenever its classical operas and paintings touched on classical myths, the enlightenment could enjoy the sly, Gibbonian pleasure of aiming at Christianity a side-swipe that was scholarly and respectable and therefore unexceptionable. In its classical fantasies it was dwelling on another body of mythology and one, moreover, whose saints and divinities were amusingly light-minded and lecherous: and thus it continually posed, without ever having to ask, the question whether the Christian myths were any more credible or edifying than the pagan.

The incredibility of the classical world in itself countered the psychological threat offered by the castrati, whose very neuter-dom perhaps gave an extra guarantee that the classical world had no power to rise again. If the remoteness of the ancient world was a re-assurance, the de-natured castrato voice em-phasised the remoteness. At the same time, since the classical myths really did represent a taboo-governed world, the castrato voice had the same aptness here as in church music: it suggested that these ancient heroes and gods were not characters so much as taboo concepts, though ones which it was, now, safe to play with for pleasure.

As a matter of fact, the enlightenment could no more give a psychological account of what the taboo concepts really did represent in ancient religion than it could in the case of Christianity. But since ancient religion was no longer alive to give it the lie by insisting that the explanation was feebly inadequate to the phenomenon, the enlightenment could take the speciously psychological short cut of interpreting the classical personages as personifications of natural forces and qualities, elevated to divine status by the people's ignorance and the opportunism of priests. This, if one discounted the more fabulous items as mere elaboration, chimed prettily with the enlightenment's own inclination to deify nature and re-inforced it by arguing that the ever-wise ancients had had the same inclination. This theory, so detrimental to psychology as a science and eventually to psychology in art, helped to produce one early and perfect artistic fruit: Handel's classical oratorio *Acis And Galatea*.[15] With its help Handel has solved what was, in one form or another, the critical problem of all eighteenth-century art, the problem of belief. Literal belief he cannot for a moment give to the Theocritian-Ovidian[16] story of the giant Polyphemus who crushes his rival, Acis, beneath a stone, whence Galatea resurrects him in the form of a stream. But the fact that the story takes place at the foot of Mount Etna allows a perfectly sophisticated duality of tone to enter Handel's treatment. In the same breath he can make fun of his Polypheme in his capacity as mythological giant and yet take him perfectly seriously, and describe him in pastoral programme music, as the activity of a volcano. This allows Handel to distil tragedy from the death of Acis in the eruption; and then again, because the work has proceeded on two planes all along, he is free at the end to create yet a third and imply that Galatea's act of resurrecting her lover is to be taken not as a piece of unbelievable myth nonsense but, movingly and seriously, as a figure of the immortality of art.

VI

Anarchy, Impotence and Classicism

———————— ✸ ————————

The enlightenment, having not the slightest conception of the unconscious emotional forces which had brought the father-figures of Christendom into being, had not the slightest conception of the unconscious emotional forces it set loose when it knocked them down. It could see that the fathers had not a rational or an intellectual leg to stand on; but to know itself justified on the level of conscious and rational psychology did not in the least protect it from an access of unconscious, irrational guilt for having committed the social equivalent of the crime which mankind has always judged more abhorrent than mere murder, namely parricide.

The punishment which little boys dread for committing this crime in fantasy and in wish is castration: a logical dread of a logical punishment, since what prompts the boy to wish his father out of the way is the boy's own sexual ambitions towards the mother. When the family is expanded into a society and the father into a god, king or patrician class, psychological analysis of the structure of society shews that the quarrel between the classes is an expansion of the quarrel between sons and father. In the family it was the sexual right to the mother which was at stake: in society it is the right to use or possess the motherland or the body politic; and the punishment the sons dread for rebelling against the political father and usurping his rights is still, though given a political form, castration. Indeed, it was this punishment, as both Homer and Edward Gibbon understood,* which was visited, under a political metaphor, on the

---

* Thus Gibbon: 'The freemen of antiquity might repeat, with generous enthusiasm, the sentence of Homer, "that, on the first day of his servitude the captive is deprived of one half of his manly virtue." But the poet had only seen the effects of civil or domestic slavery, nor could he foretell that the second moiety of manhood must be annihilated by the spiritual despotism which shackles not only the actions but even the thoughts of the prostrate votary.' (*The Decline And Fall* . . . , XLVIII.)

slave class of the ancient world—a slave being, by definition, a chattel, a thing, a neuter. Free citizens retain their political virility and may even acquire the right to exercise it through a vote. (The unconscious interpretation of girls as boys who have been castrated is precisely reflected in the fact that, long after some men had acquired votes, all women were regarded as disenfranchised *by nature*.) The free citizenry is a son's class which, being still virile, can threaten to attack the father's class and take over and enjoy its prerogatives. It can use this threat to strike a bargain with the patriciate, and secure itself a better place in the constitution. But from out-and-out rebellion, the political equivalent of parricide, it is at most times restrained by an unreasoning loyalty, a taboo dread of doing something unthinkable—of doing, that is, something which it unconsciously expects would call down on it the uncontemplatable punishment of castration.

The eighteenth-century enlightenment was an intellectual and emotional revolution in that social parricide—to withdraw belief from a god or from the authority of the Bible or the church; or to withdraw irrational loyalty from a monarch or ruling class—was suddenly no longer unthinkable. In that most thoughtful of centuries, *nothing* was unthinkable. The enlightenment was an enfant terrible, a Candide, who not merely said the unthinkable but insisted it was reasonable to do so and that the taboo embargo was unreasonable. The enlightenment was, in the most pointed sense, an *enfant*: it spoke for sons against fathers. In the individual, the Ego asserted its quest for pleasure against the unreasoning moral conscience which psychoanalysis has shewn to be an internal prolongation of the father-image, swallowed in childhood, and which had exercised an internal veto on pleasure simply from authority, from the feeling that it *is* so, without arguing the matter. In society, the enlightenment asserted the sons class, the bourgeoisie, against the hereditary rulers, and asserted the people, the laity, against the fathers of the church. Every power, religious, social, intellectual, that based itself merely on the authority of a traditional, paternal status was called in question by reason, the enlightened despot setting the fashion by emphasising the enlightenment of his rule rather than the pedigree which had made him a ruler. The intellectual history of the enlightenment

was summed up by Thomas Love Peacock, who, in 1820, wrote
one of the enlightenment's last and wittiest manifestoes, *The
Four Ages Of Poetry*: 'The subtle scepticism of Hume, the
solemn irony of Gibbon, the daring paradoxes of Rousseau,
and the biting ridicule of Voltaire, directed the energies of four
extraordinary minds to shake every portion of the reign of
authority.' All over Europe father-figures were laid intellectually low or at best were left as hollow monuments from
which the taboo power, created by the people's belief in them,
had been emptied out. It was multiple, wholesale parricide.

For this act the unconscious Ego knew what punishment to
expect, no matter how the conscious Ego might feel itself
justified by reason. It was because the enlightenment was a
concerted attack on fathers that the eighteenth century's most
acute dread was the Ego's recurrent nightmare, castration.

This dread manifested itself in the conscious in the form of an
irrational, disproportionate dread of that most infertile of
states, anarchy. Having removed the supernatural sanctions,
the enlightenment was afraid of being overwhelmed by up-
surges of naked feeling, against which it protected itself by
taste, manners and, especially in England, a denuminised stoical
version of Christianity, designed to inculcate patience and self-
control. Although the enlightenment was intellectually convinced that nature, schooled by reason, was in fact adequate to
holding society together, it was irrationally in dread of nature
unschooled. Love and pleasure-seeking, the forces on which it
chose to rely for social cohesion, terrified it in their naked state.
Education was felt to be racing anarchy. It became urgent to
forestall that terrifying vision, the enlightenment's adaptation
of the *Dies Irae*, with which Pope ended *The Dunciad*:—

> *She comes! she comes! the sable throne behold*
> *Of Night primeval, and of Chaos old!*
> *Before her, fancy's gilded clouds decay,*
> *And all its varying rainbows die away.*
> *Wit shoots in vain its momentary fires,*
> *The meteor drops, and in a flash expires . . .*
> *Thus at her felt approach, and secret might,*
> *Art after art goes out, and all is night . . .*
> *Religion blushing veils her sacred fires,*

And unawares morality expires . . .
Lo! thy dread empire, Chaos! is restored;
Light dies before thy uncreating word:
Thy hand, great Anarch! lets the curtain fall;
And universal darkness buries all.[1]

Where God the Father's had been a creating, Chaos's is an 'uncreating' word: and it was from Chaos that the enlightenment expected the infertility that should punish it for having killed God the Father.

In order to save itself from this curse, which it apprehended from wild and disorderly eruptions of feeling, including artistic feeling, the enlightenment called upon rules, regularity, order, the orders of architecture: in short, the spirit of classicism. Primarily, it applied to the classics themselves. The Grecian rule of life 'Nothing too much', so often and so felicitously broken by Greek literature, became the maxim of that quite immoderate passion for moderation which inspired Charles Jennens, when he made his contrapostal arrangement of snippets from Milton's *L'Allegro* and *Il Penseroso* for Handel to set to music,[2] to add his own section *Il Moderato*. 'Nothing too much' had its classical apotheosis not in Greek but in Latin literature. It was Horace, who 'with graceful negligence . . . Will, like a friend familiarly convey The truest notions in the easiest way',[3] that eighteenth-century England adopted for its Epicurean patron saint; among the eighteenth-century babies christened in his honour were several members of the Walpole family*— and, in 1758, a distant relation of that family, Horatio Nelson.

If the inability of classical religion to return to belief and re-establish itself in the modern world was unconsciously taken as a re-assurance against religion, the vitality of classical art was taken as a re-assurance in the opposite sense. Antique art and literature had been buried and had risen again, which proved them immortal,† and the enlightenment set about

---

* In the second edition of *The Castle Of Otranto*, the author's identity, though not stated, was signalled by an epigraph from Horace.

† The immortality of the antique shepherd Acis perhaps reverberated in eighteenth-century minds as a symbol of the immortality of antiquity itself. Handel and his librettists were not the only people to pick on the story; it was picked out so early by Pope that it seems fair to think it set the tone for the whole of his work, which itself sets the tone for the whole literature of the century. Spence's account

borrowing some of that immortality for its own arts by severely applying to them the rules of classical practice. Where Christendom had sought a blessing—a fertility—from relics of its saints, the enlightenment made almost religious use of fragments of antique statues and almost imitative-magical use of copying antique models into its own works of art.

The irony was that all the rules and regulations, intended to preserve the enlightenment from one kind of infertility, were clamping infertility of another kind tighter and tighter round it. The enlightenment was in the typical situation of the neurotic whose symptoms edge closer and closer to creating the very situation they are designed to ward off. Unconsciously, the enlightenment was bent on bringing on itself the punishment it unconsciously dreaded. Only as the mark of a neurotic situation of this kind can we understand the great (and to us, who are not trapped in it, attractive) paradox of eighteenth-century civilisation, the combination of political and philosophical libertarianism with a normative spirit prepared to regulate every last aspect of speech, conduct and art by a rule of correctness. It was in keeping with this paradox that the eighteenth century became the great age of encyclopaedias and dictionaries—ambiguous instruments, which at once store knowledge and freeze it. What Pope had called 'fancy's gilded clouds' really were banished from late-eighteenth-century Europe: but the wand before which the rococo fled belonged not to Chaos but to the obsessively strict and plodding pedantry of the neo-classic movement.

Reason had been let out of its cage only to apply itself with logical thoroughness to fabricating another. If reason is a great leveller because it is the same for everyone, it is also a great mediocritiser because it is just as reasonable at the hundredth application as at the first. The most awful thing about the eighteenth century is that it had no distaste for truisms. It could not have, because it judged them more by the truthfulness than by the newness of the truthfulness of their contents. What

---

of how Pope as a child taught himself to read and write by copying printed books is footnoted: 'When Mr. Pope got into the way of teaching himself . . . some of his first exercises were imitations of the stories that pleased him most, in Ovid, or in any other poet he was reading. I have one of these original exercises now by me, in his own hand. 'Tis the story of Acis and Galatea, from Ovid . . .' (1820 edition, 'Arranged with notes by the late Edmund Malone, Esq.', p. 53).

Horace purveyed were 'the truest notions', not the most start-
ling. If the philosophy of the eighteenth century is so uniform
through all its decades and all the countries of Europe, it is
partly because the thinkers of the end of the century thought it
no shame to be still pointing out truths Pope had enunciated at
the beginning.

Two arts wholly escaped the eighteenth-century blight:
architecture, and pure music. Since these do not make statements which can be true or false, reason could not directly judge
them; and neither was it possible directly to apply to them the
criterion of nature. No one could say that one tune was more
truthful than another, or that one house approached more
closely than another to the original and primitive design laid
down by nature, the strictly primitive and natural thing being
to have no houses at all. (Early in the century Pope had
anticipated the extreme Rousseauists by extolling the primitive
to the detriment of the arts: by his account, the primitive period,
which had been 'the reign of God', was a period without arts.[4])
In music and architecture the normative spirit of the eighteenth
century liberated a fertility of invention no period has equalled;
it presented them with classical manner and form, on which it
left the artist free to float his fantasies. In 1810, when the
normative standards of the enlightenment still held, a visitor to
Dublin could write approvingly: 'the streets are wide and
commodious, the houses uniform . . .'[5] A decade or two later
this would have been abuse; and the aesthetic atrocities licensed
by rejecting the classical spirit from architecture are still to be
seen in our streets.

The same classical spirit, however, was very nearly the
death of those arts—among them opera—which do make statements capable of being true or false. Some painters and writers
(including librettists) were driven into the mere vaporisings of
fantasy, divorced from reason not merely objectively but in the
sense that the artist has withdrawn credence from his own
fable; in some writers the study of character was driven out
by wit, and then too often wit was driven out by sententious
triteness.

Frightened by its own symptoms of infertility, the enlightenment could think of no treatment except to clap on yet another
rule, thus tightening its own constriction. Its aesthetic theories

were doing their best to extinguish imagination and at the same time to depreciate art at large. The great artists, of course, kept their imaginations alive; but the enlightenment was at small pains to keep the artists themselves alive.

VII

The Rococo Seducer

———————— ✽ ————————

Having nothing but love and the love of pleasure on which to found its hopes of social coherence, the enlightenment was particularly alert to the disruptive effects of those forces when people acted on them in personal relationships without first consulting either rationality or external constraint. The figure of whom its literature is most wary, and against whom the most stringent of its moralisings are directed, is the seducer.

The seducer was execrated no longer on the grounds of his own wickedness and the probability that seduced girls would go to hell (no doubt many of them agreed with the Duchess in Pope's *Moral Essays* who hopefully cries 'Ah, how charming if there's no such place'[1]) but for his power of disturbing the peace. By provoking animosity in his rivals or in the protectors of his victim's virtue and marriageableness, the seducer is the precursor of the dreaded Chaos. Two of the enlightenment's cardinal works, *Don Giovanni* and Samuel Richardson's enormous seduction-saga *Clarissa*,[2] open with a duel between the seducer and one of the young woman's kinsmen.

To deter the seducer the enlightenment could put up nothing more effective than the old chivalrous concept of honour, which, now totally de-Christianised and emptied of its emotive associations with paradise and the Madonna, was one of the hollow monuments of the old dispensation which the eighteenth century left standing, and to which lovers now paid much the same admittedly false and opportunist deference as writers of dedications paid to the old system of patronage. Since it was no longer re-inforced by the debt of love men owed God, honour had to be made the sole property of the Ego. The seducer must be made to abstain for his honour's sake: that is, for his own sake (the only sake the enlightenment could recognise as valid). The sanction which brought this home to him was social. Once branded as dishonourable, a man was no longer eligible to marry the highest prize the enlightened society could offer him, an educated, accomplished, sensible girl with a sufficient income. If the seducer was still not restrained, society could protect itself from him only by tightening its own bonds. It is a further aspect of the paradoxical combination of libertarianism and formality that the enlightenment, having achieved both the virtual emancipation of women and an almost free mingling of the social classes, subjected the new, extensive bourgeoisie it had thereby created to rules of protocol and niceties of polite behaviour of a finickiness which previously had troubled only the most aristocratic courts, and so meticulously governed all the occasions when the sexes might meet that a woman could hardly go for a walk in the garden without fear of being compromised.

The formality of manners reached deep into the bourgeoisie; the formal concept of honour was extended even to the proletariat. Pamela claims to be on the same footing as her master in respect of honour as well as reason. Even Masetto describes himself as 'a villager of honour' ('un villano d'onore') and is as subject as any bourgeois to the thought 'If it were not for the scandal . . .' ('Ah, se non fosse, se non fosse lo scandalo, vorrei——'[3]).

To democratise honour in this way was one of the enlightenment's great contributions to a just society: to make honour protect the poor and uneducated was an application to personal relationships of the political principle of safeguarding minorities. The scandal and affront which Beaumarchais afforded to the powers of the ancien régime with his play *Le Mariage de Figaro* was that it shewed the servants standing on a point of honour with as much nicety as their master and actually in opposition to him, thereby subverting the system which had (and in Victorian times was to do so again) preserved the honour of gentlewomen by allowing gentlemen to use the serving class as prostitutes.

However, the enlightenment did not direct its morality and its code of honour against the seducer without flattering him by the attention it paid him. He became at once its outlaw and its cult-hero. It displayed towards him the ambivalence our own society displays towards the gangster and the murderer. Long-drawn and humiliating accounts of seduction, like *Clarissa*, provided it with the same excitement thrillers do us. Seduction is one of the most persistent themes of the eighteenth century's contemporary mythology (Casanova, Byron) and its literature (Casanova, Byron, Sade, Richardson, Laclos): so persistent, indeed, that when Mozart wrote home to report 'the day before yesterday Stephanie junior gave me a libretto to compose', he misnamed it 'The Seduction . . .' instead of 'The Abduction from the Seraglio'.* Pope's masterpiece[4] concerned the *rape* of a lock. Twenty-six years after that was published, Samuel Richardson began to issue his long epistolary account of the attempt to seduce the maidservant Pamela.

Pamela[5] must be one of the most widely influential novels in history: widely and promptly translated,[6] dramatised by Goldoni,[7] plagiarised by Voltaire,† and made into an opera[8] which Mozart saw when he was a boy, by Niccolò Piccini. Perhaps Pamela, in her original pronunciation with the *e* long and accentuated,‡ reached out across Europe and down five decades to intervene in the accident whereby the heroine of *Die Zauberflöte*, intended, presumably, to be a Tamina and thus to match Tamino as exactly as Papagena matches Papageno, turned into Pamina. The influence, however, is on the name only. Pamina is a heroine who pointedly moves outside the seduction-saga convention. Mozart wrote only one opera wholly concerned with seduction: *Don Giovanni*, the eighteenth century's masterpiece on its favourite subject.

---

* *Verführung* for *Entführung* (letter from Vienna, 1 August, 1781).

† —at least according to Goldoni, who, discussing his own treatment of the story, remarks that he might have 'transferred it to another country, as it seems the famous monsieur Voltaire has done with his *Nanine*, the very same story as *Pamela*', ('. . . o trasportarlo ad altra nazione, come sembra abbia fatto il celebre monsieur Voltaire colla sua *Nanine*, argomento stessissimo di *Pamela*'—from the Preface ['L'autore a chi legge'] to *Pamela*).

‡ 'Pamela: apparently invented by Sir Philip Sidney as the name of a character in his Arcadia (1590), and pronounced *Paméla*. Richardson adopted it for the heroine of his first novel . . . There seems to have been some doubt as to its pronunciation in the 18C. Fielding, in *Joseph Andrews*, wrote: "She told me that they had a daughter of a very strange name, *Paměla* or *Paměla*; some pronounce it in one way, and some the other".' (E. G. Withycombe: *The Oxford Dictionary Of English Christian Names*.)

VIII

Compulsive Seduction

———————— ❋ ————————

Don Giovanni, a pre-enlightenment myth-figure whom Mozart and da Ponte have turned into an enlightenment individualist asserting the Ego's right to pleasure against God, honour and society, displays both the characteristics which Mr Rattray Taylor recognises as the symptoms whereby the eighteenth century attempted to deny impotence: he is both duellist and, par excellence, seducer. The enlightenment had, in fact, taken the seducer for its outlaw-hero because he was the epitome of the enlightenment's own race against impotence. It was sympathetic to him because he was trapped in its own neurosis; and it execrated him because he shewed it its doom. Don Giovanni's is the fate of emancipated eighteenth-century man.

Don Giovanni's intellectual emancipation had been fore-shadowed by Molière's Don Juan, of whom Mozart had no doubt taken note.* The opera, perhaps for politic as well as for artistic reasons, gives no account of Don Giovanni as a revolutionary and disbeliever, and has him proclaim 'Viva la libertà', only in circumstances where his meaning is merely 'This is Liberty Hall'.¹ But the original and still famous story identified him clearly enough as atheist and blasphemer, and by the eighteenth century opinions such as his were taken as signs not only of revolt but of rational and self-justifying revolt. Don Giovanni has clearly concurred in the enlightenment's multiple parricide; and, being a man of the enlightenment, he believes himself in the right and refuses to repent when the statue of the Commendatore threatens him with hell.

* Some nine years before composing *Don Giovanni* Mozart implied his wish and intention to read Molière. He reported that Fridolin Weber (who was post-humously to become Mozart's father-in-law) had given him a present of the works of Molière 'as he knew that I had not read them'. (Mozart to Leopold Mozart, from Paris, 24 March, 1778.)

Instead of describing Don Giovanni's intellectual opinions, the opera demonstrates to our eyes the act which the unconscious takes to be identical with holding such opinions: Don Giovanni (exemplifying the disruptive effect of the seducer) kills a man who is presented to us dramatically in the exclusive rôle of a father. The Commendatore comes on to the scene solely as Donna Anna's father; and it is in that capacity that he is obliged to challenge the man who has seduced or tried* to seduce her.

The Commendatore is thus an upholder of the social order; and again his rank and title emphasise that his status is paternal. After his death, his statue is even set up as one of society's ancestral father-figures; and it is this statue which, miraculously animated, comes back in the rôle of outraged father to be the instrument of Don Giovanni's punishment—Don Giovanni, the disrespectful rebel, having mocked at it.

Thus Don Giovanni is established in the very opening scene as, like the enlightenment itself, a father-murderer. But Don Giovanni does not want to kill the Commendatore, or even fight him;† he is obliged to fight in self-defence, because the Commendatore has drawn on him, and he can quite well hold himself morally guiltless of the Commendatore's death. Yet the whole point of the opera, and especially of its ending, is to hold him guilty. Let the enlightenment feel as rationally justified as it will: to kill a father-figure, even in self-defence, is a crime and breaks a taboo law; the unseen forces of the unconscious (figured in the opera as the supernatural powers of hell) will rise and exact vengeance.

Technically, Don Giovanni is guilty of murder because he would not have had to defend himself with his sword if he had not been caught in the commission of a felony. The enlightenment is making its point that seduction leads inevitably to more violently anti-social consequences. One of the enlightenment's most tediously reiterated moral lessons was that small, seemingly innocent and justified infractions of social law lead inevitably to larger ones; it was an object lesson by which it

* That most fascinating subject for gossip, whether, when the opera opens, Don Giovanni has just seduced or has just failed to seduce Donna Anna, will no doubt go on being debated for *another* two centuries.

† 'Va, non mi degno di pugnar teco' (Act I, No. 1).

bolstered up its code of honour in a world which did not really think seduction a very serious crime. The parental tyranny suffered by Clarissa Harlowe is unjust to the point of caricature; yet Richardson does not scruple to point the moral that it is her first disobedience which leads, step by inevitable and slow step, to the destruction of her honour and her person. 'This last evil', Clarissa writes incoherently when still far from the last (she has still to be trapped in a brothel, drugged and raped), 'although the *remote* yet *sure* consequence of my first—my prohibited correspondence! by a father *early* prohibited . . . I thought I could *proceed* or *stop* as I pleased . . .'² (Richardson, like Jane Austen after him,* has taken the point that it is disobedience to *fathers* which is the heart of the question.)

If Clarissa cannot proceed or stop as she pleases, it is because neither can her seducer and tormentor. The enlightenment cast off the seducer precisely because he had lost the power to proceed or stop: he could no longer do what the enlightenment most admired, namely regulate his conduct rationally in order to secure his own pleasure. The right to pursue one's own pleasure had been won by eighteenth-century man only by the act of murdering God and the lesser fathers: the unconscious knows that the punishment for this is castration: and the libertine,† in order to ward off that punishment, must continually assert his virility in order to prove that the punishment has not yet overtaken him. But he is caught in the same trap as the eighteenth-century arts: with each act of proof, he incurs a deeper guilt, and enjoys less pleasure.

The theme that one crime inevitably enslaves the criminal to the next had taken on a compulsive meaning. Mozart was quite aware of this theme: in a letter to his father³ where he protests his own chastity and insists that if he had erred he would not conceal it, he adds: 'for, after all, . . . to err once would be mere weakness—although indeed I should not undertake to promise that if I had erred in this way, I should stop short at one slip'. These words are the psychological germ of Don Giovanni; they

---

* Witness the ending of *Northanger Abbey*: 'I leave it to be settled by whomsoever it may concern, whether the tendency of this work be altogether to recommend parental tyranny or reward filial disobedience.'

† *The Libertine* is the title under which an English version of *Don Giovanni* was first performed at Covent Garden in 1817.

mark Mozart's discovery in himself of potentialities out of which he was presently to create his hero.*

Sexually as well as intellectually, enlightenment man had emancipated himself by reason only to become the prisoner of forces which, because they were unconscious, reason (short of a psycho-analytical theory) could not combat, and which in the end bound him to behaviour which neither reason nor self-love could endorse. The libertine is really courting not women but his own destruction. The opportunity to indulge in pleasure has turned into an obligation; the Ego is just as enslaved to hedonism as ever it was to the father-figures who imposed abstinence.

Leporello, when he recites the catalogue of Don Giovanni's conquests to Donna Elvira, explicitly boasts how much the course of conquest is a matter of compulsion and how little a matter of sensual pleasure: although Don Giovanni's predominant appetite is for young beginners, he conquers old women, too, 'for the pleasure of putting them in the list' ('pel piacer di porle in lista'); he does not pique himself on the point of whether a woman is rich, ugly or beautiful; so long as she wears a skirt, says Leporello, Donna Elvira knows (from experience) what he does.[4]

The belief that seduction was a duty was satirically anatomised by Jane Austen (who blames the example of Lovelace, the seducer of Clarissa Harlowe) in the character of Sir Edward Denham. 'His fancy had been early caught by all the impassioned & most exceptionable parts of Richardsons [novels]; & such Authors as have since appeared to tread in Richardson's steps, so far as Man's determined pursuit of Woman in defiance of every opposition of feeling & convenience is concerned, had since occupied the greater part of his literary hours, & formed his Character'—a character he feels to be 'quite in the line of the Lovelaces'; with the result that 'Sir Edw:'s great object in life was to be seductive . . . he regarded it as his Duty'.[5]

---

* Cf. from earlier in the same letter: 'The voice of nature speaks as loud in me as in others, louder, perhaps, than in many a big strong lout of a fellow'. There is another germ of *Don Giovanni* in Mozart's letter to his father from Vienna, 25 July, 1781 (see chapter XII).

IX

'Hé Bien! La Guerre'

————— ❀ —————

No doubt the first impetus in the eighteenth-century emancipation of women came not from their own efforts, and not from considerations of justice, but from the opportunism of men, who, if they were to pursue their own newly permitted quest for pleasure successfully, had to release women from the old obligations of virginity before and absolute fidelity during marriage.

However, the result of the emancipation of both sexes was not a paradise of pleasure freely, equally and innocently enjoyed between them. If previous centuries shew us a dispute between fathers and sons for possession of women, the eighteenth is the first to shew us conspicuously and consciously a war between men and women. Towards the end of the century[1] the war was epitomised by Choderlos de Laclos in the relationship between the Vicomte de Valmont (another of the eighteenth century's duellist-seducers) and his former mistress, the Marquise de Merteuil. 'I may add', Valmont says in one of his letters to Madame de Merteuil, 'that the least obstacle put forward on your part will be taken on mine as a veritable declaration of war; you see that the reply I ask from you requires neither long nor beautiful phrasing. Two words are enough.'[2] And she magnificently writes on the bottom of his letter: 'Hé bien! la guerre'.*

This is in fact a warfare which (except by the complete subjugation of women) cannot be wholly superseded until contraception frees the woman from the risk that she may always,

* The phrase was perhaps echoed a century later by that disapproving admirer of French novels, Henry James. In *The Golden Bowl*, the Prince's crucial telegram to Charlotte Stant is 'couched in the French tongue' and begins 'À la guerre comme à la guerre then'. James was not the only *Yellow Book* contributor influenced by *Les Liaisons Dangereuses*. It was a motif in the eighteenth-century revival conducted (cf. Chapter I) by Beardsley, whose projected title page for Laclos's novel, published in *The Savoy*, No. 8, 1896, shews Valmont in a Roman-emperor-style dressing gown which is slipping off one shoulder.

and heavily, be the loser. In the eighteenth century, when contraceptive devices of the kind used by men were used to protect not the woman from pregnancy but the man from venereal disease,[3] women were bound to defend their honour, even though men might release them from the obligation to have any.

However, although women resisted because they did not want to be proved fertile, they met in the seducer an almost irresistible force, because he did want—compulsively—to be proved virile. But the woman in whose body he should prove it was not his accomplice and re-assurer. She was, rather, the occasion of his guilt and the expected instrument of his punishment. The crime of killing God the Father had been so effective that God was no longer supposed capable of returning to avenge himself. The enlightenment might still believe in him as the principle which had created nature; but it no longer credited him with the power to thrust his arm through the fabric of his creation and strike down sinners. It believed in miracles neither of redemption nor of punishment; it held that the original creation, nature, was competent to administer both. The unconscious retained its irrational conviction that the libertine *would* be punished, but the intellectual apparatus of the conscious expected his punishment to come through natural means, through the woman herself or the kinsmen she called to her defence. The woman, therefore, figured as the castrator; it was she who was the enemy. 'To conquer' became synonymous with imposing on a woman the act of what was now hardly recognisable as love.

A woman once conquered was no longer attractive to the seducer—as Don Giovanni demonstrates when the woman who attracts him in the street proves unattractive the instant he recognises her for Donna Elvira, whom he has seduced already. The seducer has already risked and proved ineffective the punishment to be apprehended from sleeping with that particular woman. She is truly conquered in that she holds no more danger for him, and unattractive since it is really the danger he is courting.

In these conditions, the boldest women—or, perhaps, the most (though unconsciously) homosexual—abandoned the passive rôle of fortress and became active conquerors themselves, female libertines, the Joans of Arc of the sex war, campaigning both against men and against the virginity of members of their own sex. Richardson has Clarissa frightened by the 'masculine air' of the woman who abets Lovelace;[4] and Madame de Merteuil is certainly—and, such is Laclos's insight, one cannot say not intentionally—a portrait of an unconscious homosexual. Perhaps Madame de Merteuil, like the male libertine, is impelled by the need repeatedly to attest a virility which in her case really has been lost to her from the start. Unable herself to deflower the virgin Cécile Volanges, she has to call on Valmont to do it on her behalf; and it is this, rather than a direct sexual desire for him, which has drawn her into her partly hostile alliance with him. Valmont brilliantly recognises that their alliance rests on the fact that Madame de Merteuil is bound to the same course of compulsive conquest as himself. He is under no illusion that they can proceed or stop as they please. 'Conquérir', he writes[5] to Madame de Merteuil, 'est notre destin, il faut le suivre'.

The sense of tragedy in eighteenth-century literature, equally misunderstood now and at the time, is to be found in its declarations and manifestoes of the sex war, and not in those deliberate and marmoreally unmoving tragedies (the literary equivalent of opera seria) of which eighteenth-century authors were so prolific and so proud. *Così Fan Tutte* is a tragic drama; *Les Liaisons Dangereuses* a tragic novel; *The Rape Of The Lock* a tragic epic, an Iliad. In these great works, the tragic doom springs from the unconscious compulsions of the characters (just as it does in the *Oedipus Rex*, where, as Freud demonstrated,[6] it is the unconscious wishes of the hero which speak in the predicting voice of the oracle) and it consists in the fact that the men and women *cannot* lay down their arms. The dramatic tension comes from the inevitable erotic attraction which draws these enemies together. The instinct for pleasure persists in pursuing its quest; the poignancy of *Candide* is that the stupid world blots it out, the tragedy of these works of art that the characters' own unconscious doom blots it out—even while the erotic attraction they hold for one another allows the tragedy to pass for comedy, *The Rape Of The Lock* masquerading as 'an Heroi-Comical Poem', *Così Fan Tutte* as an opera buffa, and *Les Liaisons Dangereuses* as a scandalous erotic novel.

The unremitting beauty of Laclos's masterpiece is the beauty of a duel.* Valmont and Madame de Merteuil are duellists of such proficiency and in such dead earnest that thrust dictates counterthrust in a perfect and economical logic; the antagonists have been forced into collaboration; they are partners in creating the whole, the act of love whose perfectly mutual consummation is the destruction of them both.

This rapier-thrust had already been expressed by Pope— through a pair of scissors, 'the fatal engine'. In *The Rape Of The Lock*, a minor sexual perversion has become the metaphor of that perversion of sexuality from a unitive to a destructive end which was to prostrate eighteenth-century civilisation. The Baron's compulsion to mutilate Belinda's hair is witness to the libertine's compulsion to mutilate women lest women become the instruments of his own mutilation.† Pope knew quite well that this minor perversion rests on the comparison between the hair of the head and the pubic hair (which guards the region the libertine would really like to mutilate). When the ringlet is snipped from her head, Belinda cries:

> *Oh hadst thou, cruel! been content to seize*
> *Hairs less in sight, or any hairs but these!*[7]

It is, indeed, this symbolism which makes the Baron's trophy such a 'glorious prize'[8]—as though he really had been able to put the natural colour of Belinda's hair to the oldest and crudest of tests: ‡

> *Gods! shall the ravisher display your hair,*
> *While the fops envy, and the ladies stare?*[9]

Pope's method consists entirely in enforcing the contrast between macrocosm and microcosm; and it is by shocking us

---

* I admire John Weightman's remark about *Les Liaisons Dangereuses*: 'Don Giovanni and the Queen of the Night come together in a work which may not be as splendid as Mozart's operas but is clearly their contemporary and not unworthy of being placed beside them.' (*The Observer*, 1 October, 1961.)

† And in the myth of Nisus, to which Pope compares the Baron's exploit (III, 122–4), the loss of hair is as blatant a symbol of castration as it is in the story of Samson. Nisus has a lock of purple hair on whose safety depends that of his life and kingdom; his daughter cuts it off and delivers it as a love token to his enemy. (Ovid: *Metamorphoses*, VIII.)

‡ Yet in curious fact the most Homeric and at the same time the most eighteenth-century thing about *The Rape Of The Lock* is that (*fair* being ambiguous) we are nowhere told the colour of the lock.

into realising the tininess of the incident, the minorness of the sexual perversion, that he is able to make us aware of the major and tragic sexual perversion which he does not describe but wraps round the poem like a climate. The shock is repeatedly administered: both by his strategy, which consists of satirically deploying the machinery of grand epic in order to recount his storm over a coffee pot, and by his habitual tactic of deflationary zeugma, whereby his line bumps down in the middle from macrocosm to microcosm. *The Rape Of The Lock* is a fever of bathetic zeugmata:

> *Here thou! great Anna! whom three realms obey,*
> *Dost sometimes counsel take—and sometimes tea*
>
> *Not louder shrieks to pitying Heaven are cast,*
> *When husbands, or when lap-dogs, breathe their last!*
>
> *Whether the nymph shall break Diana's law,*
> *Or some frail china jar receive a flaw:*
> *Or stain her honour, or her new brocade;*
> *Forget her prayers, or miss a masquerade;*
> *Or lose her heart, or necklace at a ball . . .*[10]

The joke is that the Baron's escapade is being described in terms of the Trojan War; the tragedy that it *was* a Trojan War.

In his tragic sense, Pope is closest, perhaps, to Watteau. But Watteau's is a relenting tragedy; romantic; bathed in the light reflected from the moon faces of his clowns. In Pope there is no appeal through outcasts, none, even, to the out-of-doors: there is no pastoral; his characters are wholly *in* society. His is a city world without parks; its scents are dusty and cosmetic; indeed, it is all indoors. Even when Belinda takes the boat to Hampton Court, she is roofed over by sails and sylphs. The ironic wit has constructed round the antagonists in the sex war a masterpiece of eighteenth-century domestic architecture, in which they are caged. *The Rape Of The Lock* is a superb scheme of rococo decoration; the realm of the sylphs, whose 'airy substance' belongs literally to the elements, appears to open the poem on the open air and the sky, but is really the—exquisitely—painted ceiling.

X

Chivalry Inverted

———————— ❄ ————————

When eighteenth-century society tried to contain the libertine within the old, but now denuminised, framework of chivalry, it was lending itself to distortion by the seducer's and the sex war's purposes. Pope, needing to fit the concept of honour into the mythological machinery of *The Rape Of The Lock*, can do so only by calling on the jealousy of possessiveness. The woman guards her honour not for her own sake or society's but because she has a jealous ethereal lover in the shape of her guardian sylph—who, since Pope has already identified the sylphs as the souls of dead belles, has had to change sex in order to perform this office. Belinda's guardian tells her:

> *As now your own, our beings were of old,*
> *And once enclosed in woman's beauteous mould; . . .*
> *Know farther yet; whoever fair and chaste*
> *Rejects mankind, is by some Sylph embraced:*
> *For, spirits, freed from mortal laws, with ease*
> *Assume what sexes and what shapes they please.*
> *What guards the purity of melting maids,*
> *In courtly balls, and midnight masquerades . . . ?*
> *'Tis but their Sylph, the wise celestials know,*
> *Though honour is the word with men below.*[1]

(Madame de Merteuil would have appreciated the suggestion that a belle, once given the choice, would choose to change sex.) From a hostile contest between the seducer and the originally female guardian sylph, it is an easy step to a hostile contest between the seducer and the woman direct.

True chivalry had concerned the conquest of knight by knight: the libertine had only to distort its rules to make them apply to the knight's conquest of women. His compulsion to seduce becomes not merely a duty but a point of honour in an inverted code of chivalry. Sir Galahad believes his bodily strength will last only so long as his heart is pure: the libertine must repeatedly demonstrate the impurity of his heart in order to assure himself that his bodily virility has not yet been snatched from him. The true knight errant of medieval chivalrous romance took every man he encountered in his quests as a challenge to his courage, and every woman as a secondary challenge, this time to his chastity: Sir Gawain must face both the supernatural terrorisation of the Green Knight and the lures of the—probably magical—woman who tries to seduce him just as lecherous visions had tried to seduce the anchorites of primitive Christianity. For Don Giovanni, however, who is also a knight errant in his way (the way of the eighteenth-century quest for pleasure), it is the women who are the challenge to his courage and against whom he conducts his primary warfare. By the act of intercourse he runs them through and disposes of their reputations and, so far as he is concerned, their attractions, just as the knight at arms killed or destroyed the fighting reputations of the knights he defeated in combat. The fathers, husbands and brothers with whom Don Giovanni may have to do real combat are only secondarily and incidentally the targets of his hostility. Indeed, it does not take a very lengthy psycho-analysis to shew[2] that in unconscious terms it is these male personages who really represent sexual temptation to Don Giovanni, and that his compulsive pursuit of women is designed to counter his unconscious homosexuality and his dread of impotence. As early as 1714 Steele had recognised the century's inversion of chivalry: gallantry, he wrote, was 'turned topsie-turvey, and the knight errantry of this profligate age is destroying . . . women'.

It is in the language and conventions of chivalry that the hero and heroine of *Les Liaisons Dangereuses* pursue the enlightenment's inversion of the knightly quest. Madame de Merteuil stands in a protective relationship to Cécile Volanges, the virgin newly out of convent school. Just as, in true chivalry, the Marquise might have invoked her husband's protection for her young friend, so she now writes[3] to her former lover bidding him come and seduce Cécile, asking him to swear 'en fidèle Chevalier' not to undertake any new adventure until he shall have accomplished this, and holding out the promise of a new *rouerie* to add to his *Mémoires*, which she is determined to see printed and even undertakes to write. (The task of the medieval chronicler was performed by the memoirs, by or about its major and minor Casanovas, of which the eighteenth century was prolific: a genre which, with a stretch, includes the *Confessions* of Jean-Jacques Rousseau, and which is epitomised in the 'catalogo' Leporello keeps of Don Giovanni's successes. Don Giovanni takes old women 'for the pleasure of putting them in the list', just as Valmont is invited to take Cécile for the pleasure of putting that new *rouerie* in his memoirs.*)

Valmont's reply is that he already has another adventure in train (and is bound to it by the fact that 'conquérir est notre destin'); and the Marquise gives him leave to discharge this obligation before coming to the seduction of Cécile. Now that the knight's lady is watching him in the lists, the apex of knightly pride and pique has been touched; it is by one of the most magnificent and involuted conceits in literature that Laclos has the Marquise chide her former lover for his delay in accomplishing the preliminary seduction she has allowed him, and her reproach is couched in the proud and courtly words:[4] 'Adieu, Vicomte; bon soir et bon succès: mais, pour Dieu, avancez donc. Songez que si vous n'avez pas cette femme, les autres rougiront de vous avoir eu'.

When the enlightenment set up honour as an improvised defence against the seducer, it prepared the way for the century to end with Laclos's characters' deadly and perverted game. But the same chivalrous material also developed into a quite different end: the gothic revival. The chivalrous concepts which Valmont and Madame de Merteuil treat with so much irony and wit reappeared, quite without irony or wit, in the ballads and historical novels of Sir Walter Scott; a generation after that, the purity and chivalry of Sir Galahad were being taken with an utterly straight face by Tennyson and were helping to form the stained-glass ideal of public schoolboys. At the close of the eighteenth century and during the first decades of the nineteenth, two contemporaries, Sir Walter Scott and Jane Austen,[5] were demonstrating the two directions chivalry might take. Scott is already creating untidy canvases crowded with fancy-

---

* Cf. Simone de Beauvoir's acute remark about Sade: 'narrative plays a primary rôle in sadistic orgies'. (*Must We Burn De Sade?*, translated by A. Michelson.)

dress characters looming through romantic mist; Donizetti, Victor Hugo and even the pre-Raphaelites are already implicit. Jane Austen abides by the pure clarity, form and wit of the enlightenment. She is as ironic as Laclos, less melodramatic but equally dramatic, and perhaps even more deadly. Where Laclos is a touch in love with his characters, indulges the panache of their inverted code and reaps a bitter joy from their destruction, Jane Austen is not dazzled by her heroes and heroines for an instant. Not being infatuated, she is free to like them, and she prefers to save rather than drive them to a romantic damnation. She is clear-sightedly scathing about the social disruption wrought by the code of inverted chivalry—her Sir Edward Denham pursues women in defiance of every opposition of *convenience*. Equally, since she is never taken in, she sets her face and her skilled technique of deflationary realism against the affectations of neo-gothic chivalry as it had been sketched in the novels of Mrs Radcliffe. Against both the knight inverted and the neo-gothic knight she puts forward the round, common-sensical Johnsonian view of honour, the old eighteenth-century bastion which had proved liable to subversion by the libertine but which, in true enlightened fashion, she *cannot* abandon, simply because it *is* commonsensical. (She does her best to strengthen it with her barbed satire; but satire makes its appeal to commonsense and is of no more avail than a rapier against a romantic mist.) When she wishes to bestow a husband on the heroine whom she predicted no one but herself would much like[6] (and whom we dare guess she herself liked best of all), she gives her honourable man the significant name of Mr Knightley.

Like the true medieval knight (and like his late-Victorian imitators at the public schools, with their great concern with games and scores), the knight-libertine had a scale by which to compare the values of his conquests. (Indeed, his conquests, like those of medieval war, had a ransom value, thanks to the eighteenth-century marriage-market: if he could first seduce her, the libertine would be heartily thanked for marrying a girl to whom, while she remained uncompromised, he lacked the qualifications in income or repute to aspire.)

The highest place on the seducer's scale belonged to virgins: the eighteenth century has been described[7] as suffering from 'defloration mania'. If what the libertine feared was castration, which he expected to come on him through the woman, this deepest dread was re-inforced in the eighteenth century by the perfectly realistic fear (which Mozart cites[8] as one of his reasons for living chastely) of venereal disease[9]—apprehended as a species of castration, involving the mutilation and impairment of the sexual organs, and being transmitted by the woman. This punishment at least could not come from intercourse with virgins; and so a permissive factor was added to the compelling and positive one which actually set the high seduction value on the virgin. This was that it was impossible to make love to a virgin without also causing her pain. In seducing a virgin, not only was the libertine guaranteed against at least one form of his own expected punishment; he was even able to put the punishment at a greater distance from himself by inflicting it on the woman, the painful and bloody act of defloration being an assault of just the kind he feared falling on his own body.

Once the Ego had been liberated to pursue its own quest for pleasure, the question was bound to be raised philosophically of how far it would go in tyrannising another Ego, and cutting off that Ego's pleasures in pursuit of its own. This is the question implied by Richardson's seducer heroes. 'Ella è nelle mie mani', exults Lord Bonfil in Goldoni's version of *Pamela*;[10] Lovelace, having by trickery abducted Clarissa Harlowe and ruined her good name, writes to his confidant 'And is she not IN MY POWER?'[11] Richardson, a crypto-pornographer, does not quite admit that the victim's vulnerability is more than incidental and that the seducer is not sensitive to the charms of women unless the women can be pained and humiliated. The same fantasy was carried further along the same lines (of a hero who abducts women and holds them prisoner to his caprice) by the Marquis de Sade, who requires not only a victim but a willing victim (the ultimate humiliation) before desire is activated: 'The most divine charms are as nothing when submission and obedience do not come forth to offer them'.[12] Sade places the Ego in the extreme position of power both more pornographically and more philosophically than Richardson. The question how far the Ego will go is pushed as far as the question will go; and Sade received his answer from the French Revolution, whose liberal philosophy he supported, whose atrocities appalled him, and which in return censured him as too moderate.

However, when society attempted to use the concept of honour to protect vulnerable people, it had already tacitly admitted that their vulnerability was the supreme attraction. Honour had to be democratised in order to reduce the temptation value of the proletariat—in particular, the servant class, the domestic proletariat, the disenfranchised section of the family. The question of honour between master and maid was put forward by Richardson in *Pamela*; and (although one of the most influential versions of the story, Goldoni's dramatisation, dodges the social issue by having Pamela turn out to be the daughter of an aristocrat*) it was perhaps the pan-European fame of *Pamela* which prompted Beaumarchais to shew the vindication of the servants' honour against the tyrannical eroticism of their master in *Le Mariage de Figaro*.

The status of the serving girl, like the vulnerability of the virgin, acted not merely permissively but compulsively on the desires of the master. The libertine's unconscious wish to reiterate the castration nature had already imposed on women was given its opportunity in the opportunity to endorse the socially castrated state of the servant. In Sade the sexual significance of social class is carried to the point where he makes his valet the partner of his orgies in real life, and his fantasies run on harems and slavery (themes which occur in many eighteenth-century writings, under the pretext of the vogue for the exotic†). To cross the class barrier was, for the libertine of the

---

* Goldoni's preface (*L'autore a chi legge*) begins by attacking the anonymous English author of the novel for raising the question of a marriage between aristocrat and servant: even though London is said to be less scrupulous in such matters than other parts of Europe, 'either the English author ought not, in my opinion, to have brought the matter into dispute, or he ought to have resolved it with more decorum than his nation' ('O non doveva l'autore inglese, secondo me, disputare su tale articolo, o lo doveva risolvere con più decoro della sua nazione'). A line or two later, however, Goldoni's timidity reaches the point where he is afraid he will be censured for his timidity. 'The most perspicacious spirits' in England may not, he realises, be pleased with him; he agrees that according to natural principles virtue is preferable to nobility and wealth, but in the theatre one must uphold the morality which is in practice most commonly approved; and he hopes to be forgiven for the necessity in which he finds himself of not offending against the most applauded moeurs.

† These themes are not, of course, confined to the century's writings: witness, e.g., the two paintings by Francesco Guardi, *Scene In A Harem* and *Scene In A Seraglio*, from a Turkish sequence by Guardi. (Thyssen-Bornemisza Collection, nos. 175 A and B.)

enlightenment as for the twentieth-century homosexual, tantamount to transgressing the incest prohibition between generations. It is a conspicuous defiance of the father powers, to protect whose prerogatives the class barriers and the incest prohibition were alike created.

The virgin offered a still more pointed opportunity to affront the father. The virgin is considered essentially as some man's daughter. She is still under the protection of her father; insofar as he has the right to 'give her away' (in the eighteenth century, to a man of his own choice), she is his possession—or, in default of a father, the possession of a brother or guardian. (The common theme of guardians planning to marry their wards is an unconscious reconstruction of the primitive family situation, in which the father has not yet been obliged to renounce his personal sexual right to his daughters. The mercenary and lecherous tyranny exercised by Dr Bartolo over his ward Rosina in *Il Barbiere di Siviglia* exposes the unconscious motivations of the tyranny which such Victorian patres familias as Edward Moulton Barrett exercised over their real daughters.) To seduce a virgin is therefore to steal a daughter and violate a father's privileges. It is the father who is offended, and who challenges—and, in *Don Giovanni*, punishes—the seducer.

By this chain of unconscious reasoning, seducing virgins becomes a kind of incest. It is the next best (and worst) thing to seducing the woman who quintessentially belongs to the father, the mother herself. The married woman also offered the temptation to seduce someone else's property; but the libertine who affronted her husband was affronting an equal rather than a father; and the virgin still had the advantage in value in that her seduction must physically hurt her. Valmont has to compare the kudos of seducing Cécile Volanges with that of seducing the married woman whose virtue he is already attempting when Madame de Merteuil's invitation reaches him. He weighs the convent-educated virgin against a married woman well-known for conjugal love, religious devotion and austere principles;[13] and for the kudos at stake we may read the question of how nearly the conquest will approach incest.

Valmont has already thrown a religious factor into the valuation; and, as Casanova lets us see, the frisson of defying the incest prohibition is doubled if the class barrier to be crossed has been consecrated by the church. To seduce a nun was to seduce someone who was at once a virgin and a bride; and the father-plus-husband whose rights were offended was the enlightenment's old enemy God the Father. Voltaire was able to add this touch of blasphemous frisson to a mixture, already piquant in itself, of the code of true chivalry with the seducer's code of the obligatory conquest of virgins. The consecrated virgin was actually combined with the medieval knight at arms in the person of Joan of Arc, whose legendary reputation Voltaire pursues and deflowers through the scurrilous and funny cantos of *La Pucelle d'Orléans* (a poem which, in contrast to Pope's tragic epic, is pure comedy, and which opens with literature's most refined autobiographical understatement: 'Je ne suis né pour célébrer les saints').

The deadly stalking of virgins which was dictated by the inversion of chivalry was itself an inversion of the Mariolatry which suffused the system of historical chivalry. In its lust for virgins the eighteenth century was rebelling against Christianity's inveterate adulation of virginity—a subject which provoked from Edward Gibbon some of his most scathing and most thoroughly eighteenth-century sarcasms. But if the enlightenment was reiterating its rebellion against the father, the son is originally impelled to that rebellion by his desire for the mother; and if the pursuit of virgins was a defiance of God the Father, it was God the Father who had in the first place associated *the* Virgin with *the* Mother. This mythological fantasy in contradiction of nature meant that the fantasy of violating virgins need not be a mere approximation to the central wish to violate the mother; and the temptations it called forth can be judged by the popular scale of values by which the very worst—the most tempting—of sins was to violate the Virgin Mary.*

---

* Luther castigated the church for the looseness of its teaching, which had permitted the popular belief to arise that an indulgence would guarantee forgiveness even to one who had violated the Virgin. The same belief was still in circulation three centuries later, when Søren Kierkegaard wrote in his Journal: 'It made a terrible impression upon me the first time I heard that the *indulgences* contained the statement that they remit *all* sins: "etiam si matrem virginem violasset".' (R. H. Fife: *The Revolt Of Martin Luther*, 14; *The Journal Of Kierkegaard*, 1837, translation by A. Dru.)

Enlightenment man had found himself in the doubly criminal position of Oedipus. *Don Giovanni* describes how the rebel who infringes a father's sexual rights finds himself let in also for the crime of murdering the father, but the true position of the enlightenment was rather the other way about: it had killed God the Father and found itself let in for a sexual libertinism which verged closer and closer on incest. It is implicit in the Oedipus situation that parricide and incest are concomitants. This was the inevitability which bound the libertine to his course, once he had concurred in the assassination of God; secretly he was courting the impotence which the unconscious understands to be the punishment prescribed for both branches of the filial crime.

Not until the early part of the nineteenth century, by which time the enlightenment had suffered the incurable wound of the French Revolution, did the enlightened rebel turn into the outlaw romantic. The romantic admitted his infatuation with the mother ('He was in love with his mother', wrote Stendhal in his obituary notice of himself[14]). Equally, he admitted the doom which had fallen on him as a result—he was 'riche, mais impuissant'.[15] Indeed, the romantic condemns his own loves to impotence, by undertaking loves of such high idealism or such far-fetched and impossible fantasy that they can never be consummated. Where the libertine was a parody of the chivalrous knight, the full-blown romantic was a reconstruction of the chivalrous troubadour (of whom there is already a touch in Don Giovanni, the singer of serenades beneath balconies*). The romantic has put aside weapons in favour of a musical instrument; he is wholly and essentially an artist. He, he insists, is the one who shall suffer, and sing his suffering. He has none of the libertine's desire to inflict the mutilation he dreads on the woman; and for this reason, combined with his masochistic determination to be unlucky in love, his yearning for the unattainable mother is more likely to lead him into love with someone else's wife than with a virgin. The married woman's husband has forestalled the romantic lover, just as the father has by the very terms of the thing forestalled the son. When the Don Juan story is made into a truly romantic opera, Donna Anna becomes the Commendatore's wife instead of his

* See the end of chapter XI.

daughter.* The true romantic has given up the attempt to externalise his aggressive impulse. He turns it almost frankly on his suffering self, courts his own destruction, whether through drink, drugs, dangerous exploits or even crimes, almost directly, knows that he is at least 'half in love' with death, and takes so small an interest in society that he is not even prepared to wreak much havoc in it.

Like most revolutions, this literary revolution was inaugurated decades before it matured. The inaugurator—if we accept his claim to have 'created a new species of romance'—[16] was Horace Walpole, who published *The Castle Of Otranto*, as an anonymous chronicle purporting to be translated from the Italian, on Christmas Eve, 1764.[17] This proto-romantic farrago already puts forward all the elements of mature romanticism: doom (supernaturally signalled) is gathering upon the castle and its lord, a doom provoked by the cardinally Oedipus act of usurpation (which Walpole probably borrowed direct from *Hamlet*); and the plot glitters with intimations of incest. The wicked lord Manfred's son is killed just before his wedding ceremony; whereupon Manfred decides to marry the bride himself ('you, my lord?' she cries, 'you! my father-in-law!'[18]). Manfred goes on to plan a marriage between *her* father and his own (Manfred's) daughter. The two girls are, as one would expect, bosom friends and, moreover, in love with the same young man—who turns out to be the rightful heir to the domain Manfred has usurped. Even the pretext on which Manfred proposes to obtain from the church the divorce that will set him free to marry his all-but daughter-in-law cannot resist toying with the thought of incest: Manfred pretends to have scruples about his present marriage, on the grounds that he and his wife are 'related within the forbidden degrees'.[19] It is typical of Walpole himself, as a proto-romantic perpetually ennuyé and self-frustrated, that having created a fictitious doom he should adopt it to himself in real life by identifying his doomed castle of Otranto with his architectural romance and home, Strawberry Hill.†

* Alexander Dargomijsky (1813–69) made Pushkin's version of the Don Juan story into an opera, *The Stone Guest*, completed after his death by César Cui and Rimsky-Korsakof in 1872.

† Walpole wrote, of a visitor to Strawberry Hill, 'she desired to see the Castle of Otranto; I let her see all the antiquities of it'. (See Oswald Doughty's Introduction

Where the enlightenment was struggling to justify itself by reason, and Don Giovanni refuses to repent, the romantic pleaded guilty and punishable even before he was called to account, and refused to allow reason to convince him he was innocent. Where the enlightenment had cast off original sin, the romantic movement was subject to what Søren Kierkegaard called 'a frightful foreboding', 'the foreboding of guilt', which he defined as 'a desire for what one fears, a sympathetic antipathy'.[20]

The romantic admitted that he dwelt in the infertile region of hell; the romantic writer withdrew from the problems of society, and threw his curse at society's increasing material productiveness under industrial capitalism.* The eighteenth-century writer, on the other hand, was usually so busy drawing up plans for a just and productive society that he failed to notice that it was precisely through this busyness that the doom of infertility was falling on his art. His artistic impotence lay in his inability to pause long enough—to be, as the romantics so regularly were, bored long enough—to perform an act of imagination, just as the libertine could not pause long enough in his compulsive career of seduction to fall in love. Eighteenth-century writers tackled and disposed of logical problems, just as the seducer tackled and disposed of female reputations. That this course ended in hell Mozart demonstrated in *Don Giovanni*.

---

to his edition of *The Castle Of Otranto*.) Perhaps the first step of identification was Walpole's writing the word 'Gothic' into the title page of the second edition, when he had stopped pretending the work was a translation; the novel then became 'A Gothic Story', whereas it had first appeared as simply 'A Story'.

* Both these characteristics of romanticism had already been divined in 1820 by Peacock. In *The Four Ages Of Poetry*, he imagines 'that egregious confraternity of rhymesters, known as the Lake Poets' to be saying to themselves ' "Society is artificial, therefore we will live out of society. The mountains are natural, therefore we will live in the mountains" '. Peacock goes on to describe the romantic poet as a mole burying himself in the perpetually dark Cimmerian region which borders hell. (See further chapters XV and XXIII.)

XI

Seduction in Mozart's Operas

[with a note on Who is Cherubino, What is He?]

———————❧———————

Although *Don Giovanni* is Mozart's only opera given wholly
to the theme, seduction is also an important strand in the much
more complex thematic composition of *Le Nozze di Figaro*. The
two operas are, of course, very close in time and in their standing in Mozart's work. (*Figaro*, having had quite a success in
Vienna the previous year, had a howling success* in Prague in
January 1787; whereupon Mozart was commissioned to compose an opera specially for Prague, and produced *Don Giovanni*
by the autumn of the same year.) They are, moreover, close in
manner: both composed in long passages of continuous musical
and dramatic fabric in which several characters participate; and
both dramatic conceptions of the same *size*—grand, symphonic
opera, not chamber music for voices. And they share the Italian
language and da Ponte for librettist.

It is significant that both these operas, and only these, are set
in Spain.† If the seduction code of honour was an inversion of
chivalry, then Spain had been acknowledged ever since *Don
Quixote* as the last redoubt of true chivalry. Indeed, Spain had
long been notorious (witness, for example, Titian's painting,
now in the Prado, of 'Spain succouring religion') as a repository
of all the pre-enlightenment values—honour, superstition,
absolutism, Catholicism, tout compris. Beaumarchais, as an
agitator and infiltrator on behalf of the enlightenment, set the

———————

* The much quoted letter Mozart sent from Prague describing this success is
perhaps the origin of the cliché whereby so many novelists have registered a hit
tune in terms of errand boys whistling it in the streets. 'For here', says Mozart,
'they talk of nothing but "Figaro". Nothing is played, sung or whistled but
"Figaro" . . . Nothing, nothing but "Figaro".' (From Prague, 14 January, 1787,
to Baron Gottfried von Jacquin.)

† However, Belmonte, in *Il Seraglio*, is—again significantly—a Spaniard.

first two plays of his Figaro trilogy in Spain with the intention of shewing the ancien régime at its most ridiculous. In the first play, which became, to the almost complete loss of its social import, Rossini's *Il Barbiere di Siviglia*, Beaumarchais entered a plea that girls should be allowed to marry men of their own choosing (a point said still not to be granted in Spain). In the second, which gained so infinitely in psychology when it was taken up by da Ponte and Mozart, Beaumarchais picks on the ancient and highly respectable code of honour of Spanish aristocrats and exposes it as no more effective than open caddishness or social anarchy, since it stops short of respecting the honour of the servants. The ancien-régime conception of honour is just as liable as the enlightenment's to be perverted into the seducer's code, though the ancien-régime seducer limits his victims to members of one class. It is the seducer's code Beaumarchais condemns—not in the person of an emancipated and free-thinking libertine like Don Giovanni, but through a pillar of established society.

There was also some superficial camouflage to be had from the Spanish setting. It allows Beaumarchais to answer those who censure his audacity by disingenuously describing *Le Mariage de Figaro* as 'the lightest of intrigues' ('la plus badine des intrigues') and to recount its plot as 'A great Spanish lord, in love with a young woman',[1] etc., as though there were no more to it. The feudal remoteness of Spain from enlightened Europe permits him to create, in the 'château d'Aguas-Frescas, à trois lieues de Séville', a world-in-itself, which Mozart presently made an enchanted world. However, Beaumarchais's social purpose is not effectively disguised, or it would have defeated itself. The château could be read as society, and the sexual tyranny of the Count as the social tyranny of the ruling class; with the result that the play, so far from being accepted as a mere intrigue, was accused of infamy and sedition.[2] In *Figaro*, play and opera alike, the Spanish setting is the mark that the enlightenment is attacking the ancien régime in its last and remotest ditch.

In *Don Giovanni*, which recounts not a French eighteenth-century visitor's view of Spain but a Spanish Counter-Reformation fable, it is the other way about. The seduction code of honour is here exemplified in enlightenment man, who has cast off even the democratised code of honour; and he is the villain. True chivalry, practised by the Spanish lords and ladies whom Don Giovanni's career offends, tries to but cannot put down this seducer. Answer and punishment have to be administered by another force whose last home was Spain, supernatural religion.

In *Figaro*, the great exponent of the seduction theme is the Count. Søren Kierkegaard (in *Either/Or**) made a charming remark when he described Cherubino as Don Giovanni in youth : but the truth about Cherubino, who lives on the perpetual point of being ravished, is that he is as much seduced as seducer. He has none of Don Giovanni's active and deliberate character, and not a touch of Don Giovanni's brazenness. Intellectual self-justification in the enlightenment manner would never enter his head. He is himself the victim of the influence which through him disturbs everyone else. He is the adolescent whose sexual tension has involuntarily attracted a poltergeist into the Almaviva household. (No doubt the poltergeist is in control when Cherubino overturns a chair at so awkward a moment of Act II.)

As a matter of fact, it is possible to give a precise name to the poltergeistly influence embodied in Cherubino. Like so many fairies and spirits in the modern world, he is really a demoted god from the ancient world. The prototype on which his original creator, Beaumarchais, has unconsciously modelled him comes from the common stock of popularised classical mythology—so common that when da Ponte and Mozart took him over they unconsciously expanded him in the same terms as he had been originally conceived.

Yet although this was an unconscious process the true identity of Cherubino was evidently hovering on the tip of their consciousness. It is asking to be spoken in Figaro's farewell to Cherubino, when Cherubino has been sent off and bidden to transform himself from a page into an army officer. The dry and understated little speech Beaumarchais gives Figaro by way of farewell ('Adieu, mon petit Chérubin. Tu vas mener un train de vie bien différent . . . tu ne rôderas plus tout le jour au quartier des femmes; plus d'échaudés, de gôutés à la crème . . .'[3]) is expanded by the authors of the opera into the much more

* *Either*, 'The Immediate Stages of the Erotic or The Musical Erotic'.

dramatic and realised 'Non più andrai'.[4] The undescriptive 'mon petit Chérubin' is elaborated into a series of epithets Jamesianly searching for the mot juste to address to Cherubino. Figaro knows that at the back of his thoughts is a classical prototype, and he tries out two, Narcissus and Adonis. But he senses that the person he really has in mind is more babyish than either of these, and so he adds the diminutive ending to both names. Even so, he is not quite satisfied, because he feels that his real quarry has a more quintessential connexion with love than even Narcissus and Adonis, and so he adds 'd'amor', making a total of

Narcisetto, Adoncino d'amor.

If the line had read 'Narcisetto—Adoncino—Amor', Figaro's final shot would have hit his target. The fluttering Cherubino ('ogni donna mi fa palpitar'[5]), with his angelical and winged name (Beaumarchais's Chérubin), is the last major manifestation in European art of Cupid, the boyish god of love—whose wings, Apuleius had reported some sixteen centuries before, fluttered even while he slept.[6] By similar flutterings Cherubino, according to Figaro, disturbs the sleep of beautiful women— 'delle belle turbando il riposo'. And in fact Figaro need not have searched so hard in the fourth line of his aria for Cherubino's original name. He has made the essential point—winged love —in the first line, when he calls Cherubino a 'great amorous butterfly', 'farfallone amoroso'*.

As the name Cherubino itself bears witness, the late-classical winged god, variously a youth and a baby† ('He's still a baby', pleads Susanna on behalf of Cherubino; 'Less than you think',

---

* Properly speaking, Cupid's wings are feathered; but all he needs, to turn him into a farfallone amoroso, is to borrow the butterfly wings of his mistress Psyche. Even so, Figaro seems dissatisfied with the butterfly metaphor. Later in the aria he works his way round to the correct kind of wings and speaks of Cherubino's 'fine little feathers'—'questi bei pennacchini'.

† Both in antiquity and in the renaissance tradition, iconography is uncertain whether Cupid is a baby or an adolescent. Beaumarchais has passed on something of this uncertainty about Cupid to his Chérubin, of whom he writes (in his Préface) 'peut-être il n'est plus un enfant, mais il n'est pas encore un homme'. I have argued in my *Black Ship To Hell* that, Cupid being the most concentrated of phallic symbols, the myths' uncertainty about his size is itself a symbol of the powers of erection and detumescence. Cherubino's fluttering aria 'Non so più' is, as it were, a soliloquy by the phallos: 'I no longer know what I am, what I'm doing; One minute I'm fire, the next ice; Every woman makes me change colour; Every woman sets me aflutter.' (No. 6, Act I.)

replies the Count*), had become confused with the Jewish-Christian conception of winged baby angels. By the time of the rococo, to whose utmost development *Figaro* belongs, there is no telling sacred winged babies from profane; the air is thick with the decorative flights of indistinguishable putti and amoretti.

Cherubino, who is to be found at the bottom of every intrigue ('Fate will keep making me find this page everywhere!' exclaims the Count[7]), has fully preserved the mischief of Cupid's character. He is hardly human stuff at all, but the presiding genius of *Le Nozze di Figaro*, just as Puck, another derivative of Cupid,[8] presides over *A Midsummer Night's Dream*. Cherubino's ubiquity is the mark that all the proceedings of the 'folle journée',† all the making, shuffling and remaking of amorous couples in the night-enchanted garden of the Almaviva palace, are, like the nocturnal making and unmaking of couples in the wood near Athens, taking place under the inspiration of Eros. Eros presides over the opera just as statues of antique deities preside over the amorous couples in Watteau's paintings: and just as the pilgrim lovers on the island of Cythera have hung garlands and votive offerings on the statue of Venus,‡ so the Countess in *Figaro* addresses a prayer to Venus's son with her 'Porgi, Amor . . .'§

* 'Egli è ancora fanciullo'—'Men di quel che tu credi' (Recitative IX, Act I). Or, in Beaumarchais's play (I, x), where Susanna's protest is allotted to the Countess: 'Hélas! Il est si jeune!'—'Pas tant que vous le croyez'.

† The name by which it is always called, *Le Mariage de Figaro*, is actually the sub-title of Beaumarchais's play, and *La Folle Journée* its title—not the other way about as is often stated (by, e.g., Eric Blom on p. 228 of his selection of Mozart's letters). Mozart seems to have disapproved of the Prague management's calling his opera by the (real) title of the play. (See his letter of 15–25 October, from Prague, to Baron Gottfried von Jacquin.)

‡ —in the Louvre version. This and the version at Dahlem, Berlin, formerly called 'The Embarkation for Cythera', have now been recognised by Michael Levey as pictures of the pilgrims *on* the island. (See *The Burlington Magazine*, May, 1961.)

§ That this aria *is* a prayer is emphasised by Michael Levey ('Aspects Of Mozart's Heroines', II, *Warburg Journal*, XXII, 1–2, 1959). Belmonte, too, addresses a prayer to love (in *Die Entführung* . . . , No. 17), which is echoed by Pedrillo's 'Nun, Cupido'. In Susanna's duet with the Count (*Figaro*, No. 16) something even subtler happens: indeed, the whole duet is one of the world's miracles of psychological-dramatic subtlety. Even before Susanna accidentally betrays her deception by the slip of the tongue whereby she answers Yes and No according to her real instead of her feigned feelings, she has admitted the guilty conscience which will in a moment lead her tongue to slip, by her aside 'Scusatemi se mento, voi che intendete amor'—'Forgive me if I lie, you who understand love'. The concentration

It is not Cherubino who is Don Giovanni in potentia but Count Almaviva. There was needed only one impetus to develop Mozart's conception of this insolent aristocrat, who would like to take advantage of the droit de seigneur in order to seduce Susanna, into the insolent privateer who would like to seduce every woman he sets eyes on. And in point of fact—a point to be elaborated later—it is possible to be exact about what the impetus *was*: the death of Mozart's father, which took place between the composition of the two operas.

Already, however, the Count contains a recognisable amount of Don Giovanni; but the treatment Don Giovanni accords to all women is reserved by the Count for the peasant class on which his household draws for its servants. Towards his Countess he is coldly courteous at the half-way dénouement which closes Act II, and utterly apologetic at the final climax. But Susanna he has claimed by seignorial right. His attitude towards her is repeated in Don Giovanni's towards the peasant-girl Zerlina. The dramatic content of the miraculous duet between the Count and Susanna,[9] in which the Count is urging her to make a rendez-vous with him in his palace garden, is repeated in the Don Giovanni-Zerlina duet, in which Don Giovanni is urging Zerlina to enter his house (which he tries to make less imposing and danger-fraught by referring to it as a mere *casinetto*), where, as he says, 'we will give one another our hands'.[10]

The difference between the two intending seducers (neither of them succeeds) is that the Count, who wishes to remain a

---

of dramatic purpose is immense. On one level, Susanna's remark is addressed out of the theatrical frame to the audience, re-animating the commedia dell'arte tradition of which she is a distant derivative: and thus her remark foreshadows the aria ('Aprite un po' quegl'occhi', No. 26) in the next act, where Figaro, thinking himself deceived by Susanna, addresses *his* commedia dell'arte reflexions on women to the audience. At the same time, Susanna's 'voi che intendete amor' recalls from the previous act Cherubino's 'voi che sapete che cosa è amor'—an address to women in general *through*, in particular, Susanna and the Countess: and thus Susanna's aside begs the pardon of the particular persons in the drama, the Countess and Figaro, whose sincerity is insulted by her feigning but for whose sake it is that she feigns. And finally her aside epitomises the morality of the whole opera. The apology for lying is an epitome of the morality itself, and the 'voi che intendete amor' an explanation of the force which sanctions that morality—a translation into rational, social terms of the opera's mythology. It is as though Mozart and da Ponte were explaining that of course the god Amor to whom the Countess prays does not exist as such but that the idea he personifies nonetheless draws a binding moral and emotive force from the feelings of lovers.

pillar of society, would like a legal title to Susanna, whereas the Don has dispensed with all law except the inexhaustible dictates of his Ego. Count Almaviva regrets the liberal moment in which he renounced his droit de seigneur. Susanna knows this and lets the audience know it at the outset; when Figaro points out that the Count has abolished the droit, Susanna replies pungently 'Well, now he's sorry'—'Ebben, ora è pentito'.[11] The Count's regret is presently brought home to the audience through an equally pungent dramatic irony. At the very moment when the Count is arranging an assignation with the bride, the chorus has already started in on the celebrations for her marriage to Figaro, and the young girls are singing their thanks and praises to the Count as their 'sì saggio signor', who has given up 'a right which offends' and now 'hands us over to our sweethearts in a state of chastity'[12].

The Count would like to have his own way without disrupting society; he would simply like society to accord him wider than usual rights, in his capacity as patrician, as a father-representative in society. Don Giovanni demands—or, rather, takes—utter licence. He admits no claims on him. Donna Elvira has much in her of the Countess's regal pathos: the words which the other members (not Don Giovanni, of course) of the quartet exclaim at first sight of her, 'what a noble aspect, what sweet majesty!',[13] might describe the impression made by Countess Almaviva. But Don Giovanni's treatment of Elvira is in the utmost contrast to the submission to the Countess's claims on him which the Count makes in that great moment[14] where— 'Contessa, perdono!'—he sues for pardon.

The Count chooses to remain a Spanish grandee; and da Ponte and Mozart make marvellous use throughout the opera of the titles Count and Countess: sometimes ironic; sometimes commanding; at the end, simple and grand. It is to the obligations of his rank and honour that the Count finally submits, though he has been brought to the point of submission by the delicate and unvituperative sex warfare waged against him by his wife and Susanna—in which it is Susanna, to the credit of proletarian wit and force of character, who is general and strategist. Don Giovanni, by contrast, acknowledges no obligations of his rank. This is what shocks Don Ottavio. With a fatuousness Jane Austen might have attributed to one of her young clergymen whom she had particularly got her knife into, Don Ottavio exclaims: 'How should I ever believe a *knight* capable of so black a crime!' ('Come mai creder deggio, di sì nero delitto capace un cavaliere!'[15])

Don Giovanni, recognising no obligations of any sort,* would not give a fig for a legal title to a maidservant, being prepared to take quantities of maidservants without any justification except his desire to do so. This assertion of the Ego offers such a threat to society that, in dealing with Don Giovanni, society has to call in reinforcement from its supernatural sanction. The Count can be tamed by the women of his household because he accepts the framework of households and of society. (Indeed, the Count *has* a household, whereas the wandering Don Giovanni has by way of permanent entourage only the disreputable Leporello.) The women Don Giovanni has wronged wage against him a much bitterer and more impassioned war than Susanna and the Countess bring against the Count, but it is necessarily ineffectual, because Don Giovanni is reserved to the vengeance of heaven.[16]

Yet this is not to say that Don Giovanni has renounced the privileges of his rank and turned democrat. He is democratic in the catholicity of his sexual desires: Leporello enumerates[17] his conquest of 'peasant girls, maidservants, citizenesses . . . countesses, baronesses, marchionesses, princesses'. But in his opportunism he is quite as prepared as the Count to employ his rank as an aid to seduction; and his Egotism will accept nourishment even from the pride of being a knight and a gentleman. Whereas Molière's Don Juan had been something of an egalitarian and social reformer, Don Giovanni feels no attachment to society high or low. The opera opens with Leporello's complaint that he has to wait on Don Giovanni night and day and would prefer to give up service and turn gentleman himself.[18] Any egalitarian promptings Leporello may manifest, and any moral scruples about being an accomplice in his master's way of life, Don Giovanni corrupts with a gift of money.[19] For the benefit of his own Ego, Don Giovanni stands on his rights as a gentleman and works not only Leporello's energy but his courage hard, insisting that it must be the servant who delivers

---

* He tells Leporello (who tries to hold him to an oath sworn 'sul mio onore' not a minute before): 'Non so di giuramento' (Act I, recitative before No. 3).

the invitation to supper and opens the door when the supernatural stone guest arrives. Indeed, Don Giovanni, whose squire
has followed him, keeping a tally of victories, through Italy,
Germany, France, Turkey and Spain, insists on the privileges of
a cavaliere errant quite in the high chivalrous sense. He would
disdain to do combat with Masetto, who is too far beneath him
socially. (He has even had chivalrous, though crudely expressed,
scruples about fighting the aged Commendatore.[20]) All he will
condescend to do to Masetto is trick him and bruise him with his
own firearm, without even, as we learn from the sequel*,
deigning to damage him more seriously than can be cured by a
little petting.

Where Don Giovanni is only offhandedly aristocratic, the
Count takes an expressly patrician tone when Figaro stands in
the way of *his* desires. 'While *I* sigh', he asks himself, 'am I to
watch one of my servants being happy?' With this aristocratic
question, he provokes himself to a magnificent torrent of
aristocratic, privileged exasperation, released on the forcefully
placed and held syllable *tu*—the *tu* of master to servant.† It is,
the Count emphasises, a question of *birth*. 'You' (the lordly *tu*)
'were not born', he soliloquises to the absent Figaro, 'to give
me torment and perhaps even to laugh—to laugh!—at my
unhappiness' ('Tu non nascesti, audace, [bis] Per dar a me
tormento, E forse ancor per ridere, per ridere, Di mia
infelicità'[21]).

The Count's insolence meets much more effective human
resistance than Don Giovanni's. The plot-necessity that Don
Giovanni shall be caught out by nothing less than heaven
reduces his proletarian adversary, Masetto, to ineffectual
rusticity—which is why Masetto and his sweetheart do not
succeed in shewing anything like the character of Figaro and
his. The best Masetto can do is indicate his ironic understanding
of who is the proletarian and who the signore: 'Ho capito,
Signor, sì'.[22]

Figaro, too, at least after Susanna has alerted him,[23] is perfectly apprised of the social situation and its implications; but
the plot, which has excluded the supernatural, allows him to use
craft (he is something of an Odysseus) on a situation where he

---

* Sc. Zerlina's 'Vedrai, carino' (No. 19, Act II).
† For the source of this *tu* in Mozart's life, see chapter XXIII, p. 271.

has no power. Figaro understands his social position as well as Masetto does his. Even in soliloquy, he addresses the Count not as *tu* but with the polite *Lei*: indeed, he addresses him as *signor*, and adds his title. But where Masetto can put no more than a bitter irony into the *signore* he addresses to Don Giovanni, Figaro is free to add ironic flourish. What he has done to the Count's title is to add the mocking diminutive; and what he sings is 'Se vuol ballare, signor Contino'[24]—the aria which seemed the very essence of rebellion to Sigmund Freud, who sang it to himself on a station platform in Vienna, as an expression first of his rebellious feelings towards titled and official personages, who could get compartments on the train by bribery, and presently of 'all kinds of bold and revolutionary thoughts . . . such as would fit themselves to the words of Figaro'.[25]

Figaro, in which the alliance of the Countess, Susanna, Figaro and Cherubino, representing all the oppressed classes—servants, women and the young—triumphs over the Count, is a revolutionary document. *Don Giovanni*, for motives in Mozart's psychology which I shall discuss presently, is counter-revolutionary. No more than *Pamela* does *Don Giovanni* speak on behalf of working-class emancipation. Like *Pamela*, it merely points out that working girls may be sexually desirable to their masters. *Figaro*, on the other hand, speaks for the servants not only through their final victory (to which their mistress contributes) but through the intensity of their characterisation, which Masetto and Zerlina do not share, though they imitate it. *Figaro* establishes the servants' claim to individuality and to the sexual rights which the enlightenment had correctly recognised as inseparable from individual psychology.* This—the presidency of Eros throughout society—is the tone set when the opera opens with Susanna trying on her wedding hat and her bridegroom measuring the room for their double bed.†

Count Almaviva is following the libertine's course most exactly: he is tempted both by Susanna's virginity (the whole point of the droit de seigneur being that it is the seigneur who

---

* Cf. Freud's conjecture that it was by means of sexual rebellion that mankind originally developed out of group psychology into individual psychology. (*Group Psychology And The Analysis Of The Ego.*)

† The idea of setting the tone of the whole by opening with the image of a bed is another of *Der Rosenkavalier*'s borrowings from *Figaro*.

claims the superior pleasure of inflicting the pain of defloration) and by the class barrier, to transgress which is a species of incest. It is particularly base in Count Almaviva that the virgin he wants to seduce is his wife's maid. Susanna is, so to speak, the Countess's proletarian daughter: she has the Countess's protection in return for being herself disqualified from ever offering the Countess rivalry. It is particularly insulting to the Countess that the Count chooses to set up as her rival someone officially too low-born to enter the lists at all.

However, Susanna and the Countess have refused to be—have refused to be manœuvred into being—rivals. They decline to be trapped in either the social conventions or the code of inverted chivalry. Their reciprocal daughter-mother affection is not a class loyalty but personal to them. They have insisted on growing into personalities. It is the strength of their affection for one another which gives the opera its rarity and touchingness. At the same time, it is Susanna's and the Countess's affection which makes the opera a revolutionary document, speaking for the individuality not only of servants but of women—and indeed, actually and universally, of the human personality itself.

It was and perhaps still is rare for women in works of fiction to be capable of friendship and not to be thrust apart the instant a cause for sexual jealousy appears between them as the Count appears between Susanna and the Countess. Even in 1928[26] Virginia Woolf found it necessary to point out that 'Sometimes women do like women'. Drawing from an imaginary novel of the twentieth century the sentence 'Chloe ͵liked ͵Olivia', Virginia Woolf commented: 'And then it struck me how immense a change was there. Chloe liked Olivia perhaps for the first time in literature.' In fact, it was not the first time. There is no doubt that Susanna and the Countess like one another, and no doubt that Mozart and da Ponte made *Le Nozze di Figaro* a work not only of music but of literature.

Don Giovanni, of course, could not let the Count excel him in the scandalous transgression of class barriers which is really a question of incest. It is particularly shameless in Don Giovanni that, having married* and deserted Donna Elvira, he

---

* Whether Donna Elvira really was the one Spanish woman in 1003 to prevail on Don Giovanni to marry her is obscure. She certainly claims him (or what she

not only humiliates her when they meet again but twice chooses to administer the humiliation not in person but through his servant.* This insult he redoubles, quite in the manner of Count Almaviva, by taking the opportunity to address his own serenade to Donna Elvira's servant[27] (after he has lured the mistress out of the way by singing her a parody serenade).

It is in his serenade that Don Giovanni comes closest to the full romantic; and the serenade is another fruit of the Spanish setting. Twice in the major operas Mozart inserts a serenade as a musical set piece, using on both occasions D major, 6/8 time and a pizzicato accompaniment which simulates the serenader's own strumming. Both serenades are given to Spanish characters: Don Giovanni; and Pedrillo in *Il Seraglio*. Spain with its Moorish history preserves the chivalry of the Crusades; and Pedrillo's song,[28] which gives the signal for the rescue attempt from the seraglio, is actually a narrative ballad which recounts, in four verses, how 'in Moorish land' a maid was held captive, until there came 'from foreign land' a young knight who pitied, loved and rescued her. Don Giovanni has no story to relate, but his song, too, is cast formally: in two verses. As he invokes Donna Elvira's maidservant to appear at the window, the vocal line is erotically drawn out, carried, by the rocking rhythm, beyond where one expects the singer's breath to be exhausted, into an ecstatic, virtuoso, sensual extra twist or almost wriggle. It is with a specifically erotic meaning that Don Giovanni expresses his wish to die before his lady's eyes—'davanti agli occhi tuoi morir vogl'io'.[29]

Yet even in that wish resides a hint of the romantic's masochism. By singing a formal serenade, Don Giovanni identifies himself with the traditional troubadour, who is shut

---

takes for him: it is really Leporello in disguise) as her husband, under the name both of *marito* and of *sposo* (No. 20 and recitative before it, Act II). The accusation she makes to Don Giovanni's face is, however, the rather ambiguous one that he declared her his *sposa* ('mi dichiari tua sposa'—recitative before No. 4, Act I). *Sposa* is in any case a term which so lends itself to hyperbole that it is ambiguous: Don Ottavio addresses Donna Anna as *sposa* (No. 2, Act I) although he is only betrothed to her. Perhaps, therefore, Donna Elvira had been merely betrothed to Don Giovanni, but felt the marriage to be morally—and socially—binding because it had been consummated.

* It is in a Spanish setting but not as an insult that Cherubino sings his modified serenade, 'Voi che sapete', to Countess Almaviva while her servant, on her command, accompanies him on the Countess's guitar.

out of the house and stands looking up at his lady, just as the little boy is shut out of his mother's body and stands shorter than she. The balcony or window at which the troubadour bids his lady appear is like the balconies and window sills in dreams which Freud recognised as representations of 'the projection of the bosom'.[30] Even the wish that the lady should 'let herself at least be seen', as Don Giovanni puts it,[31] refers to the dreadful exclusion whereby the child, once weaned, may no longer even look at his mother's breasts. The complaint of the troubadour is the last, most sophisticated and most hopelessly forlorn version of the cry of the weaned child to return to the breast. After so romantic and lost a song, it is not surprising that the plot does not allow Don Giovanni to pursue his character of ruthless and efficient seducer, but imposes on him for a while the romantic's ineffectuality. Donna Elvira's maid has no sooner appeared at the window in response ('There's someone at the window; perhaps it's she', he says[32]) than his suit is interrupted by the arrival of Masetto, and we hear no more of it.

XII

Mozart Proposes a Truce

———— ✹ ————

In an age which has disposed of, or at least possesses, in psycho-analysis, the means to dispose of, the enlightenment's particular anxieties (though to step into worse of its own), the best that can be said for the eighteenth-century sex warfare is that, just as the Reformation ultimately led to victory not for either sect but for rationalism, so sex warfare led to victory not for either sex but to the dispute's being superseded. From the women's own point of view, it was probably more pleasant, as well as providing a more hopeful springboard, to be treated as adversaries than as things. In a medieval, theological world women as a class might borrow a little glamour and grace from the Virgin, but they also incurred the odium of being daughters of Eve. Valmont's angelically named victim Cécile Volanges is not so ill placed when one compares Valmont's attitude, which, insulting though it is, at least rates her a prize to be taken, with the ecclesiastically-sanctioned diatribe against women con-cocted in the fifteenth century by the authors* of the *Malleus Maleficarum*, a classical-cum-biblical hodge-podge of proofs that women are carnal, intellectually childish and vain: indeed, women are reproached even for the possession which eventually proved one of the instruments of their emancipation, their voice—which, because it is smoother than men's, is a mark of Siren-like deception.

Neither were women greatly better off when the Victorians, in disgust at the intervention of the enlightenment, made their serious attempt to reconstruct Christendom. All women began

———

* Henry Kramer and James Sprenger, whose work on the diagnosis and sup-pression of witchcraft was commissioned by a Papal Bull of 1484. The diatribe against women, who, thanks to their greater carnality, are held primarily respons-ible for witchcraft, is in Part I, question 6.

to receive a sort of diffused Mariolatry, but at the cost of being virtually credited with perpetual virginity, in the form of sexual anaesthesia. G. Rattray Taylor has found the epitome of this belief in a medical textbook of 1857, which declares it a 'vile aspersion' to call women capable of sexual feeling.[1] Even Freud, at a time* when he was well started on the career which was to demolish this superstition, could make without further explanation a passing reference to 'the sister, who as a woman is endowed with a weaker sexual instinct'.

Thus the nineteenth century did its best to exempt women from the quest for pleasure at its very core. The eighteenth century, on the other hand, had acceded to the informal emancipation of women in a society explicitly motivated by that quest. If the quest sometimes obliged the man to attempt the seduction of every woman he met, it also obliged him to wonder whether each woman, as a being no less (or actually more†) pleasure-seeking than himself, would not succumb to the seductions of all the other men she met. The 'frailty' of women, a commonplace of so many periods and literatures, remained one in the eighteenth century; and sex warfare took that stultifying form it still sometimes does among people who are only ostensibly sophisticated—a race between lover and mistress in which it is honour to abandon, and dishonour to be abandoned first.

In this world Mozart, like Susanna and the Countess, refused to be trapped. His letters to his father shew him explicitly declining the opportunity—which, he is quite aware, the age and the enlightened society have opened up—to pursue in his own life the career of a Don Giovanni. 'I simply cannot live as most young men do in these days'; 'There are people who think that no one can love a poor girl without having evil designs; and that charming word *maîtresse*, wh—e in our tongue, is really much too charming! But I am no Brunetti! no Mysliveček! I am a Mozart; and a young and clean-minded

* 1908. (*Collected Papers*, Volume II, VII.)
† Thus Pope (*Moral Essays*, II, 207–10):—

> In men we various ruling passions find;
> In women, two almost divide the kind:
> Those, only fix'd, they first and last obey,
> The love of pleasure, and the love of sway.

In women ruled by the love of sway, Pope had recognised the female libertine.

Mozart.'² Equally, his letters to his wife implicitly shew him refusing to engage in the century's great war.

Mozart's desire to marry Constanze Weber was not romantically conceived. He saw her, or at least could see her, prosaically: 'She is not ugly, but at the same time far from beautiful . . . She has no wit, but she has enough common sense to enable her to fulfil her duties as a wife and mother'. A little of the prosaicness should be discounted, because it is addressed to Mozart père,³ who was afraid the marriage would be impractical and disadvantageous, and who suspected Constanze of scheming and her mother of trapping Mozart into the engagement. Six weeks later Mozart was writing to his father:⁴ 'Please do not suspect my dear Constanze of harbouring such evil thoughts. Believe me, if she had such a disposition, I could not possibly love her. Both she and I long ago observed her mother's designs . . .' So perhaps the prosaic description of Constanze had been partly calculated to allay Leopold's fear of beautiful (equals, to Leopold's mind, extravagant and unfaithful) and brilliant (equals scheming) women. Mozart's letter to Constanze herself⁵ during their engagement makes it clear that he was determined to marry her, and persisted through being thrown over thrice.

It is true, however, that he did not reach that determination without anxiety. His letters to Leopold are special pleading; but the debate with Leopold is probably evidence of another debate within Mozart himself. He might resolve not to follow the seducer's career, but that could not relieve him of the anxiety that the woman he chose to love might not abstain from being seduced. This anxiety is a persistent theme in Mozart's life and work. It is almost violently reflected in that ostensibly anxiety-free opera *Così Fan Tutte*. Da Ponte was in the habit of writing-in to his libretti the doubts of women's constancy which were common to the period, and Mozart made of them more than a commonplace. Even the words 'così fan tutte', which form the point, the title, and the epigraph⁶ to the finale, of the opera whose explicit theme is those doubts, had already been used conversationally in the libretto of *Le Nozze di Figaro*.* (After I had noticed this, I discovered that Hans Gal had also noticed it, together with something more remarkable, namely that

---

* Basilio (in the Trio, No. 7, Act I): 'Così fan tutte le belle'.

the melodic phrase to which the words are sung in *Figaro* is actually quoted in the Overture to *Così*.⁷)

Earlier still, and at the very time when he was beginning to be interested in Constanze Weber, Mozart demonstrated that this commonplace held much more than common significance for him by employing his deepest art in the witty and tragic quartet which ends Act II of *Il Seraglio*, where the joy of reunion and the hopes for an escape change into Belmonte's and Pedrillo's doubts of their sweethearts' faithfulness in captivity: a scena which, with its complete revolutions of mood and its exploitation of the formal possibilities of regrouping two couples (the women complaining to one another of being doubted, the two men boasting to one another of having proved the women faithful, the men begging pardon of the women in succession, the final union of the four voices) is a miniature opera in itself—in fact, a miniature *Così*.

This anxiety about women's constancy is cognate with Mozart's anxiety about his own constancy. *Così* and the *Seraglio* quartet are pendants to *Don Giovanni*. Only five months before announcing his wish to marry Constanze, Mozart had been boarding in the Weber household and working on *Il Seraglio*, whose heroine (not by his choice but certainly with his concurrence) is named Constanze, in token of her character, which is attested, to the refutation of Belmonte's moment of doubt, by the events of the plot. Mozart was meanwhile flirting with Constanze Weber; and though he sent home protestations of the propriety of his actual behaviour he also sent evidence that he had come to recognise his mental inconstancy. People leap to the conclusion, he protests, that he and Constanze are going to marry; but—and it is another germ of Don Giovanni—'If', says Mozart, 'I had to marry all those with whom I have jested, I should have two hundred wives at least'.* With Don Giovanni it was not jesting, and the total for one country alone came to

* (From Vienna, 25 July, 1781.) Five days after this Stephanie gave Mozart the libretto of *Il Seraglio*. Perhaps it was the chiming of the seraglio theme with his own recent fantasy of having two hundred wives which helped to sway Mozart towards judging the libretto 'quite good'; certainly seduction was much in his mind, since he misnames the new libretto *The Seduction from the Seraglio*. (Mozart to Leopold Mozart, from Vienna, 1 August, 1781.) It took six years for the two hundred wives to multiply into the one thousand and three in Spain alone which Leporello credits to Don Giovanni.

one thousand and three—'wives' in the sense that Donna Elvira considered herself his wife.

Mozart's fears of the Don Giovanni in himself were sharpened by the fact that he had previously been in love with Constanze's elder sister, Aloysia Weber. Seven months before writing to announce his love for Constanze, Mozart confessed to his father: 'I was a fool, I admit, about Aloysia Lange' (her married name), 'but what does not a man do when he is in love? Indeed I loved her truly, and even now I feel that she is not a matter of indifference to me'.[8] Evidently Mozart did not consider Aloysia witless. For her 'beautiful voice and . . . fine method of producing it'[9] he delighted to compose arias, remarking, when he sent the score of one of them to his father, 'you cannot judge of it by the score, for it must be rendered by a singer like Mlle Weber. Please do not give to anyone, for that would be the greatest injustice, as it is written solely for her and fits her like a well-tailored garment'.[10]

When Mozart found himself falling in love with Aloysia's sister, he must have asked himself if he were not a Don Giovanni, to whom one woman, or at least one Weber girl, was as good as another. The question is, indeed, implicit in the words he uses when he breaks the news of his choice of Constanze to his father: 'But who is the object of my love? Do not be horrified again, I entreat you. Surely not one of the Webers? Yes, one of the Webers—but not Josefa, nor Sophie, but Constanze, the middle one'.[11] Unconsciously, Mozart must have suspected that the kinship between the two women he loved brought him to the verge—on which Don Giovanni hovers by unconscious symbolism—of incest.

Mozart never needed—or, rather, never had the opportunity —to choose directly between the sisters, because Aloysia foreclosed her flirtation with him and presently (in 1780) married Josef Lange. By the time Mozart was starting to flirt with Constanze, he had suffered a change in his opinion of Aloysia. He accuses her of a version of what he feared in himself, inconstancy. Aloysia, he writes to his father,[12] shewed no gratitude to her parents and, when she began to make money as a singer, deserted her widowed mother. Family inconstancy of this kind must have seemed particularly heinous to Mozart, who was always so concerned to demonstrate his continued loyalty to his father and make it clear he was not withholding more of his earnings than he needed to live on. Presently he expanded the charge against Aloysia into one which specifically includes the sexual inconstancy that so preoccupied his own fears: 'Mme Lange is a false, malicious person and a coquette'.[13]

Although the choice was officially closed, it remained open in Mozart's mind. Aloysia was already married when Mozart told his father she was still not a matter of indifference to him, and to this confession he added: 'It is, therefore, a good thing for me that her husband is a jealous fool and lets her go nowhere, so that I seldom have an opportunity of seeing her'.[14] It is as he becomes attracted by Constanze that Mozart finds it necessary to counter temptation by slandering Aloysia in writing to his father. The charge that Aloysia had deserted her family seems to have been designed solely to counter temptation: Alfred Einstein tells us that 'Mozart was completely wrong' about the facts.* When he went on to charge Aloysia with coquetry and falsity, Mozart was ostensibly denying the temptation more firmly still—but in a manner unconsciously calculated to encourage it: the charges hold out hopes to Mozart that if he presents his suit, Aloysia will listen and will be prepared to play her jealous husband false.

For Mozart's imagination, the situation remained open beyond both Aloysia's marriage and his own. It was not until *Don Giovanni* that he artistically identified himself with a hero who is inconstant to all his women, and not until *Così* that he put on the stage a love-situation hinging on a pair of sisters. *Così* is the story of two sisters who protest their constancy and fail: or, from another facet, it is, twice over, a story which was from Mozart's point of view, peculiarly autobiographical—the story of a man who wins the heart of a woman and then finds to his discomfiture that it is just as possible to win the heart of her sister.

The ultimate solution to the lover's anxiety about the woman's constancy is the one Jane Austen independently

---

* (*Mozart* . . . , 3.) No doubt Einstein is right in supposing that the slander on Aloysia originated with the girls' mother. But she, of course, was pouring it into Mozart's ears with just the same intention as he was reiterating it to himself, namely to turn him away from Aloysia (and towards Constanze). Perhaps the mother was shrewd enough to guess, from Mozart's unusual loyalty to his family, that nothing would so effectively slur Aloysia in his vision as the thought that she was false to hers.

adopted a few decades later than Mozart did, namely to endow the woman with a moral intelligence. The female libertine, though she was careful not to be enslaved by a man, and though she did become active and mobile, had merely copied the man and enslaved both him and herself to the sex war. A woman could be morally responsible in marriage only if she had chosen her husband by an informed moral choice. She must not rely merely on correct honourable behaviour, which might lead her to submit to an arranged marriage—in which case coercion would have cut her off before she ever attained to moral responsibility, and her husband would have small moral title to asking her to be faithful. But neither must she lend more credence than they would bear to her immediate, and particularly her youthful and literary, feelings—all those romantical feelings which emancipation and literacy had made it possible for women to entertain and express. If marriage were founded on nothing more solid than infatuation, then infatuation might equally justify infidelity after marriage.

To suppose oneself capable of the most high-flown constancy on the strength of an infatuation is the state of feeling which Jane Austen satirised as Affectation, and opposed to Sense. The same emotion is tragically satirised by Mozart in *Così*. Fiordiligi's arias are of such perfect beauty that they are more than parodies. They bear the weight not only of a comedic but of a tragic irony—and perhaps also of a Watteauesque regret that the nobilities and lovely idealisms she sketches are not feasible.

Così Fan Tutte, as its sub-title states, is a 'school for lovers'. It is entirely in the manner of Jane Austen, all of whose novels are schools for their heroines, and quite on the lines of her antithesis between Sense and Sensibility. The women are taught that in making protestations of fidelity, and the men that in believing in and actually betting on them, they are expecting too much of nature.* The lesson is that of Rosalind (who does not really believe it herself), that 'men have died from time to time, and worms have eaten them, but not for love', and of Jane Austen (who does). Indeed, when Jane Austen's niece†

---

* This interpretation of *Così* I owe in its entirety to Michael Levey.

† Fanny Knight, who, we have Cassandra Austen's word for it, knew Jane Austen better than anyone except Cassandra herself. (See Cassandra Austen to Fanny Knight, from Chawton, 29 July, 1817.)

was, at the age of twenty-one, dithering about rejecting a suitor, Jane Austen sent her what amounts to Rosalind's speech crisply re-written without imagery by the enlightenment: 'I have no doubt of his suffering a good deal for a time, a great deal . . . but it is no creed of mine, as you must be well aware, that such sort of Disappointments kill anybody'.[15]

That *Così* is a school is part of the enlightenment's educative programme; it enlightens its pupils by the rational exploration of nature, including the nature of their own emotions; the lesson is the almost biological one that, although sexual love seems to be aroused by so very particular an object, the species is not at all particular about which object provides it with satisfaction. What appears to the infatuate girl to be deliberate choice is only opportunity. ('Oh! dear Fanny', Jane Austen writes to her niece, 'your mistake has been one that thousands of women fall into. He was the *first* young Man who attached himself to you. That was the charm, & most powerful it is'.) True choice, the enlightenment insists, must be reasoned and informed as well as feeling. Mozart's own marriage, and his prosaic description of his fiancée, are to be interpreted in just this way: rejecting his romantical Sensibility towards Aloysia Weber, he chooses Sense and reason. Indeed, when rumours were going round about his flirtation with Constanze, Mozart expressly wrote to his cousin:[16] 'let me add, to set your mind at rest, that I never do anything without a reason—and, what is more, without a well-founded reason'.

Once the woman became capable of morally choosing her husband, the sex war could be at last composed. The woman ceased to be a possessible object, which can be lost as well as taken; her personal identity became a personal, indispensable and active constituent in a new identity, the unit of man-plus-wife, which can no more be lost than a self, and which is truly impregnable—not a mere temptation to others—because the woman's own pleasure-instinct (the basis of all moral choices) has taken the considered decision to lend itself to its creation. Having, in *Così*, posed the problems of deciding whom to marry, and having explored the education necessary to choosing rightly, Mozart stated the solution of the problem in his next opera, *Die Zauberflöte*.

He had, however, sketched this solution much earlier. When,

in the second act of *Il Seraglio*, Constanze sings 'Martern Aller Arten',[17] her splendidly coloratura defiance of all that the Pasha may do to her, she is already a much more active and self-moving personality than those eighteenth-century heroines who inertly suffer capture and incarceration by some evil power and then, equally inertly, permit themselves to be rescued by their heroic lovers, their own contribution being no more than an aria of lamentation or joy as the case may call for. Almirena, for example, the renaissance plus eighteenth-century heroine of Handel's *Rinaldo*, might be designed to illustrate the opening of the *Moral Essay* Pope addressed 'to a Lady':

> *Nothing so true as what you once let fall,*
> *Most women have no characters at all.*

By the third act, *Il Seraglio* has departed from the routine of rescue operas, and given the lie to Pedrillo's chivalrous ballad-serenade about a knight rescuing a maiden, in the most emphatic possible way: the heroic rescue fails. Now both Constanze and Belmonte are held captive and in peril of death; and when Belmonte laments that it is through him that she is lost,[18] it is Constanze's voice which comes forward in the rôle of the courageous hero, asking 'What is death?' and urging that to die side by side is a foretaste of bliss.[19] It is Constanze who leads the duet,[20] and she who swings its mood to sublime exultation.

Constanze, however, can take the lead only when both she and her lover have been forced into passivity; she is not in a position to reverse the rôles of operatic tradition and actually rescue her lover—a reversal which did not explicitly take place until 1805, when Beethoven's heroine Leonora dressed up in the hero's clothes and saved her husband from prison and murder. The duet between Constanze and Belmonte in *Il Seraglio* is a concentrated sketch of what Beethoven was to expand into *Fidelio*, namely the identity of husband and wife. (The sub-title of the Bouilly play on which *Fidelio* is based is *L'Amour Conjugal*.) Florestan's cry of 'Ein Engel, Leonoren'[21] when, lying in his dungeon, he sees an advance vision of his rescuer, is anticipated by Belmonte's 'Engels Seele!' in response to Constanze; and the very name Fidelio, under which Leonora disguises herself, is a synonym of Constanze.

However, it is only in part and indirectly from Constanze

that Beethoven borrowed Leonora. Directly, Leonora is an extension[22] of the heroine who represents Mozart's own utmost development of Constanze—Pamina in *Die Zauberflöte*. Pamina, although she sets out as the conventional heroine who is to be rescued from an evil enchanter, finishes as the active principle without whose assistance Tamino could not have come successfully through his ordeals.[23] Moreover, by a reversal of the conventions more strange (and, probably, a good deal more accidental) than what happens in *Il Seraglio*, it turns out that the power which holds Pamina captive is not the evil but the good; Tamino, so far from overcoming it, must apply for initiation into its mysteries. By this initiation Tamino receives a philosophical version of the 'schooling' the lovers receive on a domestic scale in *Così*. For all its grander and more philosophical size, *Die Zauberflöte* incarnates the same values as *Così* and contains at least one Jane Austenish stroke that might well have come out of *Così*: Tamino and Pamina, by going through the ordeals together, are finally initiated into the husband-and-wife unity Mozart is preaching; but when Tamino first falls in love with Pamina his love is of the romanticising and affected kind—so much so that what he actually falls in love with is not Pamina, whom he has not yet met, but her portrait.[24]

Die Zauberflöte makes, in a duet between a man and a woman both of whom are seeking lovers but who are not in love with one another (another break with operatic convention, and perhaps a deliberate insistence on the universality of the message), an express statement of the new identity between husband and wife which was the solution Mozart propounded to the sex war:

> *Mann und Weib, und Weib und Mann*
> *Reichen an die Gottheit an.*[25]

Man and wife attain to the godhead—that is, to the power to solve not only their own but humanity's problems. Mozart is building a monument to marriage.

It is a monument deliberately proletarian, both in the choice of the popular Singspiel form and in the actual material of the story. Mozart's own was a deliberately proletarian marriage, a marriage of people with work to do. It is significant that one of the three temples in *Die Zauberflöte* is dedicated to work—

Arbeit.[26] While still disclaiming the idea that his 'jesting' with Constanze was leading to marriage, Mozart had thrown off to his father[27] a parenthesis in which he said 'the last thing I want is a rich wife' (a hit, probably, at Aloysia's social pretensions); and when he does wish to marry Constanze he makes a point, which is no doubt true even though Mozart is emphasising it in order to placate Leopold,* of Constanze's being 'accustomed to be shabbily dressed . . . True, she would like to be neatly and cleanly dressed, but not smartly'.[28]

In *Die Zauberflöte* Mozart indicated a solution for all three of the preoccupying problems of his century. The religious problem, how to arrive at a conception of the creative godhead acceptable to enlightenment man, is solved in dramatic terms which at the same time propose a reconciliation between men and women, and between masters and men. The great duet which states that man and wife attain to the godhead is allotted to a woman and a man, a queen's daughter and the queen's birdcatcher.

How intimately Mozart must have taken that couplet from their duet,

> *Mann und Weib, und Weib und Mann*
> *Reichen an die Gottheit an,*

as a monument to his own marriage we can guess from the fact that he anticipated the libretto by some nine years, in a jingle of his own (in which the unity of husband and wife is so firmly compacted that the two together take a singular instead of a plural verb). Just after his marriage he subscribed a letter to his father:

W. A. Mozart
Mann und Weib
ist ein leib.†

The validity of Mozart's solution to the sexual problem can be judged not from his letters on the subject of his marriage but from the letters written within it. His letters to his wife achieve

---

* —who had heard rumours to the contrary. 'It is a downright lie', Mozart tells him, 'that she is inclined to be extravagant'.

† ('Man and wife . . . is one life': thus translated, to preserve the rhyme, by Emily Anderson; literally:— '. . . is one body'.) Mozart married on the 4 August, 1782, and the letter is from Vienna, 24 August. (*Die Briefe W. A. Mozarts*, Volume II, p. 183.)

(perhaps more by his inspiration than by Constanze's) an equality of tone, and an intimate naturalness about sex, which are rare enough in the eighteenth century and yet could have come from no other—until our own made it possible for a few fortunate individuals (or, rather, individual couples) to match them. Mozart can describe[29] how he has an erection at the thought of seeing Constanze again, without the subject's occasioning the smallest departure from the usual lively and self-ironic manner of his letters. Quite without tension or affectation—he might be describing the mischievous activity of Cherubino—he writes, of his 'little fellow':* 'Just picture to yourself that rascal; as I write he crawls on to the table and looks at me questioningly. I, however, box his ears properly— but the rogue is simply . . .† and now the knave burns only more fiercely and can hardly be restrained. Surely you will drive out to the first post-stage to meet me?'

This natural tone of voice civilisation had still not recaptured even in 1928. One has only to compare another letter, this time in fiction, written, on this theme and in comparable circumstances, to another Constance. People who read unblushingly through the arraigned portions of *Lady Chatterley's Lover* have been turned crimson by the strained, unsmiling sentimentality of 'John Thomas says good-night to Lady Jane, a little droopingly, but with a hopeful heart'.

---

* Cf. Freud (*The Interpretation Of Dreams*, VI, E): 'Children, too, often signify the genitals, since men and women are in the habit of fondly referring to their genital organs as "little man", "little woman", "little thing" '. With the continuation of Mozart's letter, 'I . . . box his ears . . . and now the knave burns only more fiercely', compare Freud's continuation: 'To play with or beat a little child is often the dream's representation of masturbation'.

† The words are blotted out in the autograph: which makes my point.

XIII

Hell, Love and Society—1

———————————— ✲ ————————————

Don Giovanni went much further than most of his contemporaries were prepared to go. Indeed, he went to hell—which was not where the quest for pleasure was intended to lead. It is true that the rake was prepared to defy hell—as witness his full name of rakehell; but the edge was taken off his defiance by his enlightened scepticism about whether hell existed.

Yet, in spite of its intentions, the enlightenment *did* end in hell. It ended, in other words, in the Terror, which overwhelmed the benevolent social faith of the French Revolution, and which was hell let loose in the same very precise sense in which Don Giovanni is overwhelmed by the forces of hell at the end of the opera. Like Don Giovanni, the enlightenment was the victim of underworld forces in the sense of unconscious forces. The Terror was an eruption of all the anti-reason and anti-benevolence powers in the human mind, whose existence the enlightenment had continually denied and repressed.

The eruption was followed by a philistine reaction on the part of the bourgeoisie and by a romantic reaction on the part of the artists, in the hellish light of which we can distinguish Don Giovanni, Egotist and lover, as a proto-romantic. Hence the fascination he exercised over another proto-romantic, Lord Byron, as well as over such full-opened romantics as Pushkin* and Baudelaire.† His fascination was also acknowledged by what posthumously turned out to have been one of the stormiest centres of romanticism, the fantasy-life of Søren Kierkegaard, who named Don Giovanni, together with the Wandering Jew and Faust (whose story Goethe was dramatising before Mozart

———————————

* It is on Pushkin's version of the Don Juan legend that the opera by Dargomijsky is based. (Cf. chapter X.)

† 'Don Juan aux Enfers' (*Spleen et Idéal*, XV).

was properly grown up*), as 'the three great ideas', representing 'life outside religion'.[1] (The 'life outside religion' probably meant to Kierkegaard the secular, rational life of the enlightenment, which, although the French Revolution seemed to have made it untenable, remained, to such reluctant romantics as Kierkegaard and Coleridge, nostalgically desirable.)

The Wandering Jew† is excluded from salvation and lives in a kind of earthly limbo; Faust and Don Giovanni, respectively scientist and artist (love had been an art at least since Ovid), have opted for damnation. Don Giovanni's final destination became the regular surroundings of the romantic artist, who, anguished in love and egotistically wrapped in his personal psychology, lived in the state which is the essence of hell, unproductive torment. Don Giovanni's descent at the end of Act II, scene 5, on the 29 October, 1787, (with Casanova among the first-performance audience) had pioneered the way for a rout of Satan-worshippers, Baudelaire the greatest and most devout, each determined to pass what Rimbaud was to call 'une saison en enfer'.

Don Giovanni, in proposing a counter-revolutionary quietus for the dreads of the enlightenment, anticipates the plunge, which the romantic post-Revolutionary world actually took, back into the belief that the universe is ruled by supernatural power, and that anyone who rebels will be supernaturally punished: 'Questo è il fin di chi fa mal'.[2] Romanticism brought back the belief in—and the psychological experience of—hell.

Only in *Don Giovanni*, among the major operas, is Mozart not on the enlightenment's side—though even here he cannot help shewing an emotional sympathy with Don Giovanni. He displays his hero's courage to the end, and must have known that our reaction would be admiration; he brings ‡ on the other characters to join Leporello in the final sextet as though expressly to point up the smugness of the righteous. But, however much ambiguity crept into the drama, the manifest meaning

---

* The first version of *Faust* was written in 1773–5.

† This figure also lodged himself in the romantic imagination of Coleridge, who made a note in his memorandum book 'Wandering Jew, a romance' (quoted by J. Livingston Lowes: *The Road To Xanadu*, I, I).

‡ —though he left off the final sextet for the Vienna production of 1788 (Alfred Einstein: *Mozart . . .* , 22).

of *Don Giovanni* is pro-Christianity and anti-enlightenment.

It was the power of Mozart's music that impelled Kierkegaard to weave Cherubino and Don Giovanni into *Either/Or* in 1843. Earlier still, the same power led E. T. W. Hoffmann, a Prussian civil servant turned professional musician, composer and operatic organiser, to transform himself into E. T. A. Hoffmann by replacing the last of his forenames by Amadeus. In his short fiction of 1812, *Don Giovanni*, noted by many Mozartians, his account of a performance of Mozart's opera by an Italian company in an unnamed German city is the true hero; but the first-person narrator who attends the performance is visited by the soprano who performs the rôle of Donna Anna at times when, the narrator learns from overheard conversation, she was in a swoon or dead. The fable in which Don Juan is bodily snatched into hell, leaving no corpse, was an infernal counterpart to the bodily ascension or assumption to heaven of Elijah in the Old Testament, of the risen Christ in the New Testament and of the Virgin in Christian tradition. It was a counterpart that struck the occultist or the satanist nerve in romantic aesthetes when Mozart's musical drama had turned the fable into a myth.

Mozart dealt with the orthodox Christian supernatural only in his church music and there by necessity though with inspiration. *Idomeneo* and *Die Zauberflöte* touch, respectively, oracular utterance and magic in the context of ancient-world, no-longer-believed-in religion. The magic and the ancient Egyptian doctrine in *Die Zauberflöte* were clearly not meant to be taken at their face value by audiences in 1791. How they were then and are now to be taken has been a puzzle since the first performance.

XIV
'Die Zauberflöte' Solved—1

————————— ❋ —————————

Dramatically and emotionally, *Die Zauberflöte* is not a problem-opera. It has none of *Don Giovanni*'s false climaxes, uncertainties of mood or ambiguities of moral. Opening, like *Don Giovanni*, with a running scena in which the hero is trying to escape, it proceeds through satisfactorily designed stages, creating (out of a number of contemporary elements) its own genre round it as it goes, to a triumphant finale, which is the climax of both the drama and the love-story and at the same time a solemn manifesto of moral and social principles.

Neither is there the smallest doubt what the manifesto asserts. The secret cult of Isis and Osiris, into which the hero of *Die Zauberflöte* is initiated, is blatantly intended as a symbol of the secret international fraternity of Freemasons, into which Mozart and Emanuel Schikaneder (the impresario, the first Papageno and, probably,* the librettist, of *Die Zauberflöte*) had been initiated.

Some commentators have denied or belittled the Masonic strain in *Die Zauberflöte*, but I think the question is put beyond a doubt—if one bears in mind the fondness Freemasonry shared with other secret societies for cryptic clues—by the libretto's choice of language at a moment much too solemn for verbal carelessness: the second verse of the pronouncement sung by Sarastro, who presides over the secret initiations, begins 'In diesen heil'gen Mauern'—'In this holy masonry'.†

The sense in which *Die Zauberflöte* really is a problem-opera

---

* Schikaneder's authorship, asserted by the original playbill, was afterwards challenged. (See Einstein: *Mozart . . .* , 23; E. J. Dent: *Mozart's Operas*, 14.) *Die Zauberflöte*'s is just the type of libretto that is most certainly the result of collaboration: I shall avoid controversy by referring to its authors in the plural.

† (Act II, No. 15.) Likewise one of the priests (in the dialogue before No. 11, Act II).

is twofold. First there is a technical difficulty about the plot. Internal evidence has convinced most scholars that the beginning of the opera as it now stands is the beginning of an original version of the story very different from the final result we have; in other words, the plot was radically changed about a third of the way through the writing, and the new tail was patched-on to the old head. However, no convincing reason has been advanced for why the change had to be made. The usually accepted theory will not hold water for two minutes. The second difficulty is not so much a difficulty as a blindness. The entire character of the opera has been misconceived. *Die Zauberflöte* has simply been placed in the wrong genre—mistaken for a 'fairy opera' (a theory which lends colour to the accepted but wrong theory about the change in the plot). The misconception has two sources: failure to make an intelligent and informed conjecture, based on a knowledge of the temper of eighteenth-century thought, about what eighteenth-century Freemasonry was like; and failure actually to read, as opposed to citing from previous commentators' work, an eighteenth-century novel which has long been known as one of *Die Zauberflöte*'s sources but never intelligently explored.

When these two clues *are* explored, not only does *Die Zauberflöte* turn out to be something far removed from a 'fairy opera', but its story yields up a precise, and typically eighteenth-century as well as Masonic, metaphorical meaning.

(i) *Egypt, Masonry and 'Sethos'*

The ancient Egyptian religion of Isis and Osiris, which was transported to the Greco-Roman world in the form of a mystery cult and flourished there in the early centuries A.D. (until it was overtaken by Christianity—itself a mystery cult, but the only one to be absolutely non-tolerating of all the others), identified its goddess Isis with the moon, and her consort Osiris with the sun.*

This made it easy and obvious material for the eighteenth-century passion for interpreting ancient myths as allegories of

---

* This was, at least, the statement of Diodorus Siculus (I, 11) and the interpretation known to the eighteenth century. Frazer later argued that Osiris was not originally the sun and may even have been the moon (*Adonis Attis Osiris*, Volume II).

nature. Moreover, since its deities were sources of light, it could easily be taken as a metaphor of enlightenment itself. This is, in fact, the metaphor of the ending of *Die Zauberflöte*. Light— the wisdom embodied in the cult of the sun-god Osiris—breaks through and shatters darkness.

In *Die Zauberflöte*, both the mystery cult and the enlighten- ment it sheds are identified with Freemasonry. It seems prob- able (though, since Masonry was, and still is, secret, it cannot be ascertained with certainty) that eighteenth-century Masonry had itself made the same identification. Certainly, it was a secret cult which practised initiation: where, in a passionately classicis- ing century, should it turn for a model for its initiations and rituals if not to the secret initiations of the classical world? Traditionally, Masonry traced itself back to ancient times. The Masons' attention may have been directed to Egypt by an old Masonic tradition that the Children of Israel 'lernyd ye craft of Masonry'* in Egypt. However, it was not to Egyptology directly, whose sources were largely unknown or very far to seek during the eighteenth century, that the Masons applied, but to the cult as it had been practised in the late-classical world, and which had left abundant references in lateish Latin and Greek authors like Apuleius and Diodorus Siculus, who were not merely accessible to the eighteenth century but familiar.

Whatever Masonry may have been† before the eighteenth century (it seems, a craft fraternity with unusually posh social connexions, whose secrecy was a matter of preserving trade secrets), and whatever it has since become, there is no doubt that the movement was given a complete overhaul early in the eighteenth century. However proud it may have continued of its supposed history,‡ it took on a new character. Medieval Masonry may have originated in England; eighteenth-century Masonry certainly did. The 'mother' Grand Lodge of the Masonic world is still the one which was instituted in London

---

* The words are from the fifteenth-century 'Cooke' manuscript (published by Matthew Cooke in 1861) in the British Museum. (See *Encyclopaedia Britannica*, Freemasonry.)

† See, for the history (but not the procedure, about which it is cagey) of Masonry, the article by William James Hughan, himself a Mason, in the 1910–11 edition of the *Encyclopaedia Britannica*.

‡ Claims that Masonry went back to Solomon and Moses were published in London in 1723 (*Encyclopaedia Britannica*, Freemasonry).

in 1717 and which gave Masonry its new character and declared irregular any Lodges which would not conform to its
rule.

The movement which Mozart celebrated in an opera in 1791
had, therefore, the same life-history as the enlightenment itself.
It originated early in the century in England ('you know',
Mozart wrote to his father two years before becoming a Mason,
'that I am an out-and-out Englishman'[1]) and rapidly became
international.

And in fact Masonry, in its eighteenth-century character, was
part of the enlightenment. Its initiation ceremony was nothing
but a ritualised and metaphorical version of the enlightenment's
great ideal, a philosophical education, its fraternity nothing but
a microcosm of the enlightenment's blue-print for an international, orderly, co-operative, mutually benevolent, coercion-
free society. When the enlightenment, in the absence of a
thought-out evolution theory, found it rational to postulate a
Supreme Being who had created the universe, Freemasonry
concurred and gave him the name—or, rather, the impersonal
title—of the Great Architect.

It was possible to fit-in the enlightenment's Supreme Being
with Christianity—especially in England, whose church made
small claim to be a continuing supernatural revelation; but
religion had to be accommodating if the fit was to be made, and
the result was very largely to depersonalise its mythology.
The letters and prayers written by Jane Austen; the rational
clergymen who appear in her novels and family circle (and reappeared in the flesh in the person of Sydney Smith); the very
memorial tablets (including her own) in the places of worship
she attended—Bath Abbey and Winchester Cathedral: all these
shew a religion which is far from 'insincere' but in which religious
passion is muted in favour of a religiously toned philosophical
resignation, and the specifically Christian virtues in favour of
moral and social ones. Jesus Christ, as a personality with an
anecdotal history, is barely mentioned. Similarly, it was perfectly possible—again, especially in England—to interpret the
Masonic metaphor of the Great Architect in a way that did not
conflict with Christianity. Masonry was primarily a moral
system; it did not seek clashes with religious systems. It
exacted, as a condition of initiation, a declared belief in some

sort of Supreme Being:* but it was so far from insisting that he must be taken as a Christian Supreme Being that, as early as 1723, when such tolerance was by no means common in official places, it decided to admit Deists and Jews. Its elasticity must have helped it a great deal in becoming international, by by-passing the geographical rift between Protestantism and Catholicism, but it also brought on it the wrath of the least elastic of the Christian churches.

The moral tone of Masonry in the eighteenth century sounds clearly through such Masonic or Masonesque fictions as *Die Zauberflöte* and its source-book, *The Life Of Sethos*, both of which, like most eighteenth-century fictions, leave one in no doubt of their moral. *The Life Of Sethos*, a French novel by the abbé Jean Terrasson, was published anonymously in Paris in 1731, and evidently had some success, since an English transla-tion, by Mr Lediard† (but still without the original author's name), appeared the next year.‡ The story is set in ancient Egypt, and its hero, just like Tamino in *Die Zauberflöte*, is initiated into the mysteries of Isis.§ Terrasson does not (but then one would not expect him to) explicitly connect his Isiac mysteries with Masonry; indeed, it is possible that the real influence was the other way about and the Masons borrowed hints for their own ritual from Terrasson's fictionalised Egypt.

* The French branch dispensed with this requirement in 1877, but thereby brought itself into schism with the (maternal) English branch.

† Presumably Thomas Lediard (1685–1743): 'miscellaneous writer; attached to the staff of the Duke of Marlborough, accompanying him on his visit to Charles XII of Sweden, 1707; returned to England before 1732; produced various historical and biographical works, 1735–6; author of a pamphlet dealing with a scheme for building bridge at Westminster, 1738; F.R.S., 1742; "agent and surveyor of Westminster Bridge", 1738–43; author of several works in German and an English opera "Britannia" ' (*Concise Dictionary Of National Biography*).

‡ THE LIFE OF *SETHOS*, TAKEN FROM PRIVATE MEMOIRS OF THE ANCIENT *EGYPTIANS*. Translated from a *Greek* MANUSCRIPT into FRENCH. And now faithfully done into *English* from the *Paris* EDITION; By Mr. LEDIARD. In TWO VOLUMES, *LONDON*: . . . M.DCC.XXXII.

§ In myth and cult Isis and Osiris were inseparable. (They were at once husband and wife, and brother and sister. Osiris, after his murder, owed the piecing-together of his dismembered body or even his actual resurrection to Isis.) The mysteries, however, belonged to Isis alone. Apuleius is first initiated into her mysteries, and then by a separate act consecrates himself to Osiris. The distinction is preserved in both *Sethos* and *Die Zauberflöte*, where Sarastro prays to Isis *and* Osiris, but the consecration the initiate achieves is that of Isis ('Der Isis Weihe ist nun dein!'—Act II, No. 21, second Allegro).

Sethos lent its hero's name to the disguised hero of *Thamos*,[2] for which play Mozart wrote music; and large pieces of it—some in literal translation—re-appear in *Die Zauberflöte*. Its influence on the opera seems to have been first spotted by Thomas Love Peacock,[3] and it has been known as a source of the opera ever since, though its most decisive clues have been overlooked.

Both *Sethos* and *Die Zauberflöte* take shelter behind the cult of Isis, so that no conflict between Masonry or enlightenment on the one hand and Christianity on the other can be directly raised. Even so, *Die Zauberflöte* does not endow the religion of Isis with any supernatural as opposed to moral powers (though the Queen of the Night is a supernatural figure); and it makes it clear that even the magic virtue of the flute itself is intended as an allegory of the purely natural power of music over the emotions.[4] *Sethos*, which has so much more room to explain itself, takes a militantly rationalising tone. It is crammed with rationalisations, from major ones which explain away virtually the whole body of Greek mythology to such incidental ones as this typical account of how, when the funeral cortège of the dead queen of Egypt is admitted to the burial place, 'the people, who follow'd them with their eyes, heard a noise as of thunder, which they believ'd to be real, and look'd upon it as a miracle which always happen'd when the temple of the infernal deities was open'd: But in reality it was no more than the hollow sound of the brazen gates at the entrance, which was redoubled by the repercussion of the vaults, and by the neighbouring echo's'.[5]

It is in keeping with this tone that Terrasson also makes a rational and moral stand, quite in the manner of Mozart or Jane Austen, against unreasoning romantic love. Admitting in his preface that his story is a fiction (though he attributes it not to himself but to the Greek author whose manuscript he pretends to be translating), he claims advantages—moral ones, of course—for fiction over history: fiction can display in a single hero virtues which history would have to combine many great men to demonstrate; and it can give (as he claims his fiction does) a picture of historical conditions no less accurate than the history books but twice as socially useful, since fiction can instruct readers who have no time or taste for history. Having thus established his own as the best type of fiction, Terrasson goes on to argue that it is not history but the best type of fiction which can, by its superiority, expose 'the pernicious folly of romances, when by that term we mean an advantageous, or if but a favourable representation of the frailties or disorders of love'.[6]

Die Zauberflöte, being set in an undated Egyptian antiquity, is safe from having to bring up Christianity at all. *Sethos*, however, does date its fictitious Greek manuscript: although the story is set in ancient Egypt, it was professedly written by an Alexandrian Greek in the reign of Marcus Aurelius. Terrasson has thus equipped himself with a fictitious writer of his story who *could* have chosen to set the story in Christian rather than pre-Christian times. Terrasson raises this point in his preface, in a manner highly indicative of the enlightenment's (and perhaps Freemasonry's) attitude to the subject. Since the Greek author, Terrasson remarks, has chosen to leave his hero a pagan, 'he confines himself . . . wholly to moral virtues'. Terrasson then pays some lipservice (though it sounds more Gibbonian than heartfelt) to the superiority of Christian virtues, but maintains that the decision of the novelist to limit himself to moral virtues is actually an advantage, because the moral virtues (like, we may interpolate, Freemasonry) are international, and can, besides, be accepted even by those who do not accept religion. Of course, Terrasson deplores that there *are* people who have the 'unhappiness' of not accepting religion, but this obeisance to the conventions sets him free to throw in a word against religious zealots who despise the merely moral virtues, and to warn them sharply if circumspectly that 'christian virtues are in regard to moral virtues what faith is with respect to reason; superior, but never contradictory'.

No doubt Masonry agreed with Terrasson that the quickest way round religious controversy and on to the all-important eighteenth-century questions of the public good and an international culture was to confine oneself to the moral virtues. Neither Terrasson nor Freemasonry found this a restriction. Both are luxuriantly moral. Indeed, Terrasson's preface goes into italics when he writes of (in Lediard's translation) 'the confidence I have in affirming, that this work contains *a more refined and profound moral* than has hitherto been seen in any book, the product of mere literature, or of the number of those which may be stil'd prophane'. Even the original French

Licence to print, which appears in Lediard's translation, announces that the work 'contains excellent Lessons of the most refin'd Morality'.

That Freemasonry was so highly moral was, indeed, what the Catholic church held against it—and still does: Freemasonry 'professes', according to Addis and Arnold's *Catholic Dictionary*, '. . . to lay down a code of morality founded on the brotherhood of humanity only'—that is, without reserving an exclusive and essential place for the church. That Freemasonry was secret was, moreover, an invitation to enemies of the enlightenment to call it a conspiracy. The 1952 edition of the *Catholic Dictionary*[7] still sees fit to mention, without vouching for, but also without casting doubt on, the fable that 'Freemasonry is—unknown to most of the craft—managed by five or six Jews, who bend its influence in every possible way to work against Christianity'. (Presumably it was the admission of Jews in 1723 which summoned up Catholicism's paranoid anti-Jewish fantasies.) The patent fact that Masonry is not anti- but merely non-Christian does not, of course, save it from attack. Its tolerance is its ultimate crime: even at its best, Freemasonry is bound to lead to 'indifferentism in religion'.

Not content with seeing Masonry as an anti-Christian conspiracy, the *Catholic Dictionary* finds it politically subversive, and is willing to credit the Masons with very extensive power and see their hand in a great many revolutions. In general, it finds that Masonry is 'essentially subversive of legitimate authority . . . and tends, in spite of its occasional protests of loyalty, to bring all governments into contempt'.*

It is probably true that eighteenth-century Masonry, at least, was, like the enlightenment in general, opposed to authority based on mere superstition instead of a rational morality. But if the Masonic tone may be judged from *Sethos* and *Die Zauberflöte*, it was far from revolutionary. It was, on the other hand, constitutional. The much remarked curiosity that Freemasonry was usually regarded as subversive on the continent of Europe but even during the eighteenth century enjoyed respectability and royal patronage in England is susceptible of

---

* This point of view is evidently shared by General Franco, who, on 17 June, 1962, called communism and Freemasonry 'the enemies of the greatness of Spain' (*The Guardian*, 18 June, 1962).

a simple explanation in the fact that England possessed, even if it had not written down, a constitution, to which even royal patrons knew themselves to be subordinate.

The Life Of Sethos, whose hero is a prince, is certainly not against princes,* but it is strongly against their using their power arbitrarily and, as it considers, illegitimately. The customs of ancient Egypt, which Terrasson is holding up for contemporary admiration, include one (which Terrasson has borrowed and elaborated from a hint in Diodorus Siculus[8]) which gives him the chance of expounding his political beliefs as well as repeating (a typical touch of the enlightenment's Believe-It-Or-Not type of curiosity) Diodorus's account of the process of mummification.[9] This is the custom whereby a tribunal drawn from initiates of the mysteries sits in judgment on a newly dead ruler, the people being free to bring accusations. On the basis of this trial, the tribunal decides whether the ruler's conduct has been good enough to win his corpse admission to the burial place, or whether it must be denied burial. The very idea of this denial, Terrasson remarks with strong constitutionalist implications, 'was powerful enough to keep the ancient kings within bounds of justice'.[10]

Terrasson's novel naturally makes its hero's royal mother a virtuous and popular queen, and when he comes to *her* posthumous trial Terrasson takes the opportunity to have a eulogy pronounced in which he can detail his conception of a just ruler. Good Queen Nephte was lenient; 'Vengeance never so much as enter'd into her thoughts' (an ideal which re-appears in *Die Zauberflöte*, where, 'in the holy halls' of the Isiac brotherhood, 'no one knows vengeance'†); she told the truth but did not give away secrets; she paid no heed to parasites; and, although affectionate in private life, did not allow her affections to influence state appointments, but gave posts to those best able to do the job. In this last particular, Terrasson is making the

---

* The high priest in *Sethos* gives a characteristic account of the enlightenment's attitude towards hereditary monarchy, which is justified on grounds of convenience. He finds that the principle of primogeniture in royal successions 'is even for the advantage and ease of the publick', since it makes for a more peaceful transition than 'the difficult and often dangerous estimate of personal merit' (Lediard's translation, Volume I, p. 223).

† Sarastro: 'In diesen heil'gen Hallen kennt man die Rache nicht' (Act II, No. 15). (The *Sethos* quotation is from Lediard's translation, Volume I, p. 45.)

plea which echoes through the politics and literature of the eighteenth century, that patronage and reputation be awarded on an estimate of merit alone. This in itself is only an application of the general enlightened wish that all judgments be passed on a rational basis. And in fact the whole political purpose of Terrasson's novel is to argue that authority is legitimate only if its irrational but convenient hereditary basis is confirmed by merit. Sethos is an exemplary prince because he deserves to hold authority, having prepared himself by undertaking a course of philosophical instruction and getting himself initiated into 'a body of men which', as his instructing priests tell him, 'merit alone has formed'.[11]

(ii) *The genres of 'Sethos' and 'Die Zauberflöte'*

Terrasson is thus embodying in his novel the enlightenment's ideal of the philosopher-king, whose flesh and blood manifestation was the benevolent despot. Like *Rasselas* after it, *Sethos* belongs, as its preface claims, to the genre created in the previous century by *Télémaque*[12] and the *Grand Cyrus*,[13] inasmuch as it prescribes the education of a prince. (The original originator was, of course, Xenophon.) But although *Sethos* 'is, with regard to the moral design of it, of the same species with both' *Télémaque* and the *Grand Cyrus*, Terrasson again claims to go beyond his predecessors morally; for while those 'are both properly a system of education', *Sethos* continues to the point where its hero 'is in a condition to instruct others'.[14] *Sethos*, who in the second volume circumnavigates Africa,[15] is a travelling prince who carries the tradition to perfection by being an enlightening as well as an enlightened ruler.

Die Zauberflöte likewise puts forward a travelling prince, and has him initiated. Unlike *Sethos*, the opera places no emphasis on Tamino's princeliness from the point of view of his being a future ruler, but it puts him through the same arduous course in moral virtues.

However, although the gist of *Die Zauberflöte* is as plain as can be, the detailed key is missing, thanks to the secrecy of the Masons. Mozart and Schikaneder must have been at pains not to reveal too much, and yet they must have taken care to make their symbolic representation exact and obvious enough to be picked out by their fellow-initiates. Indeed, they must have agreed with Terrasson when he accounted it a virtue in Queen Nephte that 'She never suffered a secret, or a falsity, to proceed out of her mouth'.[16]

In using that formula, Terrasson was perhaps making a deliberate statement of a Masonic virtue. Certainly he was, as an accurate historical novelist, defining a virtue considered essential by the ancient mystery cults. Initiates of the mysteries stood liable to such terrifying penalties for divulging the secrets that the secrets really are not divulged anywhere in ancient literature. Yet much can be reconstructed, because the literature is studded with what blatantly are veiled—or, rather, coded— hints. The initiates seem to have felt a compulsion to flirt with danger. The game was very precisely as Terrasson describes it, never to suffer 'a secret, or a falsity' to escape one: one must not tell out-and-out lies, and yet one must contrive to conceal the truth, except from those who know it already. Apuleius, whose novel *The Golden Ass* (properly *Metamorphoses*) sets the ancient-world pattern for both *Sethos* and *Die Zauberflöte* by ending with its hero's initiation into the mysteries of Isis, was an adept at the game. When he comes to the initiation of his narrator-hero, he says he is forbidden to satisfy the reader's curiosity by giving an account of it, and then proceeds to give one: but this is, it turns out, all in cipher, for Apuleius finishes 'There, I have told you things which, although you have heard them, you none the less cannot help remaining ignorant of'.*

Like the ancient mysteries and, indeed, all societies which share secrets, Masonry had to flaunt the existence of its secrets while hiding their content, this being the only way it could, all at the same time, preserve its secrecy, proselytise, and make its fraternity real by enabling members to recognise each other. This psychologically flirtatious attitude is displayed by the priests in *Die Zauberflöte* when Tamino arrives at their temples:

---

* It is significant that Apuleius's point was missed or at least very badly blunted by William Adlington's famous translation of 1566, which renders the passage 'Behold now have I told thee, which although thou hast heard, yet it is necessary that thou conceal it' (for 'Ecce tibi rettuli quae, quamvis audita, ignores tamen necesse est'—XI, 23). Adlington must have known perfectly well that *ignorare* has nothing to do with concealing. (According to Lewis, it occasionally means *to ignore* but regularly *to be ignorant of*—which is obviously its sense here.) Evidently Adlington could make nothing of the passage, which must have struck him as the self-contradiction it ostensibly is, because he was not au fait with the mysteries' code-game.

he is denied admission—indeed, warned off; and yet one of the priests comes out and engages him in a long conversation to such good proselytising effect that Tamino presently applies for initiation.

It is by a verbal extension of this attitude that the ancient mysteries developed their knack of alluding to the secrets in code, in a way that will seem neutral or actually nonsensical to outsiders. This knack the Masons would no doubt have spontaneously generated among themselves in any case; but in fact it is probably one of their borrowings from the ancient cults, via ancient literature. Apuleius, for instance, would have been no use to them in formulating their own rituals unless they had an understanding of his habit of talking in code.

The classicising fervour of the enlightenment did not neglect the mysteries,* and the libretto of *Die Zauberflöte* shews its authors to be familiar with what could be gathered about the ancient cults from Apuleius, Diodorus Siculus and Lucian. This information they might have taken at first hand or from common eighteenth-century classical learning; or from Terrasson, who not only crammed *Sethos* with footnotes citing ancient authorities but himself made a translation of Diodorus; or, which seems the most probable, from Masonic lore and ritual, the Masons having probably searched the ancient sources for their own ends. That *Sethos* picks on the mysteries of Isis and *Die Zauberflöte* chooses to follow it seems to drop a strong hint that the Isiac mysteries were the main model for Masonry.

Thus the inspiration of *Die Zauberflöte* and probably of eighteenth-century Masonry itself is mainly classical—but classical spiced with another flavour, calculated to make it doubly attractive to the eighteenth century, namely the flavour of the exotic and the pre-classical antique. The cult of Isis was already exotic, and already savoured of an older than classical wisdom, during its practice in the Greco-Roman world. The Egyptian trappings in *Die Zauberflöte* are not primarily, as many writers about the opera assume, native Egyptian or even native exotic, but Egyptian seen through Greco-Roman eyes. The opera is reshaping to its own use not an ancient Egyptian

---

* Even Smith's *Dictionary Of . . . Antiquities* cites, but unfortunately only to pass over disapprovingly, Sainte-Croix's *Recherches sur les Mystères du Paganisme*, of 1784.

religion but an exotic cult in classical religion. The influence of Terrasson's *Sethos* would in itself make this clear, since Terrasson purports to be translating not an Egyptian but a Greek manuscript. And as a matter of fact, Terrasson's principal source, Diodorus Siculus, had also presented his account of Egypt from a Greek point of view and for a Greek readership. Diodorus (and *Sethos* follows him) is all for demonstrating that Greek civilisation was derived from Egyptian, and all for assimilating the Greek Eleusinian mysteries to the Egyptian ones of Isis.*

Principally, therefore, *Die Zauberflöte*, although popular rather than opera-seria-like in manner, belongs to the exotic subdepartment of a favourite eighteenth-century genre, classical opera. This, again through Terrasson's influence, is crossed with another favourite eighteenth-century genre, that of stories about the education of princes, preferably princes who travel in search of their education through exotic regions. There is, however, a complication, introduced by the fact that in *Die Zauberflöte* the prince's education takes the form of initiation into a classical-exotic mystery which is standing as symbol for Freemasonry. The two common genres are really being used— they provide the neutral or nonsensical (the 'fairy-tale') façade presented to outsiders—to cloak an utterance in code.

Terrasson, whom *Die Zauberflöte* follows so faithfully, makes clear his understanding of the code-game when he takes up Diodorus's explanation of the ancient tradition that most of Greek mythology consisted of stories told by Orpheus. Both Diodorus and Terrasson maintain that Orpheus told these stories in Greece after his return from Egypt, where he had been initiated into the mysteries of Isis. (This is part of Diodorus's insistence that all things Greek were by origin Egyptian.) But where Diodorus takes the simple, rationalistic view that Orpheus just made up these improbable stories, Terrasson takes a view equally rationalistic but in accordance with the mysteries' code-game, namely that the stories Orpheus recounted, and which the non-initiated Greeks took at

---

* Isis herself Diodorus likens to Demeter, the great Eleusinian goddess (I, 13; 25); he directly identifies Osiris with Dionysos (I, 11; 15); and he holds (again followed by Terrasson) that Orpheus, the great saint and, at least in repute, the hymnologist of the Greek mysteries, had visited Egypt and been initiated there into the mysteries of Isis (I, 23; 96).

their nonsensical face value, were really 'a symbolical or disguis'd history of his initiation'.

The ingenious Terrasson may well be shewing us the thought process of the authors of *Die Zauberflöte*. The core of *Die Zauberflöte* is, no doubt, a broad allegory of nature, following the enlightenment manner of interpreting mythological or other unreasonable stories. But at the same time the authors have probably picked up Terrasson's hint about how to interpret stories of this sort, by inventing one themselves in which to conceal their Masonic purpose. Indeed, the best definition of *Die Zauberflöte* is 'an invented myth'. (As I mean to shew, it borrowed substantially from well-known myths.) To outsiders it presents a meaning which is as much moonshine as the stories told by—or the story of—Orpheus himself, but to initiates it speaks of the secrets of initiation. We must expect the details of the story to be a web of precise and deliberate code marks.

(iii) *Was the Plot Changed?*

This recognised, one comes on the great technical difficulty about the opera. It appears to be not only a story in code, but a story whose code was changed a third of the way through. The plot as it stands is not incoherent but it is gravely inconsistent, and in the very ways a moral fable (which *Die Zauberflöte* certainly is, whatever else may be uncertain) can least afford to be.

The hypothesis which most usually and economically accounts for this is that, while the opera was being composed, the whole basis of the story, including its moralising personifications, was reversed. The compelling reason to think the change took place (at a time when some music existed, with the result that the opening could not be scrapped) is the inconsistency between the first third of the opera as it now stands and the rest. The *Documentary Biography* of Mozart by O. E. Deutsch gives some, but not ironclad support to the notion of the change by including a letter of '?1840' whose writer remembered the change as fact.

The end of the opera shews the Queen of the Night as an evil power, overcome by the good power of Sarastro, the representative of the cult of Isis and Osiris. The conjecture is that the original plan, which the libretto sticks to through the first part of Act I, made the Queen good and Sarastro bad. If this is right, the three ladies (courtiers of the Queen) are following out the original plan and telling the simple truth when, in the early part of the opera, they relate how the Queen's daughter, Pamina, has been stolen by Sarastro, and describe Sarastro as 'a wicked demon', 'ein böser Dämon'[17]—a view which the Queen's birdcatcher, Papageno, quite agrees with.[18]

The change of plan is pooh-poohed by Alfred Einstein,[19] who sees no reason to doubt that Sarastro was good and Masonic from the start, epithets like 'böser Dämon' being merely slanders on him in the mouths of his adversaries; and it is true, and would make a good point for Einstein's view, that Masonry was, and is, much slandered.* The straightforward idea that the opera means and always did mean exactly what it says is seductive and, under such sponsorship, highly respectable; but it is made untenable by the inconsistencies of what the story, as it now stands, does say. It is even hard to believe that Einstein himself really did take the opera at face value—a view which makes the three ladies agents of evil: if he did, it was highly sardonic of him to dedicate his book 'To My "Three Ladies"'.

If the start of the opera was always meant to lead on to an evil Queen of the Night, the opera was demanding of its audience a subtlety which no storyteller would dare count on—least of all at the outset, when he is introducing his dramatis personae, and certainly not when the plot, contrary to a good deal of eighteenth-century practice, was an entirely new one, whose narrative and characters would be completely unknown to the audience. The opera has hardly opened, with Tamino fleeing from a serpent and appealing to the 'merciful gods',[20] when the Queen's three ladies-in-waiting appear. It would in any case be odd if the libretto had allowed the forces of evil to get such a head start over those of good in answering the hero's cry for help; and in fact the three ladies seem instantly to make themselves known as righteous by killing the serpent and saving the hero's life.

Tamino faints, the ladies withdraw to report to their Queen,

---

* Einstein sees the Queen as a portrait of the arch-Catholic Mason-persecutor, Maria Theresa herself; and even people who are convinced the plot was changed may well agree that this is what, in her second version, the Queen became.

and Papageno enters, explains himself to the now recovered Tamino as the Queen's birdcatcher, and goes on to claim that it was he who killed the serpent. The ladies thereupon return and take the opportunity to identify themselves still more clearly with righteousness by punishing Papageno for the lie. The lie seems to have been introduced with no purpose except to distinguish the ladies and the Queen they serve as, like Terrasson's Queen Nephte, champions of truth. Next time the ladies return, it is with the still more clinchingly righteous news that their Queen (again on the model of the lenient Nephte) pardons Papageno and remits his punishment. And the ladies then express the thoroughly moral wish that all liars might be so easily constrained and that in place of hate, calumny and black bile there stood love and brotherhood.[21]

This would be dangerous stuff for the librettists to put in the mouths of the three ladies if, at the time they wrote it, they already intended the ladies themselves to be liars, calumniators and enemies of the Isiac brotherhood. At least, the librettists would hardly start off in this way unless they had up their sleeves a coup de foudre which should expose the ladies' hypocrisy. But when the moment comes when the audience is required to make the volte face and accept that the ladies are, after all, evil, there is no dramatic demonstration at all. It is all managed in the clumsiest way, during conversation. We do not *see* anything to convince us of the Queen's wickedness or to cancel the very conspicuous proof the ladies gave at the outset and to our very eyes of their solicitude towards young heroes in danger from dragons. On the contrary: we are asked to accept that Sarastro is, after all, good, in defiance of the evidence of our eyes, for we do actually see that he is holding Pamina under duress—and that he has irresponsibly left her at the mercy of his lecherous underling Monostatos.

To risk confusing the two sides is the most perilous situation that can be encountered by the teller of a moral tale about the conflict of good and evil. That the authors of *Die Zauberflöte* do take this risk is certain. All we have to decide is which is more plausible: that they took it with their eyes open, having intended to do so from the start of their plans; or that they took the risk only to avoid some worse one, when it was forced on them by some compelling need to change the plot of their opera.

The three ladies tell Tamino that Pamina has been stolen by Sarastro; they bring Tamino, as a present from their Queen, a portrait of the missing princess, which kindles Tamino's desire to rescue her; and then the ladies give him, again as a present from the Queen, the talisman which is to help him in the rescue, the magic flute. Here is the cardinal difficulty about supposing the Queen was originally meant to be evil. It is by the magic of the flute that Tamino eventually comes through his initiation ordeals: can it really be that he penetrates to the secrets of wisdom thanks to a gift from an evil power? The inconsistency might well be forced on authors doing a quick job of patching, but it is a very gross inconsistency to find at the centre—at, indeed, the very title—of a moralising fable. Much more plausibly, the source of the flute—that is, the Queen—was originally meant to be good, and between this and the final version there is an imperfect join, patched over, not very satisfactorily, by Pamina's explanation (given, towards the end of the opera, to Tamino) that the flute belonged in the first place to her father (who is now dead*) and that he, in a magical hour, cut it out of the thickest part of a thousand-year-old oak during a thunderstorm.[22]

Hard as it is to believe that an originally evil Queen can be served by such righteous agents as the three ladies, it is harder still to swallow that an originally righteous Sarastro can have been served by the black and villainous Monostatos.[23] But if Sarastro originally was the villain he is called, then Monostatos becomes that typically Mozartian figure, the servant who is a doublet of his master. Tamino, to whom the Queen has lent Papageno as his squire,[24] is matched against Sarastro and *his* squire. In *Il Seraglio*, the designs of Osmin on Blonde mimic his master's designs on Blonde's mistress. It seems possible that, in *Die Zauberflöte*, Monostatos's attempt to kiss Pamina is all that is left of what was in the original story a double conception, whereby the servant grossly lusted after the daughter, while the master, whose lust was for power, plotted a dynastic marriage with the mother, the Queen herself.

The final difficulty about believing the Queen was bad from the start concerns her name. She is regularly known as the Queen of the Night; and by the end of the opera[25] Monostatos

---

* —as we are told in the dialogue before No. 14, Act II.

(who has proved a traitor to Sarastro) and her own three ladies-in-waiting are indeed rendering homage to her under this name: 'grosse Königin der Nacht'. By this name she is immediately identifiable as a personification of the powers of darkness, destined to be put to flight by the moon-and-sun enlightenment of Isis and Osiris.

However, when the Queen is first mentioned—by her ladies-in-waiting—early on in the opera, she is not called the Queen of the Night at all, but is referred to simply as 'the princess' or 'our Queen' ('die Fürstin', 'die grosse Fürstin', 'zu unsrer Fürstin', '. . . unserer Königin'[26]). Neither is this short for Queen of the Night. When[27] Papageno introduces himself as the Queen's birdcatcher, he gives his employer's full title, which Tamino repeats wonderingly: 'die Sternflammende Königin'.

This 'star-flaming Queen' is certainly not a personification of darkness (a rôle which belongs to the black-faced and black-souled* Monostatos), any more than the glittering coloratura of her arias can by any stretch of interpretation be said to represent darkness. What her arias may legitimately call to mind, as the high soprano notes fly from her spectacularly and separately, like sparks, is light suddenly manifested in darkness. Both her music and her first appearance in the opera, when she arrives as a dea ex machina out of a thunderclap,† and, presumably, airborne, suggest that most rococo of motifs, a glass chandelier, itself a permanent and seemingly frozen form of the transient rococo ornament of a firework display, which the eighteenth century often associated with music. 'Star-flaming', the Queen, was recognisable to Masons, but not to outsiders, as good and Masonic. A Masonic *Text Book* names, among the three 'ornaments' of a Lodge, 'the Blazing Star'.

(iv) *Who was the original Queen?*

We are beginning to reconstruct the Queen as she was in the original story. She was a star-flaming Queen, on the side of righteousness, who made her entrances in the air—probably on

---

* 'I know', Sarastro says to Monostatos when he is finally exposed, 'that your soul is as black as your face' ('Ich weiss, dass deine Seele ebenso schwarz als dein Gesicht ist'—Act II, dialogue after No. 14).

† '(*Donner*) *Tamino*: Ihr Götter, was ist das? . . . 1 *Dame:* Es verkündet die Ankunft unserer Königin. (*Donner*) 3 *Damen:* Sie kommt! (*Donner*) Sie kommt! (*Donner*) Sie kommt!' (Act I, dialogue before No. 4.)

a cloud, which would explain the thunder that accompanies her, though in reality the thunder would be needed to drown the noise of the machinery propelling the cloud (a piece of stage management resembling the miraculous thunder in *Sethos* which was really made by the brazen gates).

These airborne entrances would suggest that the Queen was some kind of divinity; and, as befitted a divinity, she would make only rare appearances in the opera, when the plot called for her to manifest herself ex machina. This last can be guessed because it is still true of the opera as it stands, in which the Queen is the only character to be in any way supernatural. It is not simply that hers is a brief (though, goodness knows, a spectacular) singing part—two arias and a passage in an ensemble is probably as much as a coloratura could expect, especially since there is another soprano in the cast: the point is made by her sudden disappearances as well as appearances. The Queen does not remain on stage to witness or participate in other people's activity. She has a more than regal inaccessibility, of a kind never achieved by Sarastro who, for all his augustness, is prolix and sententious. The Queen remains an important figure and is much spoken of during her absences; yet although she is inaccessible to the other characters when she is not there, she knows, as we are expressly told,[28] what they are doing in her absence; and her agents make appearances to carry out her will.

All this makes it possible to conjecture who, in the original plan, the Queen was. This personage is, as a matter of fact, still present in the opera as it stands, and still on the side of the good, but she no longer makes a personal appearance.

The original Queen really was a goddess and, in a very precise sense, a queen. She was airborne for very pertinent reasons: she is in fact the goddess whom Apuleius calls the queen of heaven, 'regina caeli'[29] (a title later appropriated by a famous and miracle-working hymn[30] for the Virgin Mary). The original Queen was not called the Queen of the Night, but, as the Sternflammende Königin, she did appear—dazzlingly star-flaming—*in* the night, and *in* heaven. She makes her appearance to Apuleius's hero-narrator in a dream—a passage to which Terrasson draws attention not by a footnote but in the very text of *Sethos*;[31] and the authors of *Die Zauberflöte* evidently heeded him, since the appearance of their queen-goddess leaves their hero feeling as though he had had a dream.*

Apuleius's description of the goddess makes it clear why the authors of *Die Zauberflöte* chose the title star-flaming: although the goddess's dress is light, she wears a cloak of gleaming black, sprinkled over with stars and with a full moon in the middle.[32] Thus the goddess is set in the midst of darkness and surrounded by stars, her subsidiaries and courtiers. (Apuleius tells us that her worshippers carried torches in honour of her starry character, and that her initiates shaved their heads so that their pates should gleam like her stars on earth.[33]) The goddess herself is a major source of light (claiming, indeed, to give light to the sun and illuminate even the Underworld[34]): she is, in fact, the goddess who was identified with the moon.† She is worshipped, so she tells Apuleius's hero,[35] under various names by the various races of men, but is known to the Egyptians by her true name (which is that of a queen): Queen Isis.

Even towards the end of the opera, the text of *Die Zauberflöte* seems to preserve a trace of the original version whereby Pamina's mother was the moon. Monostatos seems to know it: when he sees his opportunity to kiss the sleeping Pamina, he sings, as he creeps up to her (and it would be highly reasonable of him to address the words to the girl's mother): 'Moon, hide yourself at that. If it is too vexing for you, close your eyes'. Moreover, no sooner has he finished singing these words than the girl's mother appears, as though summoned by them; and her arrival foils Monostatos's attempt to kiss her daughter.‡

For it is, of course, because she never does close her eyes but is always watching from her vantage point as Queen of heaven, that Isis knows everything that goes on—or, as the Queen's

---

* As soon as the Queen has vanished, Tamino asks himself whether what he has seen is real ('Ist's denn auch Wirklichkeit, was ich sah?'—dialogue after No. 4, Act I).

† (Diodorus Siculus, I, 11.) Apuleius describes her as wearing in the middle of her forehead 'a plain circlet in fashion of a mirror, or rather resembling the moon by the light it gave forth' (Adlington's translation, *The Golden Ass*, XI, 3).

‡ Like others, the scene fails to make its dramatic point in the variously named 'translation' and 'English version' by E. J. Dent in the standard British vocal score. Divergence is inevitable between the German and the English words to be sung, but the spoken English text does not always tally with the German spoken text printed synoptically with it. Such a divergence occurs in the brief spoken dialogue for Monostatos, Pamina and the Queen that follows No. 14.

ladies-in-waiting put it, in her absence, to Tamino: 'The Princess has heard your every word; she has read every move in your face'.[36]

The authors of that dialogue may even have had vaguely in mind the passage where Diodorus ascribes[37] the same characteristic to Isis's consort and counterpart, as (Diodorus is quoting Homer) 'the sun who sees all and hears all'.

No doubt the original plan for *Die Zauberflöte* intended the Queen's entrances in the sky* to help identify her as the moon—a type of symbolism eighteenth-century audiences were well versed in reading. Something similar happens in Giambattista Tiepolo's highly operatic[38] decorative scheme at Villa Valmarana, near Vicenza, where a cloud in the sky (painted, that is, on the ceiling) brings on to the earthly scene (painted, that is, on a wall) the Greek version of the moon goddess, namely Artemis, who appears as a dea ex machina in the room which Tiepolo has transformed into a theatrical set and foils a yet worse misdeed than Monostatos's.

If this reconstruction of the Queen is right, the goddess whom Sarastro worships, in the final version, with his 'O Isis und Osiris',[39] was in the original plan opposed by a villainous Sarastro, who had stolen her daughter; and it was the goddess who represented virtue and Masonry. The presence of an Isis figure in the original plan makes it clear that the Masonic significance was not, as E. J. Dent assumed, an afterthought, introduced with the change of plot, but an inherent—and, we may guess, to Mozart the inspiring—part of the original conception of the opera. Moreover, this new view of the original Queen makes it possible to restore the outline of the original plot and to glimpse how the Masonic motif fitted in.

(v) *The Original Plot Discerned*

Isis, as the Masons no doubt knew from Apuleius and Diodorus Siculus, became identified with almost every major Greco-Roman goddess. Indeed, when she appears in the narrator's dream in *The Golden Ass*, she claims to be the constant factor in all the gods and goddesses.[40]

* A Berlin periodical described *Die Zauberflöte* in 1791 as the 'comedy with machines' (O. E. Deutsch).

Most particularly, Isis was assimilated to Demeter (Ceres),[41] through the conflation, which Diodorus insists on, of the Isiac mysteries with the Eleusinian ones held in honour of Demeter. The authors of *Die Zauberflöte* had certainly read in *Sethos* that the Eleusinian mysteries were founded by Orpheus in exact imitation of the Isiac, it being a condition of Orpheus's initiation into the cult of Isis that he should take the worship of Isis home with him to Greece.[42]

Here is a vivid clue to what went on in the mind or minds which invented *Die Zauberflöte*. Demeter, in the myth which was commemorated and re-enacted at the Eleusinia, has, like the Queen in *Die Zauberflöte*, a daughter who has been stolen away by 'ein böser Dämon'—Hades (Pluto), the god of the Underworld, who, having fallen in love with Persephone (Proserpina), snatches her and keeps her imprisoned in the underground kingdom of the dead which he rules. Meanwhile the girl's mother searches for her unhappily—with, in fact, all that unhappiness which the star-flaming Queen so marvellously expresses in her first aria when she sings 'For sufferings am I chosen, as my daughter is parted from me. Through her all my joy is lost; a wicked wight flew off with her'.[43] By the time of her second aria the Queen's character has undergone the change wrought by the change of plot, and 'hellish vengeance is seething' in her heart.[44] But about the Queen's state of heart in her first aria there is no ambiguity. It is her 'Mutterhertz'[45] which, in her sadness, has brought her to appeal to Tamino.

With Tamino's involvement in the rescue of the Queen's daughter, another myth has contributed to the outline of the plot. The Eleusinian myth does not provide a hero to rescue the stolen daughter. But *Sethos* has hinted at a hero when it maintains that the Eleusinian story and cult were taken to Greece by Orpheus; and for the continuation of their outline plot the authors of *Die Zauberflöte* needed to look no further than to the myth of Orpheus himself. In a story which is partly a doublet of the Eleusinian myth, Orpheus sets out to rescue Eurydice, another young woman who has been snatched away into the kingdom of death—where Orpheus actually penetrates in pursuit of her.

Obviously, this would be a convenient mythological model for authors casting about for a way to get the stolen heroine rescued in their own invented myth. But one can, and with certainty, go much further than that. There is a compelling reason why the story of Orpheus should have come promptly to the minds of the authors of *Die Zauberflöte*. The reason is, once again, *Sethos*, the novel which so few writers about the opera have actually read. Not content with mentioning Orpheus as an initiate of Isis and founder of the Eleusinian mysteries, Terrasson presently drops—for a considerable interlude—his own hero, Sethos, and takes up Orpheus instead. A good part of the first volume of *Sethos* is given over to telling (hand-in-hand with Terrasson's rationalised explanation, of course) the story of Orpheus and Eurydice.

(vi) *The Original Plot Takes Shape*

As soon as one discerns that the authors of *Die Zauberflöte* have borrowed, via *Sethos*, from the story of Orpheus in order to equip themselves with a rescuer of the stolen princess, it leaps to the eye that the story of Orpheus has also had a strong general influence on *Die Zauberflöte*. It is from the magic power of Orpheus's lute, symbolising, very aptly for opera, the combined powers of music and poetry, that the opera has borrowed Tamino's magic flute. Thanks to the power of music, 'a flute is more than gold and crowns';[46] and our eyes actually witness how, by playing the flute, Tamino becomes, exactly like Orpheus, capable of enchanting wild animals—'how strong is your magic tone', he sings,[47] 'since, lovely flute, through your playing the very beasts feel joy'.

Die Zauberflöte can now be recognised as one of those pieces of music, which seventeenth- and eighteenth-century composers delighted in, which set to music the compliments paid to music by literature. This fashion created an annual rite in London towards the end of the seventeenth century, when it became the custom for a poet and a composer—Dryden and Purcell were both contributors—to produce an ode for the festival of St. Cecilia as inventress of the organ. Dryden's *Song For St. Cecilia's Day*, 1687, is already playing on the power of music to provoke contrasting emotions in quick succession; and his St. Cecilia's Day *Ode* of 1697 exploits this still more dramatically, as its sub-title implies: *Alexander's Feast, or The Power of Musique*. Handel, who set the Dryden *Ode*, also converted Milton's *L'Allegro* and *Il Penseroso* into a virtuoso demonstration of the power of music, by presenting snippets of one poem interspersed, for maximum emotional contrast, with snippets of the other. No doubt one of Gluck's reasons for choosing the Orpheus story to make into an opera was that it was a large-scale compliment to music by narrative—the sense in which Milton had understood Orpheus* and in which Handel had taken Milton.

Indeed, the story of Orpheus was well established as being in itself a compliment to music, and as such it was often cited in the compliments specially written for St. Cecilia's Day. These compliments would be much in Mozart's mind at the time of *Die Zauberflöte*, as he had lately provided instrumentation for several choral pieces by Handel, among them Handel's Ode for St. Cecilia's Day. In the St. Cecilia's Day tradition, by one of those pagan-Christian dualisms (like the one between cupids and cherubs enshrined in Cherubino), in which baroque and rococo iconography abound, Orpheus had become almost St. Cecilia's pagan counterpart.

> Orpheus *cou'd lead the savage race;*
> *And Trees uprooted left their place;*
> *Sequacious of the* Lyre

says Dryden's St. Cecilia *Song*; and Pope's St. Cecilia *Ode* of 1708 narrates the story of Orpheus at length, though only to set Orpheus aside at the end in favour of his Christian pendant, with the ravishing conceit

> *Of Orpheus now no more let poets tell;*
> *To bright Cecilia greater power is given:*
> *His numbers raised a shade from hell,*
> *Hers lift the soul to heaven.*

The myth of Orpheus would be familiar to Mozart and

---

* *L'Allegro* wishes for the truly operatic combination of 'soft Lydian airs, Married to immortal verse . . . That Orpheus' self may heave his head . . . and hear Such strains as would have won the ear Of Pluto to have quite set free His half-regained Eurydice'. In Gluck's opera the strains do prevail (on Amor) to just that end.

Schikaneder from two directions, both of which influenced the opera: once from *Sethos* (and perhaps its Masonic associations); and again from its treatment in Gluck's opera *Orfeo ed Euridice*.[48]

The myth imposes on Orpheus's rescue of his wife one special condition (besides, of course, the major one of his having to brave the Underworld to fetch her): he must not, as he leads her up from the Underworld, look back. This condition is a counterpart to the one imposed on Tamino during his initiation, namely that though he may look at he must not speak to Pamina; and it is easy enough to guess that this refers to the secrecy imposed on Masonic initiates.

From the myth of Orpheus the condition about not looking back has made its way into *Sethos*, where Terrasson's account of the Isiac initiation stipulates that 'whoever goes thro' this passage alone, and without looking behind him . . . shall be intitled to the privilege of preparing his mind for the revelation of the mysteries of the great goddess Isis'.*

From the novel, however, the condition about not looking back has not made its way into *Die Zauberflöte*.† Yet a reference to this part of the myth of Orpheus *is* to be found in *Die Zauberflöte*—not, however, in its native form but by way of a reminiscence of Gluck. In the fourth act of Gluck's opera, Orpheus is leading Eurydice up from the Underworld and abiding by the rule that he is not to look back. Eurydice begs him to look at her; when he refuses, she, being ignorant of his reason, concludes that he no longer loves her, and she wishes to die. This is precisely what happens in *Die Zauberflöte*, but transmuted into the terms whereby it is speaking, not looking, which is forbidden. Tamino is under oath not to speak to Pamina. She, too, is ignorant of the circumstances, and she asks if he has not a syllable for her; when he does not utter one, she at once asks 'Do you love me no more?' and cries 'O, that is worse than illness, worse than death!'[49]—and this thought which is as a death

---

* (Lediard's translation, Volume I, p. 155.) The French text (quoted by E. J. Dent: *Mozart's Operas*, 13) reads: 'Quiconque fera cette route seul, et sans regarder derrière lui . . . aura droit de préparer son âme à la révélation des mystères de la grande Déesse Isis'.

† Neither does the opera take up the condition that the initiate must take the road *alone*, since Tamino is finally accompanied through the ordeals by Pamina, and sets out with Papageno as his companion.

leads to her lament 'Ach, ich fühls's'[50] and to her attempted suicide.[51]*

The original plan for *Die Zauberflöte*, it is becoming clear, was compiled from two myths, both of which are treated in *Sethos* and both of which, conveniently for the Masonic symbolism, are connected with mystery cults in the ancient world. The story of Demeter and Persephone supplied the opera with a queen-goddess whose daughter had been stolen and imprisoned in the Underworld; and the story of Orpheus and Eurydice supplied a hero who rescued his wife from the Underworld. The one story supplied no hero, the other a hero who was already married; Tamino was to stand between the two, and be a hero who got a wife by rescuing her from the Underworld.

Thus in the original intention *Die Zauberflöte* was to be a rescue opera—and so it still is in the first part of Act One, before the plot has been changed: the Queen tells Tamino 'You shall be the rescuer of my daughter',[52] and Tamino makes a very conspicuous declaration that to rescue Pamina is his duty.[53] The (good) Queen gives Tamino the (good) magic talisman, whereby he is to accomplish the rescue; the obvious triumphal ending is foreshadowed, whereby Tamino is successful in the rescue and is rewarded by the good Queen's blessing on his marriage to her daughter.

(vii) *Why Was the Plot Changed?*

The self-declaratory evidence of a plot-change in *Die Zauberflöte* is endorsed by the document of Ignaz von Seyfried, which O. E. Deutsch cites under '?1840'. Seyfried had known both Mozart and Schikaneder and, as Deutsch details, joined Schikaneder's company as second Kapellmeister in 1799. Schikaneder put on *Die Zauberflöte* at the Theater auf der Wieden (the Freihaus theatre). It opened on 30 September 1791.

The date of Seyfried's letter is missing, but Deutsch convincingly though tentatively deduces it from internal evidence. In

* Whereas Tamino resists the temptation to speak and therefore comes successfully through the initiation ordeals, Orpheus succumbs to the temptation to look—and as a result Eurydice, who has wished for death, does die (again). Here the myth ends: unhappily. Gluck's version, however, makes the ending happy and the final result the same as though Orpheus had come successfully through his ordeal, by arranging for Amor to take pity on him and restore Eurydice to life. Terrasson's version of the story engineers a similar result by different methods.

his sixties Seyfried vouched for both the fact of a plot-change and the reason for it : Schikaneder altered the plan of Mozart's opera because in June 1791, three months before the opening of *Die Zauberflöte*, Marinelli's rival Viennese theatre opened its production of an opera by W. Müller named *Der Fagottist* or, by some accounts, Seyfried's included, *Kaspar der Fagottist oder der Zauberzyther* (the bassoonist or the magic zither). It was based on a fairy tale by A. J. Liebeskind included in C. M. Wieland's collection. Two years earlier, in 1789, Schikaneder had successfully produced Paul Wranitsky's opera *Oberon*, to a libretto by C. L. Giesecke drawn from another story in Wieland's compilation. The story that provided the framework for *Der Fagottist* was, Deutsch records, named *Lulu oder die Zauberflöte*.

It seems, therefore, that a single story in Wieland's collection provided both the framework of Müller's *Der Fagottist* and the title of Mozart's *Die Zauberflöte*. Had Schikaneder wanted to dissociate the two operas, avoid charges of plagiarism and ward off public confusion between the magical zither and the magical flute, the direct and obvious step for him was to alter the title of *Die Zauberflöte*. That, however, is the one thing he certainly did not do.

E. J. Dent seems to imply that the original version was set in Japan, since he states (again without qualification) that Tamino, in the opera as it now is, is 'still' described as a Japanese prince 'by an oversight'. The truth is that if the original version had been set in Japan, Tamino might have been any nationality he chose *except* Japanese; and similarly in any version set in Egypt he may be no matter what but not Egyptian. The one thing which is clear about Tamino's origins is that he is not a native of whatever country it is he finds himself in at the start of the opera, since he is completely ignorant of both church and state

---

* Dent's three and a half chapters on *Die Zauberflöte* are conceivably the most inept guide to the opera ever written. People who lived through part of the period when Dent was considered the English-language authority on Mozart and his operas and when his book about them, whose first edition appeared in 1913, was kept in print like a standard work, often found it hard not to attack his misconceptions of the artist. With the recession of his influence he is recognisable as a pioneer, though an often misguided one, of Mozart studies in Britain. It is often the fate of pioneers that their successors point out they they drew the map incorrectly. Without Dent's academic prestige operas often neglected in Britain, such as *Idomeneo* and *Così*, might have been even more cold-shouldered than they were.

there and has to have both the priesthood of Isis and the great
Queen explained to him. In reality, of course, Tamino is simply
one of those exotic travelling princes, like Sethos and Johnson's
Rasselas, so dear to the enlightenment,* who travel and ask for
explanations about church and state in the countries they find
themselves in, and thereby acquire their liberal education.
Tamino is specifically Japanese simply as a fashionable, rather
Voltairean, touch of far-eastern exoticism, of the kind that
sprinkles rococo furniture; he is, indeed, Japanese in the same
mood that Sarastro's name is obviously taken from the name
of the Persian Zoroaster†—which does not, however, seem to
have suggested to E. J. Dent that any version of the opera was
ever set in Persia. If any significance beyond fashion is intended
by these outlandish touches it is probably the universal validity
of Masonry.

Often without citing Seyfried's undated and arguably shaky
assertion that Schikaneder introduced a plot-change in *Die
Zauberflöte* because he was disconcerted to find his opera
pre-empted, commentators have wildly assumed that, by the
original plan, the opera was to be not merely a fairy-tale but a
fairy work, presumably on the lines of Schikaneder's earlier
success, Wranitsky's *Oberon*. It is unlikely that *Die Zauberflöte*
was ever meant, by any plan, to include fairies. The magic that
the final and finished opera attaches to Tamino's flute is probably an allegorical representation of the moral worth of Masonic
teaching and perhaps of the benign social powers of Freemasonry. Both were secret. Their effects could be called and to
outsiders were meant to seem to be worked by magic.

If Seyfried assumed, at the time the plot was changed, that
the reason for the change was the rivalry between theatres,
perhaps Masonic discretion did not contradict him but let him
believe all his life that that was indeed the reason. I think all the
same that Seyfried *was* contradicted: by Schikaneder's not

---

* Pope, too, planned (though he did not carry out) an epic with a princely hero
on these lines—complete with a moral education got from the Egyptian mysteries.
(Spence's *Anecdotes*, 1820 edition, pp. 56–7.)

† The name Zoroaster was adopted and adapted primarily, I think, as an
exoticism. In addition, Mozart was surely reminded by his love and study of
Handel (cf. Chapter XIX) that the magician in Handel's opera *Orlando* is named
Zoroastro. I mention on page 187 a classical allusion that probably pointed Freemasonry in the same direction.

changing the title from *Die Zauberflöte* to something less blatantly like *Der Fagottist oder Die Zauberzither*.* All the other evidence apart, this in itself is enough to make nonsense of the usually accepted reason for the change which seems to have overtaken the plot of *Die Zauberflöte*.

The usual explanation having fallen to the ground, it remains to seek a better one; and the most fertile place to look is likely to be the one the commentators ignore, namely the probability that the original version of the story was already Masonic.

Here, two motives present themselves, both of which may have been active. To take the less compelling first: the star-flaming, Isis-like Queen of the first part of the opera, so long as she remained both powerful and good, was in danger of running into conflict with the rather antifeminist line taken by Masonic philosophy—which, unlike the historical cult of Isis, was not prepared to attribute the sovereignty of the universe to a female. Indeed, by making its Supreme Being an architect, Masonry had enlisted him in a then exclusively masculine profession.

The Greco-Roman cult made the worship of Osiris slightly subordinate to that of Isis—Apuleius's hero is initiated first, and with the greatest pomp, into the Isiac mysteries, and then dedicates himself to Osiris almost as an afterthought;[56] and the same is true of the Egyptian myth itself, where the story ran that Osiris was murdered and owed his resurrection to Isis—which is presumably why Isis can claim to lend her light to Osiris.

All this might pass well enough with a Masonic readership while it was damply reflected in Terrasson's abstract and philo-sophising novel: but when the supremacy of the Queen began to take on dramatic body—and nothing more dramatic than her first entrance and aria is conceivable—it may well have seemed to the authors of the opera that they were embarked on a creation which flouted the Masonic conception of women's proper place. And it is notable that later parts of the opera (that is, presumably, the revised version) lay very considerable verbal emphasis on what that proper place should be.

* Indeed, the truth may actually be that the title of *Die Zauberflöte* denotes an attempt to cash in on the success of fairy operas, whether Marinelli's or Schika-neder's own successful fairy production of two years earlier, *in spite of* the fact that *Die Zauberflöte* was never intended to be a fairy opera.

(viii) *How the Join was made*

The join between the presumptive first and second versions of the plot—and of the Queen—is made at the beginning of the long finale of Act One, the scene where Tamino, evidently in the course of searching for Pamina in order to rescue her, comes on the temples of Prudence, Work and Arts,* which so impress him that he asks himself if the gods have their seat here. That the temples concern a secret cult is made allegorically plain when Tamino is refused admission by mysterious voices inside which bid him 'Zurück!' Nonetheless, one of the priests (the Orator) comes out and engages him in a long and dramatically clumsy conversation, whose purpose is to convey to both Tamino and the audience that previous impressions of the Queen's goodness and Sarastro's wickedness are to be reversed.

The point is made in the most inept way imaginable. Tamino suddenly demands whether Sarastro is lord in this place, and is told that he is. 'Not even', Tamino persists, 'in Wisdom's temple?'; and when the answer is again Yes, Tamino exclaims 'Then it's all hypocrisy'—because, as he says, Sarastro 'is a non-man, a tyrant' ('ein Unmensch, ein Tyrann').[57]

The authors of this dialogue have run slap into the danger of actually putting words to the thought that Sarastro is a hypocrite, when what they want to impress on the audience is that the Queen is a hypocrite (this being the only way they can hope to reverse the helpful and truthtelling impression they have allowed her to make, through her ladies-in-waiting, earlier in the Act). If this risk seemed worth taking, it was presumably because it gave the authors an opportunity, which they seize in the next part of the dialogue, to score a Masonic point against the Queen. (That they are anxious to do this reinforces the argument that they have demoted her from her original position, and that Masonic antifeminism was one of their reasons for doing so.) The Orator asks Tamino his grounds for calling Sarastro names, and Tamino, who has heard the Queen's aria of lamentation for her daughter, makes the

---

* This is the gist of what Tamino reads out, during his recitative, from the inscriptions on the temples: 'Es zeigen die Pforten, es zeigen die Säulen, dass Klugheit und Arbeit und Künste hier weilen' (Act I, No. 8). The stage directions, however, ascribe the temples to wisdom, reason and nature, and Dent's 'English version' incorporates those into what he has Tamino sing.

chivalrous reply 'A woman's unhappiness': the Orator thereupon seizes the chance to state that a woman has deceived Tamino and that women do little but talk much.[58] Later in the opera, this Masonic point is reiterated in a specifically Masonic context—that is, in the interest of the brotherhood—by the duet of the two priests:[59] 'Beware the tricks of women: this is the group's first duty'.

Once the new and antifeminist version has been established by this clumsy join, Tamino is left as the hero of a rescue opera with no one to rescue. Instead, staying where he is and accepting the authenticity of Sarastro's goodness, he applies for initiation into Sarastro's order; and the initiation ordeals take the dramatic place originally designed to be filled by the ordeal of the rescue. Pamina, it turns out by the revised version, is not in need of rescuing. It is, however, too late to alter the beginning: the authors have to let it stand that Sarastro really has stolen her by force, and the best they can do is have Sarastro point out that it is for her own good to stay with him, since it would be her ruin if he were to return her to her wicked mother, whom she must forget.[60]

Sarastro, having stolen her, intends to provide Pamina with a husband, and he presently reveals to her that the man he has in mind is Tamino, whom the gods have pre-elected for the part. This, Sarastro claims, was his grounds for stealing Pamina from her mother in the first place.[61] The grounds are, however, extremely shaky (being in fact yet more evidence of a hasty join), since in reality Pamina's mother has herself pre-elected Tamino as a husband for Pamina.[62]* Imperfect patching has left the Queen and Sarastro, mortal enemies though they are supposed to be, in perfect agreement on this important point,† and it has left the righteous Sarastro guilty of snatching Pamina and holding her under duress in order to save her from her mother's designs, which are in fact exactly the same as Sarastro's.

Even before naming Tamino, Sarastro has decided that

---

* When the Queen tells Tamino that he shall be the rescuer of her daughter, she adds that she will see to it that Pamina shall be ever his (Act I, No. 4).

† However, at the last moment, by which time the authors have made her so wicked that she may forswear her earlier promises with ease, the Queen says that she has already given her word that Monostatos shall have Pamina (Act II, No. 21). Even in her second-version debasement, however, the Queen seems much too proud a character to envisage any such thing.

Pamina must marry, and he offers the thoroughly Masonic reason that a man must guide her, since without one every woman strays from her path and misses her function.[63]

(ix) *How Mozart makes the opera feminist after all*

To this sentiment of Sarastro's the opera presently gives the lie in the most dramatic fashion. In general it is a safe guess that the Mozart of the letters was unlikely to stomach the Masonic doctrine on women as anything more than a joke; and in *Die Zauberflöte* it almost seems he was at pains to counter each anti-feminine remark with a pro-feminine dramatic stroke, and, having agreed to the demotion of the Queen, made up for it by promoting her daughter into a much more prominent and moving dramatic position than, probably, either the original or the second plan of the opera allowed for.

Presumably Pamina is present in the opera, which is after all an opera as well as a Masonic cryptogram, to lend it a love interest. The Masonic meaning could quite well accommodate her as an abstract personification of wisdom, and so long as she possessed neither power nor a very high degree of characterisation she would not run into the doctrinal displeasure incurred by her mother. The probability is that neither the first nor the revised version of the plot *did* intend her to have any particular force of character: in the first version she was to be the usual inert heroine who is rescued, in the second the equally inert reward handed to the hero when he comes through the initiation ordeals—as, indeed, the text implies: when Tamino avows his wish to undergo initiation, he cries 'Wisdom's lesson be my victory, Pamina, the gracious maiden, my reward'.[64]

To such an extent does Pamina seem to have been conceived as the conventional inert *thing* that it does not seem to have occurred to the authors of the story that they might be straining the audience's sympathy for the Isiac brotherhood and casting doubts on its morality (already sufficiently muddled by the clumsy join between versions) when they let Pamina suffer Tamino's unexplained refusal to speak to her, and arrogantly describe this passage (which perhaps refers to a Masonic rule that the initiate must keep the secrets even from his wife*) as

---

* This ordeal of Tamino's has no direct equivalent in the ordeals undergone by Sethos. But a version of it, more extended in time but much less poignant—since

Tamino's ordeal and a proof of *his* courage.[65] However, although the plot may treat her as inert, Mozart makes sure that Pamina does not suffer inertly. He instantly takes her side and vindicates her by setting her cry of 'Ach, ich fühl's' to one of the most moving pieces of music ever composed, and one which not only breaks completely with the conventions of puppet-psychology but bursts through the conventions of the shape of an operatic aria. If the Queen has been made less than divine, Mozart has made her daughter fully human.

This effect, being wholly musical, is wholly Mozart's. The further dramatic development of the story moves further and further away from the antifeminism which the formal pronouncements of the brotherhood continue to insist on, until it is ruled that an exception shall be made, since a woman who does not fear death is worthy,[66] and Pamina is allowed to undergo initiation along with Tamino. One may suspect but cannot with certainty detect Mozart's personal work in swinging the story to this conclusion. What seems even more likely is that it was Mozart who added another stroke to Pamina's rehabilitation by personally writing the couplet 'Mann und Weib, und Weib und Mann Reichen an die Gottheit an' which so conspicuously resembles the doggerel couplet he had added to his signature in a letter of nine years earlier.* Mozart was capable of writing a whole letter in doggerel, and also of virtually finishing the music of an aria before telling his librettist that the aria was wanted[67] (which implies he must have settled at least the rhythm, and therefore the main outline of the words, himself): it would not be at all improbable that he was one of the writers of *Die Zauberflöte*.

Sethos is not, at this time, in love with anyone—occurs during a period of instruction which Sethos undertakes after his ordeals. During this period Sethos lives with the priests, whose wives also belong to the community. The candidate frequently meets them but is forbidden to speak to or even salute them. 'But that which will appear, without doubt, mortifying to well-bred gentlemen' is that the ladies (most of whom are of 'singular beauty') always salute Sethos, who may not reply. Terrasson tells us that this ordeal is a test of Sethos's fortitude in resisting 'the charms of the sex when they appear in competition with his duty'. This reads like a Masonic touch; so does Terrasson's account of the status of these priests' wives:— they have the courtesy title of priestess but no sacerdotal functions; they may frequent certain parts of the building only, and have 'the liberty of their husbands appartments, but not of their closets' (Lediard's translation, Volume I, pp. 181 foll.).

* See chapter XII, p. 126.

Once the ruling has been given that Pamina is worthy to be initiated, the way is open for this thoroughly Mozartian drama utterly to overturn Sarastro's pronouncement about a woman needing a man to guide her. Reunited with Pamina, and about to face the final ordeals, 'Here', sings Tamino, 'are the gates of terror, where distress and death afflict me'; and Pamina not only replies that she will go with him through it all, and not only has the wit to suggest he use the magic flute to charm their way through, but also and expressly tells him: 'I myself lead you; love guides me'.[68] It is as though Mozart were expressly telling Sarastro that, if anything, it is the man who goes astray without a woman to guide him, but that in fact both will lose their way unless directed by the presiding deity of all Mozartian dramas, love.

(x) *A more pressing reason for changing the plot*

Although we may be convinced that the second version demoted the Queen for doctrinal reasons, we cannot imagine that the authors were acting on more than a vague feeling that their star-flaming Queen was running into trouble. If the objection had been precisely formulated, the second version of the plot would hardly have been allowed to bring up the same objection all over again by taking such a subversively pro-feminine turn. We can imagine that the need to de-glorify Isis was a very important reason for *agreeing* to change the plot, but not that it was the decisive reason, which one would expect to be much more specific.

What the decisive reason was we may find by going back to the reconstruction of the original design for the opera. The three principal characters had been supplied by amalgamating Persephone and Eurydice into Pamina, and thereby combining the myth of Demeter and Persephone with that of Orpheus and Eurydice. That this story was already Masonic is clear from the many traits of Isis in the goddess-mother, and from the mystery cult associations (via *Sethos*) of both the myths which had been drawn on.

In both these myths, the idea of the Underworld, the realm of the dead, is an essential component of the story; the Orpheus myth actually includes a journey there. It is not very far-fetched to conjecture that in the original plan for *Die Zauberflöte* the 'böser Dämon' who had made off with Pamina was Hades or some personification of death, and that the rescue performed by Tamino consisted of following the example of Gluck's hero and going to the Underworld to fetch her.

This, by the way, supplies the final explanation of why Tamino is equipped with a flute which can, exactly like Orpheus's lute, enchant wild animals. Tamino was to use his magic music, as Orpheus used his, to make his way safely into the Underworld by enchanting its watchdog Cerberus. In the final version, there is neither Underworld nor watchdog; Tamino's flute music,[69] which is certainly enchanting, charms some wild animals who creep on stage and off again without any explanation or relevance to the story. Perhaps this music had already been composed for the prospective Cerberus episode in the first version and was much too excellent to be dropped from the second, even though the second could not think up an occasion for it.

From the opera as it now stands, the visit to the Underworld seems to have disappeared. The Underworld is not mentioned: Pamina is incarcerated in Sarastro's town, 'Sarastros Burg';[70] and instead of a visit to the Underworld culminating in a rescue, an initiation takes place.

Nevertheless, one item remains common to both versions: the idea of a journey. In the first version, Tamino was to make the journey to the Underworld in the steps of Orpheus and a number of other classical heroes; and it is significant that most of the myths about a living hero descending to the Underworld stress the idea of the journey there. (When[71] Odysseus makes the visit, he speaks of the road, the ὀδός, and asks who is to guide him on it.) In the final version of *Die Zauberflöte*, there is also a road which the hero must take. It is not said to lead through the mythological kingdom of the dead underneath the earth, but it is said to lead 'through death's gloomy night'.[72] It consists of the course the candidate must take during his initiation—a course which *Die Zauberflöte* and Terrasson's novel agree to call a road, 'diese Strasse'[73] or 'cette route'.

A conclusion is forcing its way up out of the comparison between the two versions of the opera: if the initiation has, in the final version, replaced the hero's visit to the Underworld, that is because, in the first version, which was already Masonic, the visit to the Underworld was one and the same thing as the initiation. Who could be better placed to preside over the initiation into the mysteries of Isis than Isis herself, who in a dream-like vision had bidden Apuleius's hero to apply for initiation? She it was, in the person of the star-flaming Queen, who appeared to Tamino in a dream-like vision and (as she still does in her first aria in the opera as it stands) invited him to undergo the ordeal of rescuing Pamina; it was this ordeal, which actually took him to the Underworld, which in the original design was to initiate him and make him worthy to attain and espouse the wisdom represented by the Queen's daughter.

This, for which I shall in a moment produce corroboration, immediately answers the problem why the plot had to be changed. The original plan was to represent the Masonic initiation as a visit to the Underworld: it had to be changed because the representation was too exact; it gave away too much of the secrets of Masonry.

XV

'Die Zauberflöte' Solved—2

So far our reconstruction reads: that the original intention was for *Die Zauberflöte* to tell the story of its hero's descent into the Underworld; that this story was meant at the same time to give an account of Masonic initiation, but an account decipherable only by initiates; that it nonetheless turned out to be too explicit, and that that was why the story was changed.

If the authors of the opera first picked on the Underworld metaphor to signify the Masonic initiation and then, after beginning work, discovered they were sailing too near the wind, it can only have been because Masonic initiation, at least in the eighteenth century, actually consisted of a symbolic visit to the Underworld or the after-life. This no one who is not privy to the secrets of eighteenth-century Masonry can hope categorically to prove (or, for the matter of that, to contradict). I can, however, hope to shew that the Masons were highly likely to choose this form for their initiation ritual, and that the philosophical purpose which might impel them to do so is thoroughly consistent with the enlightenment and with Masonic teaching. Next, I can hope to shew that, if the authors of *Die Zauberflöte* did want to depict the Masonic initiation in the form of a dramatised invented myth, they possessed not only all the information they needed but also, in *Sethos*, a very pertinent narrative model—one which they demonstrably did use and one which quite explicitly identifies the idea of initiation with the idea of descending to the Underworld: indeed, *Sethos* actually and explicitly mentions 'joining' these two ideas together. I can add a piece of external information which suggests it definitely was this part of *Sethos* the authors of the opera had in mind. Finally, I can hope to shew from internal

167

evidence that even in its second part, which evidently represents the changed version of the story, the opera has not abandoned but only further disguised its original intention of shewing a Masonic initiation as a visit to the realm of the dead.

(i) Did Masonic Initiants Visit Hell?

Hell was almost as much present to eighteenth-century imaginations as it had been to medieval ones, but for the opposite reason. Now that it was possible to disbelieve in it, hell had become a toy for producing frissons at will. It was in the same class of images as ghosts and monks, for whose effect witness 'Monk' Lewis and the painter who might well have been dubbed 'Monk' Magnasco, to whom the very figure of the monk, with his ecstasies and self-mortification, was nearly as fantastic as a ghost itself. When fashionable secret societies like the Hell Fire Club could play with the neo-gothic, medievalising paraphernalia of black masses and could amuse themselves with the romantic idea of tempting the devil, it is not improbable that a stolid, philosophising and (except, perhaps, politically) respectable secret society like Masonry should get out the classical property cupboard and use the classical images to dress up and make memorable its lessons in enlightened philosophy. And in fact at least one anti-Masonic work professes to reveal the existence of such a ceremony, based on the ancient mysteries and on ancient literature, in the higher initiations of Masonry: according to *The Mysteries Of Freemasonry*, by John Fellows, reception into 'the degree of *knights* of the *White Eagle* or *Pelican*' took place in a décor 'made as terrifying as possible, to resemble the torments of hell'.

Certainly, as Mozart's own letters make plain, eighteenth-century Masonry did offer its initiates a serious lesson about the attitude they should adopt to death. Neither can this have been, in a society wide enough to take in Deists and Jews, the orthodox and specifically Christian teaching on the subject, though it may have been compatible with Christianity, at least in the Masons' view if not the Christians'. Moreover, the standard enlightenment way round Christianity was to have recourse to the classics, a pastoral grove into which eighteenth-century minds were always glad in any case to turn aside for respite.

All this makes it not unlikely that the Masons despatched their initiants to a classically conceived representation of the Underworld. But there is also a very positive and compelling reason why they should: the classical mystery cults did so themselves. The Eleusinian mysteries, in commemoration of Persephone's sojourn in the Underworld, employed an initiation rite in which the candidate was obliged to visit the Underworld in some sort of sacred charade; and evidently the mysteries of Isis did much the same, since Apuleius's hero-narrator says that in the course of his initiation he 'approached the confine of death', 'set foot on the threshold of Persephone' and 'worshipped the infernal gods and the gods above from close to'.[1]*

Exactly what was revealed to the initiate who had successfully carried out this journey is hard to reconstruct, since the initiate was, of course, forbidden to disclose it. One can fairly guess that it was an item of mythological information accompanied by a doctrinal explanation. More certainly, it was revealed to the candidate in a dramatic form or as a tableau vivant; and evidently this was made all the more awe-inspiring because the illumination suddenly flashed before the candidate out of darkness and when he was emotionally exhausted.

For, although the revelation itself may be unknown, the ordeal the candidate underwent in attaining it is well documented, at least as far as the Eleusinian mysteries are concerned.[2] With mythological and geographical correctness, the supposed Underworld was dark. For part of the course—perhaps the beginning, since this would conveniently prevent

* Apuleius's account of Isiac initiation was drawn on by Terrasson and by Masonic ritual and lore. An undated, probably nineteenth-century volume, *The Mysteries of Freemasonry*, by John Fellows, translates the Cupid and Psyche story and Virgil's account of the Underworld visit. Probably from Masonic sources, the authors of *Die Zauberflöte* were acquainted with Apuleius and drew on his Isis for the first version of their star-flaming Queen. (See chapter XIV, iv, pp. 149 foll.) Besides its Isiac ending, Apuleius's novel contains, as a novel within a novel, the story of Cupid and Psyche. Perhaps it was in particular Apuleius's Cupid who lent his character to the markedly Cupidesque (see chapter XI, pp. 105 foll.) Cherubino of *Le Nozze di Figaro*, which Mozart composed two years after he became a Mason; in which case one might conjecture that Apuleius was virtually required reading for eighteenth-century Masons, who no doubt interpreted the story of Cupid and Psyche, as neo-Platonists had probably done before them, as some allegory of a wedding between the Soul and Love. This allegory may have been related by Apuleius to the Isiac initiation, and by the Masons to their initiation; it may even be relevant to the wedding between Tamino and Pamina which emerges from the initiation in *Die Zauberflöte*.

him from seeing where, in the real world, the start of the course was situated—the candidate was also veiled.*

The veiling is borrowed by *Die Zauberflöte*, where, as soon as Tamino and Pamina offer themselves for the ordeals, Sarastro orders their heads to be veiled, as they must first undergo purification—'bedecket ihre Häupter dann, sie müssen erst gereinigt sein'.³ Since there are no veils in *Sethos*, *Die Zauberflöte* has presumably taken them direct from the Masonic ceremony, which no doubt took them from the Eleusinia. As a matter of fact, the Masons seem to have used a blindfold. This appears in an engraving (reproduced in Lady Dilke's book on French eighteenth-century engravers) by Jacques-Philippe Le Bas (who was appointed 'graveur du Cabinet du Roi' in 1744). One of a series by Le Bas called *Les Francmaçons*, this engraving is entitled 'L'Entrée du Récipiendaire dans la Loge'. In a rococo room, several standing, hatless men and a president— who is seated, wears a hat and holds a gavel—are grouped round a chart laid on the floor. As well as various Masonic tools, the chart shews two columns, as it were of a temple, marked *Force* and *Sagesse*; between them is a star, marked *Beaute* (sic). The initiant is being led into the room, towards the group and the chart. He is blindfolded, coatless and dishevelled in keeping with the requirement that the candidate present himself with (in the words of the ritual answer he returns) 'my left breast bare'.

The mystery cults themselves evidently made a deliberate, an almost brain-washing, attempt to disorientate the candidate, who had to follow in the dark what was—or was made to seem —a long, twisting route. The experience must have been like visiting a children's 'grotto', but one that was deliberately made unnerving. The ordeal as a whole was a test of the candidate's nerve, and only if his nerve held did he become initiated and receive the illuminations waiting at the end of the course.

Here was a convenient and welcomely classical model for the Masons' own initiation rite, with certain extra advantages: it must (though *Die Zauberflöte* shews it was still a test of nerve) be taken as a philosophical allegory, since no one now lent belief to the classical gods; and at the same time it might be used to reinforce the Masonic claim to antiquity—no doubt the

---

* A terracotta relief in the Museo Nazionale, Rome, shews a priestess standing behind an Eleusinian initiant and veiling his head.

rites were claimed by descent from the Greco-Roman mysteries, or even from the ancient Egyptians themselves.

In the classical world it was natural that the mystery cults which conducted their initiants to a feigned Underworld and back should adopt for themselves, and read mystery references into, the many myths which recounted how a hero, during his lifetime, descended to the Underworld and succeeded in returning to the upper world afterwards. In Greek literature, the scriptural account of the Underworld was Homer's—though Homer, perhaps with a certain scepticism, does not vouch for it himself but puts the whole story into the mouth of Odysseus, who relates in the first person how he visited the realm of Hades and Persephone and came back. This locus classicus was copied into Latin literature by Virgil, who, in the course of his much more self-conscious national epic, has Aeneas make the Underworld visit. Greek mythology could also produce other visitors who, perhaps because they had not been treated by the pellucid Homer, were apter material for adoption as saints of the mysteries: Orpheus, reputedly the first raconteur of all Greek mythology, with the result that the mythological picture of the Underworld could purport to be his eyewitness account after his return to the surface; Theseus, who got trapped in the Underworld and had to pass some time incarcerated there; and Herakles,* who found Theseus in the Underworld and rescued him, and whose own visit there afforded the Eleusinian mysteries the occasion to claim him both as an initiate and as a founding father.†

To know that the classical world supplied these precedents for taking a hell-visiting mythological hero as a pattern of the ordinary initiant would have been highly suggestive to the authors of *Die Zauberflöte* when they contemplated inventing a myth that should describe Masonic initiation in the form of an operatic hero's visit to hell. Neither would they have to search any abstruse classical source to come by the knowledge. It was stated for them in *Sethos*, where Terrasson identifies the arduous journey of the myths with the ordeal of Isiac initiation and

---

* Herakles visited the Underworld either to rescue Alcestis or as one of his Labours, when he was required to drag up Cerberus to ground level.

† The story was that the Lesser Mysteries were instituted specially so that Herakles might be initiated, since as a foreigner he was ineligible for the Greater. (Smith's *Dictionary Of . . . Antiquities*, Eleusinia.)

remarks that 'Hercules returning with Alceste out of hell, and Theseus condemn'd to sit there for ever,* are the two different symbols of those, who either pass'd thro', or fail'd in their trials'.[4]

This was a hint of how the story should be used as a symbol, and it shewed the symbolism to be regular and respectable classical practice. But as a matter of fact Terrasson's novel also supplied a complete model of the elements the story should contain.

(ii) Terrasson's Orpheus and 'Die Zauberflöte'

Terrasson's novel is full of moral and political purpose: and part of his moral purpose is to offer a rational explanation for the supernatural stories accepted by antiquity. This was, of course, a common enlightenment game, but the enlightenment had commonly got itself into the difficulty of having to call the admired minds of antiquity either knaves or fools. While it was easy enough to argue that mythological giants like Polypheme were merely distorted accounts of perfectly natural volcanic eruptions, it was less easy to say how the distortion had crept into the account without accusing the ancients either of deliberate, priestly fraud or of possessing very small powers of reasonable analysis (or—which was almost as grave a fault in most enlightened eyes—a wild imagination).

Terrasson may not have been the first to see a way round this dilemma, but he probably produced the most elaborate and systematic account. He borrows his rationalising process, as he does the idea that Greek religion originated in Egypt, from Diodorus Siculus. But Diodorus is a small-scale and unsystematic sceptic: Terrasson at every point enlarges and improves on him. Terrasson is not above throwing in small items of physical rationalisation, like the brazen gates which explain the apparently supernatural thunder; but he only stops by the way and is anxious to sweep on to the wholesale application of his rationalising principle.

This principle is the secrecy of the mystery cults and their habit of talking in code; and it perfectly solved the enlighten-

---

* Terrasson gets this from Virgil, who discounts the story that Herakles rescued Theseus and shews Theseus as one of the permanent sights of the Underworld.

ment's knave or fool difficulty. The mystery initiate was neither knave nor fool. He told the truth, but his vow obliged him to tell it as an apparently nonsensical fairy-tale. Here was, it could be argued, the key to the myths. Their nonsensical, supernatural outer aspect had been accepted at face value by non-initiates, without the initiates' being guilty of intention to deceive; underneath, the myths were truthful and quite un-supernatural accounts of the mystery rituals.

Terrasson had invented his hero Sethos as a travelling prince, who was needed to express and exemplify Terrasson's political message. Sethos, however, was not very apt to Terrasson's secondary purpose of rationalising Greek mythology. There was no way of linking Sethos with the myths: traditionally, the myths came from Orpheus. This is why, some way through his first volume, Terrasson is obliged to drop his own hero, who is kept in reserve for political exegesis later, and devote his narrative to the story of Orpheus.

There are in fact two Orpheus passages in *Sethos*, one a short mention and the other a complete story—the one indirectly and the other directly relevant to *Die Zauberflöte*. The novel as a whole opens with the death of the good Queen Nephte, Sethos's mother. Terrasson describes her posthumous trial, and then the conveying of her body across a lake to a mausoleum (borrowed from Diodorus[5]) called the Labyrinth. The Labyrinth is divided into an upper part dedicated to the heavenly and a lower part dedicated to the infernal deities. The idea of the body being ferried across the lake and admitted to the Labyrinth is enough to convince both Terrasson and Diodorus that this Egyptian funeral custom is the basis of the Greek myth about dead souls being ferried by Charon to the Underworld; and so it is in describing the admission of Queen Nephte's corpse to the Labyrinth that Terrasson gives us his first mythological rationalisation and makes his first mention of Orpheus. According to Terrasson, Orpheus (whom he calls 'the principal author' of 'the greek mythology'[6]) was in Egypt at the time of Nephte's funeral, which he witnessed; and it was the description Orpheus gave of the funeral when he returned to Greece which became the Greek myth of the dead soul's voyage to the Underworld.

This first mention of Orpheus was not incorporated in *Die Zauberflöte*, which takes up Terrasson's second and fuller

Orpheus narrative. However, the first mention did not escape
at least one of the probable authors of *Die Zauberflöte*—though
this fact has escaped the commentators. Seven years after *Die
Zauberflöte* (and Mozart's death), Schikaneder provided *Die
Zauberflöte* with a sequel, using the same characters. For this
he evidently turned back to Terrasson's account of how
Orpheus witnessed the funeral ceremonies at the Labyrinth,
for the title of Schikaneder's continuation of the opera is *Das
Labyrinth*.[7]

After describing the funeral of the queen, Terrasson pursues
the career—or, rather, the education—of Sethos, under the
care of his mentor Amedes (one of those tutors cum confidants
who have accompanied so many princes through the Sophocles-
Racine tradition) up to the point where Sethos decides to seek
initiation into the Isiac brotherhood. Amedes, it turns out, is
an initiate himself and has been hoping all along that Sethos
would come to this decision: it is with this in mind that Amedes
has conducted the prince to the start of the initiation course. The
course itself is underground, and the way in is through a
pyramid. Sethos and Amedes climb up the outside of the
pyramid, enter by a concealed door and, once inside the
pyramid, descend by a ladder down a well which runs through
the core of the pyramid and carries them beneath ground
level.

Here the candidate finds himself at the start of an underground system of passages, and an inscription (which he has
to read by torch light since the subterranean region is, of course,
dark) explains to him what the whole business is about:
'*Whoever goes thro' this passage alone, and without looking behind
him, shall be purify'd by fire, by water, and by air; and if he can
vanquish the fears of death, he shall return from the bowels of the
earth, he shall see light again, and he shall be intitled to the privilege
of preparing his mind for the revelation of the mysteries of the great
goddess* Isis'.[8]

Prince Sethos decides that he *will* go 'thro' this passage
alone': being forbidden to look back, he does not know that his
already initiated mentor is allowed to follow him at a distance,
to make sure no physical harm comes to him. Of this there is
some danger; for as the candidate proceeds along the dark
course the inscription's promise of purification by fire, by water

and by air is fulfilled in the form of an obstacle race consisting of ordeals by fire, by water and by air.

First the candidate passes between two piles of burning wood and crosses a red-hot grating, where there is in fact space for his feet between the bars though it looks as if there is not. (Terrasson takes the opportunity to rationalise, on the same lines, other 'fiery trials, of which history makes mention'.) Next comes the ordeal by water: the candidate must swim across an underground canal. At the far side the ordeal by air awaits him. He lands on a drawbridge beside a door with two large rings in it. Naturally, he grasps the rings: but when he does so his touch sets in motion machinery which noisily begins to raise the drawbridge under his feet. The lamp which has guided him so far is inevitably overturned into the canal by the rising bridge. This is the final test of nerve. If the candidate retreats, he will break the rule about not looking back; if he holds on to the rings, he will suffer the ordeal by air, inasmuch as he will be suspended in the air—and in the dark—over the canal. But if he endures this, the machinery eventually opens the door, and he finds himself admitted to the temple of the priests.

Having launched Sethos on this adventure, Terrasson suddenly picks up his other hero Orpheus and decides to relate how Orpheus fared on the same obstacle course. He begins by giving his own, rather charming, account of the Orpheus myth. Orpheus, already a famous poet, decides to leave Greece and visit Egypt with the express purpose of seeking the Isiac initiation—being, in a thoroughly eighteenth-century way, 'persuaded that his poetry would become more sublime, when he had gain'd a thorow knowledge of theology, morality, and nature, of which he had been inform'd the Egyptians were the true and only masters'. He sails, taking his wife with him; but no sooner have they landed in Egypt than Eurydice feels 'a little smart in her heel, which she did not think of consequence enough to mention to her husband'; of this insect sting she dies that night, at the inn. Orpheus, too grief-stricken to introduce himself to anyone, lets her be buried in the catacomb reserved for foreigners. Disconsolate, he wanders by the catacombs, which are close to the pyramids, and overhears superstitious chatter about the dead walking in the underground passages linking the catacombs and the pyramids. Next night, taking a lamp and 'his lyre, which had lain unstrung for a long time', he enters a pyramid alone and makes 'its long echoing vaults ring with the name of his Eurydice'. He comes on what is, unknown to him, the well which leads to the subterranean initiation course and, determined to find either Eurydice or death, descends. At the bottom he hears 'a compleat musick', including female voices, one of which he fancies (but the rationalistic Terrasson does not support him for a second) to be Eurydice's. This affords him 'some consolation'. 'But', Terrasson continues, 'his satisfaction was yet greater, at reading the inscription'—which he also finds at the bottom of the well and which is the one beginning 'Whoever goes thro' this passage alone . . .'

It is at this point that Terrasson gives his most useful hint to the authors of *Die Zauberflöte*. When Orpheus reads the inscription, 'He saw that he was at the very gate of the initiation, which had been the occasion of his voyage, though the loss of his wife had made him forget it: But then joining both ideas, and giving up his imagination to his desires, he believ'd that the initiation would lead him to the mansion of the souls of the blessed, and that, perhaps, he might bring back Eurydice from thence.'

It was just this 'joining both ideas' which created the original plan for *Die Zauberflöte*, in which Tamino's quest for Pamina in the Underworld was at the same time to constitute his initiation.

Orpheus then goes through the ordeals, failing (where Sethos succeeds) at the final one. Instead of holding on to the rings, Orpheus retreats and looks back. He resigns himself to death and comforts himself by playing his lyre: whereupon the priests, who have, unseen themselves, been overseeing his progress, recognise that he 'can be no other than the renown'd Orpheus'. In consideration of his bereavement and of his courage in entering the pyramid alone instead of by the orthodox method in the company of an initiate, they remit the last ordeal and invite him into the temple for initiation. Terrasson allows him, however, not a whit of supernatural comfort for the death of Eurydice. 'Your only consolation', the priests tell him, 'will be in that virtue, of which our goddess, by our means, will explain to you the true principles.' The fact that, in the myth which was really a disguised account of his initiation, Orpheus afterwards claimed that he did see Eurydice in the Underworld Terrasson explains surprisingly psychologically: Orpheus connected what passed in his mind at the final ordeal with what really did happen, and came to believe that if he had not looked back he would have seen Eurydice.

(iii) '*Die Zauberflöte*' *and the Underground City*

In borrowing Terrasson's account of the Isiac initiation, *Die Zauberflöte*, with so much less space at its disposal, has had to make a marked condensation, as well as changing some of the material for dramatic purposes.

In Terrasson's novel, the candidate who succeeds in the last ordeal, that of being suspended in the air, finds himself admitted to the temple. (Evidently the machinery raises him from the subterranean to ground level, fulfilling the inscription's promise that if he comes through the ordeals 'he shall return from the bowels of the earth' and 'shall see light again'.) Just so, when Tamino and Pamina have come through their ordeals, they are immediately invited to enter the temple.

For Tamino and Pamina, however, this is the culmination: they are now initiated. 'The consecration of Isis is now yours', the Chorus announces, immediately before bidding them enter the temple—'Der Isis Weihe ist nun dein! Kommt, tretet in den Tempel ein!'[9] By the typically Mozartian idiom which Mozart had used in the couplet of his own signing his letter just after his marriage, the Chorus addresses the two in the singular, as a 'noble pair': indeed, by a typically Mozartian amalgamation, the ordeals, the initiation and the welding of husband and wife into one life are all accomplished at the same moment.

Terrasson, on the other hand, has so many philosophical points to make that he has to spin the initiation out. In fact, the inscription has promised no more than that the candidate who comes through the ordeals shall be entitled to prepare his mind for the revelation; and this preparation constitutes the second stage of the initiation. The initiation as a whole is in Terrasson threefold: the ordeals (themselves threefold); the preparation; and the revelation.

The preparation lasts fourscore and one days, during which the candidate lodges with the priests, practises a graded austerity about diet and also about talking, and receives moral instruction, on which he is examined at the end. Terrasson's notion of moral being largely social and political, the princeliness of his hero here becomes useful to him again, and it is with Sethos as its centre that he tells this part of his narrative. As a matter of fact, Sethos has already received the main lesson, that 'a king, who loves his subjects, always looks upon war as a misfortune',[10] from his tutor Amedes; but he is now given a second dose of instruction in object-lessons laid before him by the priests, who are particularly opposed to kings who make war for their own glory at the expense of their subjects' lives.

This lesson is, of course, standard enlightenment doctrine, and it is amusing that the high-priest (in defence, no doubt, of eighteenth-century imperialism) qualifies it by adding that 'To conquer nations, who are destitute of master and laws, in order to make them more happy and more polite than they were before, is allowable'.[11] Similarly, the Rousseauist paradise on earth which Bernardin de Saint-Pierre depicts in *Paul et Virginie* is compatible with slave-owning: indeed, one of the instances of Virginie's exceptional virtue is that she returns a runaway slave, though she does beg the owner to be kinder in future. In general, it is an illuminating example of the uniformity of enlightened thinking that several of Terrasson's judgments of 1731 reappear in Bernardin de Saint-Pierre's pastoral fable of 1787. Saint-Pierre's hero Paul agrees with Terrasson's preface in finding novels preferable to history.* Terrasson would have approved of Paul's choice of *Télémaque* as his favourite book of all, and also of Paul's exception to the general virtue of novels —licentious ones, by which Paul is 'tout boulversé'. Terrasson, whose Isiac priests emphasise at such length the immorality of rulers who make war vaingloriously, would have endorsed Paul's objection to history, namely that it is full of unhappinesses whose cause Paul cannot see, of 'guerres sans sujet et sans objet, des intrigues obscures, des nations sans caractère, et des princes sans humanité'.

When Terrasson's candidate has satisfied his priestly examiners, he starts on the final stage of initiation, which recompenses him for all the arduousness that has gone before

---

* Terrasson as the author and Paul as the hero of a novel may be supposed to be interested parties: as Jane Austen was to put it in the fifth chapter of *Northanger Abbey*, 'Alas! if the heroine of one novel be not patronised by the heroine of another, from whom can she expect protection and regard?'

and by which 'human curiosity' is 'fully satisfy'd'. This final manifestation of all the secrets of the sect entails a second visit to the underground region. During the ordeals, it turns out, the candidate has visited only a small portion of what is, in fact, an underground metropolis.

Here Terrasson's secondary hero, Orpheus, is brought back into play, because Terrasson wants to use the secret underground city as a rational explanation of the myth of the Underworld. Terrasson justifies the claims of Orpheus and other mythological travellers to have visited the Underworld in the sense, and only in the sense, that 'the initiates . . . travell'd, as it were, into another world'.[12] What appears in the myth as the supernatural confine and, on occasion, the torture-chamber of the dead is really, according to Terrasson, the perfectly this-worldly underground city run and inhabited by the perfectly flesh and blood officials of the secret cult.

In taking his hero to an Underworld, Terrasson is following his immediate literary model, *Les Aventures de Télémaque*, where Télémaque descends to the mythological Underworld in the course of his search for his father, Odysseus; and *Les Aventures de Télémaque* was itself, of course, following the example of Virgil and Homer (who had taken Telemachus's father on the same journey). Terrasson's, however, is an Underworld of perfectly live people; and since his concern is to rationalise away the supernatural Underworld he takes care to have Orpheus see, during his initiation-tour of the secret but natural Underworld, such sights as would readily convert into the supernatural features of the Underworld of myth.

As one would expect in a moral tale of the enlightenment, a great part of Terrasson's underground city is given over to education. The children of the priests attend an underground school, and are made accustomed to underground life from the start. Indeed, the first department of the metropolis is a lying-in hospital—which is made to explain Virgil's statement that the first department of the Underworld is reserved to babies who died at the breast.[13] There is a garden given over to sport and serious theatrical entertainments* (made out to be the original of the myth's Elysian fields) and a prison for erring

---

* These Terrasson identifies with the tableaux shewn to initiates at the Eleusinia (which he equates with the Isiac mysteries).

officers and priests of the cult (justification for Orpheus's mythological account of the punishments inflicted on dead sinners in Tartarus). Terrasson also tells us that candidates who present themselves for initiation in a spirit of vainglory, and who prove incorrigible, are kept for ever underground; the priests take 'pleasure in ridding the world of them, by sending them to exercise their valour and cunning in their subterraneous mansions. Many of those conquerors and politicians so famed in our histories', Terrasson takes the opportunity to add, 'would have been bury'd alive here'[14]—a point he has borrowed direct from *Les Aventures de Télémaque*, whose hero is perturbed to discover, during his visit to the mythological Underworld, that some of the worst-punished shades in Tartarus are those who were kings on earth.*

What *Die Zauberflöte* has done with Terrasson's three stages of initiation is to omit the middle, prosy one and amalgamate the first and last—that is, the ordeals and the final revelation, both of which, in Terrasson, take place underground. In Terrasson, the candidate who has, wittingly or, like Orpheus, unwittingly, arrived at the start of the system of underground passages first learns that what lies ahead of him is the initiation course by reading an inscription. The idea that the candidate should pick up his first clue to the whole affair by reading a written notice had not vanished from *Die Zauberflöte*, where Tamino first learns that he has come upon the Isiac brotherhood by reading the inscriptions on the doors and columns of the temples.[15] However, most of the information which in *Sethos* the candidate learns from the inscription at the start of the course is in *Die Zauberflöte* sung—not in advance of the ordeals, but during them—by the two armed men.

These two figures are themselves a condensation of the three helmeted men† in *Sethos* whom the candidate meets further

---

* With a governessy type of leniency, Fénelon makes their punishment consist of hearing a recital of their crimes together with a recital of the praise they were accustomed to receive on earth from their flatterers, because 'ils n'ont point besoin d'autres châtimens de leur fautes, que leur fautes mêmes'. What most especially perturbs Télémaque is to see a number of kings condemned in Tartarus who have passed on earth for 'des rois assez bons' but who in fact let themselves be ruled by 'des hommes méchans & artificieux' (XVIII).

† Terrasson has of course invented these three men, whose helmets bear a portrait of the dog Anubis, in such a way that they will rationalise the three-headed Underworld dog Cerberus.

along the route to the ordeals and who reinforce the inscription he has already read by telling him: 'We are not posted here to stop your passage; Go on, if the gods have given you the courage: but if you are so unfortunate as to return, we shall stop your passage: As yet you may go back, but from this moment you'll never get out of this place, unless you go on, without turning or looking back'.[16]

This subsidiary message, too, has its equivalent in *Die Zauberflöte*. It is delivered to Tamino by one of the priests who come in to visit him and Papageno when they are already groping in the dark before the ordeal of keeping silence begins. 'Prince', the priest says to Tamino, 'there is still time to turn back. One step more, and it will be too late'.[17]

However, the main outline of the proceedings is given in *Sethos* by the inscription and in *Die Zauberflöte* by the two armed men; and if one compares the *Sethos* inscription* with the text the two armed men sing,† it turns out that *Die Zauberflöte* has made in part a literal translation and in part an adaptation of Terrasson.

The *Sethos* stipulation that the candidate must not look back is dropped.‡ So is the stipulation that he must travel alone— to the obvious advantage of the opera, since an operatic hero travelling alone would be forced to soliloquise; *Die Zauberflöte* much more dramatically arranges for Tamino to start the course with Papageno as his companion and finish it with Pamina. The *Sethos* promise that the candidate who succeeds at the ordeals shall have the right to prepare himself for the final revelation has also to be omitted, because the opera omits the preparatory stage of the initiation to which it refers.

The *Sethos* inscription, outlining as it does a much more complicated initiation, mentions two distinct illuminations:

* 'Whoever goes thro' this passage alone, and without looking behind him, shall be purify'd by fire, by water, and by air: and if he can vanquish the fears of death, he shall return from the bowels of the earth, and he shall see light again, and he shall be intitled to the privilege of preparing his mind for the revelation of the mysteries of the great goddess Isis.' (Lediard's translation, Volume I, p. 155.)

† 'Der, welcher wandert diese Strasse voll Beschwerden, wird rein durch Feuer, Wasser, Luft und Erden; wenn er des Todes Schrecken überwinden kann, schwingt er sich aus der Erde himmelan.' (Act II, No. 21, Adagio.)

‡ —though, as I have already said, it appears, transmuted and by way of a reminiscence both of Gluck's Orpheus and of another part of Terrasson, in the stipulation that Tamino must not speak to Pamina.

one at the finish of the ordeals when the candidate shall come up from the bowels of the earth and see light again; and one at the final revelation. The opera, having decided to condense these two stages into one, naturally has to amalgamate the two illuminations into one; and it does so by taking the *Sethos* promise that the candidate who completes the underground ordeals shall return to the light and converting it into an intellectual apotheosis—into the enlightenment which is the object of the entire initiation. Where the *Sethos* candidate returns from the bowels to the surface of the earth, the *Zauberflöte* candidate 'swings himself out of the earth up to heaven'.

The two texts have in common: that the candidate must travel a route; that he is to undergo purificatory ordeals; that he will be initiated only if he overcomes the fear of death— 'if he can vanquish the fears of death', according to *Sethos*; 'Wenn er des Todes Schrecken überwinden kann', according to *Die Zauberflöte*.

Yet there remains a discrepancy about the ordeals themselves. *Sethos* promises purification by fire, water and air, and its narrative proceeds to shew ordeals by fire, water and suspension in the air. *Die Zauberflöte*, on the other hand, specifies that the candidate be purified by fire, water, air *and earth*—he 'wird rein durch Feuer, Wasser, Luft und Erden'.

So *Die Zauberflöte* promises three ordeals in common with *Sethos*, plus one of its own. When it comes to fulfilling the promise, the ordeals by fire and water are transferred, if not directly, at least recognisably, from the novel to the opera. The novel has already rationalised away almost any risk from the ordeal by fire; as for that by water, although a tenor cannot be expected to swim a canal as readily as the hero of a novel, stage management can turn the ordeal into a pretty and spectacular effect of some sort of cascade. Indeed, the ideas of firelight and water offered such opportunities for spectacle that the opera combines these two ordeals and, where *Sethos* had placed them first, makes them into the grand spectacular culmination of the obstacle race.

On the other hand, the ordeal by air as Terrasson describes it—hanging by two rings while a drawbridge recedes from under one's feet—was certainly too much of an ordeal to ask of a tenor.* But it is not hard to see what the opera has substituted for it (and which the authors may sardonically have thought was hardly a smaller ordeal for a tenor): the ordeal of keeping silence, of not expelling the air in one's lungs as words. This would come readily to the authors' minds as a counterpart to the ordeal of not looking imposed on Gluck's Orpheus, and as a matter of fact it is borrowed from the exercises in self-control imposed on Terrasson's candidate during the middle stage of initiation, the stage which is otherwise wholly omitted from the opera.

There remains the ordeal by earth. Not only has this no counterpart in *Sethos*: it appears to have no counterpart in *Die Zauberflöte*. The armed men seem to have introduced mention of it gratuitously. Tamino undergoes, quite recognisably, all the other ordeals they specify, but nothing in the action of the opera seems to tally with the ordeal by earth.

However, an explanation of this might occur to anyone in the audience who had read *Sethos* and would be obvious, we may conjecture, to anyone who had himself undergone Masonic initiation, though not to outsiders: the whole of the initiation in *Die Zauberflöte* is an ordeal by earth, inasmuch as all the ordeals take place, as they do in *Sethos, in* the earth.

By what I have conjectured to be the original plan for the opera, Tamino was to seek Pamina in the Underworld, in which case Act Two would naturally have been set underground. In the final version, the setting is not changed, though Sarastro is no longer a wicked Hades-figure but high priest of the Isiac brotherhood; 'Sarastro's town', where Pamina is held captive, has become the equivalent of the underground city of the brotherhood in *Sethos*. The first version was altered because, by explicitly mentioning the Underworld in connexion with initiation, it hinted too plainly that Masonic initiation consisted of a visit to the Underworld. The final version does not include an Underworld as part of its story. That its initiation ordeals are in fact taking place beneath the ground it hints only by such clues as initiates alone could decipher.

* Possibly, however, the librettists had forgotten that the *Sethos* ordeal could not be literally represented on the stage (or had not yet tackled the problem of how to do it) when they spoke of the successful candidate swinging himself up to heaven, since in *Sethos* the candidate is in the end swung by the machinery up to ground level again.

The prime clue is the darkness of the underground setting, which is explicitly said to be the darkness of death: Tamino and Pamina, in making their way through the initiation course, are going 'through death's gloomy night'—'durch des Todes düst're Nacht'.[18] At the start of the course, Papageno calls for lights.[19] Moreover, just as the initiant really was in the simulated Underworld of the mystery (or, we may conjecture, the Masonic) initiation, Papageno is quite disconcerted and disorientated by the dark: 'Tamino! Tamino!' he cries, 'will you abandon me altogether? If only I had the smallest idea where I was?'—'Wenn ich nur wenigstens wüsste, wo ich wäre?'[20]

A still more blatant hint is dropped when Papageno fails the first ordeal, that of silence. One of the priests tells him what punishment he has earned, though, in keeping with the leniency advocated by both *Sethos* and *Die Zauberflöte*, the punishment is remitted, it being punishment enough that Papageno will never now achieve initiation. What Papageno is said to deserve, however, is a punishment which scarcely makes sense unless Papageno is at the time *in* the earth: it is 'to wander for ever in the deepest clefts of the earth'—'Du hättest verdient', the priest tells him, 'auf immer in finsteren Klüften der Erde zu wandern'.[21] This is a distinct enough echo first of the warning delivered to the candidate in *Sethos* when he is already proceeding through one of the deepest clefts of the earth, that if he fails he will 'never get out of this place', and secondly of the punishment which in *Sethos* is inflicted on vainglorious candidates, who are kept where they are and sent to labour in the priests' 'subterranean mansions'.

(iv) *Had the Librettists read Lucian?*

Terrasson approaches both the myths and the mystery cults in a spirit of plodding rationalism. This was, however, by no means the mystery cults' own spirit. The Eleusinia were old and respectable, whereas the cult of Isis as described by Apuleius bore rather the relation to orthodox classical religion which spiritualism does to the Church of England: but both mysteries were extending hope of life after death, both did their utmost to impress the reality of the supernatural on their initiates' belief, and neither seems to have scrupled to impose on the initiates' credulity.

If eighteenth-century Masonry adapted the initiation rite of these supernatural religions for its own morally educative rite, it must have made a very particular adaptation which almost reversed the original content. Among its classical authorities it must have carefully picked out the information it required while for the most part ignoring the spirit. Apuleius, for all his golden storytelling, is flighty- if not positively vulgar-minded. Even Diodorus, with whose uninspired rationalism Terrasson obviously felt an affinity, is rational only piecemeal and has not built his rationalism into either an intellectual system or an emotional habit of mind.

There was, however, a late-classical authority who dealt with the mystery cults and their visit to the Underworld in a spirit not only of rationalism but of scepticism: Lucian, who, of all Greek writers, comes nearest to anticipating the enlightenment, except that he quite lacks its moralising and philosophising tone. Indeed, the enlightenment as represented by men like Terrasson (who ignores him) may well have found Lucian's satire too anarchical and sardonic and have felt that his scepticism left not even scepticism sacred. Lucian is, rather, the Voltaire of the ancient world. And it seems that his Voltairean manner and elegantly, almost manneredly pure Greek prose (together, perhaps, with his reputation—which had made his name execrated in the middle ages—of being an early opponent of Christianity) did make him popular in some enlightened circles. An edition was published in Amsterdam in 1743; there was an English translation in 1711, with a life of Lucian by Dryden; and his latest English translator[22] mentions Lucianesque compositions and borrowings by Swift and Fielding. (Fielding's sister knew of Lucian, too, as I shall mention in a moment.) It seems not unlikely that from England Lucian was carried abroad in the spread either of the enlightenment per se or of Freemasonry, which I think must have taken an interest in him for his references to the mysteries.

Lucian satirises the rich; philosophy; and people who will believe tall stories. (He is the inventor of the Sorcerer's Apprentice.) Among tall stories he includes superstitions, the myths about the gods and the revelations of the mysteries. His great satirical device is adapted from Socrates (to whom he makes acknowledgement by taking, as his favourite form, the dialogue) and anticipates Voltaire: it consists of a clear-eyed, faux-naïf hero—in fact, a Candide. To create one of these heroes, Lucian borrowed the persona of the Cynic Menippos who had lived some two centuries before. Lucian's Menippos starts life full of good will towards the established religion. He swallows everything he reads in Homer and Hesiod about the quarrels, wars, adulteries, rapes and acts of incest committed by the gods, believes all these acts must be good and feels in himself—a purely Voltairean touch—a strong desire to emulate them. But when he grows up he finds the law forbids them. Convinced, like any Candide, that philosophy must hold the answer to true morality, Menippos applies to the philosophers, only to find them contradicting one another and not practising what they preach. So he decides to inquire of the great men of antiquity: and to do so he must visit the Underworld.

Lucian first hits at the myths: Menippos's visit to the Underworld is reported in Menippos's own words, and there is nothing but his word to vouch for it: just so, Lucian hints, there is nothing to vouch for the existence of the Underworld at all except the reports of visitors like Odysseus, Orpheus and Herakles all of whom may have become, in the myth-makers' hands, as fictitious as Menippos has become in Lucian's. Menippos meets a friend who asks where he has been lately: Menippos discloses he has been in the Underworld: the friend begs for an account: Menippos replies, like an initiate of the mysteries, that he fears punishment for giving away secrets. The friend, however, urges that he knows how to keep a secret, since he is himself an initiate. Menippos lets himself be persuaded to describe his journey and how it was made possible.

Once he has decided to take the journey Menippos receives authoritative advice about the equipment he needs. He is to take a cap, a lyre and a lionskin—the emblems of, respectively, Odysseus, Orpheus and Herakles, his mythological predecessors on the visit to the Underworld, who, Lucian is implying, were invoked by the mysteries as saintly patterns for the initiant who followed in their steps. Lucian's opinion of the efficacy of this enrolment in a saintly pattern is conveyed by his making Charon so gullible as actually to mistake the lionskinned Menippos for Herakles and therefore admit him to the Underworld.

It is in the account of how Menippos comes by this advice

about how he should equip himself that there lies a tiny mark which suggests that the authors of *Die Zauberflöte* knew of this Underworld dialogue of Lucian's. Terrasson was not their informant. They may have read Lucian for themselves or, which is perhaps more likely, he may have been studied by the Masons and the information transferred to Masonic lore. However they came on it, one detail of Lucian's narrative seems to have lodged in their memory. Menippos says that when he had made up his mind to visit the Underworld he decided 'to go to Babylon and ask a favour of one of the Magi, the disciples and successors of Zoroaster' (τινος τῶν μάγων τῶν Ζωροάστρου μαθητῶν καὶ διαδόχων). 'I had heard', Menippos continues, 'that they, through certain enchantments and initiations, open the gates of Hades and lead down anyone they like in safety and send him back up again'.[23]* This presumably is why, when the authors of *Die Zauberflöte* were casting about for an exotic, wizardish and yet august name to give to a character who presides over initiations which lead the candidate down into the Underworld and then return him safely to the upper world, it was the name of Zoroaster which suggested itself to them to be reshaped into Sarastro.

(v) *The Initiation a Re-Birth*

Like most religious initiation rites, including the Christian one of baptism,† the mystery initiation was a death and a re-birth. Just as the baptised infant undergoes a token death by

---

* Lucian's idea that the way to visit the Underworld was by the help of an oriental wizard was evidently well known in the eighteenth century, since it is mentioned by Fielding's sister, Sarah. Admittedly her text, at least as reproduced in the Scholartis Press edition, misprints *Lucan* for *Lucian*; but then in the same sentence it transforms the kingdom of Pluto into 'the gloomy Realms of *Plato*'. In 1757 Sarah Fielding published a piece of historical fiction consisting of the lives of Cleopatra and Octavia as narrated in the first person by themselves. In her Introduction, she facetiously accounts for these verbatim reports thus: 'The Author begs to [sic] Leave to account for her Interview with those Heroines, as *Homer*, *Virgil*, *Aristophanes*, *Lucan* [sic], and others, have on the like Occasion, through the Assistance of an Eastern Sorcerer or Magician, who conveyed her to the gloomy Realms of *Plato* [sic] and . . . prevailed on that grand Monarch to command those celebrated Shades to give her a faithful Detail of their Lives, during their Abode on Earth'. Although all four of the authorities she names wrote narratives or dramas of a visit to the Underworld, it is only Lucian who introduces the 'Assistance of an Eastern Sorcerer'.

† —which the Anglican Catechism defines as 'a death unto sin, and a new birth unto righteousness'.

drowning while the priest prays that he 'may be born again', so the Eleusinian initiant descended into the realm of the dead and then re-emerged from the body of the earth which is so regularly recognised as a—indeed, as *the*—mother.* Similarly, the priest who prepares Apuleius's hero-narrator for initiation into the cult of Isis tells him that initiation is 'like to a voluntary death', and that even people who are on the verge of death can by its grace be brought back to health and made 'as it were new-born'.[24]

To the metaphor of death and re-birth the myths and rites contribute details of some precision. To descend into the earth is, of course, to be buried. At the same time, the darkness of the inside of the earth, in which the candidate could not see his way, signifies that dead people cannot see even if their eyes are open. 'This is extraordinary', Papageno remarks as he gropes in the darkness in which the attendants have left the candidates; 'every time the gentlemen leave one alone, one can't see a thing even with one's eyes open' ('so oft einen die Herren verlassen, so sieht man mit offenen Augen nichts').[25] When the candidate emerges from this darkness and, as the *Sethos* inscription promises he shall, sees light again, he comes to light just as the baby does at birth: it is the metaphor in which Lucretius wonderfully describes the new-born baby as 'poured out on the shores of light, like a sailor cast forth from the waves'.[26]

To the coming-to-light metaphor, Lucretius has added the metaphor on which baptism relies. Not only is the infant token-drowned in the waters of the font; his subsequent re-birth is also signified by his emerging, with obstetrical correctness, head first, from the waters which are made to break over and then recede from his head. It must have been with hardly less verisimilitude that the transparent veil slithered like water from the head of the successful Eleusinian candidate, though primarily the veil reinforced the other metaphor of entering darkness and then coming to light. The Underworld myth, though it, too, emphasises chiefly the darkness-light metaphor, does not neglect the metaphor of water: the very geography of the Underworld provides a river or lake as boundary, so that

---

* It is no doubt in order to bring out this significance in the candidate's emerging from the Eleusinian initiation that Diodorus Siculus (I, 12) insists on interpreting the name of the Eleusinian goddess Demeter as Ge-meter (= earth-mother).

none of the mythological visitors to hell can leave again without being re-born in the sense of emerging from the uterine waters.

In *Sethos* the ordeal by water, swimming across an underground canal, follows immediately after the ordeal by fire; in *Die Zauberflöte*, the ordeals by fire and by water are combined: both their juxtaposition in the novel and their combination in the opera may be references to another geographical feature of the Underworld of myth—Pyriphlegethon, the river of flaming fire. In this river, the unconscious has invented, and the conscious may have correctly understood, a condensed but accurate description of childbirth: Pyriphlegethon combines a mention of the uterine waters with the idea of the burning sensation experienced by the mother.*

When Terrasson makes over the Isiac initiation to his own moralising purpose, he quite accepts the metaphor of initiation as a re-birth for the candidate. Indeed, he draws on the very language of the Christian initiation, whose purpose is that 'the old Adam in this Child may be so buried, that the new man may be raised up in him':[27] similarly, 'an initiate', according to Terrasson, 'is a new man'. Up to a point, Terrasson even agrees with Christianity about what is to die and what is to replace it. If the Christian initiate has renounced the world, the flesh and the devil, Terrasson's initiate has ceased to be 'a man of passions'. But where the Christian has, thanks to God's grace and an act of redemption on God's part, become able to tap a supernatural source of grace (and baptism makes him eligible for the communion sacrament where he can renew his supplies), Terrasson's initiate has changed from the man of passions into the 'man of principle', and his principles draw

---

* Cf. Grantly Dick-Read (*Childbirth Without Fear*, XII):— 'The stretching of the vulva is felt as a burning sensation. A woman must be forewarned of this for it may be very frightening.' Pursuing the metaphor of the candidate's re-birth from the Underworld, the mysteries may well have come to a conscious inkling that this burning sensation was imaged in the Underworld river of flaming fire. In another context it was not beyond the understanding of the renaissance iconographer Vincenzo Cartari or his classical source, Pausanias, to take the burning sensation in the mother as an alternative to the idea of the baby's coming to light: Cartari explains that Diana, patroness of childbirth, holds a burning torch 'either because women in parturition feel very severe pains . . . or because this Goddess was the bringer of light to babies being born' (quoted by E. Panofsky: *The Iconography Of Correggio's Camera di San Paolo*, IV, d, footnote).

their sanction not from the supernatural but from the natural world.

(vi) *Original goodness*

Terrasson has, in fact, borrowed the Isiac initiation for a purpose quite opposed to what the Isiac religion intended—and equally, which was probably Terrasson's real point, to what the Christian religion intended. The ascetic tradition in Greek theology, to which the mysteries belonged, quite agreed with Christianity in finding the original and unrefined nature of man partly evil or prone to evil. Christian theology explained man's proneness to evil by the Fall of his ancestors, Adam and Eve; Greek theology explained his partially evil nature by his descent[28] from the ashes of the Titans, who had been burnt up by Zeus's thunderbolt in punishment for their having eaten Zeus's divine son Dionysos: man was, therefore, evil through the Titan in his ancestry, but also a touch divine through his descent from the fragments of the god the Titans had so eucharistically ingested.

In religions with a theology of this sort, the initiation sacrament is designed to bury (by a descent into the earth) or drown (in the baptismal font) or otherwise do to death the evil part of man's heredity, whether that part is explained as the old Adam or the old Titan; and then the sacrament accords a second, and this time unalloyed, birth to the potentially divine and immortal part.

Within the major metaphor of killing off the old Adam, the initiation may include subsidiary ordeals, at which the candidate risks or seems to risk his life again (he has already in token forfeited it by descending to the realm of the dead), as a symbol of a progressive course of purifying the divine part from its alloy. *Sethos* and *Die Zauberflöte* agree that their ordeals are purifications. The Eleusinian myth drops a large hint that the Eleusinian candidate, too, was subjected to some ordeal by refining fire when it relates how the lamenting Demeter came in disguise to Eleusis, took employment as nurse to a child and every night secretly put the child into the fire. By this baptism by fire by instalments, the goddess intended to make the child 'unageing and immortal',[29] presumably by burning away the corruptible and mortal part of his nature; and no doubt the

Eleusinian initiation included some fire rite designed to do the same for the candidate. The myth continues, however, with the child's mother finding out what the nurse was up to and putting a stop to it—whereby, presumably, the myth makes the child into a type of the initiant who loses his nerve and does not complete the course.

This view of man's nature, as partly so prone to evil as to need burning away, was the very opposite of the view taken by the enlightenment, which assailed no Christian tenet more fiercely than that of original sin. So far from seeing any need to burn away nature by supernatural, sacramental means, the enlightenment was for blazing a path back to nature by the light of reason. Terrasson allows his rationalised priests of Isis not a shred of supernatural powers—he even rationalises away their supposed gifts of divination; but he credits them with the most comprehensive scientific knowledge of nature, describes in detail their museum (a collection of botanical and mineral specimens) and the royal Egyptian zoo, and makes the priests expert mathematicians and engineers. In the eyes of the enlightenment, natural sciences go hand in hand with morality: indeed, morality—as compared with the more-than-natural science of theology—is a natural science. The moral instruction given to Terrasson's candidate rests its validity on natural discoveries, not supernatural revelation; and Terrasson makes quite clear what he means by initiation into the mysteries of Isis when he speaks of 'Isis, the mother of nature, or nature herself'.[30]

Die Zauberflöte is equally explicit on the side of the enlightenment. The enlightenment grants that there has been a Fall, or at least a falling-off, from man's original state of natural virtue; but fallen man is not evil—he is merely confused, ignorant and misled. He is, in other words, Papageno, who describes himself as 'ein Naturmensch'.[31] Lacking strength of will and intellect, Papageno will never attain enlightenment; but he does get his Papagena, and the two will breed happily and not unrighteously ever after.

Tamino, on the other hand, is capable of attaining a higher state; but Die Zauberflöte makes it quite plain that this higher state is natural and this-worldly. Where Christian theology held that the only way for fallen man to regain paradise was to avail himself of the sacraments and hope to be raised to heaven after his death by God's favour, Die Zauberflöte explicitly propounds a heaven on earth, which can be built by enlightened mortals—enlightened mortals being 'equal to the gods'. Its heaven is, in other words, the enlightenment's ideal of a just society, ordered by rational and disinterested men: and the 'path' to this heaven is the initiation course, which inculcates the natural moral virtues of enlightenment: 'When virtue and righteousness strew the path of the great with glory, then is the earth a heaven-state, and mortals equal to the gods' ('dann ist die Erd' ein Himmelreich, und Sterbliche den Göttern gleich').[32] It is in this rational sense that the successful candidate swings himself up to heaven: in the sense that earth can be made a heaven—by men who have acquired, by practising the natural sciences, the miracle-working powers, and, by practising natural morality, the virtues, which used to be attributed to the gods.

(vii) *The Metaphor of Enlightenment*

Although Die Zauberflöte sets itself such a resolutely earthly paradise, its principal event takes place in the heavens—but not in heaven. The return of Tamino and Pamina, now welded into one life, from the darkness of the Underworld is crowned by yet a further climax and a yet more powerful application of the theme of coming to light. The Queen (who has by now wholly taken on her evil character and is fully identified with the powers of darkness—her hench-women have just acclaimed her under the title Queen of the Night) admits that she and her train are defeated and have 'all fallen into eternal night' ('wir alle gestürzet in ewige Nacht');[33] whereupon Sarastro expands her metaphor by proclaiming that 'the rays of the sun drive out the night and nullify the hypocrite's power' ('Die Strahlen der Sonne vertreiben die Nacht, zernichten der Heuchler erschlichene Macht').[34]

This manifestation of the sun is in every sense the final climax of the opera: for by a metaphor of shining simplicity it *is* the revelation of the mysteries which Tamino has laboured through the darkness to attain.

The metaphor is borrowed, of course, from the moon-and-sun symbolism of the Isiac cult. Apuleius's hero tells us that during his initiation he saw the sun coruscating with white light in the middle of the night ('nocte media vidi solem candido coruscantem lumine'[35])—an effect, presumably, of priestly stagecraft. No doubt the message was that, just as the sun rises again each morning after its nightly death, so the sun-god Osiris, though murdered, was resurrected; and probably this story was interpreted as holding promise of eternal life for the initiate.

Having borrowed the metaphor, however, *Die Zauberflöte* utterly converts its meaning; and in this it presumably reflects Masonic practice. The message is now more likely to be that the sun is simply the sun, the source of light for a wholly natural universe, whose mysteries the equally natural light of reason was exploring and which, having been harmoniously designed in the first place by a supreme architect, stood in no need of miraculous resurrections or sacramental redemptions. The sun which rises at the end of *Die Zauberflöte* is the light already in the universe: what the initiate has been taught is to appreciate its proper value and put it to its proper use, in which case it proves sufficient to search out and reveal the mysteries of nature, to expose hypocrisy and to defeat evil—evil being not a power in itself but a symptom of the muddled and short-sighted condition of man while he remains in the darkness of ignorance.

Darkness is scattered and Tamino has the mysteries revealed to him by the advent of light: thus *Die Zauberflöte* converts an originally religious metaphor* into the metaphor of the idea— of the very name—of the enlightenment. Perhaps because Socrates had diagnosed that man could prefer evil to good only because he was too short-sighted to see far or clearly enough, the eighteenth century adopted, to express its similar convictions, a persistent and paramount metaphor in which the blindness of ignorance and superstition was represented by darkness and the education which could alone dispel them was an enlightenment or illumination. The image whereby those who undergo a course of moral education are *illuminated* was

---

* It is a metaphor which Christianity, too, uses on occasion: not only is Christ the light of the world but he is also, more precisely still, 'the sun of justice' which has 'risen out of' the Virgin Mary—'Felix es, sacra virgo Maria . . . quia ex te ortus est sol justitiae, Christus Deus noster' (Mass for the birthday of the Virgin).

embodied in the Order of the Illuminati which the Bavarian Adam Weishaupt founded in 1776, and which seems[36] to have been a very *Zauberflöte*ish mixture of idiosyncratic Freemasonry with a re-modelling of the classical mystery cults. Perhaps it was influenced by *Sethos*; in any case, its inmost circle of initiation was called the Mysteries. The Order (which included Cagliostro, condemned by the inquisition in 1791 for freemasonry) was suppressed but not forgotten.*

Spreading from the thought of the century—and it was very much a century dominated by thought—this paramount metaphor of enlightenment quickly touched the arts. In painting, the advent of the rococo style was nothing so much as an advent of light in the tenebrist manner which preceded it. When the rococo broke up the mathematical harmonies of classical and the weighing-scale balance of baroque composition, the visual method of signifying the break-up was to let in light to the more and more irregular spaces which were created between the masses. Tiepolo, often in the lighter medium of fresco, took the roof off the interiors in which the action of 'history paintings' had often been confined and substituted a light-irradiated sky, sometimes turning a real ceiling into a fantasy heaven. Interiors themselves were, by the use of plaster, gilt, mirrors and chandeliers, changed from static arrangements of space and solids into a glitter, manifestations of light perpetually moving and occupying time as well as space, like the actual falling of water in a cascade or sparks from a firework: glass and gilt could make a room seemingly independent of its real sources of light, which they picked up and re-issued in such incalculable, unexpected ways that they really did function as indoor fireworks and by an illusion became sources of light themselves. Francesco Guardi applied oil paint in little flickers of impasto

---

* Thomas Love Peacock (himself one of the last embers of the enlightenment, Mozartite and first remarker of the connexion between *Sethos* and *Die Zauberflöte*) remembered the Illuminati and mentioned them in *Nightmare Abbey*, where (chapter X) the conversation of Celinda Toobad (who has been in Germany) includes 'encomiums on the sublime Spartacus Weishaupt, the immortal founder of the sect of the Illuminati'. (Why Peacock calls him Spartacus or whether the text should really read 'the sublime Spartacus, Weishaupt', in reference to the rebellious nature of his teaching, I do not know.) Leo Tolstoy's researches into just-post-eighteenth-century Freemasonry led him also to a mention of the Illuminati: Pierre's proposals strike his fellow-Masons as dangerously savouring of Illuminism (*War And Peace*, VI, VII).

as though his actual medium were fireworks; Watteau snatched at the last light of a departing day, Gainsborough sometimes at the strange daylight that is about to be swallowed up in a storm: both use the creases of silk clothes to trap the last of a light that is on the point of vanishing.

Indeed, the poignancy of eighteenth-century art is the impermanence of its manifestations of light—or of reason; the characteristic of eighteenth-century composition is not so much its imbalance as its momentariness. If baroque composition had suffered an explosion, composition now consisted in the actual moment of explosion, the very act whereby the compositional elements fly apart, like the single moment at which a firework actively exists before it disintegrates into the dark. In art as in thought, the enlightenment knew itself to be impermanent. Not that it doubted the truth or justice of the illumination it gave, but the reasonable point of view had nowhere been put into permanent practice. Moreover, the realistic calculation of reason's small chances was deepened into a tragic doom whose source was the unconscious certainty that, even though reason was justified, to assert so deserved punishment. Candide's intelligence walks through the world like the flame of a candle; not only do self-interested powers conspire to blow it out; sheer stupidity lurks ready to gather again once the brief illumination has passed through. For although the darkness has no power to withstand the penetration of reason it has the inexhaustible resource of going on afterwards as though reason had never shewn it up. In the eighteenth century, the old tragedy of love blotted out by an indifferent or otherwise occupied world turned into the satirical tragedy of love justifying itself by reason and nature against a world blind to both. The reasonable point of view was (and has become again) in itself poignant: because it is so piercingly *right*; and because the world which is so probably going to extinguish it will do so not because it does not agree that reason is right but because it does not care whether it is or not.

The impermanence of rococo composition represents light which has only just, and briefly, broken through the dark. Characteristically, it is fragmentary, flickering light, and in breaking up the baroque mass it disintegrates the sculpted or moulded contours of the mass into a series, a loose chain, of appliqué ornaments. Like a firework again, rococo composition consists of what is applied, not of what it is applied to. This is what happens to the vocal line in rococo music: appliqué decorations and coloratura notes execute a fioratura over the underlying—or, rather, the merely implied—shape, so that the melody itself is impermanent and unsolid, on the verge of vanishing into the surrounding silence. The outline of the melody remains perceptible or deducible, or it may even be the only part written down, being intended as a guide for the performer like the unseen framework on which the fireworks are mounted; but it is, as one would expect it to be in the operatic century, so essentially *performer*'s music that, like a firework, it only comes into complete existence during the act of performance; and then its loose, almost disintegrating chain of appliqué ornaments, aping improvisation even when they are not really improvised, emphasises that the performance itself is a momentary manifestation, on the point of vanishing outwards into the dark.

It is this coloratura-rococo which Handel, in his Italianate and operatic mood, uses to evoke the poignancy of the quest for pleasure; the reasonable and sweet plea of hero and heroine to be allowed to love, preferably in a pastoral setting, fizzles and is briefly brilliant in the surrounding darkness of policy, tyranny, infatuation or (in *Alcina*[37]) wizardry. When he moves into his English oratorio mood, Handel thickens the pure rococo into his own solid but decorated baroque. The light of reason and pastoral nature is replaced by the steadier light of an unfevered, nonsectarian religious emotion. Handel's irresistible, oceanic religious confidence is the eighteenth century's philosophical optimism raised to ultimate exaltation. But again, though he is quite certain this exaltation is *right*, Handel does not expect it to prevail in time and numbers. The rococo impermanence still characterises it, though its poignancy has become a larger effect of pity and its intellectual rightness is reinforced by heaven; Handel still knows quite well that on earth the light is despised and rejected of men. Sometimes he makes his hero— Samson or the Children of Israel—representative of civilised man, who is civilised precisely in that he is confident of the benevolence of the deity, and who is threatened with extinction by the barbaric darkness of those whose idols are far from benevolent. Again and again Handel's imagination works within the metaphor of light piercing the darkness: 'The people that walked in darkness have seen a great light'. Not surprisingly, heaven is something he *sees*—in his famous and for ever moving account of composing the Hallelujah Chorus, 'I did think I did see all Heaven before me, and the great God Himself'. Conversely, nothing so moves his pity as darkness. In *Israel In Egypt*,[38] having treated the other plagues dramatically, decoratively, exotically, comically, he reserves his tragic chorus[39] for the thick darkness, 'even darkness which may be felt'.

In *Samson*,[40] darkness has become blindness. Milton's *Samson Agonistes* was a blind poet's dramatic poem of 'that sort . . . called tragedy' about a blind hero: Newburgh Hamilton and Handel (who himself became blind nine years after writing his musical setting) seem to have unconsciously apprehended that blindness—the punishment which, in another dramatic poem of that sort called tragedy, fell on King Oedipus—was the ultimate darkness waiting to overwhelm the enlightenment for daring to see; and they have picked out the fag end of one of Milton's lines, 'total eclipse', to fashion into one of the most famous pathetic arias of the enlightenment metaphor.

In *Die Zauberflöte*, where the Queen of the Night's arias so palpably simulate a cascade of sparks, the metaphor of light bursting through darkness underlies and shapes the whole story, as it does the whole story of *Sethos*. (It is not surprising that the person to remark the connexion between the two works was Thomas Love Peacock, who himself made a last-minute defence of the enlightenment couched in its own metaphor and even equating darkness with the Underworld—a defence of the 'light diffused . . . by the progress of reason' against the burrowings of the romantic poets into hell.)

Die Zauberflöte probably borrowed the metaphor direct from Masonic ritual, which, according to a book calling itself *The Text Book Of Freemasonry*, dramatises the candidate's search for intellectual light. When the candidate applies for admission, the inner guard asks the outer 'Whom have you there?', to which the reply is 'a poor Candidate in a state of darkness'. After his admission, the candidate is asked: 'Having been kept for a considerable time in a state of darkness, what in your present situation is the predominant wish of your heart?' The candidate's answer is 'Light'. The Worshipful Master thereupon rules 'Let that blessing be restored'; the brethren raise their hands above their heads, 'the Worshipful Master utters the words, One, two, three; on the last word they simultaneously bring them down and strike the thigh; the Junior Deacon at that moment restores the light'.

Die Zauberflöte's own use of the metaphor begins with Tamino's first encounter with the brotherhood. As soon as the Orator has withdrawn after his long conversation with Tamino outside the temples, Tamino evidently becomes aware of his own lack of illumination in comparison with the man he has been speaking to, and his first solo utterance after that conversation is 'O eternal night, when will you vanish? When will the light find my eyes?' To this the reply, 'Soon or never',[41] given by the voices inside the temples, foreshadows the initiation Tamino will volunteer to undergo. He volunteers, that is, to be taken yet deeper into darkness, and this underground darkness proves, in confirmation of Tamino's first impression of the Orator, to be dark only in the absence of the initiates who have been illuminated—as we learn from Papageno's remark that the darkness descends only when the candidates are left on their own. Like a chandelier in a rococo interior, the initiate has the property of seeming to be a source of light in himself. There follows the darkest part of the ordeals, in which Tamino and Pamina journey through death's gloomy night; and it is when the initiates emerge from that night that the metaphor bursts into its final flowering with the rout of the Queen of the Night before the rising sun.

(viii) *Why the Masons visited Hell*

Die Zauberflöte converts a sun-god into rational illumination, heaven into an ideal society on earth, and the very concept of god into enlightened man, who is equal to the gods. Instead of setting up deities and abasing man before them, it raises up man to his natural status, which superstition has debased and education can restore. Not only does it explicitly say that mortals can equal the gods; equally explicitly it says that man and wife can 'attain to the godhead', emphasises that *man* is a prouder title than the attenuated divinity which superstitious ignorance credits to royalty,* and warns that those who do not delight in the doctrine of the brotherhood 'where man loves man' are not worthy of this proud title *man*.†

So pointedly rational an opera cannot fail to convert into a rational sense the mythological Underworld full of dead souls which it has borrowed for its initiation journey. The ancient mystery cults presumably took their initiants there in charade with the purpose of assuring them the myth was true, and they were probably seeking to inspire the initiants with long-term fear as well as giving them an immediate scare: the candidate was surely given a glimpse of the posthumous tortures of the damned, with the implication that the mystery sacrament might ensure his own spirit a happier fate after death. The enlightenment, however, aiming as it was at a society on earth which should be able to do without punishments and coercion, can hardly have subscribed to these supernatural menaces, even if it had believed in any but the most generalised and philosophicalised immortality after death; and the particular branch of the enlightenment which is represented by eighteenth-century Masonry, though it may well have preached or permitted a general belief in immortality, cannot—given its multisectarian membership—have been putting forward any pronounced doctrinal or mythological picture of the life after death.

Nevertheless, if *Die Zauberflöte* is any guide to its ritual, eighteenth-century Masonry chose to include the mystery visit to the life after death in its own initiation ceremony. Why and in what sense it did so is answered, perhaps, by Terrasson. His underground city rationalises utterly away the whole Greek Underworld myth. That, however, was a myth none of Terrasson's contemporaries was in any danger of believing, since it had long before been driven out by a more potent and detailed myth, which had set aside the underground region exclusively for the wicked dead, who were no longer allowed to dwell even next door to the good, and which had elaborated the punish-

---

* One of the priests asks Sarastro whether Tamino will be able to withstand the ordeals, adding—apparently with the implication that this casts doubt on Tamino's steadfastness—'He is a prince'. Sarastro, either missing the democratic innuendo or wanting to keep all democratic pronouncements for himself, replies 'Yet more —he is a man' (Act II, dialogue before No. 10).

† Sarastro's aria (Act II, No. 15):— '. . . wo Mensch den Menschen liebt . . . Wen solche Lehren nicht erfreu'n, verdienet nicht ein Mensch zu sein'.

ments inflicted on the bad souls with all the dwelling exactitude
of a sadistic fantasy.

With this myth Terrasson must, if he is to obtain his Licence
to print, deal circumspectly; and indeed he is careful to choose
a historical setting which almost avoids a direct clash. But he
need not scruple to attack the superstitious fringe beliefs which
were in fact older than Christianity and had no central doctrinal
sanction in Christian theology; and these he does attack—and
perhaps other beliefs under cover of them—in a scene which
precedes Sethos's initiation but is closely connected to it.

What happens is that Amedes, Sethos's mentor, conducts the
prince on an educational trip to the inside of a pyramid, where
there are 'several deep and dark passages'. On the educative
value of this preliminary trip (and perhaps this is a clue to the
educative nature of the initiation trip which it foreshadows)
Amedes is of the opinion 'that this trial would be an excellent
remedy against those panick fears, which are apt to seize many
people in the dark, and against the apprehension of bugbears,
with which common report[42] then fill'd all uninhabited places,
as it does now'.[43] (The 'as it does now', though strictly speaking
it applies to the time when Terrasson's fictitious Greek author
is supposed to be writing the story, seems to point to Terrasson's having at least *some* contemporary moral to emphasise.)

It is not surprising that this scene of Terrasson's, and at least
the overt part of its lesson, should have impressed Dr Johnson,
who seems to have had personal and gloomy experience of the
fears of death. Johnson lifted the scene more or less bodily and
used it when he took *his* travelling prince, Rasselas, to Egypt
and into the inside of a pyramid. The superstitious members of
Rasselas's party demur; but ' "If all your fear be of apparitions,"
said the prince, "I will promise you safety: there is no danger
from the dead; he that is once buried will be seen no more" '.[44]

Rasselas is concerned with danger *from* the dead; and so, at
least ostensibly, is Sethos. However, Sethos's trip to this
uninhabited place which common report fills with bugbears is
the prelude to his trip to the underground city which common
report filled in classical times with the shades of the dead and
in Terrasson's own time with devils torturing damned souls.
Circumspectly as ever, Terrasson seems to hint that his real
purpose in rationalising away the Greek myth of the Under-

world is to rationalise away the Christian myth of damnation; his real message is that there is no danger *to* the dead.

When the enlightenment asked itself how Christianity had imposed on mankind, the obvious answer must have been by not merely playing on the natural fear of death but by enlarging that into a gross terror of being tortured everlastingly after death; the church which claimed the powers to bind or loose after death exercised a blackmailer's hold on man during his life and reduced him and his reasonable faculty to subservience. If man failed to follow reason and his natural instinct towards pleasure and did not, in fact, make life on earth a paradise, it must seem to be because life on earth had been corrupted, and the natural instinct towards pleasure perverted, by man's dread of a hell beneath the earth. And when Bernardin de Saint-Pierre sketched a paradise on earth in *Paul et Virginie* he took care to shew that the education which had preserved the native virtue of his ideal young pair uncorrupted, although it included the 'natural' principles of religion, excluded supernatural terrorisation: 'No one had ever frightened them by telling them God reserves terrible punishments for ungrateful children'.[45]

Although eighteenth-century Masonry was probably vague and permissive in its teaching about what happened after death, it was quite definite in giving its initiates a new way of considering death itself. Tolstoy is historically correct when he has the Masonic Rhetor (equivalent, presumably, to the Orator in *Die Zauberflöte*) teach Pierre the seven Masonic virtues, of which the last is 'the love of death': 'try by the frequent thought of death', the Rhetor explains, 'to bring yourself to regard it not as a dreaded foe, but as a friend that frees the soul grown weary in the labours of virtue from this distressful life, and leads it to its place of recompense and peace'.[46]

This is the very language of the letter Mozart wrote to his dying father,[47] a Mason writing to a Mason: 'As death, when we come to consider it closely, is the true goal of our existence, I have formed in the last few years* such close relations with this best and truest friend of mankind, that his image is not only no longer terrifying to me, but is indeed very soothing and consoling!' ('dass sein bild nicht alleine nichts schreckendes mehr für mich hat, sondern recht viel beruhigendes und tröst-

---

* Mozart had become a Mason three years before, in 1784.

endes!') Mozart continues: 'and I thank my God for graciously granting me the opportunity (you know what I mean) of learning that death is the *key* which unlocks the door to our true happiness' ('den *schlüssel* zu unserer wahren glückseligkeit').

If eighteenth-century Masonry inculcated this new and kindly image of death, it can have done so only by abolishing the fear of hell; and if it chose to conduct its candidates on an initiation journey to hell it can have been only to demonstrate, by the kind of object lesson his mentor and later his instructing priests administer to Sethos, that what is conceived of as hell is an uninhabited place whose darkness superstitious fancy has peopled with bugbears.

In its inmost meaning, *Die Zauberflöte* tells the story of its hero's visit to hell, whereby he overcomes the fear of hell. 'The gates of terror', where, Tamino says, 'distress and death' afflict him, can be none other than the gates of death—the gates of hell. The initiant is told he will succeed only if he can vanquish the fear of death—'Wenn er des Todes Schrecken überwinden kann'.[48] To do this, he must not only be willing to risk his life at the ordeals (demonstrating the fifth of Tolstoy's Masonic virtues, courage*): he must actually journey through 'death's gloomy night'. Similarly, Pamina is judged worthy of initiation because she is 'a woman who does not fear night and death'.[49] To overcome the fear of death is not merely to defy it: it is the intellectual illumination of understanding that there is nothing to fear.

The deepest meaning of *Die Zauberflöte* is its teaching about death, and this is very intimately bound to its teaching about life and society: only when the terror of hell after death is wiped out are humans set free to be 'equal to the gods' and to make 'the earth a heaven-state'.

Mozart's opera about overcoming the fear of death was first performed on 30 September, 1791, two months before his death.

---

* Similarly, in Terrasson's characterisation of 'the GENIUS OF A TRUE INITIATE':— 'Life is of no account to him' (Lediard's translation, Volume I, p. 190).

XVI

Hell, Love and Society—2

———— ❃ ————

This exploration of *Die Zauberflöte* has brought us out facing a surprising conclusion. *Die Zauberflöte* has essentially the same story as *Don Giovanni*. Both are stories in which the hero goes to hell. But they are told from opposite points of view—which are, I shall presently argue, the poles of a deep ambivalence in Mozart. It is significant of the close relation between these two opposite operas that the letter Mozart wrote his father about the Masonic view of death, so thoroughly *Zauberflöte*ish in tone, dates from just before the composition of *Don Giovanni*. Tamino and Don Giovanni are one hero seen through opposite mythologies, and Mozart never escaped their alternation.

Don Giovanni is a thorough-going Catholic opera, whose purpose is to attest the reality and horror of hell and to re-impose on its audience all those intimations of mortality and those threats of what lies beyond by means of which Catholicism rules living men through their fear of death; whereas *Die Zauberflöte* is designed, as an anti-Catholic, pro-enlightenment opera, to lift precisely that fear from mankind by attesting that life must no longer be corrupted by the fear of death because there is no hell.

Even in *Die Zauberflöte*, however, Mozart remains Catholic enough to remember that marriage is a sacrament. The new birth which ensues from the initiation is not only the emergence of an enlightened Tamino but also the creation of the new unit of husband-plus-wife. When Tamino and Pamina emerge from the last ordeal, the chorus greets them not as two but as one (with, again, that use of a singular word for a couple): 'Triumph! Triumph! Triumph! Thou noble pair'—'du edles Paar'.[1] But if at the back of Mozart's mind is a Catholic turn of thought, it is certainly not Catholic doctrine he is enunciating. He has pointedly made the marriage in *Die Zauberflöte* a secular sacrament.

A secular sacrament is, indeed, just what the Masonic initiation was. Its purpose was to activate in the members those virtues by which the Masonic society could be bound into a brotherhood, its implication that if everyone practised them society at large would become a brotherhood—or, as *Die Zauberflöte* calls it, a heaven-state on earth.

These virtues are, of course, social; and they can be liberated in man's nature only by overcoming the fear of hell and its hobgoblins. So long as man fears hell, he will devote his attention to scrambling into heaven; he will waste no energy in social love or in improving the state of society either now or for future generations; he will spread fear and superstition in place of friendship and education; he may even quit society and fail to contribute children towards its perpetuation, shutting himself up in a celibate's cell in order to make himself worthy of heaven after his death. The truest villain in *Die Zauberflöte* (the one whom both the first and the final versions agree to make a villain) is Monostatos, whose black face and soul bear witness to his obscurantism, and whose very name indicates that he is non-social man, the man who stands for himself alone. Conversely, that the three ladies are still, in the early part of the opera, playing their original part of virtuous agents seems quite clear from their choosing, as qualities to put in place of hatred, calumny and bile, the social qualities of love and brotherhood.[2]

These two qualities, erotic love, which alone can make society continue forwards through time, and social love, which alone can widen society outwards into a universal brotherhood, are the themes of *Die Zauberflöte*. 'What brings you to our walls?' (or—literally and revealingly—'to our masonry') the priest asks Tamino and Papageno; and Tamino gives the Jane Austenish reply: 'Friendship and love'.[3]

Die Zauberflöte is in complete agreement with the enlightenment: society must get rid of the supposedly supernatural (Christian eschatology) and of the artificial (the tyrannies of rulers who are qualified for their job by nothing but heredity— who, as *Sethos* keeps pointing out, are so inclined to wage aggressive wars merely for their personal glory); society must, instead, devote itself to scrutinising nature; once freed from unnatural and supernatural constraints, society will find its way back to its natural brotherly condition.

Nature was understood by the enlightenment to be inherently harmonious, just as theology had taken God to be a priori perfect. Even the straggling and uncomposed look of natural landscape, which was immediately offensive to the tidy and classicising eye of the century, was eventually tolerated, left to straggle where it liked and justified as part of a larger design by nature. By analogy, the whole universe becomes

> *A mighty maze! but not without a plan:*
> *A wild, where weeds and flowers promiscuous shoot;*[4]

and human nature, though as untidy as landscape, can be justified, exactly like landscape, as part of a larger whole:

> *Respecting man, whatever wrong we call*
> *May, must be right, as relative to all.*[5]

The business of reason was to 'First follow Nature',[6] in order to search out the principles whereby the parts were justified in relation to the grand design and liberate the natural instincts which, if man and tyrants would only leave them untampered-with, would produce a harmonious design in human society. Reason, so far from being in conflict with nature, was prepared to give its sanction only to such social and religious systems as nature, through instinct, had designed and could justify, all others being arbitrary, inorganic and therefore, like affectation itself, likely to break down in practice, through the withdrawal of human instinct from their support.

The eighteenth century was making a deliberate attempt to dispense with coercion as a principle in social organisation. It banished the two great shadows by which mankind had hitherto been kept in order: the threat of oppression extended by princes; and the threat, which *Die Zauberflöte* is trying to refute, of everlasting oppression in hell extended by 'the only ruler of princes'. These threats abolished, the century's whole reliance was placed on the force of love, of which it had a highly developed Platonic, even Freudian, conception as the instinctual force which binds living things to things outside themselves. Acting through the instinctual quest for pleasure, love was held sufficient to draw men into associations formed for mutual advantage and thus to cement a whole society. In the words of Bernardin de Saint-Pierre, 'nature, having made love the link between all beings, has made it the prime mover of our societies and the instigator of our illuminations and our pleasures' ('la nature ayant fait l'amour le lien de tous les êtres, l'a rendu le premier mobile de nos sociétés, et l'instigateur de nos lumières et de nos plaisirs').[7]

This attractive and coherent picture of man's nature was inadequate—as the French Revolution demonstrated—because it made no mention of an instinct which seeks discharge not in pleasure and not in creating relationships, but in destruction and in withdrawing from relationships. Neither did it take into account those unconscious forces, whether of love or of destruction, which have their reasons of which the conscious mind, unless it scientifically excavates for them, knows nothing. Freud was to shew that the relationship of ruled to ruler was necessarily, of its very emotional genesis, compounded of love plus hatred. But the eighteenth century was satisfied that if it could only abolish coercion by rulers it would by the same stroke automatically abolish the people's hatred of the rulers, because it would have abolished all that the conscious could see by way of cause and justification of that hatred. Equally, the philosophy of the century (except in Sade's hands) ignored the destructive impulse implicit in erotic acts—an impulse which in eighteenth-century moeurs was turning the act of sexual intercourse into an act of warfare. Bernardin de Saint-Pierre believed that women were false simply because men were tyrants. ('Women are false in countries where men are tyrants. Everywhere violence produces subterfuge'.[8]) Accordingly, he argued through *Paul et Virginie* that a society which abolished tyranny on the part of men would automatically abolish immodesty and infidelity on the part of women.

The century was baffled and fascinated by the anti-social power displayed by love, which nature had intended to be the social 'lien de tous les êtres', the moment that women yielded to its pleasures. And yet, since it had proclaimed pleasure innocent, natural and good, and had also proclaimed logical consistency obligatory, natural and good, it could not call upon ancient taboo pronouncements to prevent women from yielding

(—though one part of the enlightenment, Freemasonry, was
so scared by the problem that it plunged back into reactionary
asceticism, not only depressing the status of women but schooling men to resist sexual temptation).

In *Così Fan Tutte* Mozart raises the problem from the point
of view of women tempted to yield, and tries to formulate a
natural, anti-romantic morality which shall abide by the pleasure
principle and yet restrain women from pursuing pleasure to the
point where their behaviour sets man against man—which can
be done only by postulating that it is actually more pleasurable
not to yield to pleasure. In *Don Giovanni*, where the same
problem is raised from the seducer's point of view, the answer
is harder. *Don Giovanni* raises the whole problem of anti-social
man. Its hero is a counter-hero who is not to be seduced by
society's playing on his instinct towards pleasure into limiting
his quest for pleasure to such methods as society accepts. He
insists on pursuing his own pleasure, to society's detriment,
and even to the point where he risks forfeiting his own pleasure.
Because Don Giovanni is not deterred by this risk, he shews
himself as not acting on the conscious and rational desire for
pleasure which was all that the enlightenment could recognise
and argue with. He is acting on an unconscious compulsion
which includes the very impulse the enlightenment was determined to ignore, namely self-destruction; and so Mozart cannot
answer him in terms of enlightened morality, but has to revert
to the unreasoned beliefs of an earlier period and ends by
brandishing at his hero the very threat of hell which the
enlightenment—and *Die Zauberflöte*—were trying to do
without.

In ignoring the destructive instinct, the enlightenment had
expunged the devil from its mythology, though it kept him in
the toy cupboard. God it left standing but hardly mythological
any longer; blanched to an allegory, he is hardly more than an
alternative name for nature. To Tom Paine, 'The Almighty is
the great mechanic of the creation, the first philosopher and
original teacher of all science'.[9] To the Masons he is the
anonymous architect of the universe. If man is to turn to religion
at all, it is to a rationalised version of the religions of the
ancients, which can be interpreted as the ancients' interpretation
of nature. *Sethos* and *Die Zauberflöte* are rationalist parables

which can adopt the cloak of ancient Egyptian religion without inconsistency because the ancient Egyptians are admired as architects and scientific mechanics second only to the supreme architect and the great mechanic himself.

The natural love to which the enlightenment confided itself is set up in contrast to the supernatural love of the God who so 'loved the world that he gave his only begotten son'. In *Figaro* Mozart resolves a tangle of personal rights and claims by trusting to the natural capacity for personal sexual love, with which the artificial rights of seigneurs must not be allowed to interfere—Figaro is appealing to natural justice: and it is all accomplished under the implicit presidency of Cupid, a disbelieved-in god who of all gods is the easiest to interpret in terms of natural allegory (and with the least violence to the psychological facts). In *Die Zauberflöte* love is wider and offers a solution for the problems, which *Figaro* raises in microcosm, of all society. Love now includes social benevolence, and knowledge of its true nature needs to be diligently and deliberately sought through initiation. But by building the love story of Tamino and Pamina into the story of the initiation, the opera insists that social love is identical in natural origin with love between man and wife.

Love presides over *Die Zauberflöte* almost as palpably as it does over *Figaro*. It is neither God nor Sarastro but love which is said to join Tamino and Pamina into a unity which no man *can* put asunder;* and the presidency of love is explicitly declared at the crisis of the ordeals when Pamina tells Tamino 'I myself lead you; love guides me'.[10]

Love in *Die Zauberflöte* works miracles, but natural ones: the initiation is allegorical of the transformation love works in human psychology when it is set free from fear. *Il Seraglio* almost points the lesson that love cannot work miracles *except* through natural processes (which include reasoning and morality). Just as the Countess in *Figaro* prays to love ('Porgi, Amor') and in the end her prayer is granted but through an imbroglio of natural means, so the last act of *Il Seraglio* opens with the aria in which Belmonte, before undertaking to rescue the captives, confides himself to the power of love: 'I build

---

* Pamina and the three Genii: 'Zwei Herzen, die von Liebe brennen, kann Menschenohnmacht niemals trennen' (Act II, No. 21, first Allegro).

wholly on your strength, I confide, O love, in your might'.*
Love's answer seems to be given, and to be a disappointing one,
when the rescue fails. But Constanze reveals another and natural
sense in which love really does work miracles. In their captivity,
she and Belmonte make just the journey through the darkness
of death which Pamina and Tamino undertake at the initiation,
and, like the initiates, Constanze and Belmonte emerge having
vanquished the fear of death through the power of love. In the
end it is again the power of love, worked on by reason and
bent towards a libertarian social philosophy, which impels the
Pasha to grant the freedom Belmonte could not force from him
in defiance of the natural facts.

---

* —an aria which is, deplorably, usually left out of recordings and (except at
Glyndebourne) performances. (Act III, No. 17: 'Ich baue ganz auf deine Stärke,
vertrau', o Liebe, deiner Macht'.) Belmonte's aria is followed by Pedrillo's
serenade, which serves as the signal for the rescue; and in the spoken dialogue after
his serenade, Pedrillo, as he places the ladder at the window, makes on his own
behalf an invocation to Cupid—'Nun Cupido, du Herzensdieb! hole mir die
Leiter'—which is a brief restatement in prose of Belmonte's aria.

XVII

The Exotic

———————◆———————

It is natural love which Mozart puts forward as the solution of society's distress in both the operas which concern society in general. Both of these, *Il Seraglio* and *Die Zauberflöte*, are tinged with the most delightful and one of the most influential of enlightenment themes, the exotic; a theme which acted as apéritif to enlightened society's quest for both 'lumières' and 'plaisirs'.

The connexion between exploratory modes of thought and exploration overseas went back, as Voltaire acknowledged,* to the renaissance, when mental horizons had expanded contemporaneously with geographical, and the utopia-builders, setting off mentally in the tracks of the navigators, had begun the habit of constructing ideal commonwealths not yet to be found on any map. What first began to unseat the taboo figures of Christendom was not reason but the confrontation of opposing sets of unreasoned assertions. To Europe (which, ever since Justinian had made it an offence to 'dare to dispute publicly about the Holy Trinity', had scarcely had an opportunity to consider an alternative), it seemed the most natural thing in the world to assume that the Christian religion was the obvious inference to draw from history and from the existence and nature of the universe. The discoverers brought home news of countries where it seemed just as natural and obvious to draw quite different conclusions from the same evidence. It was the violent juxtaposition of these two statements in the mind of Europe which eventually shook reason into the conclusion that neither

* He chose a typically anglophile instance. When enlightenment man in the person of Candide discovers El Dorado, he is told that the Spaniards had 'une connaissance confuse de ce pays . . . et un Anglais, nommé le chevalier Raleigh, en a même approché il y a environ cent années' (XVIII).

set of beliefs was necessarily, and without further evidence or ratiocination, obvious or natural at all. This lesson from overseas underlined what eighteenth-century Europe was in any case concluding from the previous century's harsh experience of the stalemate between Catholicism's and protestantism's claim to authority. Both contrasts were impelling the eighteenth century to abandon the dispute over religious virtues and seek out moral ones, by-passing the question of authority and relying on reason instead.

Since it was motifs from overseas which had first awoken reason, the century set itself to exploit them as propaganda for reason; and at the same time it put them into the service of its cardinal and reasonable quest for pleasure. The recreational architecture of the enlightenment is sprigged with the exotic: from that early masterpiece, the Chinese decoration of the Pagondenburg (which the Elector Max Emanuel had Effner build him, in the grounds of Schloss Nymphenburg, between 1716 and 1719) to that last great monument to the pursuit of pleasure, the Royal Pavilion at Brighton. In the English language, China lent its name to its most appreciated and imitated export, porcelain; to the international language of the decorative arts it contributed *chinoiserie*. It is to the decorative art of cosmetics that Pope shews the contribution of the 'various offerings of the world'.* Having drawn on all the world, the taste for the exotic spilled over from the decorative arts into literature, drama and opera—in all of which it might also serve the propaganda purposes of reason. China (Horace Walpole's *Letter From Xo Ho To His Friend Lien Chi At Pekin*[1]): Turkey (whose exoticism spiced Gluck's opera *Die Pilger von Mekka* as well as Mozart's own *Zaide*,[2] where Mozart's Pasha Selim keeps his seraglio, where Don Giovanni has been in pursuit of his quest, and where Candide ends his and decides to cultivate his garden): Persia (Montesquieu's *Lettres Persanes*;† the Zoroastrian touch in Sarastro): Babylon (Voltaire's *La Princesse de Babylone*[3]): Egypt (*L'Oca del Cairo;*[4] *Thamos, König in*

---

* (*The Rape Of The Lock*, I, 130– . . . 34.) 'This casket India's glowing gems unlocks, And all Arabia breathes from yonder box'.

† (1721) When the exotic was in its oriental mode, eighteenth-century society perhaps unconsciously accepted an assonance between its own institution of the operatic castrato and the oriental one of the eunuch. Letter II of *Lettres Persanes* is from 'Usbek à son premier eunuque à son sérail d'ispahan'.

Ägypten;[5] Handel's opera on the theme of Caesar and Cleopatra; Tiepolo's pictures[6] of the meeting between Antony and Cleopatra and of the banquet at which Cleopatra dissolved a pearl and gave it to Antony to drink; *Sethos,* which provided a gloze on the dissolved pearl;* and *Die Zauberflöte* itself): South America (where Frederick the Great set his opera, and where Voltaire has Candide find El Dorado): Abyssinia (the original title of *Rasselas* being *The Prince Of Abissinia, A Tale*[7]): India (Bernardin de Saint-Pierre's *La Chaumière Indienne*): the Indies (it scarcely matters whether East or West, any more than it matters whether the hero of *Die Zauberflöte* is a Japanese or, as it is said[8] he appears in some editions, a Javanese, prince): the civilisation of the Red Indians (who provided Voltaire with a hero[9]): Mauritius (or, as it then was, under French colonisation, the île de France, which Bernardin de Saint-Pierre, who had spent some years there himself, made the paradisal setting of *Paul et Virginie*): even outer space (Voltaire's *Micromégas*[10]) —the outlandish locales spill from the spice casket to be used in an aromatic, para-geographical manner, by the same device, though to different purpose, by which Shakespeare pours forth his un-Dalmatian Illyrias and un-Czechoslovakian Bohemias.

The taste for the exotic had been well developed in the late-classical word, with its appetite for the Isiac and other foreign mystery cults. Indeed, the Roman Empire eventually succumbed, to the exclusion of all the rest, to a mystery cult which reached Rome from Palestine by way of the Hellenised Mediterranean coast, with the result that the very language of the Latin Mass is a mosaic gleaming with exotic pebbles like the Greek words *Kyrie Eleison* and the yet more outlandish *Amen, Sabaoth* and *Hosanna.* The eighteenth century could (and did, for one example, in *Die Zauberflöte*) encompass two of its favourite moods in one by combining the exotic with the classical, for doing which it could claim classical sanction. The only exotic section of *The Aeneid,* the story of Dido, was repeatedly com-

---

* Thus Terrasson—or his supposed second-century Greek—on the subject of the ancient Egyptians as chemists: 'We have at least a recent and incontestable proof of the efficacy of their dissolvents, in that pearl of inestimable value and uncommon size, which Cleopatra took from her ear, and liquify'd in an instant in prepar'd vinegar, that Mark Anthony [sic] might swallow it: And it is certain, that this vinegar was no corrosive dissolvent, because it was drunk without danger.' (Lediard's translation, Volume I, p. 69.)

posed in Metastasio's version, *Didone Abbandonata*;* there
were hardly fewer Semiramides than Didos; and Avide Perez's
Alessandro nell'Indie had a famous gala performance at Lisbon
in 1753. Another libretto which counts Alexander the Great
among its dramatis personae, Metastasio's *Il Re Pastore*, which
was composed by Mozart in 1775, is a characteristic instance
of a classical story in an exotic setting (near Sidon). Metastasio's
directions for Act Two of the libretto epitomise eighteenth-
century exotic taste and might be a description of a fresco by
Tiepolo: 'Large, and rich pavilion of Alexander to one side;
overgrown ruins of antique edifices to the other. Grecian camp
in the distance' ('Grande, e ricco padiglione d'Alessandro da
un lato; ruine inselvatichite di antichi edificj dall'altro. Campo
de' Greci in lontano').

The locus classicus for exotic antiquity is Handel's *Julius
Caesar*.[11] Stern and austere as its title makes it sound, it is in
reality a love-story in the exotic vein, being set in Egypt
('Presti omai l'Egizia terra Le sue palme al vincitor!' sings
Caesar at the outset) and concerned with Caesar and Cleopatra.
Mozart evidently knew this ravishing opera inside out: among
the many suggestions it made to him† is one for the song by
which he introduces the villagey character of Zerlina in *Don
Giovanni*,[12] which is almost literally a variation on Cleopatra's
part in her closing duet[13] with Caesar—a metamorphosis of
character less extreme than it sounds, since Handel's conception
of Cleopatra is the Shavian not the Shakespearean.

The political adventures of English and French power overseas during the eighteenth century—the struggle between
Wolfe and Montcalm, the impeachment of Warren Hastings—
which are taught to English (and, no doubt, French) school
children as so grim a part of their imperial and commercial
history, take on a much more interesting colour if one thinks of

* A quick compilation:—the index of Angus Heriot's *The Castrati In Opera*
lists seven composers of operas of this name.
† Cleopatra's cantilena (No. 17, 'V'adoro, pupille') seems to be the model for
'L'amerò, sarò constante' in Mozart's own classical-exotic opera *Il Re Pastore*.
Cleopatra's marvellously free and sad lament (No. 27, 'Se pietà di me non senti')
adumbrates Pamina's 'Ach, ich fühl's'. Even the song (No. 14, 'Va tacito e
nascosto') in which Caesar figures himself as 'the cunning hunter', 'l'astuto
cacciator', to the self-congratulatory accompaniment of a (hunting) horn, has a
rhythmical resemblance to the song sung, to a lighter accompaniment, by a different
hunter—the birdcatcher Papageno, in his 'Der Vogelfänger bin ich, ja'.

them as contributors to the vogue for the exotic. Eighteenth-
century imperialism was strongly tinged with the commercial
desire to satisfy exotic tastes, and it may also have been philosophically justified by a dash of classicism: Terrasson's argument* that it is permissible to conquer foreign races in order
to introduce them to laws and happiness is probably an apologia
for the pax Romana as well as for French and English colonial-
ism.

England was, of course, the ideal of continental liberals
throughout the enlightenment: Voltaire's own overseas ex-
plorations were limited to crossing the Channel and sending
home *Lettres Philosophiques* as from a utopia but a markedly
bizarre one. The main promoter of this continental anglophilia
(which in France in the eighties of the century went so far as to
copy the English fashion—itself a product of overseas commerce
—for plain mahogany furniture[14]) was the English possession
of parliamentary government and religious toleration. Freedom
of thought had been comparatively long established in England;
and Voltaire, as spokesman for the French branch of the
enlightenment, was generously aware that the enlightenment
was largely built on the English philosophers and natural
philosophers (especially Newton) of the preceding century. It
would have been quite uncharacteristic of the enlightenment to
enter into chauvinistic squabbles about who had been first; the
enlightenment set much more store on being right than on being
original; and it was also, most pointedly, an international—
or at least a pan-European—movement. Indeed, its great object
was an international culture that should be uniformly right. To
admire and copy foreign countries inside Europe was scarcely
less obligatory than to admire, collect and copy the exotic
products of other continents. Voltaire's satire and much of the
thought which moved towards the French Revolution had been
anticipated in England earlier in the century by Pope and Swift,
and it was to a considerable extent the English enlightenment
which Voltaire and Montesquieu took home with them after
their sojourns in England—and the influence of Lord Chester-
field which Montesquieu took home from Venice.

If parliament, philosophy, mathematics and literature were
the main causes of anglophilia, one minor strand was that

* See chapter XV, p. 178.

England, as possessor also of a fleet and great sea-borne mercantile power, was in a position to make the biggest contribution to the cult of the exotic. It was, after all, a naval victory* for England which prompted Mozart—a year after completing his exotic opera *Il Seraglio*—to write to his father that he shared Leopold's delight at the news, 'for you know that I am an out-and-out Englishman'.[15]

This, as a matter of fact, Mozart had already attested in *Il Seraglio*, where his first sketch for the liberal design—to be fulfilled in Susanna—of speaking for the emancipation at once of women and of servants, is embodied in an Englishwoman. Sketchy though she is, and shewing little of Susanna beyond liveliness and the job of lady's maid, Blonde is already quite explicit about the lesson she has to teach. (She, too, is part of the enlightenment's educative programme.) She sings to the bullying Osmin what Susanna was later to demonstrate subtly to that much nobler bully the Count: it is 'by tenderness and flattering, kindness and making jokes'[16] that one must win the hearts of good maidens. Blonde is precisely what continental liberals expected of the English: fair-haired, as her name proclaims;† and boldly libertarian, as she herself proclaims with her 'I am an Englishwoman, born to freedom—'Ich bin eine Engländerin, zur Freiheit geboren'.[17] (And perhaps it is the maritime reputation of the English which inspires her to express her joy, at the prospect of making off to sea, in a sort of hornpipe.[18])

In 1790 the character and programme of the whole enlightened movement, together with its exotic theme, were satirically summed up by Rousseau's friend Bernardin de Saint-Pierre in *La Chaumière Indienne*. With a precise eye for the enlightenment's historical genesis, Saint-Pierre opens his story in London. A group of subscribers, whose composition gives an exact analysis of the enlightened bourgeoisie—'merchants,

---

* —the relief of Gibraltar. A couple of months later (see his letter to Leopold Mozart from Vienna, 28 December, 1782) Mozart was commissioned to set an ode on this subject but found the words 'exaggerated and pompous' and never finished the music. (Cf. Alfred Einstein: *Mozart* . . . , 5.)

† —a point which, together with the widespread liberal anglophilia of the period, was overlooked by Eric Blom when he made the editorial comment that 'Blonde, for no reason that we can see, calls herself "an Englishwoman" in the second act' (p. 177 in his selection from the Emily Anderson translation of the Mozart letters).

lords, bishops, universities and the English royal family'[19]— has put up the money for twenty English savants to conduct a comprehensive inquiry into problems which need answering: the purpose of the inquiry is an epitome of the purpose of the enlightenment: 'in order to illuminate men and make them happier'—'afin d'éclairer les hommes et de les rendre plus heureux'. The Royal Society of London furnishes the savants with questions and sends them off severally to the exotic corners of the earth. The most learned of them calls, on his way, at the main intellectual centres of Europe but—a token of the reputation which made it an appropriately dark background for *Don Giovanni*—avoids Spain 'for fear of the Inquisition'. Having travelled by way of Turkey and Egypt, he arrives at the banks of the Ganges, with a list of questions calculated by Saint-Pierre to cast satire on the enlightenment's promiscuous and un-sorted-out curiosity. Among them are: 'three on the theology of the Hebrews; four hundred and eighty on those of the various communions of the Greek and Roman churches; three hundred and twelve on the ancient religion of the Brahmins; . . . three on the present state of the Indian people; two hundred and eleven on the commerce of the English in India; . . . five on the antiquity of the world; six hundred and sixty-three on the origin of ambergris . . .'

This faux naïf tone of narration, which Saint-Pierre has—not unsatirically—lifted from Voltaire, is in fact the common tone of all the enlightenment's pamphleteers. The tone itself is largely the creation of the exotic vein when that was used to make propaganda for reason. In the exotic fable, the propagandist aimed to produce artificially the juxtaposition between Christian moeurs and outlandish ones which had first shaken reason into use. He might even go further and baldly intend to shew up Christian moeurs by the contrast. This was the quite explicit intention of Frederick the Great when he turned librettist and wrote an exotic opera, *Montezuma*. One of his letters explains that he is wholly on the side of Montezuma, and has made Cortes the villain; by which method, he says, he intends to strike a blow against 'le barbarie' of the Christian religion. 'But I am forgetting', he adds (he is writing to his—and, incidentally, Tiepolo's—Italian friend, Count Algarotti) 'that you are in one of the countries of the Inquisition . . . I hope to see you soon in a heretic country where opera itself can serve to reform moeurs and destroy superstition'.[20]*

Like the fairy-tale manner of *The Emperor's New Clothes* or the childish technique of some of the Douanier Rousseau's illustrations of the fierceness of animal nature, the faux naïf tone of the enlightenment's exotic fables is designed to point out the nakedness of the contrast between Christian and pagan society. The moral, that reason is the only possible arbiter between them, is made so inevitable that even a child can see it. In a sense, *only* a child can see it. Not only the indispensability but also the rococo poignancy of reason are brought home by casting the hero or narrator in the rôle of naïf. The author carries a European hero, by a series of adventures, to a tropical shore, where he discovers that the notions and values which seem so unquestionable to the European mind have never crossed the native mind at all but that the native mind is none the worse for that:† or else the author brings to Europe an exotic foreigner, either an untutored savage or a cultivated oriental (like those who travel to Paris and Venice and send home the *Lettres Persanes*), and the established European order is tellingly undermined by the naïf questions the visitor asks about it.

Whether or not he is naïf himself, and whether he is European or outlandish, the traveller inevitably becomes a naïf when he is set down in an alien system. There he is forced to see the system through his intelligence, not his preconceptions. The absurdities of the system become patent to him, and are reflected by him to the reader, because they are not the ones he was brought up with and has become inured to. ('You Europeans', readers of *Paul et Virginie* are apostrophised by the narrator, 'whose spirit is filled, from childhood, by so many prejudices contrary to happiness' . . .[21])

In other words, it is really reason itself which is the hero, and the naïf, of the exotic vein. Only the unbending naïveté of reason can penetrate the inveterate assumptions of taboo thinking.

---

* The conquest of Mexico was the subject of an eponymous opera by Vento (see Angus Heriot: *The Castrati In Opera*, V); and Frederick's theme had been anticipated—presumably not as anti-Christian but as anti-Catholic propaganda— in England during the Commonwealth, by an opera called *The Cruelty Of The Spaniards In Peru* (see P. Scholes: *The Oxford Companion To Music*).

† Belmonte arriving in the domain of the Pasha, who turns out to be far from uncivilised, is a variation on this theme.

The childlike vision of Candide, which cannot help piercing the complacency of Pangloss's Leibnitzianly optimistic philosophy and perceiving the horrors which are actually taking place, looks clean through the accepted routine of military events and clean through the traditional and august edifice of Catholic theology: what Candide sees on a battlefield is the plain fact of brains, arms and legs strewing the ground;[22] and in the auto-da-fé which follows the earthquake at Lisbon he perceives the equally plain fact of torture plus the absurdity of its being quite irrelevant to the geological fact—'il était décidé par l'université de Coïmbre que le spectacle de quelques personnes brûlées à petit feu, en grande cérémonie, est un secret infaillible pour empêcher la terre de trembler'.[23]

Even before[24] Voltaire sent his naïf off on his tour of Europe, Latin America and Turkey, Jonathan Swift had pushed the exotic mode to the limits of fantasy in despatching his narrator-hero on his 'Travels into several Remote Nations of the WORLD', and had carried the naïf tone to the point of putting forward 'A Modest Proposal', which still shews traces of the exotic setting in which the tone was formed (the author supports his Proposal by reference to similar customs practised on 'the Island *Formosa*') and in which he liberated the most naked irony mankind has ever been shamed by.

The reasonable naïf, who was the great literary hero—or, rather, since he has no character in the naturalistic sense, the great literary device—of the enlightenment, was also its social ideal. Exotic literature gave him two forms, which, though apparently contradictory, were used to precisely the same literary purpose: primitive savage; and cultured, dignified exemplar of an old, pagan civilisation. By the same token, the ideal might be the natural man (a more extreme version of the sentimental man; the sentimental man was still a garden artfully got up to *look* wild and abandoned, whereas the natural man had really returned to the woods) or the carefully instructed and polished—and perhaps initiated—philosopher (who in ideal form *was* a king and as the next best thing had the ear, or at least the correspondence, of one).

Like the two literary devices, the two social ideals were really pursuing the same end. They are simply the Rousseauesque and the Voltairean branches of a single enlightened stem. Early in the century Pope had announced that there was no conflict between reason and instinct, both of which were working towards the happiness of individuals and societies,* and which were designed by nature to produce harmony by checking one another:

> Two principles in human nature reign;
> Self-love to urge, and reason to restrain.[25]

The contradiction between natural and philosophical man was only a dispute about priority of importance, the philosopher holding that man should sharpen his wits in order to inquire into nature's design, the natural man that he should leave them uncultivated so that nature might speak its design through his uncorrupted instinct.

(By a sad little tragi-comedy, the theory of the natural man, together with a fantasia in the exotic mode, was responsible for starting Lorenzo da Ponte on the career of journalist-versifier in the course of which he became Mozart's librettist. The Venetian Senate turned him out of his academic career, forbidding him to teach in the Republic's territory, on the strength of a Latin poem called *The American In Europe*—da Ponte himself was eventually to become a sad European in America—and an exercise he had written for his students in the seminary at Treviso on 'Whether man achieves happiness by uniting in a social system, or can count himself happier in a state of nature'.[26])

The natural man was following nature by obeying the instinct of self-love—which was no contradiction of love for others, since 'God and Nature' orginally 'bade self-love and social be the same':[27] the philosopher was equally following nature by prodding into its secrets—such as, *La Chaumière Indienne* satirically remarked, the origin of ambergris.

La Chaumière Indienne, being written by a loyal Rousseauist, ends by abandoning science: the search for wisdom finishes in a pariah's hut, a location at once primitive, exotic and proletarian. Even this, however, was not a complete abandonment of civilised fashion. Rather, it pushed to extremes a homely

---

* 'Reason or instinct operate alike to the good of each individual . . . Reason or instinct operate also to society in all animals . . . Reason instructed by instinct in the invention of arts . . .' (Pope: *Argument* to Epistle II of *Essay On Man*).

branch of the fashion for the exotic. Simulated huts, if not of pariahs at least of peasants, were a popular form of architecture, and simulated rusticity a popular recreation. The fashion was well established by 1817, when one of Jane Austen's characters 'is running up a tasteful little Cottage Ornèe [sic], on a strip of Waste Ground',[28] but it had already begun in the 1740's, when Clarissa Harlowe's grandfather 'indulged her in erecting and fitting up a dairy-house in her own taste'.[29]

The Rousseauists, however, were in earnest as well as fashion when they decided to dispense with education, formal inquiry and most of the material amenities of life in society, in order to preserve natural affections and natural reasoning-power uncontaminated. This was the lesson of Bernardin de Saint-Pierre's earlier tale, *Paul et Virginie*, where the two children, having grown up in the tropical-pastoral simplicity of Mauritius, fall in love in a natural manner, without experiencing any of the pressures towards an arranged marriage, financial calculation or subsequent infidelity which corrupt love in sophisticated societies (and without which both the novel of manners and the romantic novel would have been at a loss for subject matter).

The idyll of Paul and Virginie is, however, a touch less unsophisticated and direct than it professes to be, since Saint-Pierre has followed the classical model of *Daphnis and Chloe* not merely for his title but for the course of true love. He has learnt from Longus, not from nature, that the girl is the first to become aware of love, and he has even borrowed the occasion of her awareness. It is when she remembers that in infancy she and Paul used to be bathed in the same spring that Virginie is seized by 'un feu devorant'; Chloe, whose idyll is less modest, is seized by love when she watches Daphnis take his bath and washes his back for him.

The value of a Rousseauist upbringing is put to the test by Saint-Pierre when Virginie's mother succumbs to worldly considerations and sends her daughter to France to the care of a rich great-aunt. The virtue inculcated by a pastoral childhood proves incorruptible. Rather than submit to an arranged marriage, Virginie sails home to Mauritius, where Paul, equally faithful, is waiting. But before she can land on the island her ship is caught in a storm, and this gives Virginie the opportunity to make the ultimate demonstration of her own and her education's virtue: she refuses to swim to safety because that would mean undressing in front of a sailor, and she is modestly drowned. Saint-Pierre is still trying to exploit to a pathetic end the fragility of the natural, reasonable point of view, but in letting the reasonable be swamped by the supposedly natural he has lost Candide's tough sense of the absurd and become absurd himself. Intellectually, the appeal is still to nature, the appeal Pope had made at the beginning of the century and which continued to be made throughout the eighteenth-century movement. However, Pope's intellectual refusal to admit a clash or a non-benevolence inherent in nature opened an opportunity to soften the appearance of nature. By the end of the century the opportunity was being thoroughly exploited. Saint-Pierre has let in to literature precisely the sentimentality expressed in painting by Jean-Baptiste Greuze.

Virginie has attained her unconquerable natural virtue by being brought up illiterate: during their island idyll she and Paul 'ne savaient ni lire ni écrire'. But just as Pope had written of prehistoric primitive men

Nor think, in nature's state they blindly trod[30]

so Saint-Pierre would not have us think that his contemporary primitives, in *their* 'jardin d'Eden', have suffered any intellectual deterioration through want of intellectual exercise. The two families on the island, he assures us, 'far from being savages, had become more human'.[31] More to the point, when separation makes it necessary for Paul and Virginie to communicate through letters (though Virginie is too modest to write to Paul direct, she sends him messages when she writes to her mother), they both pick up reading and writing easily enough. Paul takes the opportunity to read novels as well;* while for her part Virginie turns into one of those profuse, grammatical and formal female correspondents without whom there would scarcely have *been* any eighteenth-century novels. She progresses in less than two years from illiteracy to signing herself

'Très chère et bien-aimée maman,
Votre obéissante et tendre fille,
VIRGINIE DE LA TOUR.

* —in judging which he so agrees with Terrasson (see chapter XV).

(As one can see from the *de*, and might expect from the romantic nature of Rousseauism, Virginie is in fact rather well born.)

In contrast to this, the Voltairean vision cannot abandon knowledge, philosophy and common sense even temporarily, because it can see nothing but the improvement of human knowledge aʌ capable of fulfilling what nature has designed, and nothing but formal education as capable of liberating naturally reasonable man from his envelope of superstition and ignorance. It fixes on benevolent despotism as the most advantageous government precisely because it is more feasible for philosophers like Aristotle and Voltaire to educate a single pupil, an Alexander or a Frederick, than to educate a whole proletariat. The Rousseauist answer to this, namely that princes and proletariats are alike untrustworthy, is given with bitter truth in *Paul et Virginie*: 'Remember what has been the lot of the majority of philosophers who have preached wisdom to men. Homer, who clothed it in such beautiful poetry, begged alms during his life. Socrates, who gave the Athenians such charming lessons in it by his conversations and his manners, was judicially poisoned by them. His sublime disciple, Plato, was delivered into slavery by command of the very prince who was his protector; and before these Pythagoras, who extended humanity even to the animals, was burnt alive by the people of Crotona'.[32]

Since the two quests are in search of the same goal, namely a social system which nature, and therefore reason, *will* support, as opposed to the father-figures of Christendom which were discredited in both visions, their two ideals—noble savage, and noble non-Christian philosopher—are continually blurring together. The intellectual and sophisticated Voltaire eventually recommends a partial return to the primitive: it is that typically eighteenth-century meeting place between artifice and nature, a garden, that we are to cultivate. (Bernardin de Saint-Pierre, so much more extreme a primitivist, was actually appointed *intendant* of the Jardin des Plantes by Louis XVI.) Again, the one decent civilisation Candide discovers in three continents is El Dorado, which has preserved its primitive innocence and naïveté by deliberately shutting itself inside its mountain frontiers, secluded from all contact with European corruption. It sets no store by the gold and precious stones which litter its landscape, and has no churches, schisms, law courts or prisons. But at the same time this simplicity of heart argues to Voltaire great advancement of intellect. El Dorado possesses a *Sethos*-type palace of sciences and mathematicians capable of constructing the amazing machines which eventually hoist Candide and his companion over the mountains and out of El Dorado[33]—though Voltaire, unlike Terrasson, and to the great advantage of his narrative, does not even make a put at describing how the machines work.

Both eighteenth-century ideals are represented in *Die Zauberflöte*. Papageno describes himself as the natural man— 'Ich bin so ein Naturmensch'—who contents himself with sleep, food and drink, though he would like a wife as well;[34] and presumably it is his rural and untutored simplicity which makes him noble enough to sing the great duet with Pamina. Nonetheless, it is the Voltairean ideal of the tutored man which the opera prefers. Tamino emerges with his nature refashioned by education, whereas the natural man fails the tests.*

Die Zauberflöte's Voltaireanism is transmitted through Masonry: in *Il Seraglio*, Mozart (little as he liked Voltaire— at least when he was in his good Catholic frame of mind and writing to his father[35]) seems to take a Voltairean tone direct. It is not simply that he shares Voltaire's anglophilia and composes, for his chorus of janissaries, a witty allusion to Turkish music† which serves the same enlivening and sophisticated purpose as the touches of exotic colour in the Voltairean conte: he has built his Pasha Selim to the precise specification of Voltaire's ideal: the noble, pagan, philosophic, exotic, benevolent despot who is amenable to education.

The actual name Selim—which perhaps is or was thought to be cognate with *Salaam*; Mozart may even have had it in mind that that greeting meant 'Peace!'—seems to have been only a popular piece of generalised near-eastern exoticism. When Sydney Smith went to the theatre in Edinburgh and saw a

---

* It is nonsense for the Introduction to the English edition of the vocal score to say that Tamino and Pamina 'stand for Everyman and Everywoman' and that their ordeals 'symbolise the sufferings and experiences of a lifetime, the fire and water, the passions and sorrows of all humanity'. If anyone is Everyman, it is Papageno; and he fails the tests.

† —according to Mozart, 'short, lively, and written to please the Viennese' (letter to Leopold Mozart, from Vienna, 26 September, 1781).

dramatisation of the story of Bluebeard, Bluebeard's rival was called Selim;[36] and the name evidently had connotations— aptly enough for Mozart's Pasha—of the thoroughbred, since it was given, presumably in tribute to Arabian steeds, to a horse painted by George Stubbs.[37] The Pasha Selim, however, is allowed to develop a good deal more character than a mere exotic touch. Moreover, his and the whole opera's development, including the Voltairean turn they are given, are to a large extent Mozart's personal work—as one can safely judge not only from the dramatic emphasis accorded them by purely musical means but also from Mozart's report to his father that 'the whole story is being altered—and, to tell the truth, at my request . . . Stephanie is arranging the libretto for me—and, what is more, as I want it—exactly'.[38]

The Pasha does not possess his Voltairean character to start with. What we watch is the education whereby he acquires it. When he is introduced, he is the raw material of nobility, aristocratic and imposing, but uninstructed: a precursor of Count Almaviva, prepared to force himself on the young woman he loves, who this time has none of Susanna's freedom to manœuvre but is wholly in the despot's power.

More perhaps than the Count, who is only genuinely infatuated, the Pasha is genuinely in love.[39] The principal love-story in *Il Seraglio*, the triangle between Constanze, Belmonte and the Pasha, is not a piece of romantic relief from the social significance of the material but an epitome of it. The enlightenment had recognised the fact which the nineteenth century buried beneath a heap of obsessively materialistic pseudo-science, whence it had to be rediscovered by Freud—namely that the bond between ruler and ruled depends fundamentally not on economics, and not on a mysterious 'herd instinct' in man, but on the well-known emotion of love, and that rulers must be supported on feelings not radically different from the erotic love which the Pasha would like to command in Constanze.

In the eyes of the enlightenment, this love of the people for the ruler must be given voluntarily—which to the enlightenment, with its passion for supposing that people act on conscious and rational motives, meant that the ruler must be worthy of it. Arbitrarily to command love to be born in someone else's breast is no more sensible than to exaggerate the love in one's own. Both are attempts to compel nature. The tyrant is as absurdly pretentious when he commands the people to love him as when he forbids the tide to advance. Tyranny is, ultimately, a species of affectation, and the tyrant is, as Tamino says, an Unmensch —a point *Il Seraglio* makes by underwriting its main love triangle with the proletarian one in which the bully Osmin is shewn up as less than a man. The enlightenment's rebellion was against anyone who tried to compel love, whether tyrannical rulers, parents arranging marriages for their children, guardians seeking to marry their wards themselves, or Marcellina trying to exact marriage from Figaro in fulfilment of a contract and a debt: and the rebellion consisted in precisely the protest Constanze makes to the Pasha's 'Tomorrow you must love me, or——'. 'Must?' she replies, 'Absurd desire!'—'Muss? Welch albernes Begehren!'[40]

It is Constanze's refusal to be compelled by political force into an emotion unnatural to her, and therefore unreasonable and absurd, which accomplishes the Pasha's transformation. (Meanwhile, in the shadow triangle, Blonde instructs Osmin in the reasonable way to win women's love, but Osmin is less teachable than his master.) The prospect of torture and death, which Constanze first faces alone and in which she is presently joined, when he has been captured too, by Belmonte, who sings with her one of the most moving of all Mozart's duets, is *Il Seraglio*'s equivalent to the ordeal which in *Die Zauberflöte* consists of entering in at the gates of terror, where distress and death afflict the traveller, passing through death's gloomy night and emerging purified from the fear of death.

Through this ordeal Constanze's voice leads Belmonte's, just as Pamina leads Tamino; and we can be in no doubt that their ordeal ratifies the love between Constanze and Belmonte, purifies them of romanticism and turns them, too, into an 'edles Paar' which has attained the godhead.

Die Zauberflöte, however, makes a point* of Tamino's under-

---

* In insisting on this point, *Die Zauberflöte* seems to be following Masonic ritual, where (according to *The Text Book Of Freemasonry*) the candidate is asked 'Do you seriously declare on your honour that, unbiassed by the improper solicitation of friends against your own inclination, and uninfluenced by mercenary or other unworthy motives, you freely and voluntarily offer yourself as a candidate for the mysteries and privileges of Freemasonry?'

taking the ordeals voluntarily,[41] and Pamina volunteers to join him. Moreover, in the final version at least, Sarastro is not a real tyrant. Probably he was designed as one, but the authors have transformed his character by a private adjustment of the story which was not meant to leave any traces. The Pasha, on the other hand, goes through just such a transformation in the course of the story: to a great extent, it *is* the story.

He begins as a real tyrant, quite prepared to impose the ordeal on the lovers, quite against their wills. For this reason, although he is peculiarly detached from the *opera* because his is not a singing part, the Pasha is much more closely involved with the *story* than Sarastro, who is a mere figurehead for the philosophic system whose ritual the lovers volunteer to go through with for their own good. When Constanze and Belmonte emerge at the end, their love, which existed before, has been ratified; but it is the Pasha who is the equivalent of the initiate and who has become a 'new man'. The Pasha's unique position as an actor but not a singer in the drama makes him a half-way step between dramatis personae and audience, a representative of the audience crept up on to the stage. It is through his reaction to the lovers' ordeal, of which the whole audience is witness, that the audience is asked to respect the rights of enlightened men and women who are prepared to die for their freedom and naturalness.

Moved by his captive's constancy ('Is this a dream?' he asks himself; 'where has she all at once got the courage to set herself against me like this?'[42]), the Pasha eventually shews himself a nobler pagan than Belmonte's father has been a Christian—for, by one of those dénouements of identity which are set off like catherine wheels by rococo plotmaking, Belmonte has turned out to be the son of an ancient enemy who used the Pasha ill. The moral purpose of the exotic vein is pointed when the ostensibly barbarian Pasha stigmatises Belmonte's father as 'dieser Barbar'.[43]

This bloody and unjust* man is, of course, a Christian of the deepest Catholic dye—a Spanish grandee.[44] Frederick the Great's opera had indicted the atrocities of the Spaniards against the Mexicans in order to shew that it was Christianity which

* —as his son admits, being prepared to die without complaint in recompense of 'das Unrecht' done by his father to the Pasha (Act III, dialogue before No. 21).

was the 'barbarie'.* *Il Seraglio* exposes a Spaniard's vindictive treatment of a Turk, and shews that it is the Turk who is capable of learning the lesson of non-vengeance.† The Pasha does not take the opportunity to avenge himself on the father through the son—because he disdains to follow the Christian barbarian's example. 'I hold your father in too much detestation', he tells Belmonte, 'to be able to tread in his footsteps'.[45] Christian and pagan moeurs have been searchingly compared; Pedrillo's narrative ballad has evoked the Crusades to the advantage not of Christian chivalry but of Selim's historical precursor in nobility, Saladin.

When he composed *Il Seraglio* Mozart's own capacity for forgiveness had recently been put to the test in his quarrel with Count Karl Arco; and the specifically Christian virtuousness of forgiving must have been much in his mind because that quarrel was itself a branch of his quarrel with 'a spiritual prince',[46] Archbishop Colloredo, whom Mozart described[47] as 'a presumptuous, conceited ecclesiastic'. Mozart's own struggle to master his feeling of insult and injustice is certainly reflected in Selim's and is perhaps the source of the psychological sympathy for Selim which Mozart marks by so strongly developing Selim's part in the drama, although there was no operatic compulsion on him to do so. In his own quarrel, Mozart could not quite bring himself to give up the code of honour in favour of the Christian virtue of forgiveness (he was not yet a Mason); but he did promise his father that he would limit himself to giving as good as he got and would not go on to administer punishment. To this promise he added a paraphrase of the words in which Selim was soon to express his disdain of following in the footsteps of Belmonte's father: 'Besides', says Mozart, 'I should be placing myself on a level with him, and really I am too proud to measure myself with such a stupid booby'.[48]

The dénouement in the last act of *Il Seraglio*, when the

---

* Paul, of *Paul et Virginie*, uses the same verbal paradox when, in the primitive bliss of Mauritius he speaks of Europe as 'ce pays barbare'; and when Virginie actually goes to France she writes home that it is 'ce pays-ci qui est pour moi un pays de sauvages'.

† One of the many anticipations of *Die Zauberflöte* in *Die Entführung* is its explicit condemnation of revenge. 'Nothing' sing the two pairs of lovers after the discomfiture of Osmin, 'is so hateful as revenge'—'Nichts ist so hässlich als die Rache' (Act III, No. 21, Andante sostenuto).

fugitives are recaptured, is the start of the test of the lovers and provokes the crucial test of the Pasha. First there is the question of Belmonte's true identity. It is here that *Il Seraglio* cardinally shews itself an anticipation of *Die Zauberflöte*, and Constanze of Pamina. When,[49] in *Die Zauberflöte*, Pamina and Papageno are caught unawares and terrified by the sound of Sarastro's august approach, Papageno shrinks, wishes he could hide like a mouse or a snail, and in confusion asks Pamina 'What shall we tell him?' Her answer, 'The truth, the truth!', is both sublime and conversational. 'Die Wahrheit' she sings in momentary near-isolation from the musical texture; for conversational emphasis she repeats both the musical and the verbal phrasing, hoisting her music marginally higher when she sings for the second time the long note for the syllable 'Wahr' which carries the verbal stress. She first accepts the perils of her advice and then confides herself and Papageno absolutely to the truth. Just so, in the last act of *Il Seraglio*, it is Constanze who deliberately reveals to Selim the truth that Belmonte is not the wandering architect he is posing as (a disguise which epitomises the enlightenment's tastes and interests) but 'my lover, my only lover'.

Beyond this, however, there is a further truth to be unveiled, which Constanze does not know—of which, indeed, no one character knows all the implications. Quite unwittingly Belmonte (in the course of hopefully explaining that his family would be rich enough to ransom him) discloses his lineage, and the Pasha recognises him to be the son of his old enemy. Here begins the test of the Pasha. At first he seizes the chance of revenge and promises to order the torture of the captives. When we next see him, he has changed his mind. Directly, we are shewn nothing of the process of the change. All that has intervened between his two appearances is an event at which the Pasha is not, within the terms of the dramatic action, even a witness, but which he has certainly witnessed and been moved by in his extra capacity of representative of the audience: the duet in which Constanze and Belmonte pass through the shadow of death and emerge to sing the happiness—'O, welche Seligkeit!' —of dying together.

Transformed by this in absentia, Selim behaves precisely as a benevolent despot—indeed, almost as a constitutional monarch

—should. He reforms his government, to the extent of giving a brisk warning to his corrupt officer, Osmin, and releases the prisoners. This last he does with a truly Voltairean declaration of rights. When[50] Candide and his companion apply to the witty king of El Dorado for permission to leave the country, the king replies that he thinks it 'une sottise' on their part to want to go, since they are happy where they are and will find it difficult to scale the mountains which surround El Dorado; nonetheless he promises to have machines constructed which will surmount the mountains, and declares: 'je n'ai pas assurément le droit de retenir des étrangers; c'est une tyrannie qui n'est ni dans nos moeurs, ni dans nos lois: tous les hommes sont libres'. Pasha Selim cannot say fairer, and he is more explicit that the basis of men's freedom is instinct, which cannot be compelled, even when it refuses to attach itself to what should naturally attract it: 'If you can't win people by kindness, it's best to rid yourself of them.'[51]

XVIII
Near the Core

———————— ❋ ————————

Opera was created by the enlightenment in its own image. Even Samuel Taylor Coleridge planned to write a libretto;* and Mozart, true to the enlightenment, intended himself to be principally an operatic composer. When Mozart was eight, his father reported[1] that the child's head was full of operatic projects. At twenty-one, he told his father[2] direct: 'You know my greatest desire is—to write operas'.

Mozart's passion for opera is stamped by the enlightenment: yet his five major operas, taken together and searched in relation to the enlightenment, reveal a deep ambivalence towards it. Three concern the enlightenment's major social preoccupations, and openly argue the enlightenment's case; one is an out-and-out counter-enlightenment manifesto; and *Così*, which embodies Mozart's personal anxiety about choosing between the Weber sisters, also embodies the enlightenment's sexual anxieties about the results of its rebellion against fathers. The sub-title of the opera puts forward the enlightenment's lesson that an enlightened education is a remedy against the flights, affectations and frailties of romantic love, while its title and its tragedy insist that in the present state of female nature there is no hope of the enlightenment's sexual problem being solved.

Constanze and Aloysia Weber figured to Mozart, especially after Aloysia's marriage, as sacred and profane love. Mozart can defend himself against profane love only by blackening its image and even then has to be grateful for avoiding temptation because he does not often meet Aloysia. The choice between the women, which remained open in Mozart's imagination at least until he had finished *Così*, is a particularisation of another choice,

* He made a note, under the heading 'My Works', 'Carthon an Opera' (quoted by J. Livingston Lowes: *The Road To Xanadu*, I, I).

which remained open all his life and in which he never decided which *was* the sacred and which the profane: the choice between the Catholic church and the enlightenment. In his own sexual life, Mozart definitely chose sacred love in the person of Constanze; yet the public monument he built to their marriage in *Die Zauberflöte* was couched in terms of Freemasonry, which, by the standards—prudence, tradition, the Christian rules of behaviour —which counted Constanze sacred, was definitely profane.

At the end of his life Mozart was still committed to both sides: he was both a Catholic and a Mason. During the eighteenth century two Papal Bulls were directed against Masonry 'by name' (the specification is the *Catholic Dictionary's**); and in Austria towards the end of the century, where the ultra-Catholic policy pursued by Maria Theresa and kept up by her son Leopold II was busy persecuting Masonry,[3] Mozart can have been in no doubt that the two were, at least according to the Catholic side, incompatible.

The internal contradiction in Mozart reached almost from the start of his career to the very end. In the last year of his life, 1791, when he received commissions from both the authorities and the popular side, his major works make an almost violently contradictory list. He produced, in *La Clemenza di Tito*, a justification and celebration of the monarchy; in his unfinished Requiem, a token of his own submission to the church before dying; and, in *Die Zauberflöte*, a justification of the proletariat and Freemasonry.

This is the richest manifestation of an ambivalence which had, in fact, shewn itself much earlier. Three years before incarnating the Voltairean ideal in the Pasha Selim, Mozart had sent his father[4] news from Paris of Voltaire's death, and had employed the conventional Catholic tone of execration. Here, too, Mozart is defending himself by blackening the image which, as he was to shew in *Il Seraglio*, attracted him. That 'godless arch-rascal Voltaire has pegged out like a dog, like a beast!' he writes. 'That is his reward!'—or, as he was to have the pious sextet sing after Don Giovanni goes to *his* reward, 'Questo è il fin di chi fa mal!' Just before his death, Voltaire,† on his last

* It cites 'In eminenti' (Clement XI, 1738) and 'Providas' (Benedict XIV, 1751).
† Voltaire is reputed to have been initiated into Masonry himself during his visit to England.

triumphal visit to Paris, had been received en fête by the Masons, in honour of his services to the enlightenment. Six years after celebrating Voltaire's death, Mozart himself became a Mason.

Such enduring contradictoriness is not merely intellect-deep but a manifestation of an emotional ambivalence which penetrated Mozart's whole psychology. In Mozart's work, as Mr Donald Mitchell points out,[5] the ambivalence issues in irony —which is most concentrated of all in *Così*: in Mr Mitchell's words, 'it is *Così*'s two-sided truth which is, perhaps, the very quintessence of Mozart's ambiguity, his ambivalence, his love of paradox'. The ambivalence of Mozart's nature did not escape the notice of Leopold Mozart, who wrote[6] about his son: 'Two opposing elements rule his nature, I mean, there is either too *much* or too *little*, never the golden mean'. Leopold could hardly be expected to recognise his own part in the puzzle of Mozart's personality. That Leopold is crucially involved we are entitled to guess straight away, if only because the enlightenment was quintessentially a rebellion of sons against fathers; and it is fair to surmise that the source of Mozart's ambivalence towards that rebellion was the particular combination in his life of two facts, that he was an artist, and that he was the son of an artist.

The high point of the puzzle, where it may be most boldly attacked, is the period of *Figaro* and *Don Giovanni*. Taken together, these two operas constitute the crucial display of Mozart's ambivalence. In the space of a year, at the centre of his career, he passed from the enlightened extreme, in *Figaro*, to its counter-revolutionary opposite, in *Don Giovanni*.

As da Ponte remembered long afterwards, it was Mozart who made the proposal that they should turn Beaumarchais's notoriously revolutionary *Le Mariage de Figaro* into an opera* —and this in spite of the fact that the Emperor had just forbidden the play to be acted in Vienna as being 'too outspoken for a polite audience'.[7] Yet when Mozart asked da Ponte for another libretto to follow up *Figaro*, he was exceedingly pleased[8] by da Ponte's suggestion of the reactionary Don Juan

---

* Mozart's mind had been running on the fashionable figure of Beaumarchais's Barber some four years before *Figaro*: witness the letter where he tells his father 'The barber of Salzburg (not of Seville) called on me . . .' (from Vienna, 19 October, 1782).

story, a theme so old-fashioned, so almost medievally Catholic
in its hell-fire message, that da Ponte compared working on it
to reading Dante's *Inferno*.

That da Ponte should choose it is not surprising. His memoirs
shew to perfection the character of the timid seminarist, who
had never felt really the master of his environment since being
turned out of his seminary. By the time he wrote the memoirs,*
age, neglect, the nineteenth century and the puritanism of his
American surroundings had reduced him to trying to laugh
away the youthful Rousseauism which had cost him his job in
the seminary; but he cannot have been a bold man even in his
Vienna days, and it is easy to reconstruct that he was eager to
repeat his success by writing another libretto for Mozart while
hoping to turn Mozart away from the dangerous subjects
Mozart had led him into with *Figaro*. Besides, the Don Juan
story held two practical advantages for da Ponte: it was in-
veterately popular; and, since there already existed several
models, including a highly usable one by Bertati,[9] it would
demand the minimum original invention and labour from da
Ponte, who had two other libretti to work on at the same time.

That Mozart should welcome the subject, however, would be
very strange if Mozart had remained in his *Figaro* mood. In
that case even the popularity of the Don Juan theme would
probably have told against it. Whereas the Figaro theme was
fashionable and avant-garde, Don Juan's was a popularity which
had persisted, like superstition, beneath the rational and
educated surface of the enlightenment. Indeed, its popularity
was, to even superficially enlightened minds like Carlo Goldoni's, quite inexplicable. Jane Austen, of course, did not dream
of taking Don Juan seriously and, after seeing his story at the
Lyceum in London, irreverently reported leaving him 'in hell
at half-past eleven' and that the performance 'did very well' for
the two little girls in the party;[10] but even the much naïver
Goldoni wrote in his Memoirs, about the Italian version of
'cette mauvaise Pièce espagnole': 'I have never been able to
understand how this farce could hold its own for such a long
time, could draw crowds, and could be the delight of a cultivated nation'.[11]

All the same, Goldoni himself treated the story, but he was

* They were issued in 1823–7.

at pains to smooth out its supernatural melodrama and make it susceptible to swallowing by enlightened gullets. As he carefully sets out in his Memoirs, he assimilates all the supernatural events to events which might have a natural explanation: in his play, the statue 'does not speak, or walk, or go into town to supper'; and while it remains imperative for the wicked Don Juan to be punished Goldoni has 'arranged this event in such a way that it could be the immediate effect of the wrath of God, and that it could also arise from a combination of secondary causes always governed by the laws of providence'.[12] In other words, Goldoni is just as timid with Don Juan as with Pamela, and wants to have both enlightenment and popular approval.

Providing the supernaturalisms could be given a possible (though Goldoni will not insist on an obligatory) natural explanation, there was much in the Don Juan story that was to the enlightenment's own, as well as to the popular, taste—notably the seduction motif, with or without connotations of intellectual rebellion. Even the moralistic ending was only the sort which novel-readers quite expected to find tacked-on to stories of sexual licence. Miscreants in eighteenth-century literature regularly come to a punitive end, by a convention which was usually the most arbitrary bit of applied moralising but which Choderlos de Laclos exploited to the far from conventional purpose of thoroughly working out the thanatic compulsions inherent in the personalities of his hero and heroine.

In the Don Juan legend it was only the supernatural method of pointing the moral which was disconcerting. Most of the eighteenth-century minds which took up the story either rode its supernaturalism as an assured though hackneyed vehicle to popular success (which is probably how da Ponte thought of it) or else minimised the supernaturalism—in Goldoni's case by rationalisations within the story, in Gluck's by choosing to treat it in the form where story goes for least, ballet. (Gluck's Don Juan ballet[13] is still danced at Vienna.) Mozart alone seems to have embraced the supernaturalism for its own sake. He does nothing to minimise it; indeed, musically he exploits it to the utmost. Yet his fastidiousness about his libretti, and the number of texts he abandoned half-composed because, presumably or explicitly, they did not suit him, make it clear that he would not have accepted da Ponte's suggestion of the theme if it had not suited him. And of course the opera he made of it proves that it did suit him. But what it suited in him was the other extreme of his ambivalence, the opposite face of the creator of *Figaro*.

There is, as I have already said, an event in Mozart's life psychologically momentous enough to have impelled him from one extreme to the other. Leopold Mozart died between the composition of the two operas; and his death seems likely to have been what precipitated Mozart into accepting Don Juan as the theme of the second. Mozart had contracted to compose *an* opera before Leopold died, but the subject had evidently not been fixed, since it is not mentioned in the final letters between Mozart and his father. It would be consistent with both Mozart's and da Ponte's methods of work if they left starting on the opera until the last possible moment before their deadline. The chronology is: Mozart received the commission to compose a new opera for Prague while he was there in January of 1787; by April of that year he knew that Leopold was seriously and probably mortally ill—it was on receiving that news that he wrote and sent to Leopold his Masonic reflexions on death; Leopold died on the 28th of May; *Don Giovanni* had its first performance in October.

It seems to me that the best hope of throwing any light into the material of *Don Giovanni*, 'in which', in the words of Alfred Einstein,[14] 'such dark, primeval, and demonic forces are inextricably combined', is to take it, like *Hamlet*,* as one of those works of art created by a son in the complex emotions following on his father's death. I must admonish my readers in advance, however, that this will, precisely, throw light: nothing less, nothing more. It will not explain away either the masterpiece which is *Don Giovanni* or the genius which was Mozart. The common reproach that psycho-analysis explains away the greatness of great works of art is a very curious one. Perhaps it rests on a very flimsy conviction of the validity of art, since it seems convinced that the beauty can be vaporised at a touch; and certainly it rests on a very extensive ignorance of psycho-analysis, since the briefest exploration of psycho-analytical writing is enough to reveal that, even if psycho-analysis for

---

* See further the next chapter.

some reason should want to explain away art, it is totally
incapable of doing so.

When[15] Freud analysed the relationship of survivors to their
dead, and, in particular, the primitive fear of the ghosts of dead
people, he picked out a paradox: the friend or kinsman who is
loved and welcomed during his life as a well-wisher is, after
his death, transformed into something so malevolent and
dangerous that the most intense magical precautions have to
be taken to prevent his returning with hostile intentions against
the survivors. This transformation does not really take place
in the dead person but in the minds of the survivors. If he is
now apprehended as hostile to them, it is really because they
are hostile to him. Moreover, this hostility on their part, which
shews itself after his death, really existed during his life, but
was unconscious: it co-existed with, and hid behind, the love
which was consciously entertained towards him. The unconscious hostility which lurks behind every intense conscious love
'represents', Freud diagnosed, 'the classic case, the prototype
of the ambivalence of human emotions'.

The actual death of the loved-hated person is a crisis for the
survivor because in the unconscious a wish is as good as a deed.
The unconscious hatred can express itself only by the graphic,
the almost cinematographic, means of an unconscious wish:
unconsciously to hate somebody is to create a wish-fantasy in
which he keeps away—dies. When this wish is met by the
person's actual death, the unconscious holds itself responsible
for the deed which it has already acted out on its fantasy screen:
'in the unconscious mode of thinking even a natural death is
perceived as murder; the person was killed by evil wishes'.[16]
Unconsciously, the survivor accuses himself as the murderer.
Granted the unconscious mode of thinking, it is perfectly
reasonable of him to dread and protect himself from the return
of the ghost. In the same way, Freud pointed out, mourners are
sometimes subject to 'tormenting scruples' about whether they
really have done everything in their power to prevent the death;
and these scruples are 'immune to refutation or objections'
because they are 'in a certain sense justified'.

The high classic cases of such tormenting scruples, where
the person who was subject to them could find a quietus only in
actually being punished, were analysed by Freud elsewhere:[17]

the scruples which eat into the awareness of King Oedipus until they bring it home to him that the distress afflicting his kingdom is really a punishment on himself provoked by his own unwitting (that is—unconscious) acts of killing his father and marrying his mother; and the scrupulous hesitations which hold back Prince Hamlet from avenging the murder of his father—because he is unconsciously convinced that he himself is guilty, in wish, of the murder.

It is not accident that both these high classic cases concern sons and dead fathers. The very quintessential prototype of the ambivalence of human emotions is the unconscious murderous wish an infant son entertains, on account of the mother, towards the father whom he may consciously love, admire and imitate; and the very quintessential prototype of tormenting scruples among mourners is the reproach the son unconsciously addresses to himself when the infantile situation is given a recrudescence by the actual death of the father.

This was Mozart's situation when he created *Don Giovanni*; and there is analogous material in the story itself which made the subject, contrary to everything one would expect after *Figaro*, not merely acceptable but precisely apt to him. The ghost in *Hamlet* and the ghostly statue of the murdered Commendatore in *Don Giovanni* are no exceptions to the usual psychological genesis of ghosts.

Whereas Hamlet has really lost a father by murder, though it is only in unconscious wish that Hamlet himself is a murderer, Don Giovanni is really a murderer, but not of his father. Yet, as I have argued already, the Commendatore, with his commanding title and rank, is precisely one of those social father-figures the enlightenment laid low. Besides, he is Donna Anna's father. It comes nearer to parricide on Don Giovanni's part to have killed the father of a woman he has seduced or tried to seduce than to have killed an ordinary—as it were, an unrelated —person. By the same token as Don Giovanni's mistresses are his quasi-wives, the Commendatore is his quasi-father-in-law. Don Giovanni is guilty of a private quasi-parricide and at the same time of social parricide—and this not merely against rank and chivalry, but against their supernatural sanction. The Don Juan legend was a Counter-Reformation parable, an atheist's tragedy: Don Juan sets up as the enemy of God; and the father he really assaults, and who comes back to punish him, is God the Father.

The material and history of this legend permitted Mozart to offer an apology to his own father through the medium of offering an apology to God for that worse-than-the-Reformation, the enlightenment. I have already cited the germs of *Don Giovanni* which shew Mozart identifying his own impulses towards sexual promiscuity with Don Juan's utter violation of the sexual code; and in his propaganda for the enlightenment and for social revolt, especially in the recent *Figaro*, Mozart had concurred in and identified himself with Don Juan's blasphemy. For him to undertake, immediately after *Figaro*, to tell the story of Don Juan's punishment was a punishment of himself.

A tiny symptom of Mozart's identification with his hero erupted in the form of a joke Mozart had used, without significance, before,[18] and which now recurred in a letter[19] to his friend the bass singer Jacquin, at the very time Mozart was engaged on the final rehearsals for *Don Giovanni*. Mozart is teasing Jacquin by expressing amazement at actually receiving a letter from him. 'A letter from—— I am almost rubbing my eyes sore—— Why, it is——'. The sentence goes on to conclude: 'It actually is from you—— indeed!' But into the chain of parentheses Mozart has inserted another: 'Why, it is—— the devil take me': and after this reminder of the fate of his hero, he has tossed in, between the magical signs of the cross, the spell which is to ward off his hero's fate from himself: 'Why, it is—— The devil take me † God protect us † It actually is from you'. It is, of course, the merest nothing, an application of folk-superstition, like the conventional and now vulgar 'Gesundheit!' after someone sneezes. Yet this faint, burlesqued return of superstition is probably a long-distance echo of Mozart's remorse towards his newly dead father.

The logical amends for a son to make to a father whom he has unconsciously wished dead is to bring him back to life in deliberate fantasy. It is not enough to set up (even with that remarkable despatch the commentators have all noticed) a memorial-statue to the Commendatore, like one of those hollow monuments which the enlightenment left standing but jeered at as openly as Don Giovanni sneers at the Commendatore's memorial: the memorial must be re-animated and made capable of movement and speech.

The power which animates the dead Commendatore is divine vengeance—which historically has been given its mythological animation by just the same need to compensate paternal authority for the sons' murderous wishes against it. When guilt towards the father and fear of the revenant become too strong to be borne, the ghost is promoted god and becomes not merely immortal but eternal—the utmost apology which can be made to him for the unconscious wish to prove him, by the most practical method, mortal. Within the legend's own dramatic action, the animation of the Commendatore's statue is a vindication of God: Don Juan's blasphemous attacks have not succeeded in murdering God. When Mozart chose to re-animate this incredible old legend in which the re-animation of a stone memorial was turned to the greater glory of God, he was re-animating the God whom he and the enlightenment had considered stone cold dead.

It is possible, however, that it was Mozart's pro- and not his anti-enlightenment eye which was first caught by the Don Juan story. A theme very similar to the statue which moves, namely the legend of Venus's granting Pygmalion's request for the animation of the statue he has sculpted, has been documented (by Mr J. L. Carr in the *Warburg Journal*) as a great favourite with the enlightenment, much treated by librettists and dramatists (including Jean-Jacques Rousseau), versifiers (including Voltaire) and painters (including Boucher and Fragonard). Mr Carr adds that the sceptical philosophers welcomed, as propaganda for a materialist view of life, the motif of Pygmalion's creating life by his own art[20] (or science or—which is pseudo-science—magic).

And indeed Pygmalion represents enlightened man at his most daring. He has actually usurped God the Father's creative prerogative, just as the infant son would like to usurp his father's procreative prerogative. What is more, Pygmalion exercises it through a blatantly sexual metaphor. For the inert and passive substance of a statue to stir, to move, to take on a life of its own, is a metaphor of erection—the ultimate objective of all magical conjuration. The 'remarkable phenomenon of erection', wrote Freud in interpreting the sexual significance of dreams of flying,[21] 'which constantly occupies human phantasy, cannot fail to be impressive as an apparent suspension of the laws of gravity'. The eighteenth century, which was so deeply terrified of losing the natural power, betrayed its preoccupation with it (as well as with Newton and the laws of gravity) in its fascination with the apparently magical and self-moving activity of automata and mechanical toys, metaphors under which it sought to ensure the continuation of its own threatened potency. Pygmalion, who had actually usurped the procreative powers of God and brought to life the most life-like as well as the most gratifying of all toys (he was an Adam who had independently provided himself with an Eve) became a hero to the enlightenment because he personified the assurance it was always seeking of fertility for its own arts and sciences.

At first sight the animation of the statue of the Commendatore offers the same assurance. This first sight may well have drawn Mozart to the subject, because he was very probably in need of just such an assurance. Unconsciously holding himself guilty of Leopold's recent death, he might well dread the punishment of artistic impotence. He had always been a fertile and confident composer. But in 1787 he faced the obligation of the commission he had accepted in Prague, conscious that it must be his first major work to be carried through without Leopold's support and unconsciously holding himself to blame for Leopold's absence. Circumstance must have re-inforced this internal anxiety: he was pressed for time and found da Ponte almost too busy to get down to the libretto. In these pressures Mozart must have doubted, as artists with a commission so regularly do, whether he could rise to the occasion; and the Commendatore's ability to rise (indeed, by the metaphor of automata, to rise in the sexual sense) even after death must have figured to him as a magic talisman of his own ability to transcend Leopold's death.

However, although Pygmalion's usurpation made him an enlightenment hero, it was an act which incurred the punishment reserved for rebellious sons. This became clear in 1818, when the legend of Pygmalion was developed by Mary (Wollstonecraft Godwin) Shelley, into her novel *Frankenstein*, whose subtitle, *The Modern Prometheus*, associates its hero with another mythical usurper and one whose myth does punish him, most bitterly, for the usurpation. Where Pygmalion was the daring artist-scientist of the enlightenment, Frankenstein is the criminally arrogant modern scientist. He, too, conjures inert substance into life; but he is punished when his creature uses the life he has given it to destroy all that is dear to its creator. Similarly, the animated statue of the Commendatore moves only to destroy the hero with whom the creator of the opera was so closely identified. But where *Frankenstein* represents the next stage on from the Pygmalion legend, *Don Giovanni* makes a retreat from it. The animation of the statue re-asserts the creative power of God and his right and ability to punish, the moral being that the enlightenment should never have tried to steal his privileges in the first place. Mozart's imagination is affirming that his magic talisman has led him back into the fertile mythology of Catholicism.

XIX

'Don Giovanni' and 'Hamlet'

———————— ✵ ————————

The circumstances in which Mozart composed his Oedipal music-drama *Don Giovanni* are astonishingly similar to those in which Shakespeare composed his Oedipal poetry-drama *Hamlet*. Mozart's father had just died. Shakespeare's father was buried ten months before 'A booke called "*the Revenge of HAMLETT Prince Denmarke*" as yt was latelie Acted' was entered in the Stationers' Register.*

It was Freud who pointed out the psychological significance of John Shakespeare's death to the composition of *Hamlet*.[1] Freud took it, on the authority of 'a work on Shakespeare by Georg Brandes [1896]', that Shakespeare wrote *Hamlet* immediately after his father's death. This is probably the outline of the truth, but the detailed facts seem to be more complicated —and even more closely parallel to Mozart's biography.†

Mozart, it is safe to suppose, knew nothing about the Oedipal crisis in Shakespeare's life. But he did know its artistic result, *Hamlet*. The Oedipal forces which were probably activated in Shakespeare's personality by his father's death were poured into his treatment of the son-father theme in the legend of Hamlet. When the son-father situation reached its crisis in Mozart's personality at the death of Leopold Mozart, Mozart was about to start work on the legend of Don Juan, with *its* son-father theme; and quite evidently Shakespeare's treatment of the same theme in *Hamlet* was summoned to Mozart's mind. *Hamlet* can be clearly recognised—though it is so surprising to find it there

———————————————

* Mr Johannes Shakespeare is recorded as buried on 8 September, 1601. The entry in the Stationers' Register is for 'xxvjto Iulij', 1602. (Charles Williams: *A Short Life Of Shakespeare With The Sources*; G. B. Harrison's edition of the First Quarto *Hamlet*).

† See the Note at the end of this chapter.

that it has been overlooked—as one of the sources of *Don Giovanni*.

The memories of a performance of *Hamlet* which returned to Mozart during the composition of *Don Giovanni* were seven years old (though of course Mozart might have read the play at any time). Schikaneder's company performed *Hamlet* in Salzburg in September, 1780, and Mozart presumably saw it then; in any case, Mozart referred to *Hamlet* in a letter two months later.[2] Mozart had by then left Salzburg for Munich, where he was occupied in composing *Idomeneo*. He wrote home to his father his reflexions on the 'subterranean voice' in his opera: 'Picture to yourself the theatre, and remember that the voice must be terrifying—must penetrate—that the audience must believe it really exists'. Already given to improving his libretti, he tells his father that he wants the subterranean speech in *Idomeneo* shortened; and he adduces the speech of the ghost in *Hamlet*, which he thinks 'would be far more effective' if it were not so long.

When, years later, Mozart came to compose *Don Giovanni*, he encountered the same sort of theatrical problem as he had done with *Idomeneo*.[3] Another voice, not subterranean but sepulchral, had to be rendered terrifying; the audience had to be made to believe that another improbability really existed. The similarity of the problems would naturally turn Mozart's thoughts back to *Idomeneo*, and *Idomeneo* happened to be fresh in his mind because he had brought it out again for a private performance only the year before.[4] From *Idomeneo* his thoughts evidently went to *Hamlet*. Perhaps he even remembered, consciously or unconsciously, writing a letter which compared *Idomeneo* and *Hamlet* to the father whose absence he was now mourning.

However, in *Don Giovanni* it is not the ghostly Commendatore who shews the influence of *Hamlet*, except insofar as Mozart has taken the advice he offered Shakespeare and keeps the utterances of his revenant short. The suppressed link in Mozart's mental association between *Don Giovanni*, *Idomeneo* and *Hamlet* is the idea of a *subterranean* voice. This idea occurs in both *Idomeneo* and *Hamlet*. It was not the subterranean utterance of the *Hamlet* ghost which Mozart had criticised as long-winded, but the *Hamlet* ghost does make a subterranean utterance. Perhaps this one met with Mozart's approval; in any case, it is the subterranean remarks of the *Hamlet* ghost which, though they are no longer subterranean, reappear in *Don Giovanni*.

The ghost in *Hamlet*, who has already secured a private interview with his son, disclosed the crime and charged Hamlet with the duty of revenge, speaks subterraneanly when Hamlet is swearing Horatio and Marcellus to secrecy about the ghost's existence. 'Nay, but swear't', says Hamlet. They give their word. 'Upon my sword', Hamlet insists. 'We have sworn, my lord, already', says Marcellus. 'Indeed, upon my sword, indeed', Hamlet reiterates: and from beneath the stage the ghost's voice cries 'Swear'. Through the formulation of the oath, and through the repeated shifts of the oath-takers' ground, the ghost interposes with his 'Swear', 'Swear by his sword', 'Swear'—until at last the oath is composed to his satisfaction and Hamlet can call down to him 'Rest, rest perturbed spirit'.

It is this scene[5] which is transposed into *Don Giovanni*, Act one, scene one. Donna Anna has just found the body of *her* murdered father, and she calls upon Don Ottavio to swear vengeance. 'Lo giuro', 'I swear it', he sings, and repeats the words; but not to the satisfaction of Donna Anna's perturbed spirit, for he feels obliged to go off into the rococo elaborations of 'I swear it by your eyes, I swear it by our love'—'lo giuro agli occhi tuoi, lo giuro al nostro amor'. Donna Anna, satisfied for the moment, joins him for the quatrain of duet which begins 'Che giuramento, o Dei!' But then she breaks away from the duet to command, all over again, solo, that he swear; and ringing emphasis falls on the very word Hamlet's ghost cries from the cellarage, 'swear'—'giura!' Like Marcellus, Don Ottavio repeats 'lo giuro'; and only after he has repeated his elaboration of the oath (an elaboration which fills the same dramatic place as Hamlet's re-formulations and shifts of ground) is Donna Anna sufficiently appeased to unite her voice to his in a repetition and working-out of their duet.

Thus it is Donna Anna, the woman wronged, who plays in *Don Giovanni* some of the nagging and insistent rôle of the wronged ghost in *Hamlet*, with his insistence on oaths and vengeance. The shift of psychological interest from heroes to

heroines is typical of opera and quintessentially typical of
Mozart's operas; and something of the part of the younger
Hamlet himself, the usurped prince who yet hesitates to take
his revenge, falls to the other wronged woman in *Don Giovanni*,
herself the victim of a usurpation, Donna Elvira.

In Hamlet's case, his hesitation is a mystery to himself; it
rests on the fact, of which he is unconscious, that he identifies
himself in point of guiltiness with the murderer he would
punish. Donna Elvira, on the other hand, knows perfectly well
that the reason she hesitates to prosecute Don Giovanni's
punishment is that she is still in love with him. It is for this
reason that she alone pities him as punishment gathers about
him: 'Pietà, pietà', she intercedes, and on the express grounds
that he is her husband, in the great sextet where the others
threaten death to the person who is passing himself off as Don
Giovanni;[6] and it is for this reason that she makes a final attempt
to save Don Giovanni and is his last visitor before the stone
guest. Donna Elvira describes her emotional dilemma quite
explicitly in the recitative before her great aria 'Mi tradì'—
'Unhappy Elvira', she apostrophises herself, 'what a contrast of
emotions is born in your breast', 'che contrasto d'affetti in sen
ti nasce': whereupon she launches into a sustained and controlled
exposition of the two contrasting emotions, the definite 'He
betrayed me . . .' and the rather bumpy, unwilling, grudged
'But, betrayed and abandoned, I still feel pity for him'.[7]

Donna Elvira's moving and psychological aria 'Mi tradì' did
not exist when *Don Giovanni* had its first production at Prague
in 1787. Mozart composed 'Mi tradì' for the Vienna production
of 1788—at the request of Katharina (or Caterina) Cavalieri,
the Vienna Elvira, for an extra aria. The written-in aria could
not veer from the existing operatic structure. Mozart used the
opportunity to display the balancing point where the structure
and the psychology of the opera turn. Because the aria must
mark time in the plot development, he can make it a still or a
revolving-on-its-own-axis point in a headlong world. Elvira,
like all the other avengers (and most of all Don Ottavio, who
is reduced by it—and the additional disadvantage of being a
tenor—to the most milksoppy hero in operatic history), suffers
from the impotence imposed on human effort by Don Giovanni's
being reserved for the vengeance of heaven.

Fluently and originally, Mozart is, in 'Mi tradì', archaising. Like a heroine of earlier in the century, Elvira contrasts her duty and her love. Mozart's invention has a merry-go-round compulsion to keep going that mirrors the circling of her emotions. It might be an invention by J. S. Bach or by Handel. With the work of both those seemingly out-of-date masters Mozart owed some of his deep acquaintance to Gottfried van Swieten, imperial civil servant and librarian at Vienna. The Vienna *Don Giovanni* for which Mozart composed 'Mi tradì' opened on 7 May 1788. For performance on 30 December 1788 van Swieten commissioned the first of Mozart's four arrangements of choral works by Handel, *Acis and Galatea*; the soprano was the Vienna Donna Elvira.

'Mi tradì' is a sign, unconsciously given, that Mozart had reverted also to the performance he had witnessed seven years before of an out-of-date play by Shakespeare. Certainly it is in 'Mi tradì' that the influence of *Hamlet* expresses itself most strongly : 'Mi tradì' is, in fact, an epitome of all Hamlet's soliloquies. It is hesitation caught in the act of hesitating; a pendulum; a series of decisions, each formally counterbalanced by an objection, which in turn impels, like a piece of mechanism, a contrary decision.

The agonised, insoluble and mysteriously motivated hesitation Mozart expresses so brilliantly in 'Mi tradì' is not solely Donna Elvira's own, which is quite unmysterious and of the routine order of agony suffered by love-and-duty sopranos, but the composer's. 'Mi tradì' is *Mozart*'s Hamlet-like soliloquy. Just as Hamlet cannot bring himself to punish Claudius because he unconsciously holds himself as guilty as Claudius, so Mozart cannot bring himself to have Don Giovanni punished in human terms because he is in conscious sympathy with Don Giovanni's enlightenment crimes of blasphemy and parricide, and in unconscious collusion with the wish for the death of the father.

This hesitation on Mozart's part is responsible for the long-drawn impotence of the human avengers in *Don Giovanni*, the very impotence which obscures the dramatic strength of 'Mi tradì': but we have only to recognise that aria as Mozart's own soliloquy to recognise not only its psychological but its dramatic significance. As a confession that Mozart is identified with Don Giovanni, it explains to us why Mozart cannot allow Don

Giovanni to be punished within the conscious, rational and natural framework of the drama: consciously and rationally he believes Don Giovanni to be in the right. It is of unconscious guilt that neither Mozart nor Don Giovanni can be absolved. Mozart cannot administer punishment to his hero except by calling on the forces of the unconscious—calling up, that is, the supernatural powers of hell: and Donna Elvira's aria marks the exact place where he does so.

'Mi tradì' is the turning-point not only of the second half but of the opera as a whole. (Formally, it is the end of the first act which is the half-way climax, but that has all dissolved into dramatic nothingness because Don Giovanni makes his escape so facilely; it has merely pointed up the impotence of his human pursuers.) 'Mi tradì' marks the last attempt of human vengeance to bring itself to punish Don Giovanni; and the attempt ends in hesitation. But when the curtain rises again after 'Mi tradì', it is on the scene in the graveyard (which may be not without a memory of the graveyard scene in *Hamlet*) where Don Giovanni invites the statue of the Commendatore to supper, and it is here that the vengeance of heaven takes over.

It is Donna Elvira who leads up to the graveyard scene, but its effects are shewn in the character of the other wronged woman, Donna Anna. Within the action of the opera, Donna Anna has no more idea than Donna Elvira that the graveyard scene has taken place; neither of them is present at it. Yet it is the graveyard scene which releases both women from the obligation to pursue vengeance, an obligation which Donna Anna has fulfilled much more whole-heartedly than Donna Elvira. In the dramatic pattern of the opera, the graveyard scene establishes that Don Giovanni may from now on be left to heaven, and the result is that Donna Anna need no longer play the part of a Fury goading Don Ottavio to revenge, but is free to present the gentler aspect of her personality (an aspect we already know of Donna Elvira's, because she has been unable all along to bring herself to play the Fury). The graveyard episode is followed immediately by the miraculous domestic scena, the only truly domestic passage in *Don Giovanni*, where Don Ottavio reproaches Donna Anna with 'Crudele', and she replies with her heart-cry 'Crudele? Ah, no, mio bene!' and then sings her incomparably moving 'Non mi dir'.[9] This immense change in Donna Anna's character, beautifully justified in dramatic terms by the intervention of the graveyard scene, means that singers who undertake Donna Anna have to be capable of being Queens of the Night for 'Or sai chi l'onore' in the first part and Countesses Almaviva for 'Non mi dir'.

NOTE TO CHAPTER XIX

The difficulty about exploring the relation of *Hamlet* to the death of Shakespeare's father is the difficulty of discovering when Shakespeare wrote *Hamlet*; and here the main trouble seems to be that he probably wrote it several times.

It appears (I am relying on G. B. Harrison's Introduction to his edition of the First Quarto text of *Hamlet*) that an old play on the Hamlet story, known to scholars as the *Ur-Hamlet*, was performed in 1594; a quotation from it (of 1596) establishes that this was not Shakespeare's play. However, it presumably was the material which Shakespeare took up and re-fashioned. *A* version, and presumably a new one, of the Hamlet story was registered and had lately been acted in 1602. The entry does not mention Shakespeare, but probably the new play was by him, and it probably represented his first re-fashioning of the *Ur-Hamlet*. The first printed text—which does name Shakespeare—appeared in 1603 (not earlier than May); but this was the First Quarto, a 'bad text' differing considerably from the Second Quarto of 1604, which, together with the subsequent First Folio, is the basis of the received text. It seems that the First Quarto is a bad text in two distinct ways: it reads like a pirated text, taken down at a performance or put together from an actor's memories; and it also differs *in story* from the received text.

All of this suggests that Shakespeare first re-fashioned the *Ur-Hamlet* and then, perhaps more than once, re-fashioned his own re-fashioning. It is possible that these textual probabilities coincide with psychological probabilities which can be extracted from Shakespeare's life history, and that one can point to events which probably directed Shakespeare's attention to the

Hamlet theme and then impelled him to re-work his earlier treatment of the theme.

In 1596 Thomas Lodge referred to 'yᵉ ghost which cried . . . at yᵉ Theator . . . *Hamlet, reuenge'*—words which do not come from any text of Shakespeare's play and presumably do come from the *Ur-Hamlet*. It seems, therefore, that the *Ur-Hamlet* was still in the repertory or at least in recent memory in 1596 and had not yet been replaced in either of them by a new version by Shakespeare. Shakespeare's first version thus probably dates from after 1596. And it was in fact in 1596 that an event occurred which might very well turn Shakespeare's attention towards the old Hamlet play and urge him to re-make it: the death of Shakespeare's son, who was named, to the vindication of the emphasis psycho-analysis lays on the significance of names, Hamnet.

This first Shakespearean *Hamlet*, written after 1596, is quite probably the one which had lately been acted in 1602. The psychological probability is that this version was written out of the emotions provoked by Hamnet Shakespeare's death. In that case, it seems likely, again on psychological grounds (though also on grounds of general probability), that the text of the First Quarto of 1603 was pirated from Shakespeare's *first* version of the play. The story told by this First Quarto text differs from the later text chiefly in the character of Gertrude, whom it makes wholly and definitely, instead of ambiguously, innocent of complicity in the murder—indeed, ignorant that it *was* a murder. As soon as Hamlet discloses the truth to her, the First Quarto Gertrude places herself at his disposal and agrees to play up to his stratagems. ('. . . I sweare by heauen, I never knew of this most horride murder . . . I will conceale, consent, and doe my best, What stratagem so'ere thou shalt deuise.') Psychologically, the conclusion is irresistible that Shakespeare wrote this version as a father and a husband, more particularly as a bereaved father. Gertrude is still seen sympathetically as a wife, her innocence guaranteed and her honour vindicated by her taking sides with Hamlet.

It is possible, however, that by the time this version was pirated and printed, Shakespeare was already making it out-of-date by writing his second version, which was printed as the Second Quarto of 1604, and in which the story has been changed.

Gertrude is now ambivalently regarded by her son, and the author is deeply identified with the son's emotions. The impulse to Shakespeare to produce this altered version, writing this time as a son, probably came in 1601, with the death of Shakespeare's father.

That the deaths of both Shakespeare's son and his father should be involved in the composition of *Hamlet* is a further astonishing biographical coincidence. Mozart's third child, Johann Thomas Leopold, died in November 1786—eleven months before *Don Giovanni* appeared. This son was called, in the continental fashion, by the last of his Christian names. (Leopold Mozart, in a letter to his daughter from Salzburg, 1–2 March, 1787, refers to the child as 'little Leopold'.) The boy was thus the namesake of Mozart's father; and we can conjecture that thereby his son's and his father's death acquired for Mozart the psychological assonance that the death of *his* father and *his* son held for Shakespeare, for whom the point of fusion was that his son was the namesake of a hero whose relation to his father was so significant.

Like Mozart, Shakespeare makes amends to a father unconsciously wished away by resurrecting a murdered father in ghostly form in a drama. If, like Mozart, he attempted to heal the son-father quarrel by identifying himself with his father, then we can credit on psychological grounds the tradition that Shakespeare himself played the part of the ghost in his play—which part, Nicholas Rowe had heard in 1709, was 'the top of his performance' as an actor.

XX

Mozart and Brimstone

————————❄————————

In consigning Don Giovanni to hell, Mozart was punishing his
infantile and unconscious self for parricidal wishes against
Leopold Mozart, and his enlightened self for parricidal wishes
against the established order. However, the act of expiation did
not align Mozart with the reaction; yet neither did it pay the
debt once and for all and free Mozart to become an out-and-out
revolutionary. The impulse of expiation and submission revived
again, when it was Mozart's own death that he was expecting,
in his Requiem; though even so he was unable to make his submission final by completing the music. And the rebellious
impulse proved equally irrepressible and immortal when it went
on from its burial in *Don Giovanni* to create *Die Zauberflöte*.

For a rebellious impulse which is immortal Mozart chose a
very apt symbol in Don Giovanni. Don Giovanni, though quite
literally repressed in hell (mythology's representation of the
unconscious[1]) is unkillable. That, of course, is true of all
repressed wishes or, mythologically speaking, of all dead souls:
they all continue immortal in their incarceration. But Don
Giovanni has not descended into hell in the normal mythological
manner of souls after death (who have no hope of getting out
again): he has not died. The special supernatural intervention,
which Mozart, unlike Goldoni, has made no attempt to iron out
of the story, consists in the fact that Don Giovanni is carried off
without leaving a body behind him. The survivors rush on
demanding where he is; and Leporello tells them 'Hope no
more to find him; search no more; he has gone far away'.[2]

In other words, Don Giovanni is half-way to joining the
company of Greek heroes whom the Masonic enlightenment
adopted as prototypes for its own initiants. He has descended
into hell in his lifetime; if he could only achieve the return
journey, he would change—at least in enlightened eyes—from

outlaw into hero. Just as the legend of King Arthur, by refusing him a physical death, holds out hopes of his second coming and makes him *rex quondam rexque futurus*, so the legend of Don Juan makes him anti-rex quondam and hints at his being anti-rex futurus by suggesting hopes—or fears—of his return. Mozart's opera of submission to the reaction had indeed taken an ambiguous form. The resurrection-value of the rebellious impulse he had sent to hell in *Don Giovanni* was proved when, in *Die Zauberflöte*, he took up the same mythological metaphor and shewed the enlightened hero's triumphant return from the realm of death.

In Mozart's personal psychology, the material which created his ambivalence, and held it open and unhealed his life long, is to be found in the extraordinary closeness of his relation to Leopold Mozart. 'Cheer up your son', Mozart wrote to Leopold[3] after they had differed about Mozart's behaviour to the Archbishop, 'for it is only the thought of displeasing you that can make him unhappy in his very promising circumstances'. His circumstances were more promising still when he was asked to provide an opera to follow up *Figaro*'s success in Prague; and then it was the unconscious thought of having displeased Leopold to the point of having killed him in wish which turned the new opera into *Don Giovanni*.

Leopold's minute superintendence, in person or by letter, of his son's life and career was the guarantor that the rebellious impulse in Mozart would be perpetually provoked and renewed. One outlet for rebellion was enlightenment: the other was the scatology which for so long kept Mozart's letters from being read or, if read, appreciated—to the neglect of not only an unparalleled personal revelation by a supreme artist but also one of the most lively and penetrating social reports ever written.

Mozart's scatological fantasies offer no confirmation to the psychologist of types, who would expect on the strength of them that Mozart's talent was for the plastic arts and his character parsimonious—whereas in fact he inclined, so far as his poverty allowed, towards an extravagance he was always having to defend against Leopold's prudence.* What these letters really

* And he hoped to win Leopold to the idea of his marriage by urging that Constanze would provide 'economy and good management, which cannot be expected from a young fellow, particularly if he is in love' (from Vienna, 27 July, 1782).

betray in Mozart is the eternal infant prodigy, whose training at the clavier had begun almost as early as his training at the lavatory. From the obligation to report the progress of his career to Leopold with almost a book-keeper's constancy, Mozart escapes into his letters to his contemporaries, his sister and his cousin, where his excretory nonsense-fantasies denote a retreat into the naughtiness of the nursery.

It was naughtiness, as the inconsequent turn of the fantasies shews, in its most literal sense—a lack of purpose and of concern with what Leopold regarded as the serious affairs of life. 'I have detected in my son', Leopold wrote[4] when Mozart was twenty-six, 'an outstanding fault, which is, that he is far too *patient* or rather *easy-going*, too *indolent*, perhaps even too *proud*, in short, that he has the sum total of all those traits, which render a man *inactive*'.*

Leopold, perhaps, really did have the characteristics of an anal-erotic psychology; and in him the infantile high valuation of excrement had been converted, as unconscious symbolism regularly converts it in dreams and myths,[5] into a high valuation of another but antithetical earthy substance, gold. It was precisely against this conversion of values that Mozart was protesting. His scatological jokes with his cousin, which were later replaced by persistent questions and advice to his wife on this subject in relation to her health, are an attempt to form a nursery conspiracy which shall preserve the nursery values against the adult values of Leopold. Perhaps Mozart's persistent inquiries of his wife were a nursery caricature of Leopold's persistent inquiries of Mozart, but Mozart related them to a subject, Constanze's health, which in his eyes did really matter. In his scatological fantasies, on the other hand, he was flaunting his preoccupation with the substance which, to Leopold's mind, was the least valuable of all substances in the world, sheer waste matter on which one should not waste one's time.

Only in *Don Giovanni*, where Mozart was accusing himself of having wronged Leopold, does this infantile conception of

---

* Perhaps Leopold felt that *proud* was rather a contradiction of the other epithets; it is by refining on this string of characteristics that he arrives at the formulation of a general contradictoriness in Mozart's character which I have already cited (in chapter XVIII).

naughtiness shew signs of shaping a serious conception of evil. If we read through the Don Juan legend to the Christian mythology which the legend was intended to vindicate, the real hero of *Don Giovanni* is the devil. It is the devil whose attentions Mozart had superstitiously warded off from himself in the letter he wrote while he was rehearsing *Don Giovanni*, and the devil of whom Don Giovanni says—prophetically and with dramatic irony—'I think the devil is amusing himself today by frustrating my pleasurable progress', 'Mi par ch'oggi il demonio si diverta d'opporsi a' miei piacevoli progressi'.[6]

The less canonical portions of Christian mythology had long associated[7] the devil with a bad smell, with the anal kiss, supposedly a part of the ritual of witchcraft, and with sodomy. In *Don Giovanni*, Mozart, who elsewhere uses the explosion of air from brass instruments in a comic sense unmistakably parallel to his comic letters, employs the trombones in a terrifying sense to signify the nearness of the gates of hell. Earlier, he had employed trombones to convey the supernatural quality of the oracle in *Idomeneo*. 'The accompaniment to the subterranean voice', Mozart wrote to his father[8] during the composition of *Idomeneo*, 'consists of five instruments only, that is, three trombones and two French horns, which are placed in the same quarter as that from which the voice proceeds'. The trombones, as E. J. Dent pointed out,[9] were not part of the normal operatic orchestra but were considered almost as a stage property; the trombones in *Don Giovanni* are, in Dent's words, 'treated as if they were played on the stage, or even under the stage, like Purcell's in *The Libertine*'. Perhaps when he deployed the trombones in this way for *Don Giovanni* Mozart's mind had gone back, via the subterranean voice in *Idomeneo*, to the voice that comes from under the stage in *Hamlet*.

It is not unexpected, therefore, that Don Giovanni, alone of Mozart's heroes, should be—like Hamlet—an unconscious homosexual.[10] Neither is it unexpected that Hamlet himself shews some of the preoccupation found in Mozart's letters with 'things rank and gross in nature': particularly with the smell of dead bodies ('if indeed you find him not within this month, you shall nose him as you go up the stairs into the lobby'); more particularly still, with the smell of dead father-representatives ('Dost thou think Alexander looked o' this fashion i' the earth?

. . . And smelt so?'). Death, to Hamlet, is a gigantic act of defecation, which turns the whole body—even the body of an empire's political father—into unregarded waste matter:

> *Imperious Caesar, dead and turn'd to clay,*
> *Might stop a hole, to keep the wind away.*

The whole nexus has a perfectly logical coherence in the psychology of the unconscious. Don Juanism itself is an attempt to ward off, to postpone the day of, the punishment it has already earned; and this punishment is, to the unconscious, equivalent to being turned into a woman or a passive homosexual. Inevitably the devil turns his victims into sodomites; that is the consequence of the punishment he administers, since, as Freud remarked,[11] 'every punishment is ultimately castration'. Don Giovanni's prophetic utterance that the devil is opposing himself to his pleasurable progress gives a precise account of imprisonment and punishment. Whether they take place on earth or in hell, their purpose is to frustrate pleasurable progress. Mozart is frustrating and punishing the enlightenment's essential hedonism in having Don Giovanni interrupted in the middle of his invertedly knightly quest for pleasure.

However, the punishment of castration, the negation of all pleasure, which the small boy expects to visit him as a result of his ambitions towards the mother, is also capable of being turned to pleasurable account. The small boy can actually improve on it by understanding it as something which turns him into a woman. If he is to be obliged by the father to give up his desires towards the mother, then he will put himself in her place vis-à-vis the father. This versatility, this almost duplicity, on the part of the infantile Ego makes it less surprising that Mozart should offer his submission to his father in *Don Giovanni* by exploiting—through the mythological material—those anal preoccupations which in his letters he employed to express rebellion against the father. No doubt Mozart had often heard in person from Leopold that he was *'indolent'* and *'inactive'*, and no doubt he had interpreted these as the characteristics of effeminacy: and when the myth bundles off Don Giovanni to an everlasting union with the father of lies in the reek of brimstone and sulphur, it implicitly postulates a homosexual union between them.

Through and through, *Don Giovanni* is an ambiguous act of submission. Does its reek of brimstone signify the closest possible union between devilish father and renegade son; or is it the mark of the son's rebellion against the heavenly father? Through which of the unseen fatherly protagonists, God or the devil, are we to discern the figure of Leopold, returning to claim his son as the Commendatore returns to claim his quasi-son-in-law and murderer? It is Mozart's ancient problem of which *is* the sacred, which the profane. *Don Giovanni*, ending either on its hero's last terrified shout or on the pious and smug epitaph after his removal, cannot help pointing the question whether the heavenly father is heavenly and benevolent at all. It is God who unremittingly and efficiently pursues vengeance; it is ultimately he who, in his omnipotence, is responsible for hell-fire; and it is he who condemns Don Giovanni to it because Don Giovanni sticks bravely to his Egotism and refuses the hypocritical tribute of repentance under threat.

Read in this sense—and the opera cannot help suggesting this reading through its ostensible message, because of the dramatic emphasis it places on Don Giovanni's courage—Don Giovanni is really the bravest of all Mozart's liberal, truth-telling heroes and heroines. He is bold and moral enough to affirm his undying belief in the pleasure-principle, even though all the evidence goes to shew that his own quest for pleasure has been too compulsive to yield him much real enjoyment—even though he knows it has led him, as all compulsions do in a psychological sense, to hell. Even in the opera which constitutes his act of submission, Mozart shadowily sets forth the anti-God answer he was to make openly in *Die Zauberflöte*, where the message of the ordeals is that this bullying God who tries and fails to overawe Don Giovanni is in any case a false pretender, since hell-fire, the fear of which is the great corrupter of human morals and happiness, does not really exist.

XXI

'Such as the Father is, Such is the Son . . . the Father Eternal, the Son Eternal . . .'

―――――――――❊―――――――――

We do not, of course, possess a 'solution' to the puzzle of an artistic personality. The elements we can pick out as the unconscious sources of Mozart's supreme creativity are just those we would have to pick out as the unconscious sources of the peculiar behaviour of dozens of neurotics or hysterics. If we did not have a record of the works of each, and if we had not judged the works by other—by social and aesthetic—criteria, we should be unable to guess which was the Mozart and which the hysteric. Psycho-analysis informs us that the infant does not die in any personality but continues to spin its wish-fantasies in the unconscious so long as the personality lives. We can guess that in great artists the infantile material is unusually accessible to conscious control, whereas in the hysteric or neurotic the infant has risen up and intruded itself on the conscious in the form of an involuntary symptom. But art itself often seems to be, and perhaps even must be, an involuntary activity, only the form it takes being consciously directed. We do not know through what mechanism the great artist exercises the high degree of conscious control which distinguishes him from the mere fluent fantaisiste, who may be equally 'inspired'—that is, equally dependent on an unconscious impulse and unconscious material. Neither do we know what element it is in the structure of a personality which makes the difference between an artist—good or bad—and a hysteric.*

The non-resolution—the very active non-resolution—of an

―――――

* Cf. Freud (*Totem And Taboo*, II):— 'We may say that hysteria is a caricature of an artistic creation, a compulsion neurosis a caricature of a religion, and a paranoiac delusion a caricature of a philosophic system'.

unconscious and infantile dilemma, which has brought many neurotics to prostration and immobility, became in Mozart the principle of an artistic perpetual motion. The influence of Leopold Mozart, for ever driving Mozart to rebel and for ever pulling him back on the strings of filial piety, could not be removed by physical distance (which was bridged by letters) or even finally by Leopold's death. The father was indeed eternal—in the son. And equally Mozart was eternally a son: a personality, an Ego, whose existence was psychically possible only in and through the filial relationship.

The mechanism through which this worked was the very thing which allows most sons to patch up a solution to the Oedipus conflict, the son's identification with the father. Mozart could not achieve such an identification, for the reason that it already existed and had been proposed—by Leopold—from the start.

Artists' biographies often read 'His father intended him for the law/the church/medicine/commerce, but after studying/ practising for a year or two, he broke away, to his father's displeasure . . .' Sometimes there is an eventual reconciliation and a measure of mutual identification between father and son on the point of their both recognising the rightness of the son's break-away. Even when the father observes and approves of the son's talent, it is often a case—very often, for instance, in the biographies of the painters of the Italian renaissance—of the father's handing the boy over to a pseudo-father: he takes the boy into the nearest big town and places him in the workshop of the local master.

With Leopold Mozart and Wolfgang Mozart not a touch of all this could apply. Both were artists in the same medium (a situation which is perhaps less rare among musicians and composers than in the other arts); their art was one which demands a great deal of technical instruction (whereas a writer can be instructed only by himself); and they belonged to a small family, without a quantity of siblings to set father and son at a distance and tap off into cross-relationships the intense identity between them. Leopold was both the real father and the master of the apprentice. There was no question of his being displeased by his son's choice of profession: it was his own choice, both for himself and, more important, for his son.

Art is by psychogenesis[1] a rebellion against paternal forces in society and in the artist's own psyche. For Mozart, however, art could not wholly express rebellion against his father in person, because Leopold, as artist, was likewise a rebel. (With the same effect, no sooner had Mozart become a Freemason than Leopold followed his example.) Mozart had no occasion to usurp Leopold's place: Leopold had destined him to occupy it —including the place of breadwinner—from the start. When, at the age of twenty-one, Mozart went off with his mother to Munich, leaving Leopold behind at Salzburg, Mozart could not unconsciously interpret this as a break-away on his own part, in which he carried off his mother and thrust himself into Leopold's position: rather, it was to Leopold that he wrote, during the journey, with proud obedience and as a proof that he was doing as Leopold wanted him to do: 'I am most attentive to my duty. I am quite a second Papa . . .'[2]

A year later, Mozart was again abroad with his mother, this time in Paris. Again it was Mozart's duty to take care of his mother on his father's behalf; and his mother died. Mozart's own relationship to his mother was swallowed up in his more than identification with, his actual impersonation of, Leopold. His own grief loses the opportunity to express itself in his duty to make Leopold's grief as bearable as it can be by preparing him for the news: a tortured, touching symptom of the eternal son. By an unparalleled act not so much of self-control as of self-negation, as though he could not bring himself to admit the separateness of his own existence from Leopold's by knowing a fact which was not yet known to Leopold, Mozart wrote to Leopold 'My dear mother is very ill' at a time when she was already dead.

Keeping up the pretence, and also no doubt to the relief of his own feelings, Mozart continues this extraordinary letter[3] with the sort of thing Leopold would expect from it and must find in it if the fiction were to be passed off. A paragraph of reportage about musical affairs tails away into chit-chat ('I went to the Palais Royal, where I had a large ice . . .'). At this point of relaxation, the violence of Mozart's remorse towards his father is able to break suddenly and apparently irrelevantly through, and it takes the characteristic form of an outburst against the enlightenment: it is in this letter, under the pretext of chattering

on,* that Mozart gives his vindictive account of the death of
Voltaire.

The death of his mother, whom Leopold had entrusted to
him, figures to Mozart as a dereliction of his duty to Leopold.
Mozart unconsciously expects that Leopold will accuse him, as
tormented mourners accuse themselves, of not having done all
he might to prevent the death—of having, in fact, wished the
death. The unconscious relevance by which he drags in Voltaire's
death in order to appease Leopold is that Mozart thereby
makes, as it were, the declaration: Now here is a death which I
would not be ashamed of your thinking I had wished. Writing
to a father, Mozart sacrifices to him a figure of the enlightenment. Voltaire's is, precisely, a death which the enlightened
Mozart would *not* have wished; to seem to concur and delight
in it is one of the most apt tokens he could have used for his
desire to submit to his father.

The death alike of his mother and of Leopold increased
Mozart's sense of debt to Leopold; and in both cases the debt
was paid by a plunge into reaction. It was his mother's death
which provoked the epitaph on Voltaire, 'That is his reward!',
his father's death the epitaph on Don Giovanni, 'Questo è il
fin di chi fa mal!'

Mozart's was a double burden: his own identification with
Leopold, and Leopold's with him. Leopold had chosen to pursue
his own career through his son's. He demanded the right to
supervise and control Mozart's career because that was his own
career as well; the talent was not Mozart's but *theirs*. Mozart
himself held, no doubt seriously though he says it jokingly, that
God had given him his talent and laid him under certain obligations towards it.† Through his obligations to the heavenly, we
can read his obligations to his earthly, father.

Indeed, Mozart was capable of making to his earthly father as
complete a submission, as thorough a 'Thy will be done', as
ever a man made to God. Leopold, however, was not in fact

---

* It was the merest pretext, since the news was a month out of date. (Voltaire had
died on 30 May and Mozart was writing on the 3 July, 1778.) Indeed Mozart
introduces the subject with 'Now I have a piece of news for you which you may
have heard already'.

† At the period when he was still insisting he was not in love with Constanze
Weber, Mozart wrote to his father 'God has not given me my talent that I might
attach it to a wife and waste my youth in idleness' (from Vienna, 25 July, 1781).

immortal; and therefore Mozart is driven to express his identification of his father's will with his own through ideas and images which clearly betray his terror of the remorse he knows will fall on him when Leopold does die. On Leopold's name-day in 1781 Mozart sent him congratulations which, although their hyperboles are intended as pleasantries, make an extraordinarily tense, convoluted, neurotically intellectualised and apprehensive statement of the strains in the son's unusual identification with the father. 'Dearest, most beloved father!' writes Mozart, 'I wish you every imaginable good that one can possibly wish. Nay rather, I wish nothing for you, but everything for myself. So I wish for my own sake that you may continue to enjoy good health, and that you may live many, many years for my happiness and my infinite pleasure. I wish for my own sake that everything I do and undertake may be in accordance with your desire and pleasure, or rather that I may never do anything which may not cause you the very greatest joy. I hope it may be so, for whatever contributes to your son's happiness must naturally be agreeable to you'.[4]

So completely does Mozart accept identification with his father that he admits that it would be 'selfishness' in him if he kept his earnings to himself: 'Believe me, I would gladly deprive myself of everything, if only I had it!'[5] And for 'all the fatherly love which you have lavished on me so richly from my childhood . . . I can never thank you enough'.[6]

Mozart owed his talent in a particular sense to Leopold, since it must have been clear to him—and this was reinforced by the example of the Bach family whom he so much admired—that his musical bent was hereditary. It was equally clear, however, and to both Mozarts, that the son was much *more* talented than the father. Precisely that was why Leopold, though for financial reasons he could not drop his own career, gave his heart to teaching and promoting Mozart. Like the activity of any literary or musical agent, Leopold's activity on behalf of Mozart's career can be seen—and no doubt Mozart in his ambivalence did see it—both as self-sacrifice and as the exploitation of somebody else's talent. But the argument that Leopold himself had possessed no great talent to sacrifice to his son's cannot have reduced Mozart's sense of debt: in his own capacity as artist, and through the identification of his own with his father's feelings, Mozart perfectly appreciated artistic Egoism and knew that greater love than this hath no artist than to lay down his own artistic ambitions and take up his son's.

We can understand what psychological affinity with Mozart it was that gave Kierkegaard his interest in, and understanding of, the theme of Don Giovanni. Mozart after his father's death must have had just the feelings Kierkegaard wrote down[7] after *his* father's death: 'I look upon his death as the last sacrifice which he made to his love for me; for he . . . *died for me* in order that if possible I might still turn into something'.

If Mozart had remorseful reactions in favour of the established order it was because his father, who represented the established order in Mozart's personal life, had taught him all he knew, which not only filled up the son's mind but emptied out the father's. It was probably this which, although Mozart quickly outgrew Leopold's style of composition (according to Einstein,[8] that of 'a provincial schoolmaster trying to appear fashionable'), held Mozart back from ever becoming, in the strictly musical sense, a technical innovator.

Mozart was caught in the dilemma that he could please and satisfy Leopold only by surpassing him. Even his infantilism, his playing the family fool, his determination to see and sign himself as 'the same old buffoon',[9] are attempts to do precisely what he did in the letter he wrote after his mother's death, namely soften the blow he could not help inflicting on Leopold. At the same time, his reverence towards the great composers who belonged to the generation before or, roughly, contemporary with his father*—his study and imitation of the works of Handel, J. S. Bach and Joseph Haydn (in the last case combined with personal respect and affection)—indicates that he was casting about for an adoptive musical father† whose music he could more genuinely admire and learn from than Leopold's.

Both the great works of Mozart's reactionary impulse, *Don Giovanni* and the Requiem, express the reaction by casting back in time. With *Don Giovanni*, it is a case of casting back

---

* Bach and Handel were both born in 1685, Leopold Mozart in 1719, Haydn in 1732.

† The letter in which Mozart dedicated six string quartets (K. 458, K. 464–5) to Haydn employs the conceit whereby the works are Mozart's sons and he commends them to the guardianship of Haydn. (From Vienna, 1 September, 1785.)

historically—a comparatively rare case in the eighteenth century, which was not much interested in 'period atmosphere' unless the period concerned were classical or that generalised but distinctively Venetian high renaissance in which Sebastiano Ricci and Giambattista Tiepolo set their (highly operatic) personages, dressed and painted in a 'maniera Paolesca'[10] (sc. Paolo Veronese). Modern producers of *Don Giovanni* regularly recognise its archaism of feeling by dressing it in the period of the legend, not the composer. With the Requiem, the archaism is stylistic—under the influence of Handel, for several of whose choral works Mozart had lately provided instrumentation.[11] After the rococo of much of Mozart's other church music, the style of the Requiem makes almost as ghostly an effect of resurrection as the return of the Commendatore himself.

The Requiem, however, is not wholly a work of reaction; and neither is its counterpart, simultaneously composed, *Die Zauberflöte*, wholly a work of the enlightenment. In this last year of his life Mozart achieved or suffered a certain fusion between the opposite poles of his ambivalence. In *Die Zauberflöte*, whose message is so strongly against violence and in favour of reconciliation, Mozart was certainly reaching out deliberately for this fusion. The initiation is designed to set on rebellion a cast so reasonable and so disciplined as to make it acceptable even to father-figures—to, we may be sure, Leopold himself. But the great father-figure in *Die Zauberflöte*, Sarastro, is seen by no means unambiguously.

Indeed, the opera's presentation of Sarastro perfectly illustrates how an unconscious impulse may take advantage of external and fortuitous circumstance. If it is correct to deduce that the plot of *Die Zauberflöte* was altered, then it is this quite external fact which made the opening for the doubts we cannot help feeling about Sarastro. The final intention may be to make him ultra-virtuous and ultra-paternal (in the rosy view of paternity); but the authors have not given him quite time to shake off their first plan, in which he was to be the villain; and the plot as a whole obliges us to remark that he does appear, after all, to have really stolen Pamina.

In this first breach in the image of a virtuous Sarastro, Mozart's responsibility does not go beyond passive complicity. He has merely failed to insist that the two versions be more adroitly patched and the image of Sarastro properly mended. However, having once let the crack remain, he has not resisted its being enlarged. Having stolen Pamina, Sarastro exposes her to the insults of Monostatos, allows her to be tortured by the thought that Tamino no longer loves her, and himself preaches at her—both about her mother's wickedness and, most unfairly, as the story finally shews, about the shortcomings of the female sex. In our total impression of him, Sarastro is not very far short of a sanctimonious bully. Mozart has not resisted raising or allowing to be raised just the doubts about his Masonic father-figure which *Don Giovanni* raises about God the Father.

The reconciliation towards which *Die Zauberflöte* reaches out is, once again, to be achieved by Mozart's identification of himself with Leopold. (This theme is, as a matter of fact, implicit in the initiation in *Die Zauberflöte*, since it is the identification of the initiant-son with the divine father which furnishes the psychological content of religious initiation rituals.[12] Probably it was an unconscious understanding of this theme which in the first place attracted Mozart not only to the story of *Die Zauberflöte* but to the whole Masonic movement which lies behind it.) And yet Leopold cannot manifest himself in his son's dramatic work except as an ambiguous figure whose ambiguity is created by Mozart's ambivalence towards him.

In the Requiem, on the other hand, the coalescence between his opposite points of view has been agonisingly forced on Mozart. That Mozart died before he could finish the Requiem almost suggests that the coalescence could not be made—almost that Mozart died rather than finish the Requiem. Like the death of Dickens before he could finish *The Mystery Of Edwin Drood*, it seems to offer an insight into the psychology of the artist's genius too deep and too dazzling to take advantage of: it is a puzzle one dare not solve because the tragedy is too stunning. Mozart's intention in the Requiem is to retreat from the rococo of his own ecclesiastical manner to the baroque assurance of Handel's. The Requiem is the music of a man who would like to assert 'I *know* that my redeemer liveth'. But for Mozart this retreat into Handel is itself dangerous, because it carries him away from the Catholic church and towards protestantism. From there he is carried, by way of the greater emphasis protestantism (and Handel) placed on the Old Testament, back almost beyond Christianity into the ancient Jewish world with its uncheerful uncertainties about life after death.

Once again in the Requiem Mozart employs the trombones to announce supernatural and deadly terror. The strange circumstances of the Requiem's commissioning—the arrival of an unknown man bearing the invitation to write the music from an anonymous authority—are said to have been received by Mozart as a premonition of his own death. To understand in precisely what sense he received the commission we have only to think of *Don Giovanni*. The visitor bearing an invitation is merged with the visitor who comes in answer to Don Giovanni's invitation—the revenant father, come to seek vengeance and carry off his quasi-son. For the last time Mozart cannot decide whether the ghostly influence of Leopold is sacred or profane. The Requiem is Mozart's most convulsive attempt to submit himself to the Catholic church and accept the consolation and terror of heaven and hell in place of the Masonic revelation that the life after death was a baseless legend. And yet the music of the Requiem contains, according to Einstein,[13] Masonic allusions.

The effect the Requiem makes is quite beyond both Christianity and enlightenment, and almost beyond art. The music is very nearly too naked to be judged as art; Mozart's retreat into the solid conventions of the baroque has nearly burst the conventions of art itself. It is impossible to say whether the Requiem is good art. It is certainly great.

The whole work is an elaboration and intensification of Don Giovanni's last shout. It is Mozart on the subject of his own death, which Masonry had taught him to conceive of as the mere extinction of the brief rococo flame, and which Catholicism promised would mean, precisely because of his unrepentant adherence to Masonry and enlightenment, the endless flames of hell.

XXII

Society's Guilt

———— ❋ ————

In Mozart, as in Antoine Watteau, that other great doomed artist of the century, the enlightenment's pilgrimage in quest of pleasure is made poignant by his awareness of his own life's fragility. Watteau is the height of the early rococo, Mozart the height of its development; and both incarnate the conscious impermanence which *is* the rococo. 'I never lie down at night', Mozart wrote to his father,* 'without reflecting that—young as I am—I may not live to see another day'. That is the implicit epigraph of all his music.

Mozart was ill, and the strains of his relationship with Leopold perhaps accelerated his illness—even, it may be, creating an unconscious remorseful resolve to outlive Leopold by as little as possible. Society can be blamed for none of that. But the strains were reinforced, the acceleration increased and Leopold's own calls on Mozart made more compelling in their effect as a result of the pernicious values of European society, which was and still is inclined to believe that the only good artist is a dead one. The early and still persistent rumour that Mozart was poisoned by a rival is perhaps an unconscious confession, on the part of the society which gives it credence, of guilt. The legend has picked on the wrong villain, but it tells a truth when it insists there *was* a villain.

Like Watteau, who so evidently identifies himself with the isolated and unhappy clowns he paints, Mozart knew that to society he was no more than a clown, no more than 'the same

* It is in this letter (from Vienna, 4 April, 1787) that Mozart gives his reflexions on death. They are prompted by the thought of Leopold's death, but this brings with it—no doubt it was psychologically inseparable from—the thought of Mozart's own. This thought makes its appearance through a reference to the death of 'my dearest and most beloved friend, Count von Hatzfeld'; Mozart assimilates himself to the dead friend, who 'was just thirty-one, my own age'.

old buffoon'. He entertained. 'I play and hear them exclaim: *"Oh, c'est un prodige, c'est inconcevable, c'est étonnant!"*, and then it is—*Adieu'*. This from Paris.[1] After giving a concert in Strasbourg he wrote:[2] 'The chief receipts consisted in the shouts of *Bravo* and *Bravissimo!* which echoed on all sides'.

Towards the end of his life, all the pressures increase so sharply, and are so courageously met, that the letters become a tragedy we could hardly bear to read even if we were uninvolved. (In fact we are involved, both through Mozart's music, which is still alive, and again because our own society, though directing them to different ends, so largely maintains the values of the eighteenth century.) Mozart is so poor that he has both to borrow and to work continually. He writes a begging letter[3] and adds the postscript: 'O God!—I can hardly bring myself to despatch this letter!—and yet I must! If this illness had not befallen me, I should not have been obliged to beg so shamelessly from my only friend. Yet I hope for your forgiveness, for you know both the good and the bad prospects of my situation. The bad is temporary . . .'

To Constanze, from whom he is separated while he is in Frankfurt, he promises:[4] 'Dearest, most beloved little Wife of my Heart! . . . I am firmly resolved to make as much money as I can here and then return to you with great joy. What a life we shall have then! I will work—work so hard—that no unforeseen accidents shall ever reduce us to such desperate straits again . . .'

This promise of a life without desperation was written in the year before his death. Already he had experienced not being able to work, and had written to the fellow-Mason[5] from whom he borrowed: 'I could not sleep all night for pain . . . Picture to yourself my condition—ill and consumed with worries and anxieties. Such a state quite definitely prevents me from recovering . . .'

XXIII

Enlightenment and Psychology

———————⊛———————

If eighteenth-century society undervalued its artists to the extent of applauding Mozart but neglecting to pay him a living wage, that was only a symptom of its persistent undervaluation of art itself, and its neglect of the whole realm of human psychology which produces and is expressed in it. One highly practical reason why Mozart could never wholly overcome his duty to the idea of *father* and commit himself wholly to the cause of the enlightenment is that this neglect of art was actually more stringent, or at least more a matter of principle, on the enlightenment's side than on the reaction's.

It is true that eighteenth-century princes and prelates, whenever they could afford to, called on the arts to celebrate princely occasions by an apt piece of political propaganda for absolutism. (Mozart supplied in this genre *La Clemenza di Tito* and *Il Re Pastore*, both to libretti by Metastasio, the one for a coronation and the other for the visit of an Archduke to an Archbishop.) But this, on the monarchies' part, was merely counter-propaganda. They had borrowed the habit itself from their opponents. The enlightenment both anticipated and outdid them in chaining the arts—especially literature, which was so much cheaper than opera—to a social or philosophical purpose. The forces of the reaction, by their very nature, went in for splendour —courtly operas, apotheoses on ceilings—often in the very places and palaces where they could preach the glory of absolutism only to the converted. The enlightenment limited its audience by nothing except literacy, and flooded Europe with pamphlets.

The characteristic literary form invented by the enlightenment is the long short story perfected by Voltaire, and it is really not a story at all but a pamphlet and parable, in which the hero is not a character but a peephole for the intelligence. Even novels proper, which were making vast efforts to re-emerge during the eighteenth century (and in Laclos's unique and inimitable masterpiece did emerge, but in epistolary form that had soon to be discarded) linked art to the moral purpose of 'improvement' and usually chose to resolve the story in accordance with external morality rather than internal necessity. Madame de Staël, one of the enlightenment's most active propagandists through her pamphlets and her pamphlets disguised as novels, believed that literature had achieved a higher status in the eighteenth century by ceasing to be 'a mere art' and becoming 'a weapon in the service of the spirit of man'.[1] In the last year of the century Jacques-Louis David was putting forward, in his own art of painting, a new style, but one often coupled with it the inveterate enlightenment view of the true destiny of all arts—'which is to serve morality and elevate men's souls'.[2] Bernadin de Saint-Pierre is angry with 'les gens riches' and the 'gens du monde' for failing to prize literature, which, according to Saint-Pierre, has 'the most august function with which heaven can honour a mortal on earth': but when he describes this function it is, yet again, the inartistic, less-than-imaginative business of 'comforting the unhappy, illuminating nations, telling the truth even to kings . . . serving as a barrier to error and tyrants'.[3] Only a literature which had, with the noblest motives, sold itself to these purposes could have perpetrated Virginie's death through modesty and then tried to make a touching movement out of the recovery of her body, which, when it is washed ashore, is found to have one hand still modestly holding down her clothes.

The enlightenment was not merely inviting literature to serve propagandist ends. An invitation would have been legitimate enough; and no one in his senses would wish the lively pamphleteering literature of the eighteenth century unwritten. Its crime begins only when it drives out—or, rather, prevents the rebirth of—a psychologising literature. The enlightenment refused to make any place for art in its own right and would not even grant it a raison d'être except as propaganda or—a still more belittling slavery—as a divertissement and refreshment, no more to be taken seriously than a beautifully executed icecream.

In offering nothing but these alternatives, the enlightenment was behaving exactly like the princely courts. Mozart's appalled shout when he looks into his own death is the cry of a man to whom the enlightenment promised deserts of vast eternity and Catholicism hell-fire; and likewise he could not derive hope of an artistic immortality either from the enlightenment's anti-artistic intellectualism or from the flippant and fickle fashionableness of aristocratic patronage. When John Keats considered his fears of ceasing to be before finishing his work as an artist, he consoled himself by the thought that he would be among the English poets when he died; but society had given him so little cause to think it accepted his claim to the title, or even ranked the title itself very high, that one of his last wishes was to have inscribed on his grave 'HERE LIES ONE WHOSE NAME WAS WRIT IN WATER'. Mozart can have taken small comfort from the hope of being remembered, if fashion did not swing against his being remembered at all, among the Austrian court composers; and he was buried in a pauper's grave, whose whereabouts society quickly forgot and has never remembered.

The princely courts had merely adapted to their own interest the enlightenment's valuation of art. In their view art must be either a parable in justification of princely courts or one of the icecreams a magnificent prince provided for the refreshment of his guests. As court-musician to Archbishop Colloredo, Mozart sat at table with the Archbishop's valets, private messenger, confectioner and cooks: below the valets but, he noted,[4] above the cooks.

The essence of Mozart's disagreement with Leopold Mozart on the subject of their relations with their Archbishop patron was that Leopold was content for himself and his son to remain in the Archbishop's service on fundamentally the same terms as the Archbishop's pastrycooks, whereas Mozart asserted himself as a man of honour ('My honour is more precious to me than anything else', he explained to his father[5]) and refused to be treated as a valet. ('I just want to set down the chief accusation which was brought against me in respect of my service. I did not know that I was a valet—and that was the last straw. I ought to have idled away a couple of hours every morning in the ante-chamber'.[6])

Writing to Leopold, Mozart expressed his rebellion against these terms of service by a hypothetical choice which, of all hypothetical choices in the world, was calculated to shock Leopold: 'If I were offered a salary of 2,000 *gulden* by the Archbishop of Salzburg and only 1,000 *gulden* somewhere else, I should still take the second offer'.* The public expression of his rebellion was held over until Beaumarchais's play gave him the opportunity artistically to impersonate a valet who finally triumphs over an insolent master. The insolent form of address, the *tu*, which Count Almaviva hurls, de haut en bas, at Figaro, is a translation of the *Er* which the Archbishop had—according to Mozart's verbatim report to Leopold[7]—employed in speaking to Mozart.

If the enlightenment agreed with or excelled the princelings in misprizing art, it was because it could not conceive what to make of fiction—in, that is to say, the wide sense wherein all works of art, in whatever medium, are fictions, being composed of material which is not true and which did not exist anywhere in the perceptible world, not even the artist's conscious mind, until it was suddenly set loose from the hidden world of the artist's unconscious. The enlightenment was ill at ease with art because it was ill at ease with the unconscious.

Not that it was so foolish as to think that conscious and reasoned motives were enough to constitute a human being. Obviously some other motive directed the desire to live in animals and babies, which might be virtually without reason and consciousness; and reason alone was incapable of offering even the adult a sufficiently compelling reason to stay alive. But although the enlightenment did recognise a force of natural instinct, it was convinced that instinct worked in the same direction as reason, and had in fact been implanted for that purpose by that supremely reasonable director, the non-denominational God it held to be the designer of the universe. It was ignoring not only the anti-benevolent instinct but every

---

* (From Vienna, 12 May, 1781.) Similarly, Mozart had to explain to Leopold his concern to keep up his prices as a teacher. 'At present' (Vienna, 16 June, 1781) 'I have only one pupil . . . I could have many more, it is true, if I chose to lower my terms, but by doing so, I should lose credit . . . I would rather have three pupils who pay me well than six who pay badly . . . I simply mention this in order that you may not think me guilty of selfishness in sending you only thirty ducats . . .'

instinctual motive which was not admissible to consciousness or capable of being summoned at will by the commands of conscious reason. In such a view, art, inasmuch as it was partly a product of instinct, *could* have only two purposes in the overall design: it could actively forward reason, or it could passively refresh the active warriors in the battle for reason.

Against this, Catholicism, if not absolute monarchy, had one tremendous advantage, the fruit of which Gibbon remarked in his Memoirs when he compared London with Paris in point of architecture and other works of art: 'All superfluous ornament is rejected by the cold frugality of the Protestants; but the Catholic superstition, which is always the enemy of reason, is often the parent of the arts'. Catholicism could not ignore the unconscious or the unconscious's destructive impulses, because it was itself a manifestation of them. It could not misprize fantasy completely, because it was itself a fantasy. The enlightenment was busy arguing that in a state of nature, if instinct were given its benevolent head, there would be no necessary conflict between a sons class and a fathers class: but Catholicism was a mythology exclusively concerned with the relationship of a Son to a Father (and to the Father's generative powers, represented by the Holy Ghost); on this mythology it had built a religion exclusively concerned with the relationship of men, as sons, to their father in heaven; and within the framework of the religion itself it offered men the utmost opportunity to express their ambivalent feelings towards the father, since the central sacrament consisted of commemorating the agonising death men had inflicted on the Son who was somehow identical with the Father, and ingesting a piece of his body.

For this reason the harness in which Christianity rode the arts was—at least until the seclusion of Christendom was incurably burst open—much less deleterious to art than the straitjacket the enlightenment imposed. Secular art had virtually ceased to exist with the disruption of antiquity; but the arts of painting, sculpture, architecture and, embryonically, drama were re-born for the modern world within the enfolding cloak of Christendom, and were full-grown and ready to step into independence the moment secular art became feasible again. The painters and sculptors of early Christendom might be more or less obliged to channel their fantasies through the Christian myth and their aesthetics through religion; but the prime Christian subjects—the Crucifixion and the mother-and-son group (the father has significantly been suppressed from the picture)—lent themselves to the expression of precisely the same Oedipal motifs which Sophocles had expressed through a theme selected from the looser and wider canon of Greek mythology and Shakespeare through a free selection from history and legend. The enlightenment, on the other hand, clamped down on these free or comparatively free selections and expressions; and when Mozart found himself in the psychological position of a Shakespeare with a *Hamlet* to write, he had to revert to the less hampering restrictions of Catholicism.

What the archaic superstitions of the Catholic world offer to Shakespeare in *Hamlet* and to Mozart in *Don Giovanni* is a convention in which to represent what is really the unconscious mode of thinking, whose existence the enlightenment refused to take into account. The unconscious, like children, never comprehends the irrevocability of death. To the unconscious, dead people are always liable to come back—and they do come back, with the utmost, convincing vividness, in our dreams.

When enlightened princes like Sethos and Rasselas demonstrated by object lesson that the dead cannot return, they were at no pains to distinguish between the untruth that the dead can return in the material and objective world and the manifest truth that they can and do return in our psychic world, but simply trampled down the psychological fact along with the superstition. But it was precisely the persistence of this superstition into the age of Shakespeare which gave Shakespeare the chance to express through it the psychological truth. He can shew us Hamlet's conscious and unconscious emotions at once: Hamlet can see the ghost within the same framework as he sees Horatio and Bernardo. When science dispels superstition from popular culture, dramatists like Ibsen have to resort to symbolism if they are to represent the unconscious ideas of their characters, and they run the risk of the audience's misunderstanding—or even of their misunderstanding themselves—this characterisation on two levels.

Catholicism and the side-superstitions which went with it left a certain free play to fantasy and much free play to artistic rationality exercised within the terms of the fantasy. What it did not leave was any freedom whatever to reason exercising itself *on* the fantasy from outside. It had the advantage of being a fantasy but not of knowing and admitting it was one. Indeed, it was prepared to persecute anybody who could not accept its insistence that its fantasy was literal truth.

This was partly what put the enlightenment in a position of malaise whenever it turned its attention to fantasy of any kind, regardless of whether or not the fantasy claimed to be literally true. The enlightenment's most urgent business was, as Voltaire insisted, écraser l'infâme by pointing out that Christianity was *not* literally true—and not only the Christian myth itself, but the whole pre-scientific picture of the world which accompanied it. Christianity had under its nose, and pushed under the enlightenment's, all the material which was eventually explored to the end of formulating a scientific psychology. Christendom had been strongly impressed by dreams and hallucinatory visions, and by the hysterical seizures and stigmata suffered by witches and saints. In one sense it knew all about taboo, and its heretic- and witch-hunters all about paranoia. But of course it kept its interest in these phenomena within the terms of the illusion. The enlightenment was devoted to piercing the illusion. It insisted that dreams were not prophetic of true events and that visions do not come truthfully from God: and so busy was it denying that the Christian fantasy was true and divinely revealed that it never asked where the fantasy, though untrue, *had* come from, and never enlarged its own picture of nature and instinct into a biological science of psychology which *could* take into account the existence of fantasy. Mozart's family friend, Franz Anton Mesmer, might have provided the eighteenth century with most of the data Freud eventually did work on; but the century chose to treat him, like Mozart himself, as an entertainer, and as such he touches the buffoonery in *Così*.

From developing a comprehensive biological theory the enlightenment was held back because, while it threw away the psychological advantages of his mythology, it stuck to the philosophical concept of a Creator. More than one eighteenth-century mind sketched a theory of evolution; but so long as there was no generally received and coherent evolutionary picture to put in the place of the supreme mechanic of the creation, the century was cut off from approaching a psycho-analytical theory, which is essentially evolutionary in conception.

In the absence of such a psychology, the enlightenment was no less disconcerted when artists confronted it with fantasies than when religionists did. Here were fictions every bit as fictitious as the Christian myth. They did not invite direct attack in the interests of truth, because they did not claim to be literally true; but that was the very thing which made it hard to see their relevance to a benevolently ordered society. So long as society had not achieved a benevolent order, the arts might pro-pagandise for it. Literature was given—and fulfilled—the function of satire. But the eighteenth century misunderstood its own satires, seizing on the social, and ignoring the artistic, purpose. And in fact the social purpose for which literature was invited to propagandise was working towards a state where literature and art in general would no longer have any occasion for existing—a complete return to the primitively blissful state of society of which Pope had approvingly written:

Pride then was not; nor arts, that pride to aid.[8]

When the enlightenment considered religious fantasies, the only explanations it could suggest of their genesis were the unpsychological ones that classical mythology was primitive science in allegorical dress and that the Christian myth was a deliberate invention for purposes of fraud. The artist, ad-mittedly, did not ask to be literally believed, and yet these explanations of religious fantasy rubbed off on to art, with the result that whenever the artist was not blatantly allegorical or socially purposeful he risked being suspected of self-interested fraud. Against the possibility of being gulled by him the eighteenth century took the precaution of underpaying and undervaluing him, like people who habitually refuse alms to beggars in case one of the beggars should be only pretending.

All eighteenth-century art shews signs of the problem, which authors had to tackle no less than audiences, of how—if not literally—it *was* to be taken. Catholicism had provided at least a conventionally accepted framework of literal belief; and when it invited painters to illustrate its myths it lent itself to their personal fantasies, unwittingly initiating secular art and in-voluntarily educating artists and audiences in that 'willing suspension of disbelief' which is the basis of art. But when the enlightenment abolished that compulsory suspension of disbelief which constitutes religious faith, it took no care to separate out and preserve, from the combined religious-artistic tradition, the capacity for artistic faith.

It was largely against Coleridge, proponent and definer of 'that willing suspension of disbelief for the moment, which constitutes poetic faith',[9] that Thomas Love Peacock directed one of the enlightenment's last shafts in *The Four Ages Of Poetry*—though it was Shelley who was provoked into answering Peacock with *A Defence Of Poetry*. Peacock's essay has been as unjustly neglected and disparaged as Shelley's has been unjustly praised and kept famous. Victory has been awarded to Shelley because he was a great poet and Peacock was not— a manifest truth which has nothing to do with the case of the two essays and which has led posterity into a perverse verdict on them, ignoring the no less manifest truth that Shelley's essay is a meaningless farrago of amorphous mysticism, couched in vile prose, whereas Peacock's is a penetrating and witty application of common sense written in a prose almost worthy of Jane Austen. Indeed, Peacock adopts not merely the sentiments but the very cadence of Jane Austen—it is her disapproval of Sir Edward Denham's choice of reading* all over again—when he expresses his distaste for the Coleridge-type epic compiled 'by extracting from a perfunctory and desultory perusal of a collection of voyages and travels, all that useful investigation would not seek for and that common sense would reject'.

All the same, Shelley was right: but right in *Adonais*, not in *A Defence Of Poetry*; and, in *Adonais*, right by virtue of the poetry not of the argument—which is also a defence of poetry and every bit as misty as the one in his essay. Conversely, Peacock's essay, cogent, lucid and rational as it is, exemplifies precisely the enlightenment's failure to comprehend art. Peacock simply cannot grasp that Coleridge came back with great poetry—as well as with much abysmal poetry—from his 'perfunctory and desultory' perusals of old travellers' tales, and that it was just because Coleridge's attention was *not* concentrated on 'useful investigation' that his reading mind could constitute an immense dragnet of free association, catching

* See chapter VIII.

quantities of dross, which undoubtedly 'common sense would reject', but also moments of unmatched poetry which only the purblind common sense of Peacock would reject equally with the dross.

Peacock begins by pointing out that in its golden—its Homeric—age, epic poetry is without competitors: the other arts are rudimentary, other branches of literature do not yet exist, and poetry 'has no rivals in history, nor in philosophy, nor in science'. For a primitive culture, its poetry *is* its history, philosophy and science. However, 'with the progress of reason and civilisation, facts become more interesting than fiction'—a perfect statement of the enlightenment's point of view, except that the truth was more probably that facts had become less disturbing than fiction. According to Peacock, the instant that accurate history, argument and 'sciences of morals and of mind' come into being, ancient poetry stands discredited as purveying inaccurate and fabulous versions of them and modern poetry cannot adapt itself to purveying the new, accurate versions, since 'Pure reason and dispassionate truth would be perfectly ridiculous in verse, as we may judge by versifying one of Euclid's demonstrations'. Thus, Peacock claims, all poetry, old or new, is an anachronism from the moment society becomes capable of reason. Poetry 'can never make a philosopher, nor a statesman, nor in any class of life an useful or rational man'. There is no place for fiction in the rational society except as 'ornamental' and deserving 'to be cultivated for the pleasure it yields'. Even this pleasure, Peacock argues, is to be had more from ancient than from contemporary poetry, because ancient poetry has the advantage that it was created in genuinely poetical —that is, credulous and barbaric—times, whereas the modern poet is 'a semi-barbarian in a civilised community'.

In Peacock we catch the enlightenment at its favourite anti-psychological game. Discovering that a fiction is not true, it thereupon dumps it in the wastepaper basket, without bothering to ask what, in the civilisation and the author which created it, obliged the fantasy to take this one particular form and none of the millions of other, equally untrue, forms it might have taken. This question, when Freud asked it about the fictions everyone creates, namely dreams, led to the foundation of a science of psychology which shewed that, while dreams are nonsense by the standards of the objective world, they are by no means arbitrary nonsense but subject to laws which science can discern. But the enlightenment had relegated dreams to the rubbish, along with religious myths and poetic visions, as soon as it had found out that dreams no more truthfully foretell the future than the Homeric myths truthfully recount the past.

Peacock's description of the contemporary poet as a semi-barbarian who 'lives in the days that are past' and whose 'ideas, thoughts, feelings, associations, are all with barbarous manners, obsolete customs, and exploded superstitions' is perfectly accurate. If to Peacock's mind this is disparagement and not appreciation, that is because Peacock's mind, governed by the enlightenment, has not permitted itself to discover that barbarous manners and exploded superstitions are what constitute the mental world of every infant and of the infantile unconscious on which every rational and conscious adult mind is economically and historically dependent. When he adds 'The brighter the light diffused round' the poet 'by the progress of reason, the thicker is the darkness of antiquated barbarism, in which he buries himself like a mole, to throw up the barren hillocks of his Cimmerian labours', Peacock has added, to the enlightenment's own metaphor of enlightenment, the very metaphor of the Underworld by which the Homeric myth unwittingly figures the unconscious; and by describing the poet's power to throw up material from that region Peacock unwittingly explains what he denies—both the psychological function of literature in a civilised community, and why poetry continues to move our emotions no matter how far our rationality has progressed.

Jane Austenish as his style is, Peacock has not advanced with her into psychology but stays behind in the pure, strict and strangled enlightenment. Neither he, straitjacketed in eighteenth-century rationalism, nor Shelley, swirling in romantic irrationalism, has divined that the true successor to the Homeric epic as a psychological vehicle is not the epic as practised by the Lake Poets (a form Peacock punctures with some justice) but the novel; and Peacock's own entertaining and inventive novels, by remaining true to the pamphleteering tradition of the eighteenth century, became just such anachronisms as he held poetry to be.

The great artistic problem of the enlightenment was how to

reconcile idealisation (or the grand manner, or sheer propaganda) with naturalism (literal reportage blessed by the deification of nature and the belief that the dullest fact must be more interesting than the liveliest fiction). Middle-class taste inclined more and more to avoid the problem by sticking to the genres which in themselves lay the greater emphasis on reportage: portraiture or genre painting rather than the misnominated history painting; history rather than novels—which the bourgeoisie gobbled up, but disparagingly, like someone helping himself to two chocolate creams while murmuring 'Well, perhaps—a small one'. The whole tendency of the eighteenth century and its long afterglow—a tendency resisted by Mozart and Tiepolo, but at great cost—was to exclude imaginary fictions. Yet since the enlightenment was crushing the religious and political myths which had been the vehicle for psychological knowledge, though that knowledge went unrecognised in them, it was to the artists that it fell to keep psychology alive in an anti-psychological world.

XXIV

Mozart as Literature — and as
Super-Literature

————————— ❋ —————————

While the enlightenment was doing its best to squeeze it out
of the other arts, the obvious medium in which to keep the power
of fantasy alive was opera. Throughout the century, the enlightenment hurled at opera a bombardment of unkind epithets
or half unkind ones, like Voltaire's 'beau monstre',* and it did
so precisely on the grounds that opera was fantastic to the point
of being preposterous. When the imagination did resist en-
croachment in other arts, it was often through the inspiration
or direct influence of opera. Perhaps it was because their own
art denied them the opportunity of being imaginatively preposterous that eighteenth-century writers were so easily tempted
to turn librettist; and it was to a very large extent opera which
provided the costumes and décor for the imaginative world
realised in paint by Tiepolo.[1]

The war between facts and fictions, which made its acute
appearance in the eighteenth century and is still widely waged
today, rests chiefly on the enlightenment's misconception of
nature—indeed, on its ignorance of our psychological nature.
The artist and the scientist, both of whom depend on unconscious
motives to impel them into activity at all, are also both dependent on the accessibility of fantasy-material from the
unconscious. The scientist must have a supply of it if he is to
create hypotheses, and the artist if he is to create that different

* Voltaire's remark was quoted (from the *Réponse à M. de la Lindelle*) by
J. Cooper Walker in support of his own unkinder eighteenth-century lamentations
over the fashion for opera (*Historical Memoir On Italian Tragedy*, 1799). Other
objections to the absurdity of opera came from Addison, Dr Burney and Metastasio's English translator, John Hoole. (See Michael Levey: 'Tiepolo's Treatment
Of Classical Story . . .' in the *Warburg Journal*.)

type of hypothesis which we call fiction. Scientist and artist direct the fantasy-material to utterly different ends: the scientist works on the fantasy from outside, the artist from inside, the fantasy-illusion: yet not only is the source of the material the same in both cases, but in both cases what works on it is intelligence, though an intelligence specialised and temporarily narrowed down for a particular purpose. Our false assumption that art is a matter of feeling and science a matter of thinking has turned hundreds of scientists into philistines and hundreds of artists into fools, at the same time producing a one-eyed science and quantities of unintelligent—that is, bad—art.

When one scrutinises works of art which have failed artistically, they turn out to fail through a failure of intelligence: and conversely the supreme artistic successes of Shakespeare and Mozart rest on an intelligence which is quite of the same order of mental processes as Aristotle's or Freud's. We appreciate *Le Nozze di Figaro* through the same faculties as we acknowledge the truth of a syllogism or a theorem—but in appreciating *Figaro* we have agreed to suspend direct reference to the outside world. Our sense of the just-rightness of *Figaro's* structure is an acquiescence in the internal logicalness of its structure (and the same is true when we recognise a melody as just right: we are applauding its internal consistency). We acknowledge Mozart's super-intelligent penetration of the form of his fantasy world, just as we acknowledge Euclid's or Freud's seizing on the form, the essential principles, of the objective world.

Mozart's supreme intelligence set to work to enlarge opera until it was capable of carrying those psychological perceptions which the enlightenment refused to deposit in a body of scientifically collected and classified information, and which Catholicism had certainly collected but had insisted on classifying according to literal belief in their face value.

The burden of carrying an implicit psychology usually falls chiefly to literature, which is more immediately flexible in the business of conveying characters. It *had* been carried, and virtually single-handed, by Shakespeare, whose blend of drama with poetry is the counterpart of Mozart's blend of drama with music, and who transcends the literary conventions of his time just as Mozart transcends the musical ones of his. In the nineteenth century, the burden returned to literature and was carried, by an extraordinary number of extraordinarily able hands, in the novel. But in the eighteenth century, literature without music was precluded from the task to which it is the most apt of arts because literature, of all the arts, had been first and furthest colonised by the enlightenment, which wanted to exploit literature's particular fluency for its own purposes. When the enlightenment cluttered up fictitious narrative with homilies and moral points, and squeezed the character out of the Voltairean hero, it was depriving literature of the very qualities which eventually became the strength of the nineteenth-century novel.

Equally, the eighteenth century could not revert to the Shakespearean method of embodying psychology in literature— and this not only because the enlightenment turned as stern a face against poetic fantasies as any other kind, but also because of a difficulty about languages. The break-up of the Christian monopoly had resulted, from the first stirrings of the renaissance on, in the progressive disuse of Latin in favour of the various national vernaculars. Dante broke into Italian, and Chaucer into English, as secular artists—who have not, of course, thrown off Christianity but who are emphatically laymen and are neither appointed nor self-appointed as spokesmen of the church and its mythology. The Reformation announced itself in Germany and England by nationalising the language of the Bible. Shakespeare's colossal creative act of virtually forming modern English was part of the intensely nationalistic culture of Elizabethan England, for which he was a hard-working propagandist.

The enlightenment, on the other hand, was trying to go back on all these earlier centrifugal forces and to re-create a united Europe, a new Christendom without Christ but under the uniform governance of the reasonable architect of the universe. It was concerned to patch up the rivalries between nation-states and transcend the Catholic-protestant split which had given nationalism such impetus. Insofar as reason entailed science, the enlightenment had actually come back to needing Latin, which now had to serve as an international scientific language. Insofar as reason ordained toleration and a uniformly polite society, the enlightenment was multilingual. Its culture is typified in Mozart's pan-European travels and multilingual correspondence and compositions.

This international* cultural purpose produced a special use of the various national languages. Writers could make themselves understood to an international audience only by giving up a good part of the emotive and metaphorical use of words, which is almost the whole of Shakespeare's method. A metaphor may be misunderstood by foreigners—and it was as foreigners that Gibbon published his first work, and that Goldoni wrote his memoirs and Frederick the Great his letters, in French. The local associations which are so great a part of Shakespeare's linguistic music are lost altogether on any but native ears. Indeed, to a foreigner any concrete and specific word is harder than any abstract. Abstracts announce their derivation from frequently-met verbs or perhaps from Latin or Greek roots, but the foreigner who stumbles for the first time on oxlips or eglantine may well think them rootless. He has small hope of guessing what they mean (hence the need to translate them, by way of the Linnaean classification, into Latin), let alone what they emotionally mean; and through their very lack of relationship to less rare words they will with difficulty stick in his mind to wait for a second meeting. To oblige its foreigners, in a culture where everyone was a foreigner in some important section of it, the vocabulary of the enlightenment took to abstraction. By a less soulless step of the process which translation by machines may presently impose on our languages, the writers of the enlightenment pruned words down to their nonfiction content, which could be translated rapidly and without loss of substance or could be directly understood by a foreigner who had had the benefit of a few of those language lessons which Mozart was always taking and which da Ponte ended up by giving. Under the enlightenment, even English and French achieved, by pruning on both sides, a homogeneity; a stylistic lingua franca was created by writing both languages as though they were Ciceronian Latin filtered through Erasmus.

This treatment of language was bound to damage the psychological potentialities of literature, by facilitating the enlightenment's tendency to squeeze character out of characters and

* Otto Jespersen points out that the word *international* was coined (by Bentham) in 1780, and comments: 'it marks linguistically the first beginning of the era when relations between nations came to be considered like relations between citizens, capable of peaceful arrangement according to right rather than according to might' (*Growth And Structure Of The English Language*, VI).

atmosphere out of descriptions. The genius loci in eighteenth-century pastoral literature is highly *un*-local; through its very vocabulary, it cannot help being evocative less of pastoral experience than of Theocritus. Equally, the characters in eighteenth-century novels, on the few occasions when they achieve an idiosyncratic psychology, have to do so despite the handicap of not possessing an idiosyncratic way of talking or writing letters.

The eighteenth-century treatment of language was to the benefit only of the enlightenment's precision tool, wit, whose ideal was to be international. Against that ideal puns offended, which is no doubt one reason why they fell into opprobrium. The other is that they come into the mind by means of an illogical, quirky and perhaps even unconscious train of associations, which takes no account of meaning—meaning being the only element in words which the enlightenment *did* take account of. Wit, on the other hand, follows a train of thought which is perfectly reasonable. The witty person is original only in seeing it more quickly than anyone else. Language had no part in wit, and therefore foreignness of language did not obstruct it. It is part of the ideal quality of El Dorado that, at the supper party its king gives to Candide and Cacambo, 'Cacambo explained the king's bons mots to Candide, and, though translated, they still seemed bons mots'—'quoique traduits, ils paraissaient toujours des bons mots'.[2]

For eighteenth-century purposes, music, which was the occasion of Mozart's travels and language lessons, had the advantage of being international without undergoing even the moment's time-lag of translation. For artistic purposes, which formed no part of most eighteenth-century purposes, it also had the advantage that it was resistant to the enlightenment's pruning. It was impossible to cut away the fiction content of a musical statement, because to do so would leave nothing. A tune is purest fantasy, without any concrete imagery whatever. For this reason music, though it did not escape undervaluation, did escape being colonised by the enlightenment and exploited, and was not subjected to the reproaches by which the enlightenment nagged away at the concrete images it encountered in painting and literature. The question which so disconcerted the enlightenment, whether the statement made by the image was true or false, was simply not provoked by music. Architecture escaped distortion for the opposite reason—that its images always were, in a sense, true: there really is a tangible roof literally keeping out the rain. This turned out to provide shelter for architecture as an art. Although the enlightenment did enlist it to serve the classicising and exoticising ideals, it was not the propaganda, which was perhaps too large to be effective, but the art which triumphed and achieved in the eighteenth century its most graceful and highly imaginative fictions.

When music married itself to words and drama, and turned into opera, it acquired the concrete imagery it lacks in its single state. Promptly it incurred the enlightenment's contempt. But the enlightenment did not bother to crush it, because it was not sufficiently badly frightened by it. Even more than the eighteenth-century novel, eighteenth-century opera remained both fashionable and popular even while everyone threw fashionable intellectual bricks at it. Cécile Volanges has caught a touch of this modish disparagement: her politeness to her correspondent just overbalances into impoliteness to opera when she writes to Madame de Merteuil[3] 'Mama is indisposed . . . so I shall not have the honour of going to the Opera with you. I assure you that I regret your company much more than the Spectacle'— 'je regrette bien plus de ne pas être avec vous que le Spectacle'.

If there had not been disparagement for opera itself, there would have been for the extravagancies of some operatic and musical partisans—extravagancies which Jane Austen diagnosed as thoroughly affected. Music as an art she never disparages, though it is not the art most to her own liking. It is as an artist and on behalf of art that she resents the supposition that affected feeling can substitute for talent, knowledge and work. The most professional of literary artists herself, she has had her teeth set on edge in the dreadful suburban garden of amateur accomplishment (in drawing as well as music) which is so large a part of the social life she shews in her novels and comments on in her letters.* It is with the anger of righteous satire that she refuses mercy to amateur singers and pianists who make displays of a

---

* 'It is the fashion to think them both'—a Mrs Holder and Miss Holder— 'very detestable, but they are so civil . . . that I cannot utterly abhor them, especially as Miss Holder owns that she has no taste for Music' (Jane Austen to Miss Austen, from Bath, 21 May, 1801).

musical sensibility which is belied by their performance. Against their raptures she propounds a heroine who makes the down-to-earth admission 'Malbrook . . . is the only tune I ever really liked'.[4] The penchant for romantic operas affected by the romantic heroines of romantic novels she deflates by 'the Noise of the Coach & 4 . . . was to Catherine a more interesting sound, than the Music of an Italian Opera, which to most Heroines is the hight of Enjoyment'.[5]

However, if enthusiasm for opera might be ignorant and affected, so might disparagement of it; and likewise disparagement of novels. When the disdain which Cécile Volanges hints towards opera was displayed by other girls in other novels towards novels themselves, Jane Austen replied with the lethal question, 'if the heroine of one novel be not patronized by the heroine of another, from whom can she expect protection and regard?'

In framing her defence of novels, Jane Austen shews herself wholly and exactly aware that the cultural task performed by novels is to be psychological.

> 'Such is the common cant. "And what are you reading, Miss ——?" "Oh! it is only a novel!" replies the young lady; while she lays down her book with affected indifference, or momentary shame. "It is only *Cecilia*, or *Camilla*, or *Belinda*": or, in short, only some work in which the greatest powers of the mind are displayed, in which the most thorough knowledge of human nature, the happiest delineation of its varieties, the liveliest effusions of wit and humour, are conveyed to the world in the best chosen language.'[6]

(Jane Austen's lesson has still not been learnt. One can still read, in an ostensibly cultured context: 'Novels are the least in demand; reading is serious'.[7])

Fanny Burney, the author of *Cecilia* and *Camilla*, had herself set the precedent for Jane Austen's defence of *Cecilia* and *Camilla* by protesting against the low estimation of the novel as a form. 'In the republic of letters', she writes[8] (borrowing Addison's phrase for the literary-egalitarian society of the enlightenment), 'there is no member of such inferior rank . . . as the humble Novelist; . . . among the whole class of writers, perhaps not one can be named of which the votaries are more numerous but less respectable'. (It took Jane Austen to transform this oratory into the fine irony of 'Let us not desert one another; we are an injured body'. The change epitomises the change she made in the form.)

As the daughter of a musicologist, though one who tilted at opera himself, Fanny Burney was also aware of the similar disparagement which was directed at opera. Defending the novel in the preface, she defends opera in the text of *Evelina*. A stout propagandist, she puts the criticisms of opera in the mouth of the proletarian Branghton family (who infuriate Evelina by talking through the performance). Thus Fanny Burney implies not only that such judgments are ignorant but that—in which she is true to the enlightenment—only ignorance *could* produce such bad judgment. Here, however, she was more noble-minded than observant. As a matter of fact, the most stringently educated minds of the enlightenment were for ever bringing against opera just the objections urged by the Branghtons.

' "What a jabbering they make!" cried Mr. Branghton . . . "Pray what's the reason they can't as well sing in English?— but I suppose the fine folks would not like it, if they could understand it."

' "How unnatural their action is!" said the son; "why now who ever saw an Englishman put himself in such out-of-the-way postures?" '

And again:

' "So, Miss," said Mr. Branghton, "you're quite in the fashion, I see; — so you like Operas? well, I'm not so polite; I can't like nonsense, let it be never so much the taste."

' "But pray, Miss," said the son, "what makes that fellow look so doleful while he is singing?"

' "Probably because the character he performs is in distress."

' "Why then I think he might as well let alone singing till he's in better cue: it's out of all nature for a man to be piping when he's in distress." '

As a novelist, Fanny Burney suffers in our eyes from Jane Austen's having developed her idiom to such immeasurably greater penetration and subtlety. Fanny Burney's harping on the Branghtons' crassness merely turns Evelina into a prig—of which the author remains naïvely unaware. Sadly, this hardly matters, since in any case Evelina does not possess the elements of a coherent character; it only forces us to notice that Fanny Burney does not put forward so much as a germinal hint of that marvellously conscious and moral battle between priggishness and self-awareness which came into existence when Jane Austen created, in Emma, one of the most coherent characters in literature. In our eyes, therefore, Jane Austen is too kind to her predecessor when she chooses Fanny Burney's novels as the planks on which to mount her defence of the novel as a genre. Her happy phrase about 'the happiest delineation' of the varieties of human nature, excellently as it suits her own work, looks awkward on Fanny Burney's; psychological felicities occur in novels and operas of the period, but only in Jane Austen and Mozart can you be sure they appear by design.

Yet it is with perfect historical precision that Jane Austen picks on Cecilia, Camilla and Belinda. The exploration of the heroine's feelings was the plinth on which novels rose to psychology. Mozart was no less explicit (and this time it is an author talking about his own work) in distinguishing the heroines as where the serious import of his comedic operas should reside. In 1783 he sent his father[9] a specification for the type of libretto he would like the Abbate Varesco to provide for him in the comedic genre.* (He names Varesco in default of da Ponte, whom he had already picked out as the better librettist, but who he feared would be too busy.) It should be 'a new libretto for seven characters'; and Mozart goes on to give virtually a recipe for the libretto with which da Ponte eventually did provide him in *Così*. 'The most essential thing is that on the whole the story should be really *comic*; and, if possible, he ought to introduce *two equally good female parts*, one of these to be *seria*, the other *mezzo carattere*, but both parts equal *in importance and excellence*. The third female *character*, however, may be entirely buffa, and so may all the male ones if necessary.'

(If this is taken as an anatomy avant la lettre of *Così*, it makes it abundantly clear that Fiordiligi's part is no mere caricature of opera seria. The demand for two equally important female parts shews how early Mozart had it in mind to express his feelings towards Constanze and Aloysia Weber in an opera—and in fact his situation between the two sisters was very freshly in his mind at the time he wrote this letter.)

* Varesco had already provided Mozart with an opera-seria libretto—*Idemeneo*.

Mozart's willingness to throw to the dogs the high-dramatic —the opera-seria—potentialities of his male characters recognises something which was already implicit in opera as a form. Against recognising and realising the obvious future development of opera, the old, heroic, rhetorical, statuesque tradition fought a noble reactionary battle. But the heroine was in the most literal sense crying out to become the focus point of operatic drama. Because of the cult of the soprano voice, the soprano already had the dominant singing part; and the use of castrati could only put off the moment when the heroine should step into the principal dramatic interest as well. It was not purely musical considerations, which could be served by male sopranos, that impelled the heroine towards domination, but those social and psychological forces which had already made her victorious in novels—where the equivalent of the soprano aria was the letter, into which the heroine so fluently poured her emotions the instant Richardson or Fanny Burney put a pen in her hand.

The public was more than willing to read what the heroine had to say about herself: both because women as an oppressed class excited the enlightenment's liberal sympathy; and also through sheer sexual curiosity. (Perhaps it was a too nearly naked knowledge that sexual curiosity was involved in reading it which made the young lady caught with a novel lay it down with 'momentary shame'.) Once the enlightenment had recognised women as pleasure-seeking creatures, the public was agog to be informed what pleasures appealed to them.

Since the start of the century, the two closely related traditions of opera seria and history painting had shewn a predilection for subjects which made the heroine—and the very question of her pleasure—the centre of a drama. In the sacrifice of Iphigenia (one of Tiepolo's subjects at Villa Valmarana), the crucial question is whether the heroine shall live or die; but some of the subject's appeal, and also the reason why the artist need not treat it sombrely, lies in the simple metaphor which gives a sexual sense and interest to the question whether or not the young woman is to be penetrated by the sacrificial knife. Another favourite subject, the continence of Scipio (which Sebastiano Ricci treated about 1695, setting a fashion which lasted deep into the eighteenth century[10]), explicitly concentrates interest on whether or not the heroine shall be allowed to retain her chastity. Like the clemency of Titus, the continence of Scipio could be used as an argument in favour of absolute power, which it shews not to preclude generosity and self-control. Scipio refuses to take advantage of his power over his attractive prisoner and allows her to return to her sweetheart chaste—just as the Pasha returns Constanze to Belmonte, and as the village girls in *Figaro* think Count Almaviva is now prepared to let them come to *their* sweethearts. (They are, however, mistaken, *Figaro* being propaganda for the other side.)

These themes place the heroine in the centre of the composition and focus on her the audience's slightly titillated and two-edged curiosity (which outcome, after all, *is* more to the heroine's pleasure?) But they have not yet made the heroine an active force in her own drama. The fate which excites such interest is still settled by the men or deities grouped round the central point, not by the central point herself. In the pre-Mozart opera and the pre-Jane-Austen novel, the heroine has been given arias and letters through which she can actually express herself. But in dramatic terms she remains inert. Evelina not only is but regards herself—not without priggishness—as a prize to be carried off by the most highly qualified suitor. In *Clarissa*, Richardson makes the heroine a sacrificial victim subjected to a more lingering torment—and with no happy intervention from heaven at the end—than Iphigenia herself. Although the elements of a great novel are concealed, unorganised, inside it, *Clarissa* is hardly more than an enormous sadistic daydream. The public, hanging on each instalment, assisted at the degradation and thrillingly postponed ruin of the attractive victim. The very lingering quality of the torments her seducer inflicts on Clarissa is symptomatic of the seducer's own dread of being punished by impotence.

Subjects like the continence of Scipio and the sacrifice of Iphigenia, while they focus curiosity on the heroine, leave the dramatic or tragic struggle to take place in the mind of Scipio, in the mind of Agamemnon, called on to sacrifice his own daughter, or among the Olympians, one of whom eventually steps in as saviour. Equally, the titillation takes place in the mind of the onlooker. In a painting, there is not time for titillation to develop beyond a hint—though that was probably enough to be one of the agencies which towards the end of the eighteenth century provoked the severe reaction of the neo-classic movement against everything associated with the rococo. Even in a painting, the division of interest between the do-ers and the heroine who passively suffers opens up a tiny invitation to sadism. In a long novel this becomes sadistic pornography. If the neo-classic reaction in painting was partly based on the unspoken suspicion that the rococo was an erotic style, it was—at the start of the next century—on the express grounds of Lovelace's sexual libertinism that Jane Austen joined the middle-class reaction against Richardson. Richardson lets most of the story and all of the heroine's sufferings be related through Clarissa's own letters, but he leaves all the actions which determine her sufferings to Lovelace. What is artistically worse is that Richardson cannot live up to the implications of doing this. Not having put Lovelace into classical dress, he lacks all the trappings and the classical-renaissance-operatic tradition which enables Tiepolo to make his heroes into—at least—gorgeous dummies, even if they do lack the interest and sympathy he gives to his women. The failure of *Clarissa* as a work of art turns on Richardson's perfunctory treatment of Lovelace, which refuses either to explain his motives or even vivify his character.

The heroine could be freed from sadistic exploitation and also from the rôle of mere chattel only by herself taking to the dimension of moral consciousness and becoming an active mover in the moral debate. This liberation the heroine achieves in Jane Austen's novels and in Mozart's operas, which are innovations very largely by virtue of their heroines' activeness as personalities.[11]

The new freedom was within reach of both the novel and the opera—when they were taken up by supreme intelligences—because both had a tradition of absolute preposterousness. The convention from which Jane Austen's novels developed was not the Voltairean conte, even though Voltaire was Jane Austen's equal in reasonableness. The Voltairean story, for all its deliberate and dispassionate touches of the fabulous, was imaginatively unrealised and stuck strictly to its intellectual, non-fiction thesis. Instead, Jane Austen took up the despised and often despicable romantic novel, which she began satirising before she was well into adolescence. Her persistent satire of it does more than betray that it was the influence most continually present to her thoughts; the satire actually constitutes the process by which she refined and enlarged the form until its propensities for fantasy became capable of carrying not childish daydreams but imaginative psychological information. Her own novels, as their bare plots make clear, are very far from the realistic novel as that was developed later in the nineteenth century. While her psychological acumen is as 'true to life' as Mozart's, her stories, like his, obey beautifully artificial conventions which she disciplines and works out in the realm of pure artistic fantasy. These conventions she had borrowed, refined and, above all, enlarged, as she was quite aware herself, from the undisciplined dream-spinning of her romantic predecessors.

In blowing the bubble of its own autonomous world, opera was even more fortunately placed than the romantic novel—and often even more preposterous. Its strength lay in the very thing the Branghtons in *Evelina* urge against it: it was 'out of all nature'. If it was to exist at all, it could not exist naturalistically. The great eighteenth-century canon, 'Nature', was powerless—was irrelevant—against it. Although in opera there were images capable of being true or false, and capable therefore of disconcerting the enlightenment while it wondered *which*, the presence of the music so slowed down and distorted their presentation as to remove all claims to verisimilitude. Rationalistic puritanism could attack opera as a whole from the outside, but it could not go through an opera piece by piece suggesting that this or that was unnatural, because the entire form had taken to the air. Loves and deaths which waited for an orchestral 'symphony' before taking place, and conversations guided by a continuo or repetitively sung by four people talking at once, were not even putting forward a claim to be 'real'.

Secure within this convention, Mozart was able to enlarge the convention to the point where he could represent non-realistically the realities of a human psychology which includes the fantasy material the enlightenment tried to discount. Moreover, Mozart's personal convention of opera made it possible to represent dialogue—not, of course, in a speaking likeness, but in its essence. To this day, good dialogue is a rarity in literature. It is possible to write an excellent novel, a goodish film and even a passable play with no ear for dialogue whatever. Above all, dialogue was the weak point of the eighteenth-century novel. To supplement this lack, it often preferred to stay behind in the straitening epistolary convention it had outgrown, where the exchange of letters excuses the author from attempting an exchange of tones of voice.

Eventually, the novel—beginning, yet again, with Jane Austen's novels—developed its own non-naturalistic convention for rendering dialogue. Before that properly happened, Mozart had remoulded the rhetorical convention of opera, in which one da capo aria followed another in a debate as formal as the alternation of letter and reply in the epistolary novel. What his new convention allowed him to catch—through the weaving together of singing voices—was, precisely, the exchange of tones of voice in dialogue. In the duet between Susanna and Marcellina,[12] he captures, through the orchestra as much as through the singing voices, the very tone of a spoken, or almost shrieked, altercation between female rivals. Indeed, he goes further and captures the very gestures of female rivals wearing long skirts. Indeed, he goes further still: he sketches the very outline of the situation, the relationship, which is meant by *rivalry*. In the opening hasty conversation on the run between Donna Anna and Don Giovanni, which Einstein called 'one of the wonders of the world',[13] Mozart actually incarnates the running duel between the sexes which is the social history of the eighteenth century.

The essence of Mozart's, as of all good, dialogue is that it embodies not only more than the outward appearance of dialogue but more than is, or ever would be in the real world, spoken. Into one conversation between Susanna and the Count[14] Mozart condenses the whole of their relationship—to do which he has had to make himself so much the psychologist that he incidentally tosses in an implicit anticipation of a principle not explicitly formulated until Freud wrote *Psychopathology Of Everyday Life*.

Elsewhere in the operas Mozart delineates the nuances of social psychology. In the shewing-up of the Count, the various discomfitures of Figaro, and the embarrassments and uncertainties of the lovers in *Così*, he puts on record the emotion of personal malaise in a social setting which is so important in modern life and which was probably brought into it for the first time by the enlightenment. For if the enlightened society made it possible for almost any interesting person to meet any other interesting person, it also put on the individual personality the onus to be interesting. Fame-snobbery succeeded to place-snobbery. The nobody who met a somebody suffered the obligation of saying something apt at the meeting. Formal politeness helped only negatively: the nobody would hardly be remarkable for mere good manners, though he would be un-unpleasantly conspicuous for lacking them.

These particular forms of social embarrassment were probably a new experience. Under the impersonal dispensations of a taboo system, the chances are that the villein does not have to endure embarrassment in addition to his graver disabilities when he finds himself measured with his master. His behaviour is prescribed by ritual, as the Catholic's is when he enters the presence of his God. Enlightened man, on the other hand, suffered in society the lack of ease of a protestant in church. The protestant fumbles because nothing is prescribed for him in the way of action, and he can mark his respect only by his politely hesitant bearing. Although the enlightenment worked slowly in changing a taboo-ridden into an egalitarian society, and a diehard Archbishop could still make an unwitting contribution to a masterpiece by addressing Mozart by the form *Er*, eighteenth-century society was tending, often against its will, towards a condition where everyone was accorded the polite pronoun *you* and the polite titles *Mr* and *Esquire*.* In doing so, it isolated everyone in a sea where he owed everyone else the respect previously payable only to a lord and master and through prescribed forms. Eighteenth-century Freemasonry was perhaps protesting, among its other protests, against the embarrassments of polite society when it made all men brothers, and eighteenth-century Quakerism against the embarrassments both of polite society and of Anglican protestantism when it insisted on meeting other human beings as Friends, dispensing with both *Mr* and churches, and reverting to the pronoun *thou*.

By developing a convention of dialogue which could represent

* By 1818 Lady Susan O'Brien, looking back to 1760 when the change had not yet been accomplished, lamented that now 'Every man, tradesman, or Farmer is Esqr.' (quoted by G. Rattray Taylor: *The Angel-Makers*, 2). Similarly, Gibbon, in his Memoirs, on the subject of his ancestors:— 'they held the rank of Esquire in an age when that title was less promiscuously assumed'.

not merely dialogue itself but the psychological relationships which issue in dialogue, Mozart made himself able to express character through its relationships to other characters—an innovation and a great increase in dramatic power in a century which still often fell into imitating the static, descriptive method of defining character as it had been practised by Theophrastus and, more economically, by Tacitus. For dramatic and narrative purposes, Mozart's music-drama, like Shakespeare's poetry-drama, is not only infinitely rich in content but actually pithier in expression than works where the dramatic line has to be supplemented by explanation and by descriptive summings-up of character. Mozart's innovating impulse, which the weight of Leopold's influence prevented from issuing in technical innovations, was pushed into a super-innovation of form. Handelian opera remains a parliamentary debate, in which each singer in turn catches the conductor's eye and makes a speech. Mozart borrowed deeply from Handel's great device of capturing atmosphere and even character in the preludes and accompaniments to arias; but Mozart's own convention is so much more elastic that he can, like Shakespeare, reserve his right to reveal his characters either through soliloquy or through an ensemble of soliloquies or through dialogue; either through their reflexions or through their repartee or through cries and improvisations wrung from them by the dramatic action. For unrolling his dramatic action he invents his wonderful continuous musical fabric, which wraps not only different characters but different musical forms and themes into the integral mood of the whole. By supremely musical means he subordinates even his incomparable melodies to the music-drama, and there is not one of them which yields up everything that is in it when it is considered out of dramatic context. As early as *Idomeneo*, itself a dramatic masterpiece, Mozart was protesting that, while he would shape solo arias to the singer's voice, 'as far as trios and quartets are concerned, the composer must have a free hand'; and on his tenor's[15] complaint that his part in a quartet gave him no opportunity to let his voice go, Mozart comments: 'As if in a quartet the words should not be spoken much more than sung'.[16]

In Mozart's hands, opera was carrying the psychologising burden of literature; and the next time his themes of social discomfiture, the puncture of romantic affectations, being shewn up and—the private equivalent of the last—coming to self-knowledge appear in the world history of art it is in the novels of Jane Austen. Fortunately I can do no harm to Mozart's reputation by pointing out that his operas are also literature. He is too secure in his technical virtuosity, and too well established as (in the words[17] of the music critic, Bernard Shaw) 'the master beloved of masters', to incur the ignorant slander of not knowing his musical business which was attached to Wagner because he also took a responsible attitude towards his libretti and dramatic effects—and this despite the evident absurdity of Wagner's claim to literary talent.

Mozart, who had the good sense not to write his own libretti but merely had his writers write them according to his requirements ('I have explained to Stephanie the words I require for this aria'[18]), was not a *talented* writer, either. But unlike Wagner he was an excellently unpretentious and lively one, using a serviceable version of the enlightenment's lingua franca, in which, true to the enlightenment, the vitality lies not in the vocabulary or metaphors but in the sheer content and precision of his observations. (This is the Mozart of the letters; Mozart the dramatist is, of course, a metaphorist of metaphorists.) His interest in words as such remained at an infantile level. It is a primitive and formalistic, almost mathematical, cast of mind which, in his letters, exploits words for rhymes and puns. This childish facility with words probably helped him to assimilate foreign languages early in life; but perhaps it was in turn that early multilingualism which fixed his facility for ever at the childish. All the same, it *was* facility. Mozart was quite unawed by words, did not become awkward in their presence* and was prepared to juggle the vocabularies of several languages in the air to amuse his family. Obviously it was his unusual combination of word-fluency with music-fluency which directed his genius towards opera.

---

* The contrast is with Beethoven, of whom J. W. N. Sullivan wrote: 'It is difficult for the ordinary man, who is always predominantly a word-user, to understand that to Beethoven language was a clumsy device for communication . . . we must remember that he was, to an altogether unusual extent, without the "language mentality".' (*Beethoven*, 3.) If Sullivan is right, the wonder is that Beethoven undertook to compose an opera—or, even more, that it is such a moving one.

Mozart as Literature—and as Super-Literature

No one would dare suppose that the literature in Mozart's operas removes a semiquaver of the music in them. But it is foolish to let the music obscure the literature, especially as it is only in the presence of the literature that the music lets itself be completely heard. Indeed, the fusion is closer still: the music *is* the literature. Mozart's operas are literature written in music—or music composed in words, characters and actions. A deeply searching approach to the music will in fact* come up with information about the plot and characters; and vice versa. It occasionally happens with nineteenth-century operas that the only tolerable approach is to try to ignore the plot and characters —to treat the opera as instrumental music which happens to be partly for voices: but such an approach to Mozart, which no truly musical musician could make, would be not only an insult to the self-knowledge of a composer who deliberately chose to pour his genius into opera above all, but also a crypto-philistinism, a secret destructiveness against an art whose supreme excellence is discernible only in, indeed consists in, its perfect wedding of music to drama. Even the counter-movement, which wants all operas to be played in a language the audience can understand, and which thereby does place some emphasis on the plot, does not place it nicely enough. It will do for some plots, but not for Mozart's. A singing version in another language can never be faithful enough either to the sense or to the historical period to report exactly what it was that Mozart set to music. The only solution is that cure by education which the enlightenment universally prescribed. English audiences must, however roughly, learn the rudiments of German and Italian. It is the only way to read Mozart. That alone justifies the pain. Mozart knew his own genius when he chose opera. He was a creative psychologist whose characters, who exist only in music plus drama, deserve the serious and searching affection—passion, even—we give to Shakespeare's.

Mozart's unique historical importance is that, at a time when the enlightenment was squeezing psychology out of literature, he carried, and carried forward, psychology for European civilisation. This holds a lesson for us at a time when other forces, equally blind in practice but much less enlightened in purpose, are beginning to squeeze psychology out of all the

* Witness Siegmund Levarie's *Mozart's Le Nozze di Figaro.*

arts and art itself out of society. But where Mozart's absolute importance is concerned, what his contemporaries were doing is neither here nor there. We should still have to apply to the unique delights and poignancies of his operas, even if Shakespeare and Proust had been psychologising at the same time. To us, Shakespeare, Mozart and Proust *are* contemporaries—both of one another and of ourselves: culture is precisely the power to make our great artists eternal. We, as the only one of the group to be literally alive, have to carry the burden of preserving the eternity of the others. It is not only posterity we shall make secure if we can now prevent the dark ages from closing down, but also the great artists of the past which their greatness makes ever-present.

Appendix: A Note on Professor Chailley's 'Magic Flute'

In 1972 a volume was published in Britain under the title *The Magic Flute, Masonic Opera*. The author was Jacques Chailley, whom a note on the dust jacket described as 'professor of the history of music at the Sorbonne', the translation into English by Herbert Weinstock and the spelling North American.

Rejecting Seyfried's reminiscence that in 1791 (the year of the opera's first production) Schikaneder imposed a change on the plot because it was pre-empted by a rival theatre, Professor Chailley's book holds that the libretto was complete before and remained intact during the composition of the music.

The discrepancies in the plot as it now stands are, the book insists, deliberate and would be meaningful to members of the audience who had followed the internal discussions and disputes of Freemasonry.

The music, the author claims, represents Mozart's 'feelings about' and the plot reflects in detail 'the problems then agitating Viennese Masonry with respect to woman's role in the Order'.

The volume locates Masonic disputes on that subject in France during the period 1770 to 1780 and again in the 1840s. It does not, however, shew that such a dispute was 'agitating' Masons in Vienna in 1791.

The French Masonic dispute was between an aspiration to an independent branch of Masonry for women and the orthodox Masonic assignment to women of a subsidiary position. Mozart, the book claims, and the libretto were on the side of orthodoxy, represented in the opera by Sarastro.

The book interprets the Queen of the Night as representative of the aspiration to an independent female Masonry and Pamina as representative of female submission. Kidnapped by Sarastro and removed from her mother's influence, Pamina submits to her kidnapper and, purified by her ordeals, is admitted to orthodox initiation as half of a pair—in the company, that is, of the lover whom Sarastro has allotted to her.

Tamino, in the Chailley version, becomes disabused of his trust in the plausible hypocrisy of the Queen of the Night. He continues, however, to love Pamina, whom he has fallen in love with via the portrait of her given him by the Queen, and he undergoes his ordeals with the help of another gift of the Queen's to him, the flute.

I cannot believe in a dramatic allegory that chooses, as Professor Chailley insists it does, to represent the submission of women by means of a heroine who leads her lover through the ordeals with the words 'Ich selbsten führe dich'.

Neither can I believe Professor Chailley's account of Mozart's use of key in the opera. The keys are interpreted, rigidly, in terms of Masonic moralism without heed to the practical imperatives. G major, associated with Papageno, is called 'the key of futility', but no mention is made of the limitations placed on a free choice of key for any musical texture that incorporates the five fixed notes of Papageno's pipe.

The opening third of Professor Chailley's book concerns the German-language Singspiel form. He maintains that the Singspiel was 'very simply the German equivalent of the French *opéra-comique*' and denigrates Mozart's operas with Italian texts.

Defying the multilingual letters of the composer who, in his letter to his mother and sister from Milan on 10 February 1770, signed himself 'Wolfgang in Germany, Amadeo in Italy, De Mozartini', Professor Chailley asserts that Mozart, in his poverty, was 'ready to accept any way of earning a living, even that of composing a boring *opera seria* to a libretto (*La Clemenza di Tito*) by Metastasio'.

He is contradicted by Mozart's own cataloguing note that Metastasio's text was editorially made into a 'real opera' by Mazzolà and by the letter of 26 January 1770 in which Mozart, at fourteen, tells his sister that he has composed an aria from Metastasio's *Demetrio*, a performance of which, to J. A. Hasse's music, Mozart found 'charming'.

Professor Chailley asserts that the choosing of a text for an Italian opera 'counted less with the composer' than the consideration of texts 'for the "German operas", each word of which had significance for the audience'.

His words are contradicted by the series of letters from November 1780 to January 1781 in which Mozart, through his father as go-between, makes his librettist, Varesco, improve the Italian text of *Idomeneo* to Mozart's requirements. The Chailley assertion is further contradicted by Mozart's letter of 7 May 1783 in which he says 'I should dearly love to show what I can do in an Italian opera!' (to shew, that is, to Vienna; *Idomeneo* had shewn Munich), reports that he has 'looked through at least a hundred libretti and more' and makes clear, three years in advance of its fulfilment, his wish to secure da Ponte as his Italian librettist.

Professor Chailley gives his view of da Ponte, which contrasts with Mozart's, in his statement that, in *Le Nozze di Figaro*, da Ponte 'blunted the piquancies of the French play somewhat' and in his statement that 'the stupidity of the action of *Così Fan Tutte* does not prevent it from presenting a well-defined social message, if only in its title: that of proclaiming the moral fragility of the fair sex'. That mission, as Professor Chailley calls it, was, he says, developed in *Die Zauberflöte*, with the addition of 'the conclusion and corrective that had been lacking'.

Those assertions suggest to me that the cardinal point is not, as he mistakenly supposes, that Mozart expected his audiences to take in every word of his operas in German but that Professor Chailley does not understand the words of his operas in Italian.

The spoken words of an opera in German no doubt were instantly apprehensible to a German-speaking audience— provided it could hear them; spoken words lack the carrying power of the sung recitative that replaces them in Italian operas. The sung words, however, particularly when sung by more than one person at a time, do not instantly yield their significance to an audience, no matter what their or the audience's language. Professor Chailley's exaggerated belief in the comprehensibility of German opera to German-speaking audiences is contradicted by a fact he does not mention: in the fashion common at the time, the libretto of *Die Zauberflöte* was on sale to the public at the first production. Professor Chailley should have consulted Mozart's letter of 8-9 October 1791, in which he tells his wife, who was taking the cure at Baden, that he is 'tomorrow' to take her mother to *Die Zauberflöte* and that her other son-in-law, Franz de Paula Hofer (the court violinist at Vienna who was the first husband of Josepha Hofer, née Weber, the first production's Queen of the Night), had already given her the libretto to read in advance.

The playbill for the first production of *Die Zauberflöte*, which is reproduced in *Mozart und seine Welt in zeitgenössischen Bildern* (Bärenreiter, Kassel-Basel, 1961), describes the work not as a Singspiel but as 'eine grosse Oper'. Mozart's letter of 14 October 1791 records his delight when his guests at the theatre pronounce it an 'operone'.

Professor Chailley's commentary is one of the few to pay fairly detailed attention to Terrasson's *Sethos*, of which he includes a page, in its French text, in his illustrations. He shews sparse acquaintance with the Latin and ancient Greek sources emphasised by eighteenth-century Masonry. Almost the only assertion in his book that cannot be questioned is that the standard French title for the opera, *La Flûte Enchantée*, is a mistranslation since the German title implies not that the flute is enchanted but that it administers enchantment.

Notes

———————❈———————

CHAPTER I

1 Preface to *Back to Methuselah*
2 Alma Mahler: *Gustav Mahler*, pp. 17; 169
3 The original poster was for *The Comedy of Sighs* by Dr John Todhunter, 1894. See the Beardsley 'Iconography' by Aymer Vallance in the Robert Ross book
4 The first of Beardsley's many Wagner drawings were *Götter-dämmerung* and *Tannhäuser* decorative compositions in 1890 or 1891. (See the Vallance 'Iconography')
5 Harold Nicolson (of Gertrude Bell) in *The Observer* of 30 July, 1961
6 *Beethoven: His Spiritual Development*, II, 2
7 *Beethoven* . . . , II, 1
8 Mozart to Leopold Mozart, from Vienna, 13 October, 1781
9 from Vienna, 26 September, 1781
10 —though in the text where Mozart found the poem it was not ascribed to Goethe. See Einstein: *Mozart* . . . , 19
11 See Einstein: *Mozart* . . . , 22
12 See Mozart to Leopold Mozart, from Vienna, 28 December, 1782

CHAPTER II

1 Angus Heriot: *The Castrati In Opera*, III
2 Mozart to Leopold Mozart, from Munich, 15 November and 22 November, 1780
3 *Group Psychology And The Analysis Of The Ego*, IX
4 *Group Psychology* . . . , V

CHAPTER III

1 J. Christopher Herold: *Mistress To An Age*, 5
2 Boswell's *Tour Of The Hebrides*, 4 October
3 Boswell: *Life* . . . , 9 May, 1778
4 Boswell: *Life* . . . , 11 April, 1776
5 'Signore, io sono una povera serva, voi siete il mio padrone. Voi

cavaliere, io nata sono una misera donna; ma due cose eguali abbiam noi, e sono queste, la ragione e l'onore' (*Pamela*, I vi)

6 Boswell: *Life* . . . , 7 February, 1754
7 Letter to Lady Mary Bennet, from Foston, September, 1817
8 Built in 1760 (*City of Bath, Official Guide Book*)
9 Boswell: *Life* . . . , 20 September, 1777
10 Cf. Constantia Maxwell: *Dublin Under The Georges*, II; VIII
11 Cf. Walter Ison: *The Georgian Buildings Of Bath*
12 1778
13 Letter XVI
14 Letter XXI
15 e.g. by E. J. Dent: *Opera*, II

CHAPTER IV

1 'CHÉRUBIN. Ce rôle ne peut être joué, comme il l'a été, que par une jeune et très-jolie femme; nous n'avons point à nos théâtres de très-jeune homme assez formé pour en sentir bien les finesses.' (Caractères et Habillements de la Pièce)
2 The cardinal reference for the whole subject is Sigmund Freud: *Collected Papers*, Volume II, VI
3 I take this information from N. Pevsner: *An Outline Of European Architecture*, III
4 otherwise Bartholomew de Glanville; minorite friar, flourished 1230–50 (*Concise Dictionary Of National Biography*)

CHAPTER V

1 *The Complaint, or Night Thoughts*, VIII (1742–4)
2 *Essay On Man*, II, 161–2 (1733)
3 *David Copperfield*, XIX (1849–50)
4 Pope: *Essay On Man*, III, 318
5 *Essay On Man*, III, 109–10
6 *Essay On Man*, IV, 1 (Epistle IV was added in 1734)
7 *A Hymne To God The Father*
8 *The Age Of Reason*, I (1794–5)
9 1790
10 Letter the 12th
11 Letter the 9th
12 *Sex In History*, IX
13 1791
14 Freud: *The Interpretation Of Dreams*, V, D, c
15 first performed circa 1718–20
16 Theocritus: Idyll XI; Ovid: *Metamorphoses*, XIII, 738 foll.

CHAPTER VI

1 IV, 629– . . . 56. (First version 1728; complete edition 1729)
2 1740
3 Pope: *Essay On Criticism,* 653– . . . 6 (written 1709, published 1711)
4 *Essay On Man,* III, 148–51
5 Quoted by Constantia Maxwell: *Dublin Under The Georges,* VIII

CHAPTER VII

1 II, 108 (1735)
2 *or, The History Of A Young Lady* (1747–8)
3 *Don Giovanni,* Act I, recitative before No. 13
4 First version 1712; complete edition 1714
5 *or, Virtue Rewarded* (1740–2)
6 e.g. Italian version, Venice, 1744–5
7 *Pamela,* 1750—later (i.e. after Goldoni had added a sequel, *Pamela Maritata*) called *Pamela Fanciulla*
8 *Cecchina, o La Buona Figliuola,* Rome, 1760. (See Angus Heriot: *The Castrati In Opera,* I.) The opera seems to have used Goldoni's play as libretto (see E. J. Dent: *Mozart's Operas,* 2)

CHAPTER VIII

1 Don Ottavio and his 'compagne belle', all masked, thank Don Giovanni for inviting them to his party, to which Don Giovanni replies that it is open to all and 'Viva la libertà' (Act I, No. 14, Part Two)
2 I, Letter XCIV
3 from Vienna, 15 December, 1781
4 'Delle vecchie fa conquista/pel piacer di porle in lista,/sua passion predominante/è la giovin principiante;/non si picca, se sia ricca,/se sia brutta, se sia bella;/purchè porti la gonnella/voi sapete quel che fa' (Act I, No. 4)
5 *Sanditon,* 8

CHAPTER IX

1 *Les Liaisons Dangereuses* (1782)
2 'J'ajoute donc que le moindre obstacle mis de votre part sera

pris de la mienne pour une véritable déclaration de guerre; vous
voyez que la réponse que je vous demande n'exige ni longues ni
belles phrases. Deux mots suffisent.' (*Les Liaisons Dangereuses,*
Lettre CLIII)

3 See G. Rattray Taylor: *Sex In History*, IX
4 III, Letter XXVIII
5 Lettre IV
6 *The Interpretation Of Dreams*, V, D, b
7 IV, 175–6
8 III, 162
9 IV, 103–4
10 III, 7–8; III, 157–8; II, 105–9

CHAPTER X

1 I, 47– . . . 78
2 Cf. my *Black Ship To Hell*, I, 2
3 Lettre II
4 Lettre XX
5 Scott 1771–1832; Jane Austen 1775–1817
6 J. E. Austen-Leigh's *Memoir*, quoted in R. W. Chapman's edition
of Jane Austen's letters
7 by I. Bloch, quoted in G. Rattray Taylor's *Sex In History*, IX
8 Letter to Leopold Mozart from Vienna, 15 December, 1781
9 Cf. Boswell's *London Journal*, 25 November, 1762, etc.
10 I, vi
11 *Clarissa*, I, Letter XCIX
12 quoted by Simone de Beauvoir: *Must We Burn De Sade?* translated by A. Michelson, p. 47
13 Lettre IV
14 *Memoirs Of An Egotist*, translated by T. W. Earp, p. 143
15 Baudelaire: 'Je suis comme le roi d'un pays pluvieux . . .' (*Spleen
et Idéal*, LXXIX)
16 in his Preface to the second edition, 1765
17 This date is given by Oswald Doughty, quoting a Walpole letter,
though the title page of the first edition is dated 1765. (See the
Introduction to Doughty's Scholartis Press edition, which also
reprints the original title page.)
18 Chapter I
19 Chapter III
20 Journals, 1843; 1842, translated by A. Dru

CHAPTER XI

1 'La plus badine des intrigues. Un grand seigneur espagnol, amoureux d'une jeune fille . . .' (Préface)

2 Thus, according to the critics, 'dans le *Barbier de Séville* je n'avais qu'ébranlé l'État; dans ce nouvel essai, plus infâme et plus séditieux, je le renversais de fond en comble. Il n'y avait plus rien de sacré si l'on permettait cet ouvrage.' (Préface)

3 I, x

4 No. 9, Act I

5 Cherubino's aria 'Non so più', No. 6, Act I

6 *The Golden Ass*, V, 22

7 'E mi farà il destino ritrovar questo paggio in ogni loco' (Recitative XV)

8 in particular, of Apuleius's Cupid (as I have tried to shew in *Black Ship To Hell*, IV, 11; 16)

9 'Crudel! perchè finora', No. 16, Act III

10 'Là ci darem la mano', No. 7, Act I. Einstein points out that the theme of an aristocrat trying to seduce a peasant bride, together with much of the social criticism in Mozart's operas, had been anticipated in Bertati's libretto for Bianchi's *La Villanella Rapita*, for the Viennese production of which Mozart wrote two interpolations, including a duet between the peasant-girl and her Count, which, 'like the better-known duet between Zerlina and Don Giovanni, is in A major, and is full of the same seductive sweetness' (*Mozart . . .* , 22)

11 'Ebben, ora è pentito' (Act I, recitative II)

12 No. 22, finale of Act III

13 'Che aspetto nobile! che dolce maestà!' (No. 9, Act I)

14 No. 28, Finale

15 Recitative after No. 10, Act I

16 See Bernard Shaw: Epistle Dedicatory to *Man And Superman*

17 No. 4, Act I

18 'Notte e giorno fatticar . . . Voglio far il gentiluomo E non voglio più servir' (No. 1)

19 Recitative after No. 15, Act II

20 'Va, non mi degno di pugnar teco' (No. 1)

21 No. 17, Act III

22 No. 6, Act I

23 No. 2, Act I, 'Se a caso madama'

24 No. 3, Act I

25 *The Interpretation Of Dreams*, V, B

26 1928 is the date of the lectures which were published in 1929 as *A Room Of One's Own*
27 Recitative after No. 15; No. 17 (Act II)
28 No. 18, Act III
29 No. 17, Act II
30 e.g. *The Interpretation Of Dreams*, VI, E
31 'lasciati almen veder'
32 'V'è gente alla finestra: forse è dessa' (recitative after No. 17, Act II)

CHAPTER XII

1 *Sex In History*, XI, quoting W. Acton in *The Functions And Disorders Of the Re-Productive Organs*
2 from Vienna, 15 December, 1781; from Mannheim, 22 February, 1778
3 from Vienna, 15 December, 1781
4 from Vienna, 30 January, 1782
5 from Vienna, 29 April, 1782
6 Act II, No. 30
7 Hans Gal: *The Golden Age of Vienna*, IV
8 from Vienna, 16 May, 1781
9 Letter to Aloysia Weber from Paris, 30 July, 1778
10 from Mannheim, 3 December, 1778
11 from Vienna, 15 December, 1781
12 from Vienna, 9 July, 1781
13 to Leopold Mozart, from Vienna, 15 December, 1781
14 from Vienna, 16 May, 1781
15 from Chawton, 18 November, 1814
16 to Maria Anna Thekla Mozart from Vienna, 21 October, 1781— but Emily Anderson notes that it is doubtful if this dateline is correct
17 No. 11
18 'Ach Constanze! durch mich bist du verloren'
19 'Was ist der Tod? . . . und dann an deiner Seite ist er Vorgeschmack der Seligkeit'
20 No. 20
21 No. 11, Act II
22 Cf. Michael Levey's article *Fidelio and Léonore* in the *Musical Times* of February, 1961
23 Michael Levey: 'Aspects Of Mozart's Heroines', I (*Warburg Journal* XXII, 1-2, 1959)
24 'Dies Bildnis ist bezaubernd schön' (Act I, No. 3)

25 Act I, No. 7, 'Bei Männern'
26 Act I, Finale
27 from Vienna, 25 July, 1781
28 from Vienna, 15 December, 1781
29 from Berlin, 23 May, 1789

CHAPTER XIII

1 Journal, 1836, A. Dru's translation
2 Act II, Finale (No. 26)

CHAPTER XIV

1 from Vienna, 19 October, 1782
2 which concerns the cult of Osiris. See Philips ABL 3089
3 E. J. Dent: *Mozart's Operas*, 225 note 1
4 Act I, No. 5; No. 8
5 Lediard's translation, Vol. I, p. 51
6 Lediard's translation, Preface
7 1952 edition, with *Nihil Obstat* and *Imprimatur* of 1950
8 I, 92
9 Terrasson admits that his account (in Lediard, Volume I, p. 31 foll.) is based on Diodorus (in whom it comes in I, 91)
10 Lediard's translation, Vol. I, p. 34
11 Lediard's translation, Vol. I, p. 187
12 F. de S. de la Motte Fénelon's *Les Aventures de Télémaque*, published (inadvertently) in 1698
13 Madeleine de Scudéry (1607–1701)
14 Preface, Lediard's translation
15 He does this under the name Cheres and in the company of Phoenicians. Left for dead and resuscitated by Phoenicians, Sethos takes the name Cheres on p. 378 of Volume I (Lediard's translation) though Terrasson has accidentally called him Cheres forty-two pages earlier.
16 Lediard's translation, Vol. I, p. 46
17 Act I, dialogue before No. 4
18 Quintet, No. 5, Act I
19 *Mozart* . . . , 23
20 'Barmherzige Götter!'
21 'Bekämen doch die Lügner alle/ein solches Schloss vor ihren Mund:/Statt Hass, Verleumdung, schwarzer Galle/bestünde Lieb' und Bruderbund.' (Quintet, No. 5, Act I)
22 'Es schnitt in einer Zauberstunde/mein Vater sie aus tiefstem

Grunde/der tausendjähr'gen Eiche aus,/bei Blitz und Donner, Sturm und Braus' (Act II, No. 21, second Andante)

23 —though Einstein (*Mozart* . . . , 23) explains Monostatos as a traitor in the Masonic camp and, like the Queen herself, a portrait of an historical (but not in this case nameable) personage.

24 Act I, No. 5

25 Act II, No. 21, Più moderato after the third Allegro

26 Act I, dialogue after No. 2; No. 1; dialogue before No. 4

27 Act I, dialogue after No. 2

28 Act I, dialogue before No. 4

29 *The Golden Ass*, XI, 2

30 During a plague, Pope Gregory the Great led a procession through Rome to St. Peter's. Angels appeared, singing the anthem *Regina Coeli*; and the saintly Pope's ability to complete the quotation persuaded the angel of the plague to sheathe his sword—just over what is for that reason known as Castel Sant'Angelo.

31 —which refers to a statue of the goddess 'much the same as Apuleius, in his Metamorphosis, represents the goddess appearing to him in a dream' (Lediard's translation, Vol. I, p. 274)

32 *The Golden Ass*, XI, 3–4

33 *The Golden Ass*, XI, 9; 10

34 *The Golden Ass*, XI, 25; 6

35 '. . . Aegyptii . . . appellant vero nomine reginam Isidem' (*The Golden Ass*, XI, 4–5)

36 Act I, dialogue before No. 4. But in No. 1 the ladies resolve to take the news to their Princess ('Lasst uns zu unsrer Fürstin eilen, ihr diese Nachricht zu erteilen')

37 I, 11

38 See Michael Levey: 'Tiepolo's Treatment Of Classical Story At Villa Valmarana' (*Warburg Journal*, XX, 3–4, 1957)

39 Act II, No. 10

40 'deorum dearumque facies uniformis' (XI, 5)

41 —as Diodorus Siculus points out. Lucius, in *The Golden Ass*, is determined to invoke the goddess by every possible name and evidently thinks Demeter the most likely, since he begins his prayer 'Queen of heaven, whether you are Ceres . . . or Venus . . .', etc. (XI, 2)

42 Lediard's translation, Vol. I, p. 174 foll.

43 'Zum Leiden bin ich auserkoren,/denn meine Tochter fehlet mir./ Durch sie ging all mein Glück verloren,/ein Bösewicht entfloh mit ihr.' (Act I, No. 4)

44 'Der Hölle Rache kocht in meinem Herzen' (Act II, No. 14)

45 Act I, recitative to the Queen's aria, No. 4

46 '. . . so eine Flöte ist mehr als Gold und Kronen wert' (Act I, quintet, No. 5)

47 'Wie stark ist nicht dein Zauberton, weil, holde Flöte, durch dein Spielen, selbst wilde Tiere Freude fühlen!' (Act I, No. 8)

48 Vienna, 1762 (new version Paris, 1774)

49 'Sprichst nicht eine Silbe mit deiner Pamina? Liebst du mich nicht mehr? O das ist mehr als Kränkung, mehr als Tod!' (Act II, dialogue after No. 16)

50 Act II, No. 17

51 Act II, No. 21

52 'du wirst der Tochter Retter sein' (Act I, No. 4)

53 'Pamina retten, Pamina retten, ist mein Pflicht' (Act I, No. 8)

54 E. J. Dent: *Mozart's Operas*, 13

55 1789 (E. J. Dent: *Mozart's Operas*, 13)

56 'I was only religious to the goddess Isis, but not yet sacred to the religion of great Osiris, the sovereign father of all gods . . .' (*The Golden Ass*, XI, 27, William Adlington's translation)

57 'Sarastro herrscht in diesen Gründen? . . . Doch in dem Weisheits-tempel nicht? . . . So ist denn alles Heuchelei! . . . Er ist ein Unmensch, ein Tyrann!'

58 The Orator: 'So gieb mir deine Gründe an! . . . Ist das, was du gesagt, erwiesen?' Tamino: 'Durch ein unglücklich Weib bewiesen, das Gram und Jammer niederdrückt.' The Orator: 'Ein Weib hat also dich berückt? Ein Weib tut wenig, plaudert viel. Du, Jüngling, glaubst dem Zungenspiel?' (Act I, No. 8)

59 Act II, No. 11: 'Bewahret euch vor Weibertücken, dies ist des Bundes erste Pflicht!'

60 end of Act I; Act II, dialogue after No. 9a

61 'Pamina . . . haben die Götter dem holden Jünglinge bestimmt; dies ist der Grund, warum ich sie der stolzen Mutter entriss' (Act II, dialogue after No. 9a)

62 'du wirst der Tochter Retter sein; und werd' ich dich als Sieger sehen, so sei sie dann auf ewig dein' (Act I, No. 4)

63 'Ein Mann muss eure Herzen leiten, denn ohne ihn pflegt jedes Weib aus seinem Wirkungskreis zu schreiten' (Act I, No. 8, Larghetto)

64 'Weisheitslehre sei mein Sieg; Pamina, das holde Mädchen, mein Lohn.' (Act II, dialogue before No. 11)

65 Act II, dialogue after No. 10

66 Act II, No. 21, first Allegretto

67 Mozart wrote an entire letter in doggerel to his sister from Salzburg, 31 July, 1783; for his composing an aria in *Il Seraglio*

before mentioning it to Stephanie, see the letter (already cited) to Leopold Mozart, from Vienna, 26 September, 1781.

68 Tamino: 'Hier sind die Schreckenspforten, die Not und Tod mir dräu'n.' Pamina: 'Ich werde aller Orten an deiner Seite sein. Ich selbsten führe dich, die Liebe leitet mich . . . Nun komm und spiel' die Flöte an . . .' (Act II, No. 21, second Andante)
69 Act I, No. 8, Andante
70 Act I, No. 5
71 *Odyssey*, X, 501
72 Pamina and Tamino: 'Wir wandeln . . . froh durch des Todes düst're Nacht' (Act II, No. 21, second Andante)
73 Thus the two men in armour, Act II, No. 21, Adagio

CHAPTER XV

1 'Accessi confinium mortis et calcato Proserpinae limine . . . deos inferos et deos superos accessi coram et adoravi de proxumo' (*The Golden Ass*, XI, 23)
2 Smith's *Dictionary Of . . . Antiquities*, Eleusinia
3 Act I, No. 8, Allegro-Adagio, a tempo
4 Lediard's translation, Vol. I, p. 175
5 I, 61
6 Lediard's translation, Vol. I, p. 174
7 E. J. Dent (*Mozart's Operas*, 15) records that *Das Labyrinth*, with music by Peter von Winter, was produced at Schikaneder's own theatre in 1798. Dent does not remark the connexion of its title with the story of *Sethos*.
8 Lediard's translation, Vol. I, p. 155
9 Act II, No. 21, second Allegro
10 Lediard's translation, Vol. I, p. 121
11 Lediard's translation, Vol. I, p. 224
12 Lediard's translation, Vol. I, p. 248
13 *Aeneid*, VI, 426–9
14 Lediard's translation, Vol. I, pp. 198–9
15 'Es zeigen die Pforten, es zeigen die Säulen' (Act I, No. 8)
16 Lediard's translation, Vol. I, p. 158
17 Act II, dialogue before No. 11 : 'Prinz! Noch ist's Zeit zu weichen —einen Schritt weiter, und es ist zu spät'.
18 Act II, No. 21, second Andante
19 Act II, dialogue after No. 11
20 Act II, dialogue before No. 20
21 Act II, dialogue before No. 20
22 Paul Turner, in the Introduction to his (Penguin) translation of selections from Lucian

23 *Menippos*, 6
24 Adlington's translation of 'voluntariae mortis . . . quodam modo renatos . . .' (*The Golden Ass*, XI, 21)
25 Act II, dialogue after No. 11
26 '. . . ut saevis proiectus ab undis/navita, . . . cum primum in luminis oras . . . natura profudit' (V, 222–5)
27 Book of Common Prayer
28 E. R. Dodds: *The Greeks And The Irrational*, V; H. J. Rose: *A Handbook Of Greek Mythology* . . . , III; VI
29 'Homeric' Hymn *To Demeter*, 242: καί κέν μιν ποίησεν ἀγήρων τ' ἀθάνατόν τε
30 Lediard's translation, Vol. I, p. 274
31 Act II, dialogue before No. 11
32 Act I, No. 8, Presto
33 Act II, No. 21, Più moderato
34 Act II, No. 21, Recitative—Maestoso—Andante
35 *The Golden Ass*, XI, 23
36 A. Einstein: *Mozart* . . . , 4; *Catholic Dictionary*, Freemasonry
37 first performed 1735
38 first performed 1739
39 No. 8
40 first performed 1743
41 Tamino: 'O ew'ge Nacht, wann wirst du schwinden? Wann wird das Licht mein Auge finden?' Voices: 'Bald, bald, Jüngling, oder nie!' (Act I, No. 8, second Andante a tempo)
42 Misprinted 'reports' in the original edition of Lediard's translation
43 Lediard's translation, Vol. I, pp. 117–18
44 XXXI
45 'On ne les avait jamais effrayés en leur disant que Dieu réserve des punitions terribles aux enfants ingrats'
46 *War And Peace*, V, III
47 from Vienna, 4 April, 1787
48 · The two armed men, Act II, No. 21, Adagio
49 'Ein Weib, das Nacht und Tod nicht scheut, ist würdig und wird eingeweiht' (Act II, No. 21, first Allegretto)

CHAPTER XVI

1 Act II, No. 21, second Allegro
2 Act I, No. 5
3 '1 *Priester*: . . . Was treibt euch an, in unsere Mauern zu dringen? *Tamino*: Freundschaft und Liebe' (Act II, dialogue before No. 11)

4 Pope: *Essay On Man*, I, 6–7
5 Pope: *Essay On Man*, I, 51–2
6 Pope: *An Essay On Criticism*, 68 (1711)
7 *Paul et Virginie*
8 ' "Les femmes sont fausses dans les pays où les hommes sont tyrans. Partout la violence produit la ruse." ' (*Paul et Virginie*)
9 *The Age Of Reason*, II (1795)
10 'Ich selbsten führe dich, die Liebe leitet mich' (Act II, No. 21, second Andante)

CHAPTER XVII

1 1757
2 K. 344
3 1768
4 Mozart's unfinished opera buffa (K. 422) begun in 1783
5 the play by Tobias Philipp (Baron) von Gebler for which Mozart composed incidental music (K. 345) in 1773 and 1779
6 at Palazzo Labia, Venice, painted between 1740 and 1750. Compare the modello for the *Meeting Of Antony and Cleopatra* at the National Gallery of Scotland, Edinburgh; and the other *Banquet of Cleopatra*, at Melbourne, National Gallery of Victoria.
7 1759
8 E. J. Dent: *Mozart's Operas*, 13
9 the Huron in *L'Ingénu* (1767)
10 1750
11 first performed London, 1724
12 Act I, No. 5, 'Giovinette che fatte all'amore'
13 No. 39
14 F. J. B. Watson's Introduction (p. xliii) to his Catalogue of Furniture in the Wallace Collection
15 from Vienna, 19 October, 1782
16 Act II, No. 8, 'Durch Zärtlichkeit und Schmeicheln, Gefälligkeit und Scherzen . . .'
17 dialogue following No. 8, Act II
18 'Welche Wonne, welche Lust' (No. 12, Act II)
19 'une compagnie de souscripteurs . . . composée de négotiants, de lords, d'évêques, d'universités et de la famille royale d'Angleterre . . .'
20 The French text is quoted by Alan Yorke-Long: *Music At Court*, IV
21 'Vous autres, Européens, dont l'esprit se remplit, dès l'enfance, de tant de préjugés contraires au bonheur . . .'

22 III

23 VI

24 *Gulliver's Travels*, 1726; *A Modest Proposal* . . . , 1729; **Candide;**
    ou L'Optimisme, 1759

25 *Essay On Man*, II, 53–4

26 da Ponte's *Memoirs*, L. A. Sheppard's translation

27 Pope: *Essay On Man*, 111, 317–18

28 *Sanditon*, 3

29 Richardson's note to Letter II of *Clarissa* (1747–8)

30 *Essay On Man*, III, 147–8

31 'loin d'être sauvages, elles étaient devenues plus humaines'

32 ' "Rappelez-vous quel a été le sort de la plupart des philosophes
    qui leur" ' (sc. aux hommes) ' "ont prêché la sagesse. Homère,
    qui l'a revêtue de vers si beaux, demandait l'aumône pendant sa
    vie. Socrate, qui en donna aux Athéniens de si aimables leçons
    par ses discours et par ses moeurs, fut empoisonné juridiquement
    par eux. Son sublime disciple, Platon, fut livré à l'esclavage par
    l'ordre du prince même qui le protégeait; et avant eux, Pythagore,
    qui étendait l'humanité jusqu'aux animaux, fut brûlé vif par les
    Crotoniates." '

33 XVIII

34 'Ich bin so ein Naturmensch, der sich mit Schlaf, Speise und
    Trank begnügt; und wenn es ja sein könnte, dass ich mir einmal
    ein schönes Weibchen fange—' (Act II, dialogue before No. 11)

35 from Paris, 3 July, 1778

36 Letter to Mrs Beach, 21 February, 1799

37 I am grateful to Michael Levey for pointing out this picture,
    which is signed and dated 1802 and was sold at Christie's, 21 July,
    1944 (102)

38 from Vienna, 26 September, 1781

39 Witness his soliloquy after her 'Ach, ich liebe' (No. 6)

40 After No. 10

41 Act II, dialogue before No. 11

42 'Ist das ein Traum? Woher hat sie auf einmal den Muth, sich so
    gegen mich zu betragen?' (soliloquy after No. 9)

43 Act III, dialogue before No. 20

44 'ich bin von einer grossen Spanischen Familie', says Belmonte
    (Act III, dialogue before No. 20)

45 'Ich habe deinem Vater viel zu sehr verabscheut, als dass ich in
    seine Fusstapfen treten könnte' (Act III, dialogue before No. 21)

46 Mozart's letter to his father, from Vienna, 19 May, 1781

47 to Leopold Mozart, from Vienna, between 26 May and 2 June,
    1781

48 from Vienna, 20 June, 1781
49 Act I, Finale, Allegro maestoso
50 XVIII
51 'Wen man durch Wohlthun nicht gewinnen kann, den muss man
   sich vom Halse schaffen' (before No. 21)

CHAPTER XVIII

1 Leopold Mozart's letter to Lorenz Hagenauer, from London,
   28 May, 1764
2 from Mannheim, 4 February, 1778
3 A. Einstein: *Mozart* . . . , 23
4 3 July, 1778
5 Donald Mitchell's Foreword to *The Mozart Companion*
6 Leopold Mozart to Baroness von Waldstädten, from Salzburg,
   23 August, 1782
7 da Ponte's *Memoirs*, L. A. Sheppard's translation
8 Cf. da Ponte's *Memoirs*, VI
9 See A. Einstein: *Mozart* . . . , 22
10 However, Jane Austen was not specifically condemning the story
   as such but the pantomime it had been turned into. (R. W.
   Chapman annotates this as being *Don Juan, or The Libertine
   Destroyed*, 1792, based on Shadwell's *Libertine*.) Jane Austen told
   her sister Cassandra (15 September, 1813) that it contained
   'scaramouch and a ghost'. She described it to Francis Austen
   (25 September, 1813) as 'sing-song & trumpery' and said that
   she 'wanted better acting'.
11 Einstein's translation (*Mozart* . . . , 22) of Goldoni's *Mémoires*,
   I, 39 (1787), of which Einstein quotes the French text.
12 Einstein's translation of Goldoni. The French text is quoted in
   Einstein: *Mozart* . . . , 22
13 1761
14 *Mozart* . . . , 22
15 *Totem And Taboo*
16 *Totem And Taboo*, A. A. Brill's translation
17 *The Interpretation Of Dreams*, V, D, b
18 e.g. in his letter to Leopold Mozart, from Munich, 13 November,
   1780
19 from Prague, 15–25 October, 1787
20 J. L. Carr: 'Pygmalion and the "Philosophes"', *Warburg Journal*,
   XXIII, 3–4, 1960
21 *The Interpretation of Dreams*, VI, E, (A. A. Brill's translation)

CHAPTER XIX

1 *The Interpretation Of Dreams*, V, D, b. Freud disowned the emphasis he had placed on this when he came to believe that Shakespeare was not the author of the plays.
2 See Mozart's letter of 29 November, 1780, and Emily Anderson's editorial note to it
3 where he solved it, according to Einstein (*Mozart* . . . , 21) largely on the model of the voice of the oracle in Gluck's *Alceste*.
4 i.e. in 1786, the year before *Don Giovanni* (Einstein: *Mozart* . . . , 19)
5 Act I, v
6 Act II, No. 20
7 'Mi tradì . . . Ma tradita e abbandonata provo ancor per lui pietà'
8 Act II, No. 23
9 No. 25

CHAPTER XX

1 Cf. my *Black Ship To Hell*, IV, 12
2 'Più non sperate di ritrovarlo, più non cercate, lontano andò' (Act II, No. 26)
3 from Vienna, 16 May, 1781
4 to Baroness von Waldstädten, from Salzburg, 23 August, 1782
5 Freud: *Collected Papers*, Vol. II, IV
6 Recitative after No. 8, Act I
7 G. Rattray Taylor: *Sex In History*, VI; VIII
8 from Munich, 3 January, 1781
9 *Mozart's Operas*, 9
10 Cf. my *Black Ship To Hell*, I, 2
11 *Collected Papers*, Vol. V, XXI

CHAPTER XXI

1 Freud: *Group Psychology And The Analysis Of The Ego*, XII
2 from Wasserburg, 23 September, 1777
3 from Paris, 3 July, 1778
4 from Vienna, 10 September, 1781
5 to Leopold Mozart, from Vienna, 16 June, 1781
6 to Leopold Mozart, from Vienna, 12 May, 1781
7 Journal, 1838, A. Dru's translation
8 *Mozart* . . . , 7

9   Letter to his mother and sister, from Milan, 10 February, 1770
10 See Michael Levey: *Painting In XVIII Century Venice*, VI
11 for *Acis And Galatea* (K. 566), *Messiah* (K. 572), *Alexander's Feast* (K. 591) and *Ode To Saint Caecilia* (K. 592) see XIX
12 Cf. my *Black Ship To Hell*, IV, 11
13 *Mozart* . . . , 18

CHAPTER XXII

1   to Leopold Mozart, 1 May, 1778
2   to Leopold Mozart, 26 October–2 November, 1778
3   to Michael Puchberg, from Vienna, 12–14 July, 1789
4   28 September, 1790
5   to Michael Puchberg, from Vienna, 14 August, 1790

CHAPTER XXIII

1   J. Christopher Herold: *Mistress To An Age*, 11
2   *Artists On Art*, compiled and edited by R. Goldwater and M. Treves
3   ' ". . . de consoler les malheureux, d'éclairer les nations et de dire la vérité même aux rois. C'est, sans contredit, la fonction la plus auguste dont le ciel puisse honorer un mortel sur la terre . . . servir de barrière à l'erreur et aux tyrans" ' (*Paul et Virginie*)
4   to Leopold Mozart, from Vienna, 17 March, 1781
5   from Vienna, 9 May, 1781
6   from Vienna, 12 May, 1781
7   from Vienna, 9 May, 1781
8   *Essay On Man*, III, 151
9   *Biographia Literaria*, XIV

CHAPTER XXIV

1   Cf. Michael Levey: 'Tiepolo's Treatment Of Classical Story At Villa Valmarana', II (*Warburg Journal*, XX, 3–4, 1957)
2   XVIII
3   *Les Liaisons Dangereuses*, Lettre XII
4   *Lesley Castle*, Letter the Sixth
5   *Catharine* (1792). The inconsistency whereby the text spells her Catherine and the title Catharine is Jane Austen's.
6   *Northanger Abbey*, 5
7   from an article in *The Guardian*, 26 June, 1961. It did, however, provoke a letter of protest.

8 Preface to *Evelina*
9 from Vienna, 7 May
10 Michael Levey: *Painting In XVIII Century Venice*, I
11 Cf. Michael Levey: 'Aspects Of Mozart's Heroines' (*Warburg Journal*, XXII, 1–2, 1959)
12 *Le Nozze di Figaro*, Act I, No. 5, 'Via resti servita'
13 *Mozart* . . . , 22
14 *Le Nozze di Figaro*, Act III, No. 16, 'Crudel, perchè finora'
15 Anton Raaff
16 to Leopold Mozart, from Munich, 27 December, 1780
17 Epistle Dedicatory to *Man And Superman*
18 to Leopold Mozart, from Vienna, 26 September, 1781

Articles and Books Cited

―――――――❋―――――――

Adlington, *see* Apuleius
Emily Anderson, ed., *see* Mozart
Apuleius: *The Golden Ass* (*Metamorphoses*), Loeb edn. with William
    Adlington's translation, Heinemann, 1958
Jane Austen: *Northanger Abbey* (written 1798–9, first publd. 1818),
    Heffer
    Minor Works, Oxford, 1954
    Jane Austen's Letters To Her Sister Cassandra And Others, ed.
    R. W. Chapman, 2nd edn., Oxford, 1952

Memoirs Of Madame Du Barri (1829), anonymous transln., Cassell
    (1928), 1930
Pierre-Augustin Caron de Beaumarchais: *Oeuvres Complètes*, ed.
    E. Fournier, Garnier, Paris
Simone de Beauvoir: *Must We Burn De Sade?* transl. A. Michelson,
    Peter Nevill, 1953
Ludwig van Beethoven: *Fidelio* (first perf. 1805, revd. version 1814),
    vocal score, Boosey & Hawkes
Eric Blom, ed.: *Mozart's Letters*, selection from the Emily Anderson
    edn., Penguin, 1956
James Boswell: *The Life Of Samuel Johnson, LL.D.* (1791), Everyman
    London Journal, ed. F. A. Pottle (Heinemann, 1950), Ace Books,
    1958
Brigid Brophy: *Black Ship To Hell*, Secker & Warburg, 1962
Fanny Burney: *Evelina* (1778), Everyman

J. L. Carr: 'Pygmalion And The "Philosophes"', *Warburg Journal*,
    XXIII, 3–4, 1960
Cassell Opera Guides (*Die Zauberflöte, Die Entführung aus dem Serail*,
    introductions by Brigid Brophy), Cassell, 1971
A Catholic Dictionary, 15th edn., Virtue, 1952
Jacques Chailley: *The Magic Flute, Masonic Opera*, translated
    H. Weinstock, Gollancz, 1972
City of Bath, Official Guide Book, 1961
The Concise Dictionary Of National Biography, Oxford, 1930

Articles and Books Cited

da Ponte, *see* Ponte

E. J. Dent: *Mozart's Operas* (1947), Oxford, 1949
  Opera (1940), Penguin, 1945

Otto Erich Deutsch : *Mozart, A Documentary Biography*, Black, 1965

Grantly Dick-Read: *Childbirth Without Fear*, Heinemann, 1960

Lady (Emilia F. S.) Dilke: *French Engravers And Draughtsmen Of The XVIIIth Century*, George Bell, 1902

E. R. Dodds: *The Greeks And The Irrational*, University of California, 1956

Doughty, *see* Walpole

John Dryden, selected edn., Hart-Davis, 1952

Alfred Einstein: *Mozart His Character His Work*, transl. A. Mendel & N. Broder (1946), Cassell, 1956

John Fellows: *The Mysteries Of Freemasonry* . . . , Reeves & Turner, undated

François de Salignac de la Motte Fénelon: *Les Aventures de Télémaque* (1698), Geneva, 1777

Sarah Fielding: *The Lives Of Cleopatra And Octavia* (1757), ed. R. B. Johnson, Scholartis Press, 1928

R. H. Fife: *The Revolt Of Martin Luther*, Columbia University, 1957

J. G. Frazer: *Adonis Attis Osiris* (3rd edn. 1914), Macmillan, 1919

Sigmund Freud: *Group Psychology And The Analysis Of The Ego* (1921), transl. J. Strachey (1922), Hogarth Press, 1949
  The Interpretation Of Dreams (1900), transl. A. A. Brill (1913), Allen & Unwin, 1945
  Psychopathology Of Everyday Life (1914), transl. A. A. Brill, Penguin (1938), 1942
  Totem And Taboo, transl. A. A. Brill, Penguin, 1942
  Collected Papers, translation supervised J. Rivière, 5 vols., 1924–5–50, Hogarth Press, 1953

Hans Gal: *The Golden Age Of Vienna*, Max Parrish, 1948

Edward Gibbon: *The History Of The Decline And Fall Of The Roman Empire* (1776–88), Henry Frowde, 1903–6, 7 vols.
  Memoirs Of My Life And Writings (1796), Everyman

Carlo Goldoni: *Opere*, ed. F. Zampieri, Ricciardi edn., Milan-Naples, 1945

R. Goldwater & M. Treves, compilers and eds.: *Artists On Art*, Kegan Paul, 1947

G. F. Handel: *Acis And Galatea* (first perf. c. 1720), vocal score, Novello

G. B. Harrison, *see* Shakespeare

Articles and Books Cited

Angus Heriot: *The Castrati In Opera* (Secker & Warburg, 1956), John Calder, 1960

J. Christopher Herold: *Mistress To An Age, A Life Of Madame De Staël.* Hamish Hamilton, 1959

E. T. A. Hoffmann, See R. Taylor

Homer: *Odyssey*, Oxford text, 1954

Walter Ison: *The Georgian Buildings Of Bath From* 1700 *To* 1830, Faber, 1948

Henry James: *The Golden Bowl*, Methuen, 1905

Otto Jespersen: *Growth And Structure Of The English Language*, Blackwell, Oxford, 9th edn., 1948

Samuel Johnson, selected edn., Hart-Davis, 1950

Søren Kierkegaard: *Journals* (1835–54), ed. & transl. A. Dru (1938), Collins (Fontana), 1958

Either/Or, translated by D. F. Swenson and L. M. Swenson (vol. I) and Walter Lowrie (vol. II), revised and with a foreword by Howard A. Johnson, Princeton University Press 1971

Henry Kramer and James Sprenger: *Malleus Maleficarum*, transl. M. Summers, Pushkin Press, 1951

Choderlos de Laclos: *Les Liaisons Dangereuses* (1782), Charlot, Paris

Siegmund Levarie: *Mozart's Le Nozze di Figaro*, University of Chicago, 1952

Michael Levey: 'Aspects Of Mozart's Heroines', *Warburg Journal*, XXII, 1–2, 1959

'Fidelio And Léonore', *Musical Times*, Feb. 1961

Painting in XVIII Century Venice, Phaidon, 1959

'The Real Theme Of Watteau's "Embarkation For Cythera"', *Burlington Magazine*, May, 1961

'Tiepolo's Treatment Of Classical Story At Villa Valmarana', *Warburg Journal*, XX, 3–4, 1957

The Life and Death of Mozart, Weidenfeld and Nicolson, 1971; Cardinal, 1988

Charlton T. Lewis: *A Latin Dictionary For Schools*, Oxford, 1889

J. L. Lowes: *The Road To Xanadu* . . . (1927), Constable, 1951

Lucian, Loeb edn. vol. IV, Heinemann, 1925

Satirical Sketches (selection, transl., etc., P. Turner), Penguin, 1961

Alma Mahler: *Gustav Mahler* (1940), transl. B. Creighton, John Murray, 1946

Constantia Maxwell: *Dublin Under The Georges* . . . , revd. edn., Faber, 1956

Pietro Metastasio: *Opere*, Venice, 1802

Articles and Books Cited

Donald Mitchell, ed. (with H. C. Robbins Landon): *The Mozart Companion*, Rockliff, 1956
Charles de Secondat Montesquieu: *Lettres Persanes* (1721), ed. G. Truc, Garnier, Paris
W. A. Mozart: *Die Briefe W. A. Mozarts*, Georg Müller, Munich-Leipzig, 1914
   Mozarts Briefe, herausgegeben W. A. Bauer & O. E. Deutsch, Fischer, Frankfurt, 1960
   Mozart und seine Welt in zeitgenössischen Bildern, Bärenreiter, Kassel-Basel, 1961
   The Letters Of Mozart And His Family, transl. & ed. Emily Anderson, 3 vols., Macmillan, 1938

   Così Fan Tutte, vocal score, Boosey & Hawkes
   Die Entführung aus dem Serail (*Il Seraglio*), vocal score, Novello
   Don Giovanni, vocal score, Boosey & Hawkes
   Le Nozze di Figaro, vocal score, Novello
   Die Zauberflöte (*The Magic Flute*), vocal score, Boosey & Hawkes

National Gallery (loan exhibition catalogue): *From Van Eyck To Tiepolo*, An Exhibition of Pictures from the Thyssen-Bornemisza Collection, 1961

Thomas Paine: *The Age Of Reason* (1794–5), Watts, 1945
Erwin Panofsky: *The Iconography Of Correggio's Camera Di San Paolo*. Warburg Institute, 1961
Thomas Love Peacock: *The Four Ages Of Poetry* (1820), ed. H. F. B. Brett-Smith, Blackwell, Oxford, 1921 (edn. containing also essays by Shelley and Browning)
   Nightmare Abbey (1818), Hamish Hamilton, 1947
N. Pevsner: *An Outline Of European Architecture*, Penguin, 1961
Lorenzo da Ponte: *Memoirs* (first publ. 1823–7), transl. L. A. Sheppard, Routledge, 1929
Alexander Pope: *Poetical Works*, M'Lean, 1821

G. Rattray Taylor: *The Angel-Makers*, Heinemann, 1958
   Sex In History, Thames & Hudson, 1953
Samuel Richardson: *Clarissa, or The History Of A Young Lady* (1747–8), Everyman, 4 vols.
H. J. Rose: *A Handbook Of Greek Mythology* . . . , Methuen, 1926
Robert Ross; *Aubrey Beardsley* . . . with a revised iconography by Aymer Vallance, John Lane, The Bodley Head, 1909

Bernardin de Saint-Pierre: *Paul et Virginie* (1787) and *La Chaumière Indienne* (1790), Gründ, Paris

Articles and Books Cited

P. A. Scholes: *The Oxford Companion To Music*, 4th edn., 1950

Bernard Shaw: *Man And Superman* (1903), Penguin, 1946

William Shakespeare: *The Tragicall Historie Of Hamlet Prince Of Denmarke* (First Quarto, 1603), ed. G. B. Harrison, John Lane, 1923

Margaret Shenfield: *Bernard Shaw A Pictorial Biography*, Thames & Hudson, 1962

Sydney Smith, Letters, selected & ed. N. C. Smith, Oxford, 1956

William Smith, ed. (with others): *A Dictionary Of Greek And Roman Antiquities*, 3rd edn., Murray, 1890

    A Classical Dictionary, Murray, 1904

Joseph Spence: *Observations, Anecdotes, And Characters, Of Books And Men*, ed. E. Malone, John Murray, 1820

Stendhal: *Memoirs Of An Egotist*, transl. T. W. Earp, Turnstile, 1949

J. W. N. Sullivan: *Beethoven: His Spiritual Development* (1927), Mentor, 1956

Jonathan Swift, selected edn., Nonesuch, 1944

Ronald Taylor (translation and introduction): *Six German Romantic Tales* (Kleist, Tieck, E. T. A. Hoffmann), Angel, 1985

The Text Book Of Freemasonry . . ., compiled by a Member of the Craft, William Reeves, 7th edn., undated

Thyssen-Bornemisza, *see* National Gallery

M. A. R. Tuker & H. Malleson: *Handbook To Christian And Ecclesiastical Rome*, III & IV, Black, 1900

Virgil, Oxford text, 1942

J. F. M. Arouet de Voltaire, *Romans*, Livre de Poche, Paris

    La Pucelle d'Orléans, Paris, 1808

Horace Walpole: *The Castle Of Otranto* (1764), ed. O. Doughty, Scholartis Press, 1929

F. J. B. Watson: Wallace Collection catalogues, *Furniture*, 1956

Charles Williams, ed.: *A Short Life Of Shakespeare With The Sources*, Oxford, 1933, abridged from Edmund Chambers: *William Shakespeare: A Study Of Facts And Problems*

E. G. Withycombe: *The Oxford Dictionary Of English Christian Names*, 1945

Mary Wollstonecraft: *A Vindication Of The Rights Of Woman*, vol. I, 1792

Virginia Woolf: *A Room Of One's Own*, Hogarth Press, 1929

Alan Yorke-Long: *Music At Court . . .*, Weidenfeld & Nicolson, 1954.

Edward Young: *The Complaint, or Night Thoughts* (1742–4), Tegg, 1812

Index

Index

Don Giovanni. *See* Giovanni
Don Jouan. *See* Giovanni
Don Juan. *See* Giovanni
Don Ottavio. *See* Ottavio
Don Quixote. See Quixote
Donizetti, Gaetano, 16, 95
Donna Anna. *See* Anna
Donna Elvira. *See* Elvira
Donne, John, 28, 66
Doughty, Oswald, 101
Dorabella, 37, 68
Drood. *See Mystery* . . .
Dryden, John, 153, 154, 185
Dunciad, The, 75

Einstein, Alfred, 27, 59, 121, 145, 235, 262, 265, 293
Either/Or, 105, 130
Eisen, Charles, 17
Effner, J., 211
El Dorado, King of, 229, 284
El Greco (Domenikos Theotoco-poulos), 27
Elijah, 130
Elvira, Donna, 68, 86, 88, 109, 113, 114, 115, 120, 245–7
Emma Woodhouse, 95, 288
Empedocles, 66
Entführung aus dem Serail, Die (*see also* under names of characters), 17, 20, 30, 31, 82, 103, 107, 114, 119, 124, 125, 147, 208, 210, 215, 223–9, 231
Epicurus, 66
Erasmus, 283
Eros. *See* Cupid
Euclid, 277, 281
Eurydice, 153, 155, 156, 164, 175–7
Evelina, 50, 51, 287–8, 290
Evelina (*see also* under names of characters), 50, 287, 292

Fagottist, Der (*oder Die Zauberzither*), 156, 157–8
Faust, 128, 129
Fellows, John, 168
Fénelon, F. de S. de la M., 140, 180
Fielding, Henry, 82, 185
Fielding, Sarah, 187
Fidelio (*see also* under names of characters), 124, 296
Figaro, 105, 106, 108, 109, 111, 112, 208, 225, 271, 293
Figaro. See Nozze

Fiordiligi, 37, 68, 122, 288
Firbank, Ronald, 17
Florestan, 124
Folle Journée, La. See Mariage de Figaro
Four Ages Of Poetry, The, 75, 276–8
Fragonard, Jean Honoré, 239
Franco, General, 138
Frankenstein, 240–1
Frazer, Sir James George, 132
Frederick the Great, 52, 53, 212, 216, 217, 222, 227, 283
Freud, Sigmund, 29, 38, 39, 40, 69, 89, 112, 115, 117, 127, 205, 224, 236, 239, 242, 255, 256, 274, 277, 281, 293

Gainsborough, Thomas, 21, 195
Gal, Hans, 42, 118–9
Galahad, Sir, 93, 94
Gawain, Sir, 93
Genii, 208
George IV, 49
Gertrude, 249
Gibbon, Edward, 70, 73, 75, 99, 137, 272, 283, 294
Giesecke, C. L., 157
Giovanni, Don, 16, 31, 59, 83–6, 88, 90, 93, 94, 100, 102, 103, 105, 108, 109, 110, 111, 113, 114, 115, 117, 119, 120, 128, 129, 203, 207, 211, 231, 233–4, 242, 245, 251, 254–6, 265, 293
Giovanni, Don (*see also* under names of characters), 23, 29, 59, 68, 80, 82, 98, 100, 102, 104, 112, 119, 121, 129, 130, 131, 203, 207, 213, 216, 232, 235–41, 242–9, 251, 252, 253–6, 262–3, 264, 265
Giulio Cesare. See Julius Caesar
Gluck, Christoph Willibald von (*see also* under names of works and characters), 26, 154, 155, 165, 181, 183, 211, 234
Godwin, William, 46
Goethe, Johann Wolfgang von, 18, 30, 128
Golden Ass, The (*Metamorphoses*) (*see also* Apuleius), 141, 152
Golden Bowl, The (*see also* under names of characters), 87
Goldoni, Carlo (*see also* under names of works and characters), 48, 82, 96, 97, 233–4, 251, 283

Index

Index